GIANT BOOK OF GAMES AND PUZZLES FOR SMART KIDS

GIANT BOOK OF GAMES AND PUZZLES FOR SMART KIDS

MORE THAN 1000 FUN AND EDUCATIONAL ACTIVITIES

DIEGO JOURDAN PEREIRA

FOR YOUNG READERS

DEDICATED TO THE MEMORY OF JASON SCOTT SCHNEIDER (1975-2019).

10 9 8 7 6 5 4 3 2

LIBRARY OF CONGRESS CATALOGING-IN-PUBLICATION DATA IS AVAILABLE ON FILE.

COVER DESIGN BY DIEGO JOURDAN PEREIRA
COVER AND INTERIOR ARTWORK BY DIEGO JOURDAN PEREIRA
"10CENT COMICS" AND "GRAVESIDE" FONTS DESIGNED BY NATE PIEKOS. USED UNDER LICENSE.

ISBN: 978-1-63158-329-2

PRINTED IN CHINA

THE POOR ZEBRA GOT SCARED AND LOST HER STRIPES!
CAN YOU DRAW THEM?

WHAT ABOUT THE TIGER'S?

COLOR THEM BOTH!

COLOR THE CUTE CATERPILLAR.

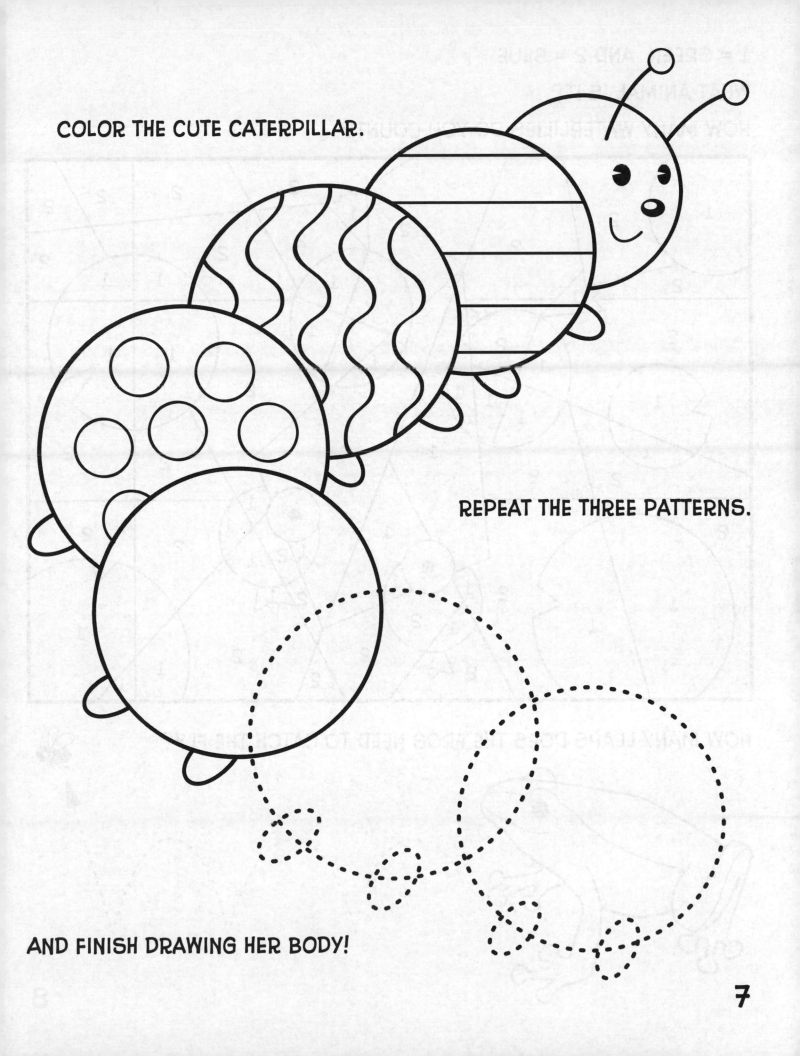

REPEAT THE THREE PATTERNS.

AND FINISH DRAWING HER BODY!

1 = GREEN AND 2 = BLUE

WHAT ANIMAL IS IT?

HOW MANY WATERLILIES DO YOU COUNT?

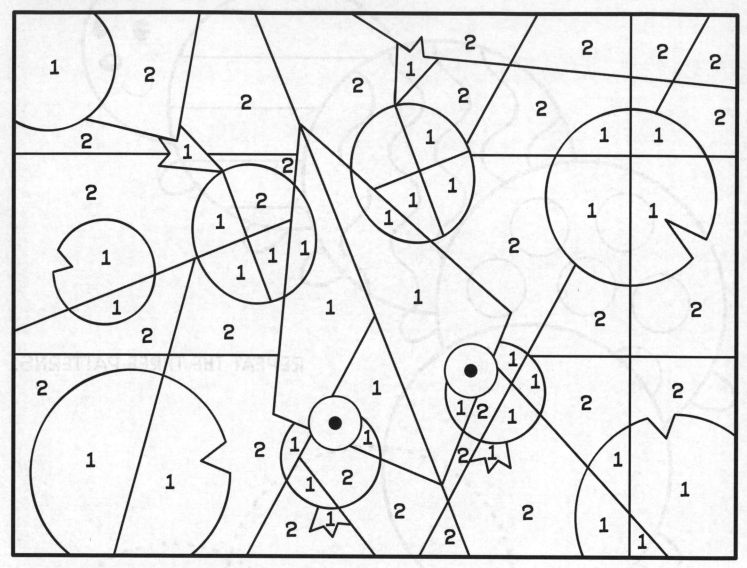

HOW MANY LEAPS DOES THE FROG NEED TO CATCH THE FLY?

FILL EACH FISH WITH A DIFFERENT PATTERN.

HOW MANY FISH DO YOU COUNT?

DECORATE AND COLOR THE SEASHELLS TOO!

COLOR THE INSECTS IN EACH GROUP.
THEN COUNT THEM, AND COLOR THE RIGHT NUMBER.

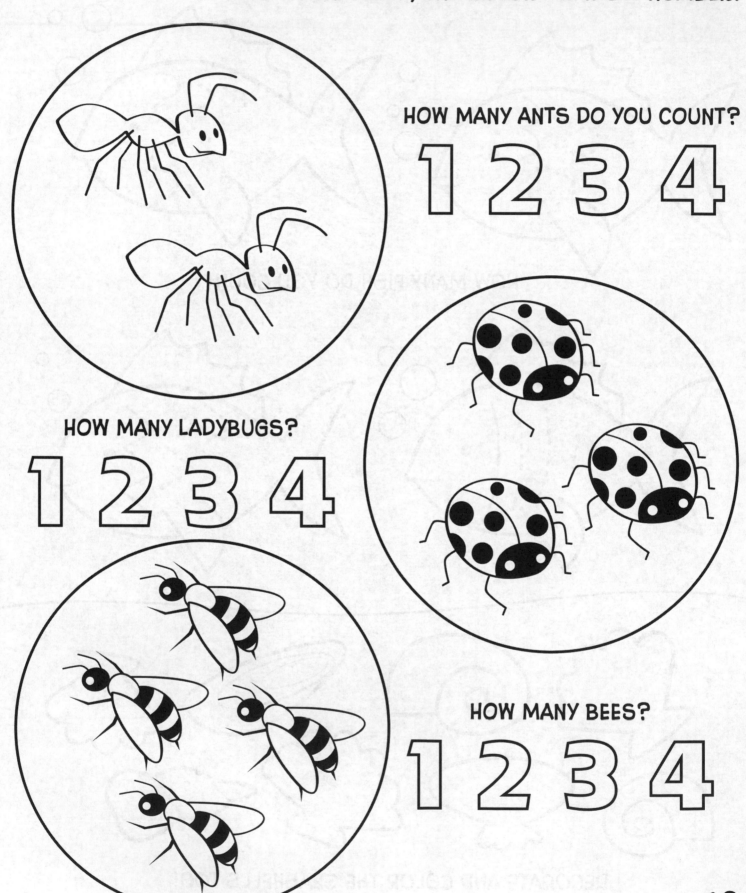

HOW MANY ANTS DO YOU COUNT?

1 2 3 4

HOW MANY LADYBUGS?

1 2 3 4

HOW MANY BEES?

1 2 3 4

10

COLOR THE FOODS YOU HAVE EATEN.

WHICH TEDDY BEAR DOES NOT LOOK LIKE THE OTHERS?

WHAT IS THIS?
WHERE DOES IT LIVE?

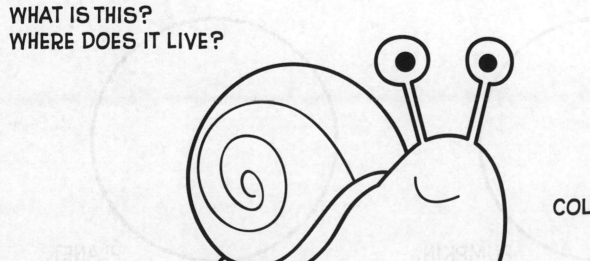

COLOR IT!

TURN THESE CIRCLES INTO FUN STUFF AND COLOR THEM ALL!

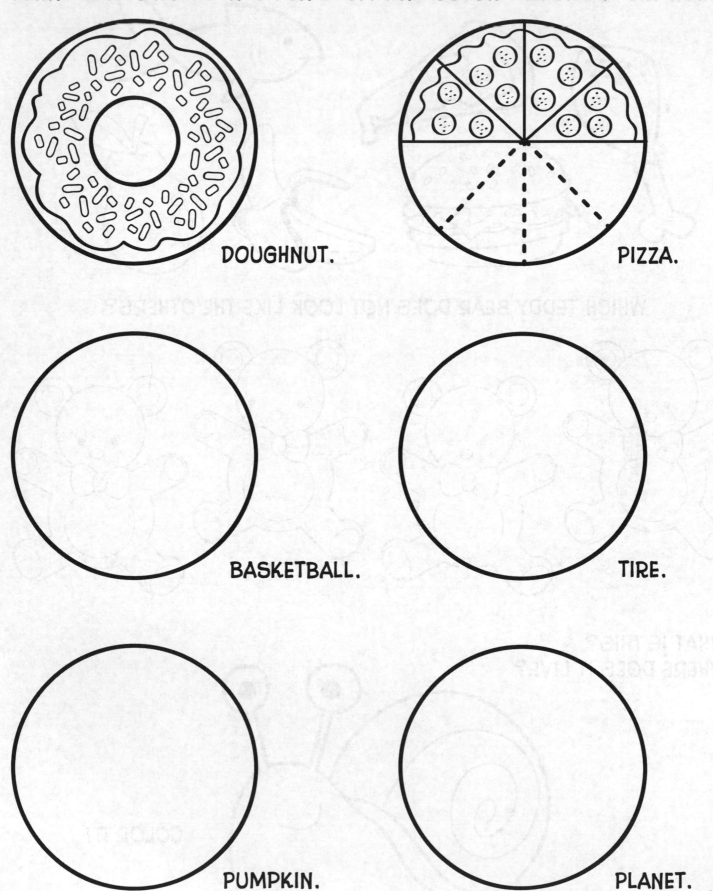

DOUGHNUT.

PIZZA.

BASKETBALL.

TIRE.

PUMPKIN.

PLANET.

12

IF THE CABBAGE IS ALL GREEN, WHAT COLORS IS THE CARROT?

DECORATE THE GHOST'S SHEET TO MAKE HIM HAPPY!

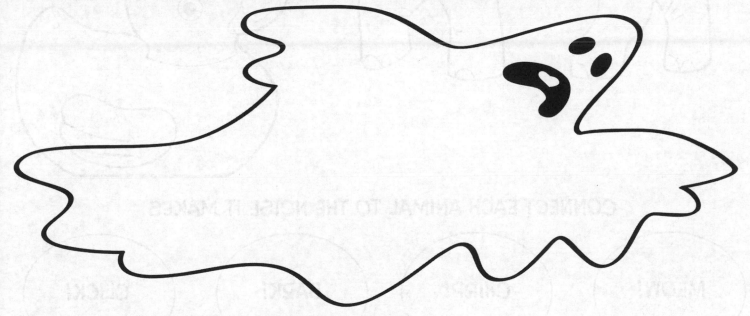

COUNT AND COLOR THE STARS YOU SEE.

13

TRACE THE DOTS TO DRAW THE WATER
THE ELEPHANT IS SPRAYING.

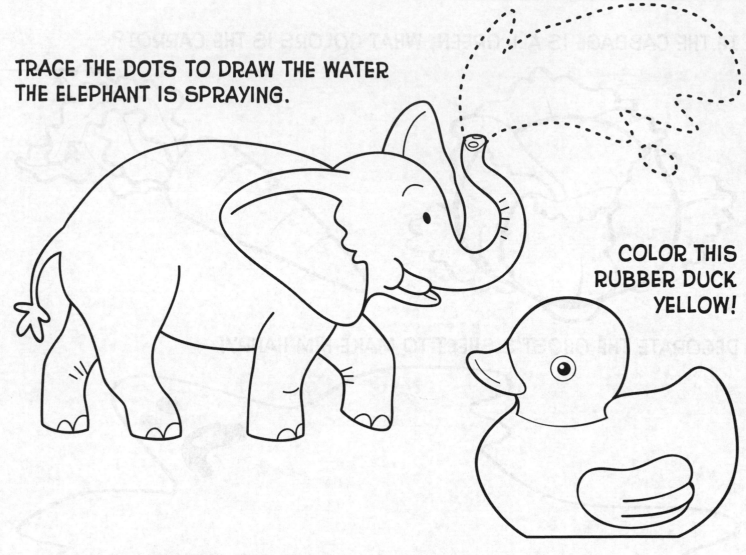

COLOR THIS
RUBBER DUCK
YELLOW!

CONNECT EACH ANIMAL TO THE NOISE IT MAKES.

MEOW!   CHIRP!   BARK!   CLICK!

14

DRAW THE MYSTERIOUS TREASURE
HIDDEN UNDERGROUND.
WHAT ELSE CAN BE FOUND BELOW? DRAW IT!

ABOVE.

BELOW.

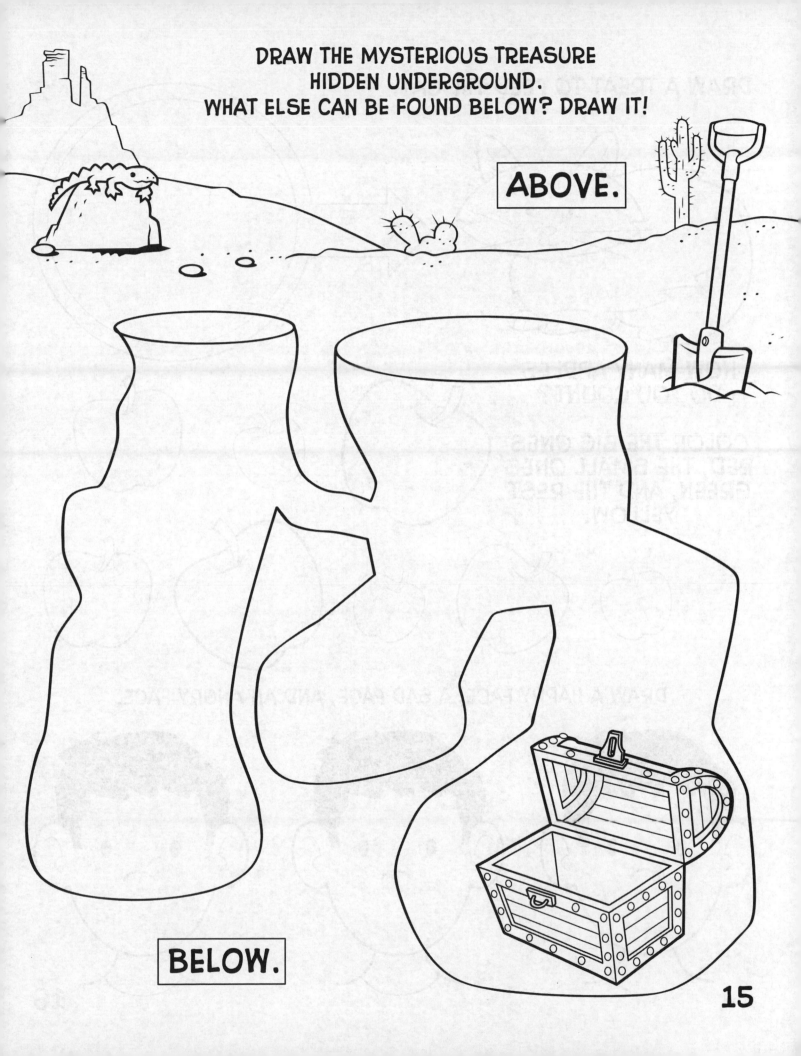

DRAW A TREAT TO FEED THE CAT.

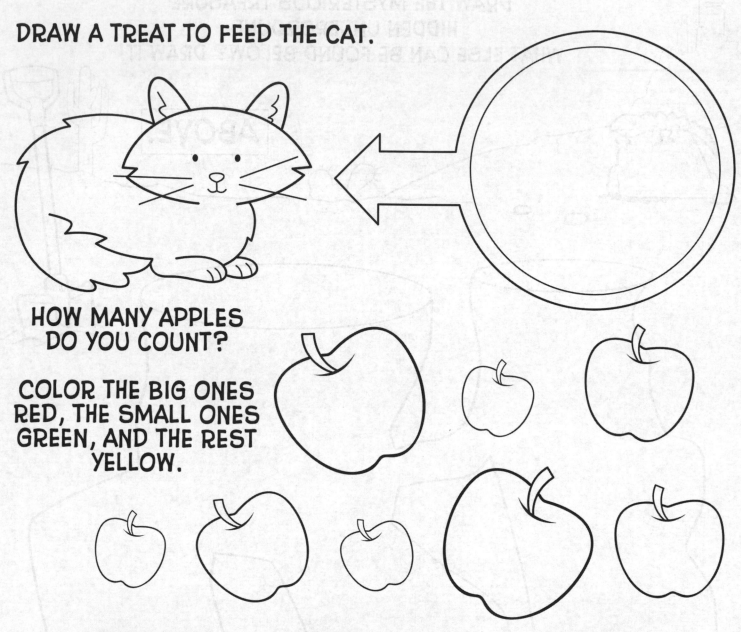

HOW MANY APPLES DO YOU COUNT?

COLOR THE BIG ONES RED, THE SMALL ONES GREEN, AND THE REST YELLOW.

DRAW A HAPPY FACE, A SAD FACE, AND AN ANGRY FACE.

WHICH PUPPY DOES NOT LOOK LIKE THE OTHERS?

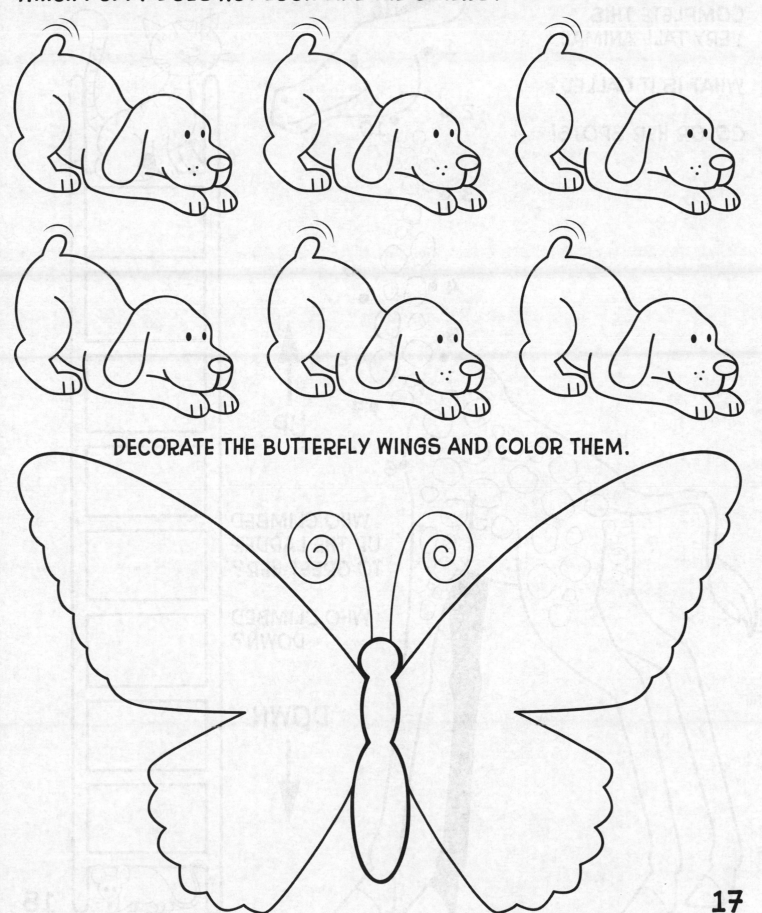

DECORATE THE BUTTERFLY WINGS AND COLOR THEM.

17

CONNECT THE DOTS TO
COMPLETE THIS
VERY TALL ANIMAL.

WHAT IS IT CALLED?

COLOR HER SPOTS!

UP

DOWN

WHO CLIMBED
UP THE LADDER
TO GREET HER?

WHO CLIMBED
DOWN?

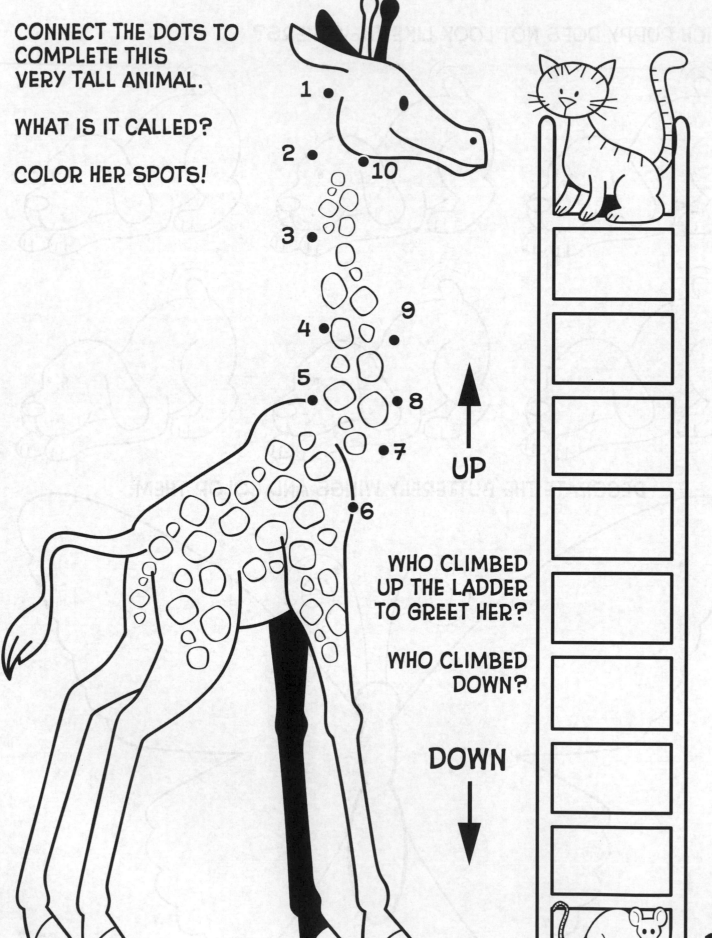

18

DRAW THE LIONS' MANE —
ONE STRAIGHT AND THE OTHER CURLY.

DRAW TWO MORE LIONS
WITH DIFFERENT MANES.

1 = BLUE , 2 = GREEN, AND 3 = BROWN

WHAT IS IT?

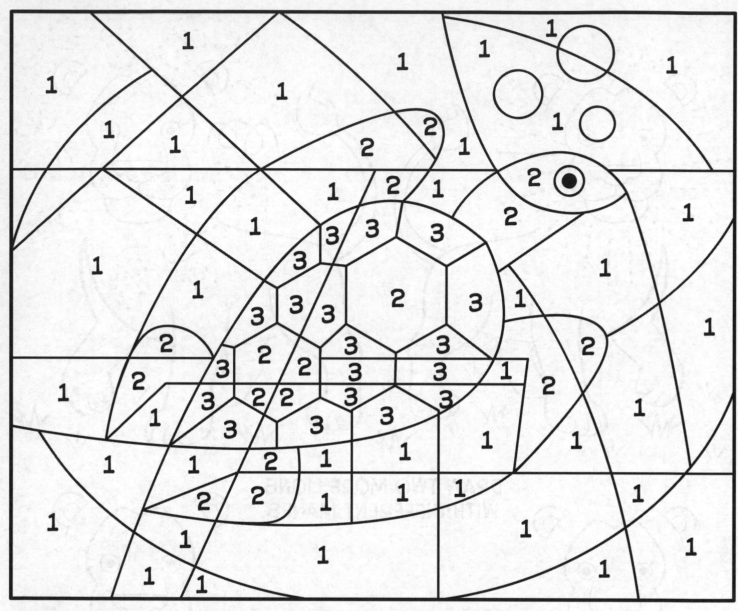

WHICH PATH WILL TAKE THE BUNNY TO THE EASTER EGG?

CONNECT THE DOTS TO DRAW THE ROCKET,
THEN DRAW THE ASTRONAUT LOOKING OUT THE WINDOW
AND COLOR EVERYTHING!

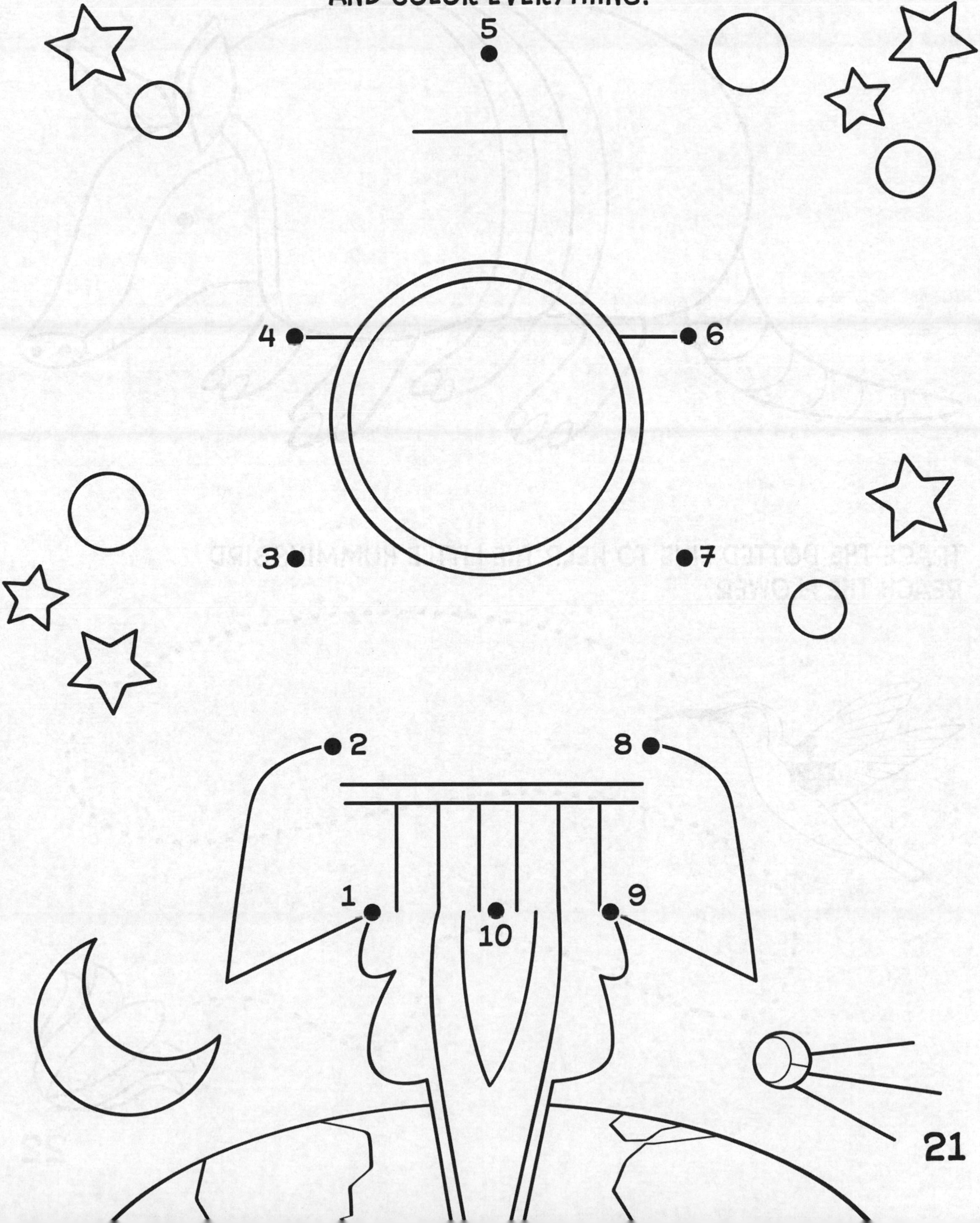

5

4   6

3   7

2   8

1   9

10

WHAT ANIMAL IS THIS?

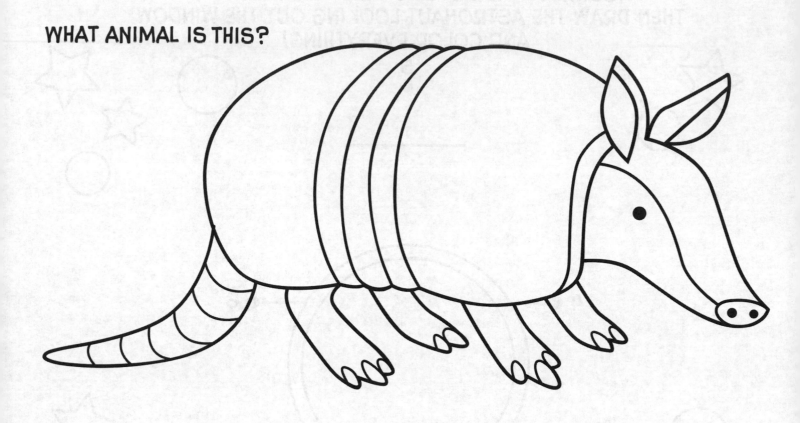

TRACE THE DOTTED LINE TO HELP THE LITTLE HUMMINGBIRD REACH THE FLOWER.

COLOR THE FRUITS IN EACH GROUP.
COUNT THEM AND COLOR THE RIGHT NUMBER.

HOW MANY APPLES DO YOU COUNT?

1 2 3 4
5 6 7 8

HOW MANY BANANAS DO YOU COUNT?

1 2 3 4
5 6 7 8

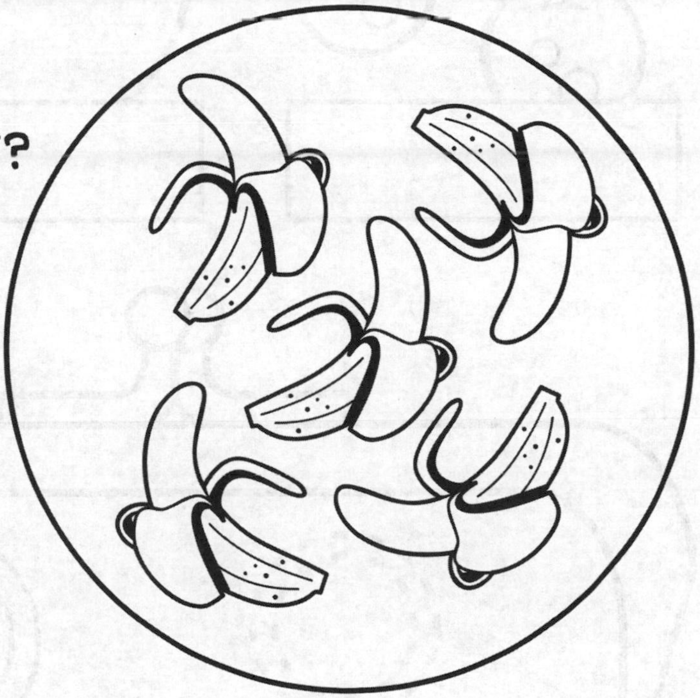

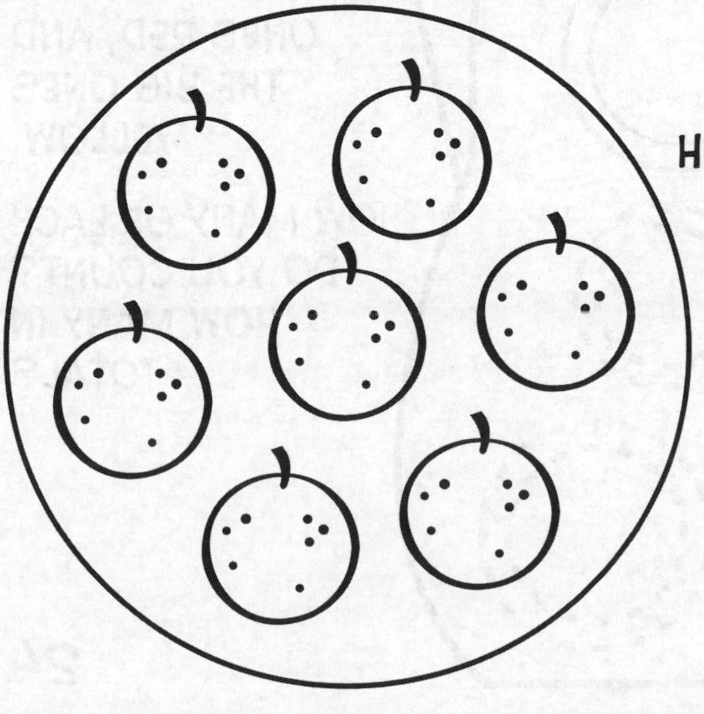

HOW MANY ORANGES DO YOU COUNT?

1 2 3 4
5 6 7 8

23

COLOR AND NAME
EACH FRUIT.

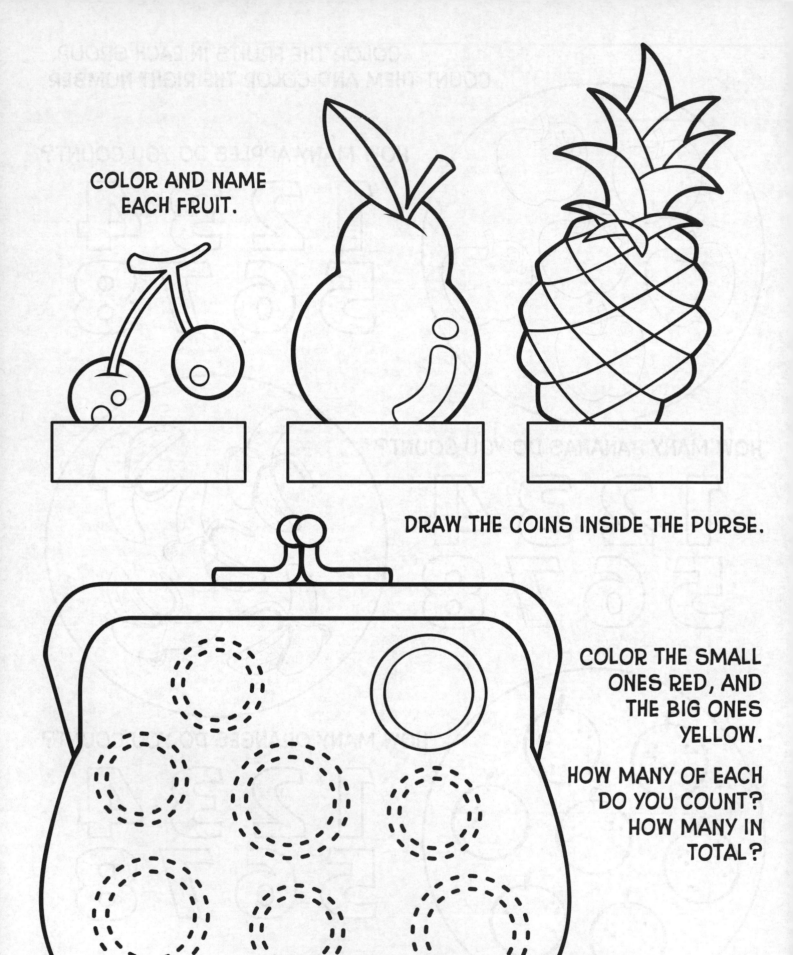

DRAW THE COINS INSIDE THE PURSE.

COLOR THE SMALL
ONES RED, AND
THE BIG ONES
YELLOW.

HOW MANY OF EACH
DO YOU COUNT?
HOW MANY IN
TOTAL?

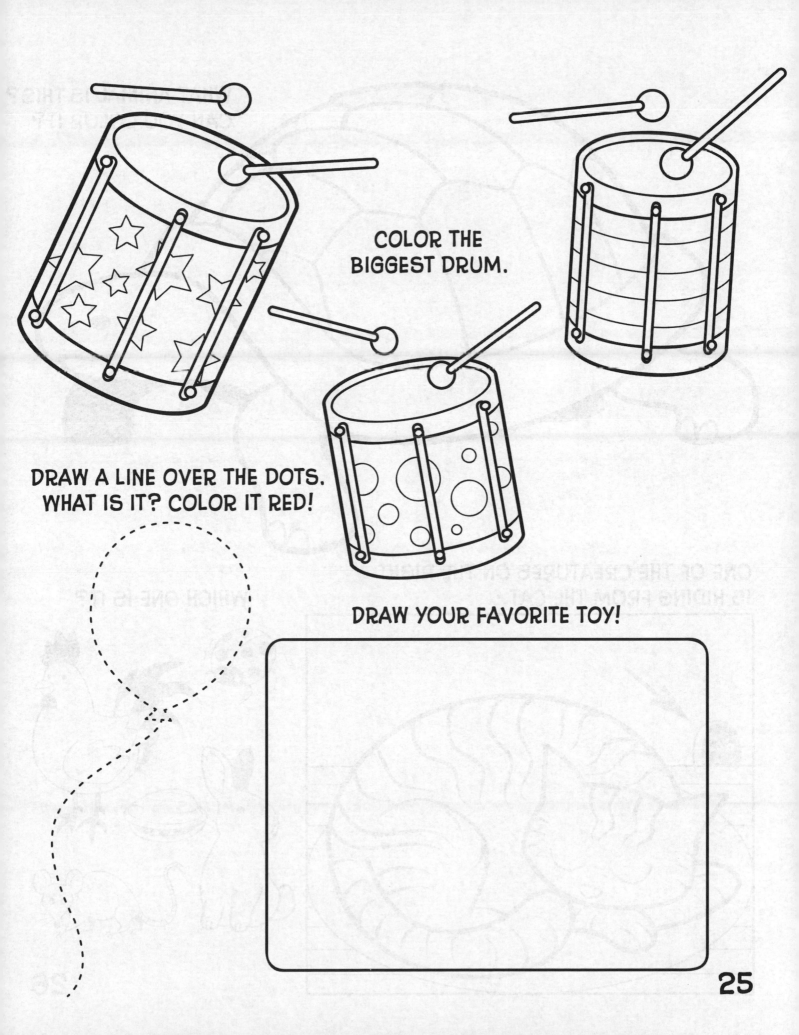

COLOR THE
BIGGEST DRUM.

DRAW A LINE OVER THE DOTS.
WHAT IS IT? COLOR IT RED!

DRAW YOUR FAVORITE TOY!

25

WHAT ANIMAL IS THIS?
CAN YOU COLOR IT?

ONE OF THE CREATURES ON THE RIGHT
IS HIDING FROM THE CAT.

WHICH ONE IS IT?

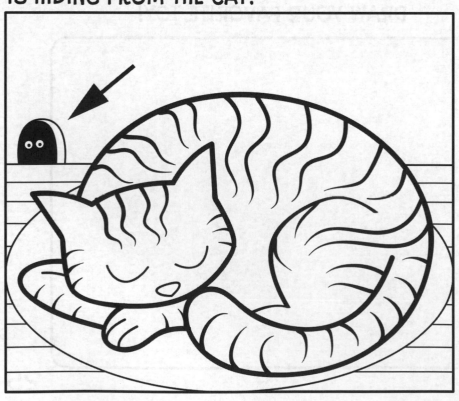

26

FILL THIS PAGE WITH THE DOG'S MUD PRINTS! →

DRAW FOUR RAISINS ON TOP OF THE ROLL AND THEN COLOR THE CUP.

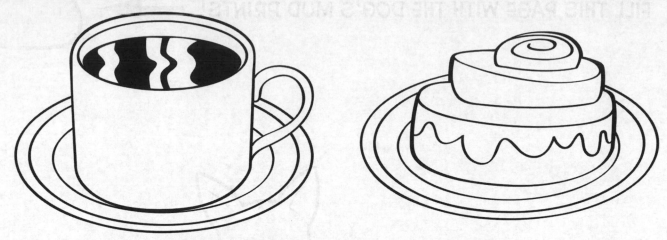

FILL THE HEDGEHOG'S BACK WITH SPINES AND DRAW ANOTHER ONE JUST LIKE IT.

WHICH PENGUIN DOES NOT LOOK LIKE THE OTHERS?

TRACE THE DOTS TO DRAW THE SAIL AND THE FLAG.

WHAT SHOULD BILLY USE AS BAIT TO CATCH FISH?

DRAW THE MISSING FISHING LINE.

COLOR ALL SIMILAR FISH THE SAME.
HOW MANY OF EACH GROUP CAN YOU COUNT?

DRAW THE BAIT!

ONE OF THEM IS MISSING!
WHERE IS IT?

WHAT KIND OF FISH IS THIS?

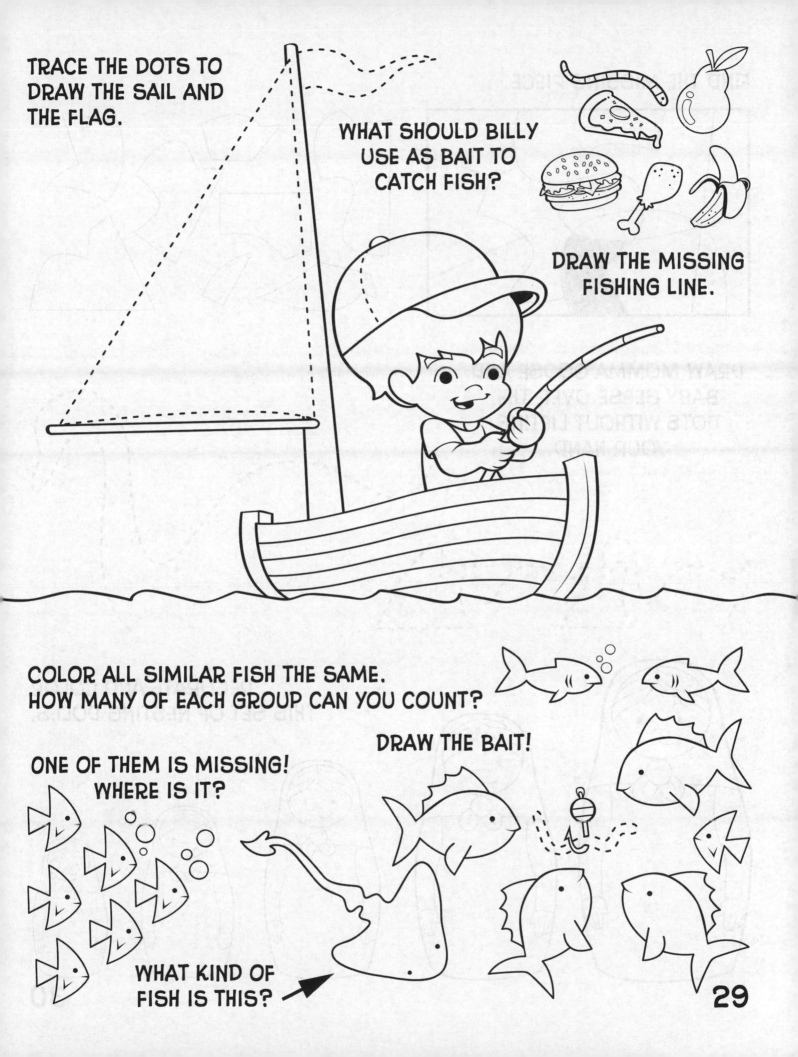

29

FIND THE MISSING PIECE.

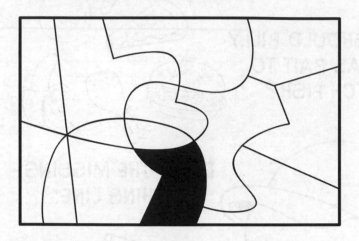 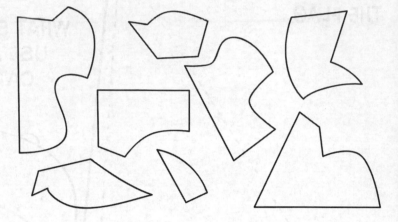

DRAW MOMMA GOOSE AND BABY GEESE OVER THE DOTS WITHOUT LIFTING YOUR HAND.

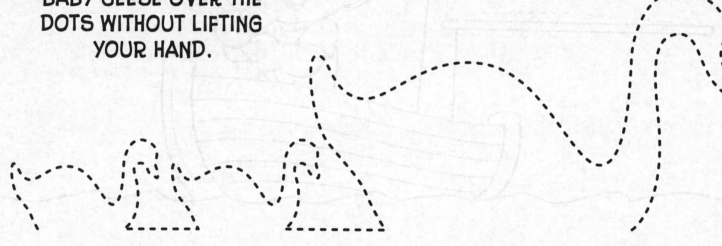

DECORATE AND COLOR THIS SET OF NESTING DOLLS.

A WHOLE LOT OF HATS! CAN YOU GUESS THEIR NAMES?

C

F

B

F

T

DRAW THREE SCOOPS OF ICE CREAM ON THE FIRST CONE,
TWO ON THE SECOND ONE, AND ONE ON THE THIRD ONE.
COLOR EACH LIKE YOUR FAVORITE FLAVORS!

WHICH ONES ARE NOT FRUITS?

WRITE THE NUMBERS MISSING ON THE CARS.
COLOR ONE LOCOMOTIVE RED
AND THE OTHER GREEN.

1   2   4

6   9

DRAW THE SPOTS
MISSING FROM THIS COW!

HOW MANY CUBES
CAN YOU COUNT?
WHICH TOWER IS THE TALLEST?

COLOR ALL HEARTS RED,
ALL STARS YELLOW,
ALL WATER DROPS BLUE,
AND ALL LEAVES GREEN.

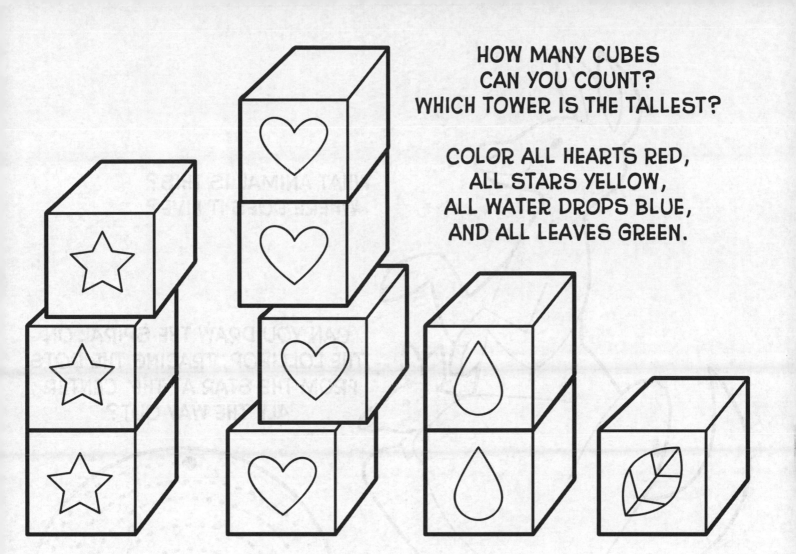

WHICH OF THESE ANIMALS STANDS
ON ONLY TWO LEGS?

33

WHAT ANIMAL IS THIS?
WHERE DOES IT LIVE?

CAN YOU DRAW THE SPIRAL ON
THE LOLLIPOP, TRACING THE DOTS
FROM THE STAR AT THE CENTER
ALL THE WAY OUT?

DECORATE AND COLOR
THE GIFT WRAPPING!

WHAT DOES THE MOUSE EAT?

DRAW YOUR MOM'S PORTRAIT.

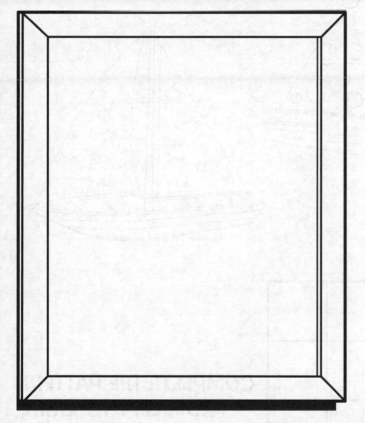

DRAW YOUR DAD'S PORTRAIT.

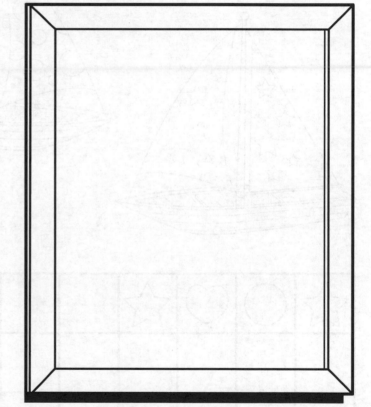

HOW MANY TIMES DID THE RABBIT LEAP TO GET THE CARROT?

FIND THE MATCHING
SAILBOATS AND
COLOR THEM ALIKE!

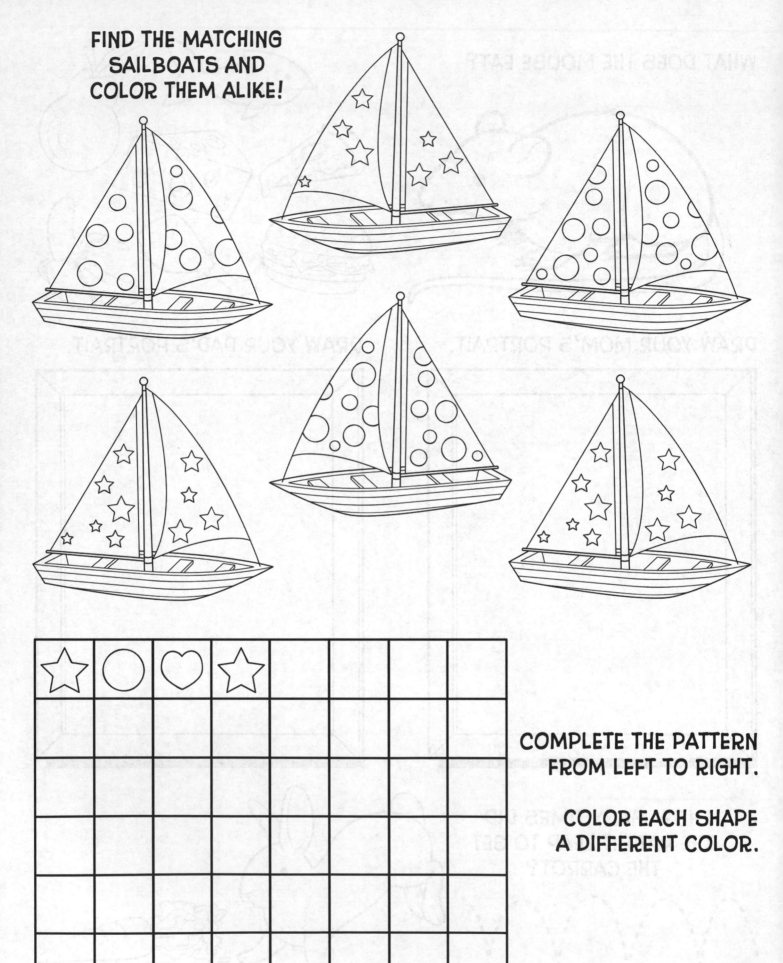

COMPLETE THE PATTERN
FROM LEFT TO RIGHT.

COLOR EACH SHAPE
A DIFFERENT COLOR.

36

FIND THE IDENTICAL TWIN BIRDS.

HELP MINDY GET HOME BY TRACING THE SUN'S DOTTED LINES YELLOW, AND THE CAR'S RED. COLOR THE WHOLE SCENE.

HOW MANY BALLOONS DO YOU SEE? COLOR THEM RED!

CONNECT THE DOTS TO FIND OUT WHAT CREATURE THIS IS.
WHERE DOES IT LIVE?

THE SEA IS VERY BUSY TODAY.
DRAW CIRCLES AROUND THE FISH.

WHAT IS NOT POSSIBLE
IN THIS PICTURE?
COLOR EVERYTHING BUT!

THERE'S AN INTRUDER AND THE BEES ARE SLEEPING! CAN YOU DRAW THE ONES MISSING FROM THE HIVE AND WAKE THEM UP? CAN YOU COUNT THEM ALL? WHERE IS THE QUEEN?

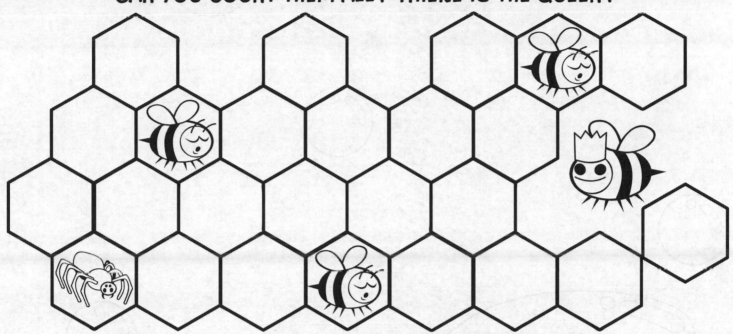

GIVE NUMBERS TO THE BIRDS FROM THE SMALLEST (1) TO THE BIGGEST (4) IN REAL LIFE.

WHAT IS THE NAME OF THIS ANIMAL? WHERE DOES IT LIVE?

39

FILL THIS PAGE WITH BLUE BUBBLES! ➡️

WHAT ARE BUBBLES MADE OF?
UNSCRAMBLE THE LETTERS TO FIND OUT!

COLOR THE SQUIRRELS BROWN AND THE HEDGEHOGS GRAY. HOW MANY OF EACH DO YOU COUNT?

WHAT HUNGRY ANIMAL IS THIS? CONNECT THE DOTS TO FIND OUT AND COLOR IT.

FINISH DRAWING THE SCALES ON ITS BACK TOO!

WHICH BUNNY DOES NOT LOOK LIKE THE OTHERS?

HELP JIMMY FIND HIS SNEAKERS
BY COLORING THEM BLUE!

COLOR THE COWBOY BOOTS BROWN,
THE HIGH HEELS RED,
AND THE REST AS YOU WISH!

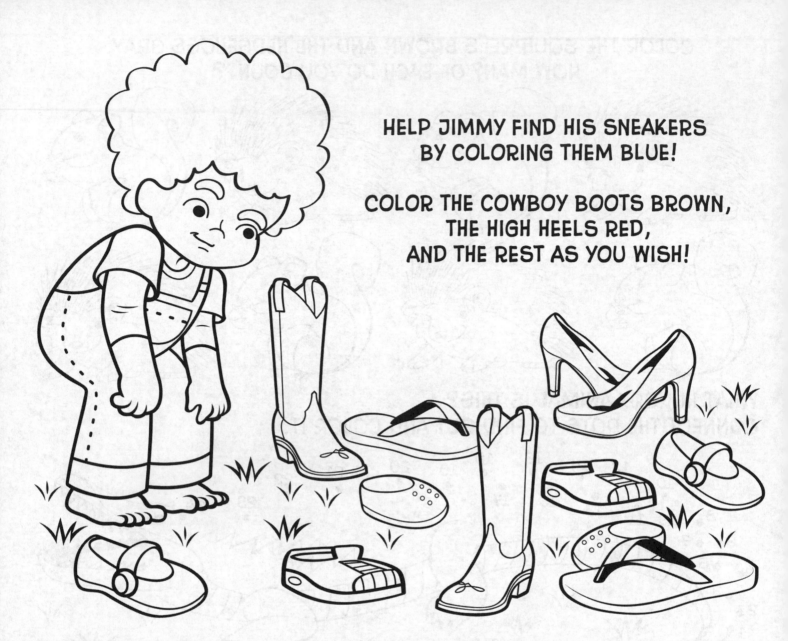

DRAW THE GARDEN SNAIL'S SHELL BY TRACING THE DOTTED LINE.
WHAT DOES IT EAT?

GUIDE THE PLANE THROUGH THE CLOUDS
SO IT LANDS SAFELY!

43

1 = BROWN
2 = BLUE
3 = GREEN
4 = YELLOW

WHAT ANIMAL IS IT?

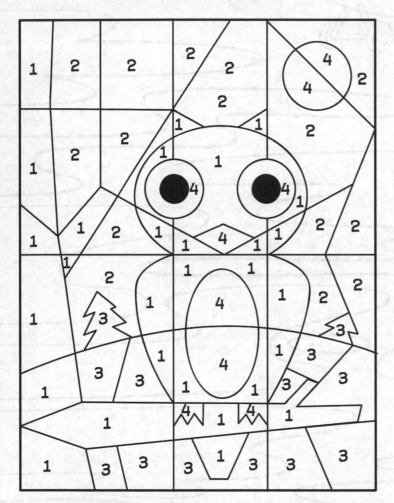

FIND THE EAGLE'S SHADOW.

DRAW A SLEEPY FACE, A SURPRISED FACE, AND A SERIOUS FACE.

44

FIND THE SEVEN DIFFERENCES.

CAN YOU DRAW A DINOSAUR IN THIS PREHISTORIC LANDSCAPE?

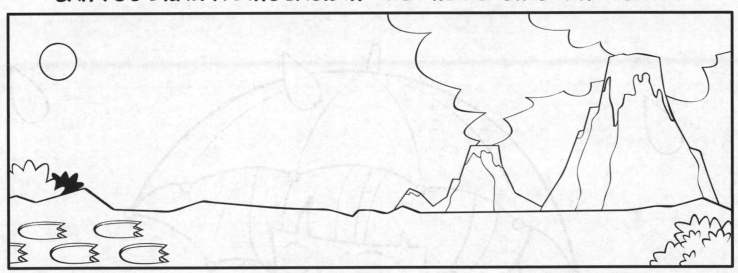

COLOR THE OBJECTS YOU CAN OPEN.

45

FILL THIS PAGE WITH BLUE RAINDROPS! ———➤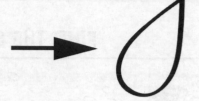

COLOR ANNIE'S
UMBRELLA RED,
HER COAT YELLOW,
AND HER BOOTS GREEN.

TRACE THE DOTTED LINES
TO DRAW THE HIVE.

WHAT SWEET TREAT
DO THE BEES MAKE?
NAME IT!

H _ _ _ _

WHAT IS THIS ANIMAL CALLED?   DRAW ANOTHER ONE JUST LIKE IT!

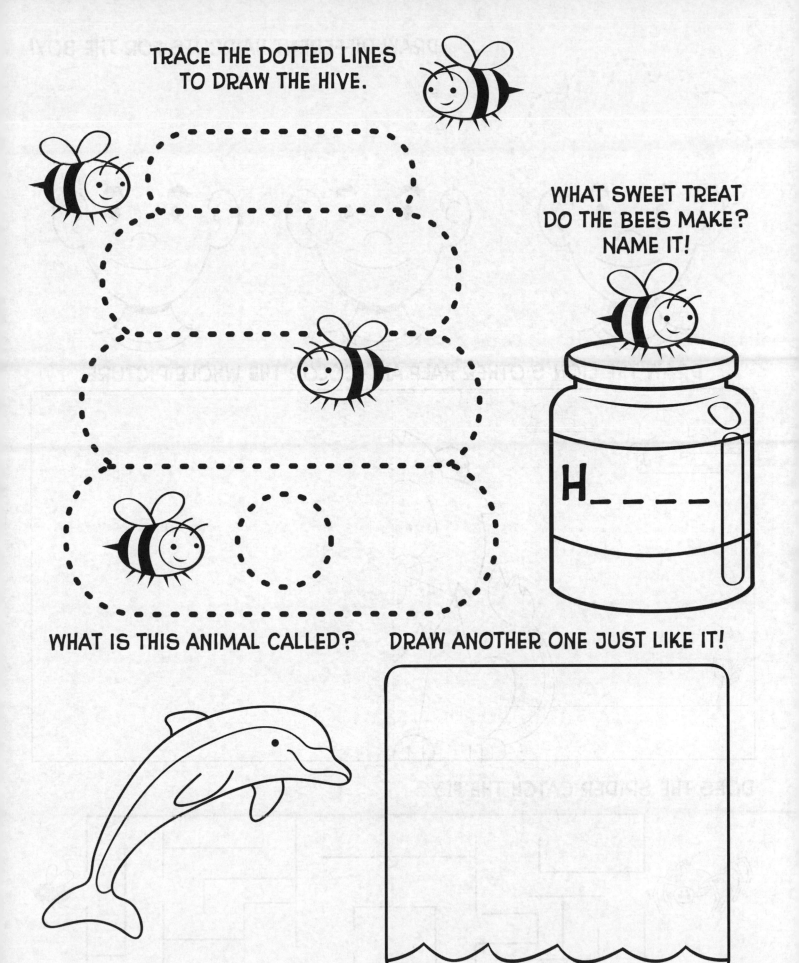

47

DRAW DIFFERENT HAIRCUTS FOR THE BOY!

DRAW THE LION'S OTHER HALF AND COLOR THE WHOLE PICTURE.

DOES THE SPIDER CATCH THE FLY?

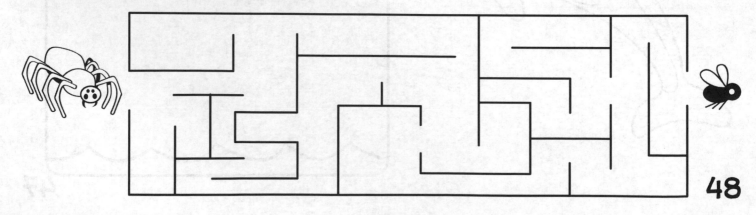

WHAT'S MISSING FROM THIS CAMEL? CAN YOU DRAW IT?

WHICH ONE OF THESE ANIMALS DOES NOT LAY EGGS?

COLOR THE FOODS THAT TASTE SWEET.

COLOR ONLY THE STRIPED T-SHIRTS.

DECORATE THE ONE
IN THE MIDDLE
ANY WAY YOU LIKE!

COLOR THE BENT WANDS ORANGE AND THE STRAIGHT ONES YELLOW.

DRAW THE RAYS OF SUNSHINE THROUGH THE CLOUDS.

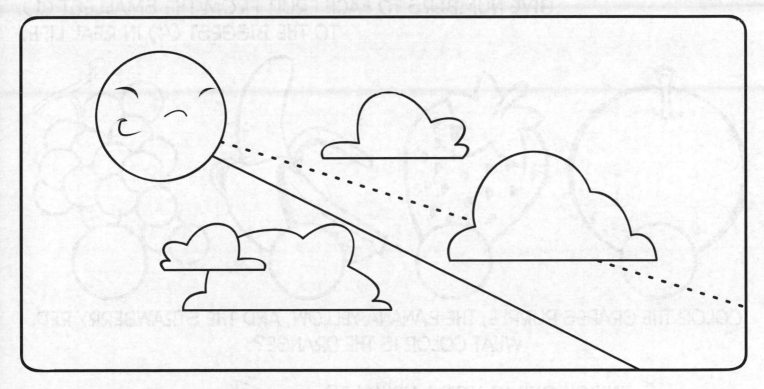

WHAT ANIMAL IS THIS?
WHERE DOES IT LIVE?

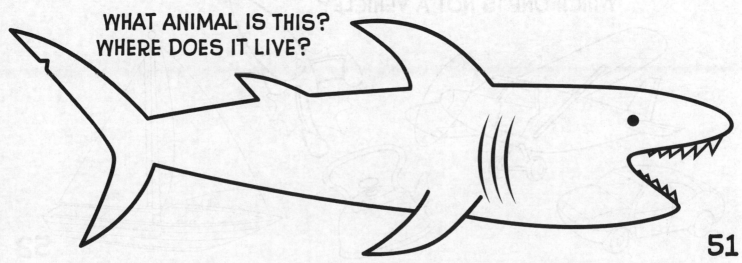

TRACE THE FIRST FLOWER AND THEN FOLLOW
THE BEE'S FLIGHT PATH TO THE NEXT FLOWER.

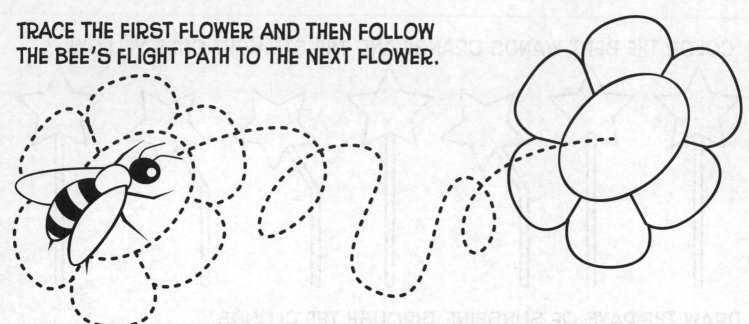

GIVE NUMBERS TO EACH FRUIT FROM THE SMALLEST (1)
TO THE BIGGEST (4) IN REAL LIFE.

COLOR THE GRAPES PURPLE, THE BANANA YELLOW, AND THE STRAWBERRY RED.
WHAT COLOR IS THE ORANGE?

WHICH ONE IS NOT A VEHICLE?

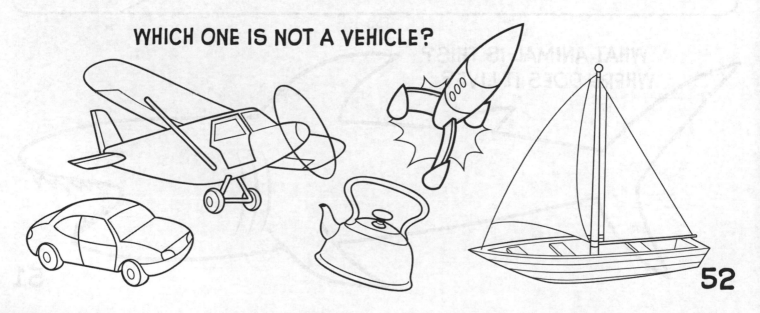

52

TURN THESE SQUARES INTO FUN STUFF, AND COLOR IT ALL!

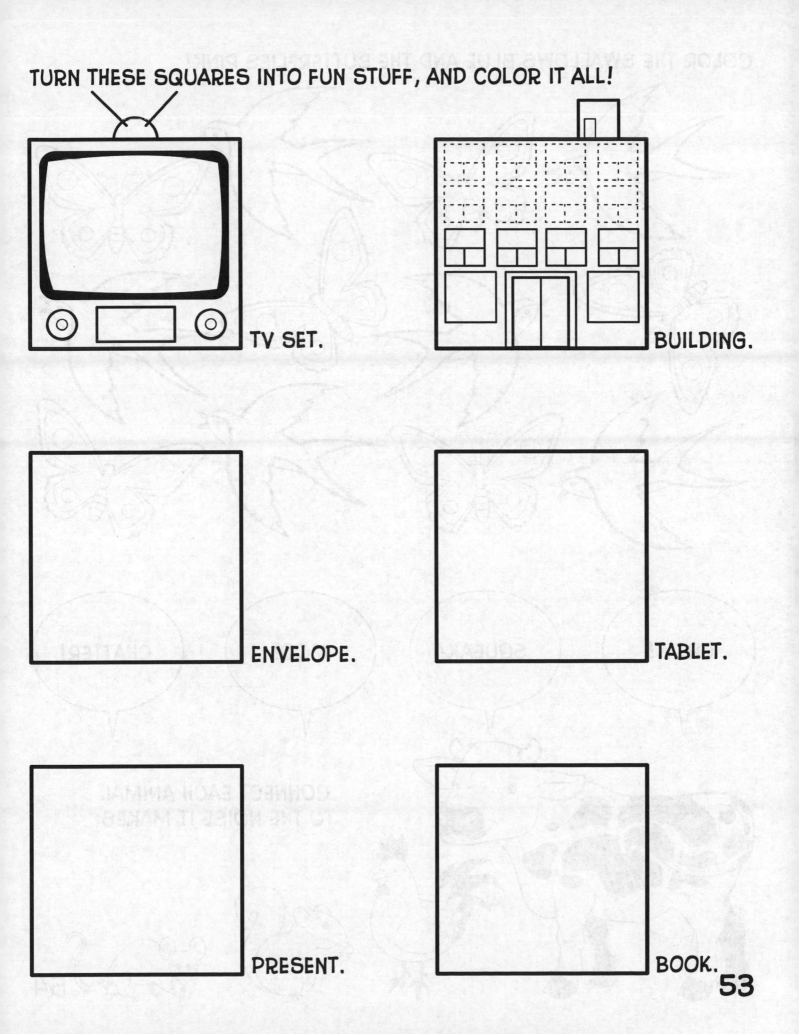

TV SET.

BUILDING.

ENVELOPE.

TABLET.

PRESENT.

BOOK.

53

COLOR THE SWALLOWS BLUE AND THE BUTTERFLIES PINK!

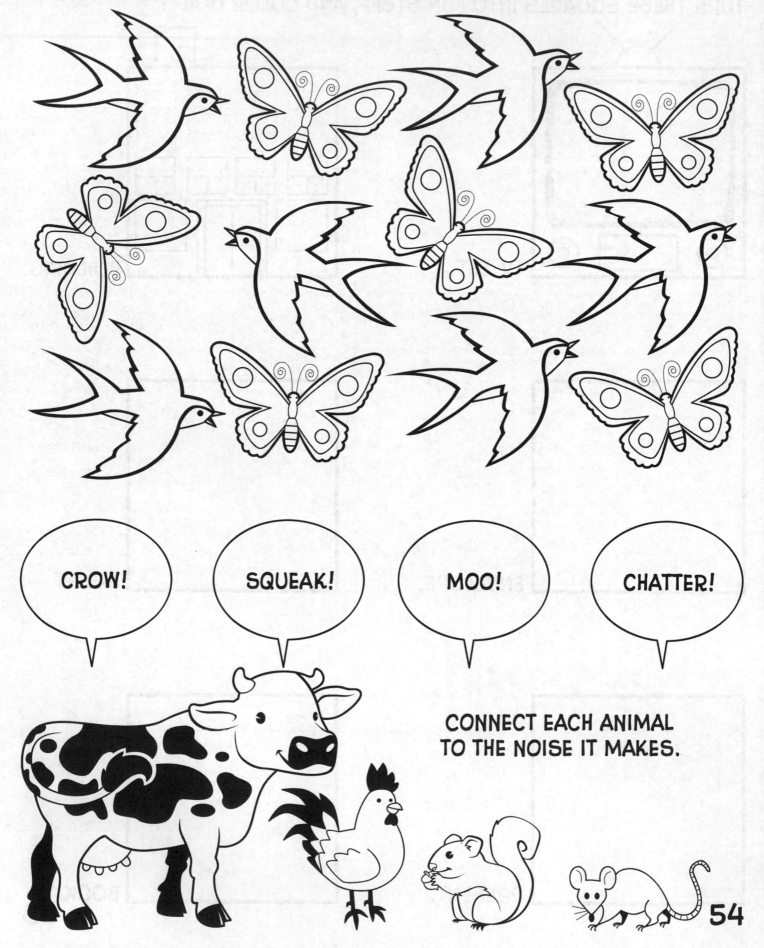

CROW!

SQUEAK!

MOO!

CHATTER!

CONNECT EACH ANIMAL TO THE NOISE IT MAKES.

54

DRAW THE KITTY'S
LONG TAIL, AND THEN
COLOR HIM ORANGE.

DO YOU HAVE A PET?
DRAW IT HERE.

FILL THE JAR WITH CANDY.
COLOR HALF OF THEM RED
AND THE REST BLUE.

COUNT THEM ALL.

WHOOPS!
HOW MANY DOUGHNUTS
DID SALLY DROP?

WHICH ONE OF THESE DOES NOT
BELONG IN THE KITCHEN?

DRAW THE SHEEP'S COAT OF WOOL— ONE WAVY AND THE OTHER CURLY.

DRAW TWO MORE SHEEP WITH DIFFERENT COATS.

WHAT IS NOT POSSIBLE IN THIS PICTURE? WHY?

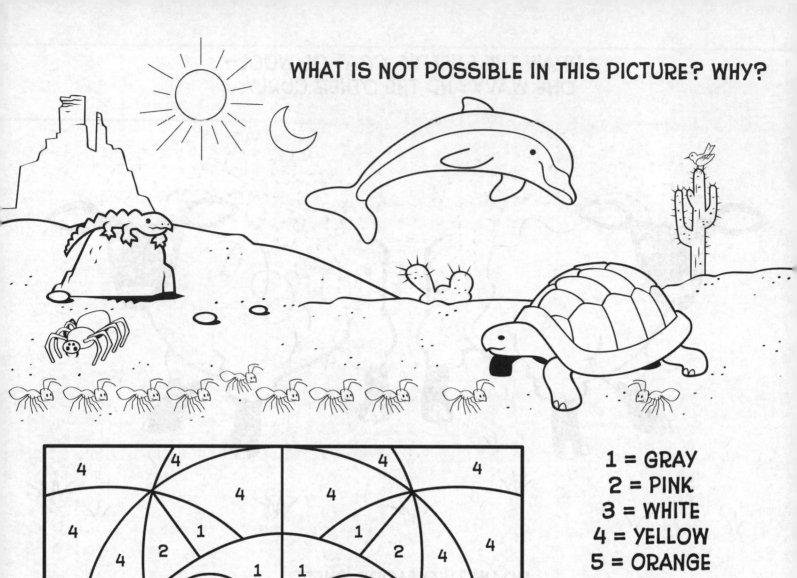

1 = GRAY
2 = PINK
3 = WHITE
4 = YELLOW
5 = ORANGE

WHAT ANIMAL IS IT?
DRAW A CIRCLE
AROUND ITS FAVORITE
FOOD BELOW.

58

ONE OF THESE ANIMALS CAN'T SWIM. CAN YOU GUESS WHICH ONE?

WHAT IS THIS ANIMAL CALLED?   DRAW ANOTHER ONE JUST LIKE IT!

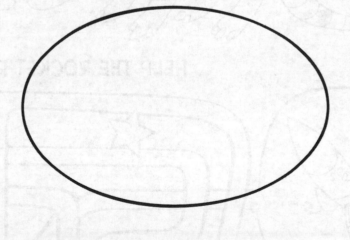

FINISH THIS DRAWING.

WHICH ARMADILLO DOES NOT LOOK LIKE THE OTHERS?

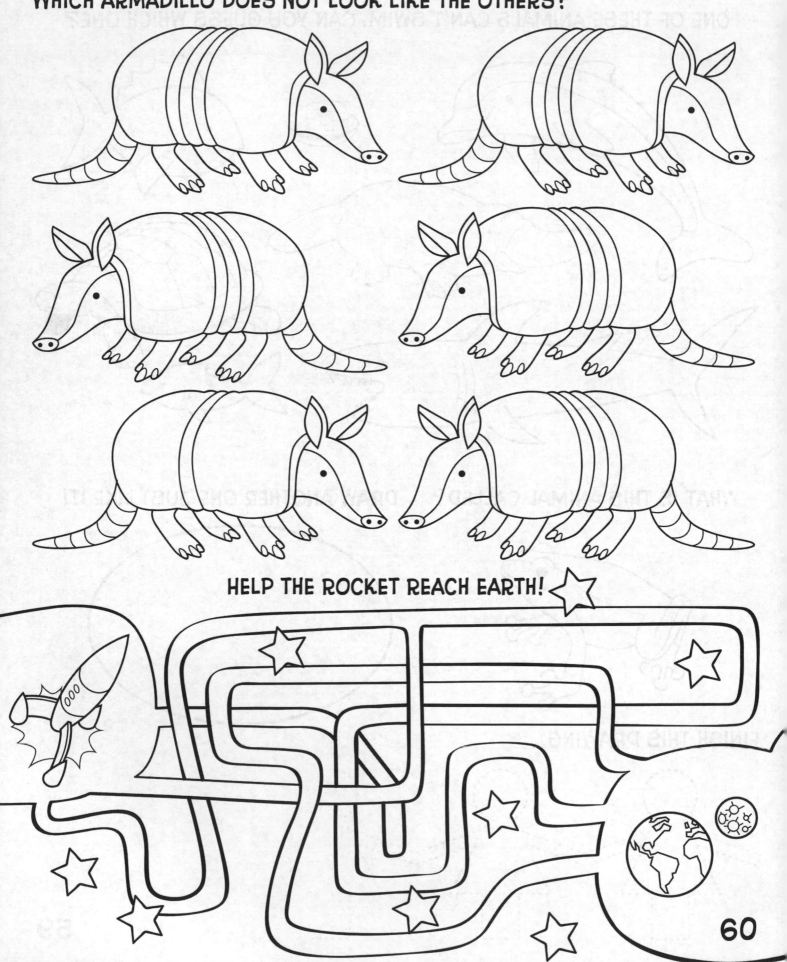

HELP THE ROCKET REACH EARTH!

FILL THE SKY WITH FALLING SNOWFLAKES! →

COLOR THE CARROT ORANGE
AND THE PINE TREES GREEN.

COLOR THE CABIN
BROWN
AND THE SNOWMAN'S
BUTTONS RED.

DRAW A LINE TO MATCH EACH WORD TO DIFFERENT PARTS OF THE TEDDY BEAR.

RIGHT ARM

RIGHT LEG

TUMMY

MOUTH

LEFT LEG

HEAD

EYES

EARS

NOSE

LEFT ARM

COMPLETE THE NIGHT VIEW WITH STARS, BATS, AND OWLS!

HELP THE LITTLE MONKEY REACH THE BANANA!

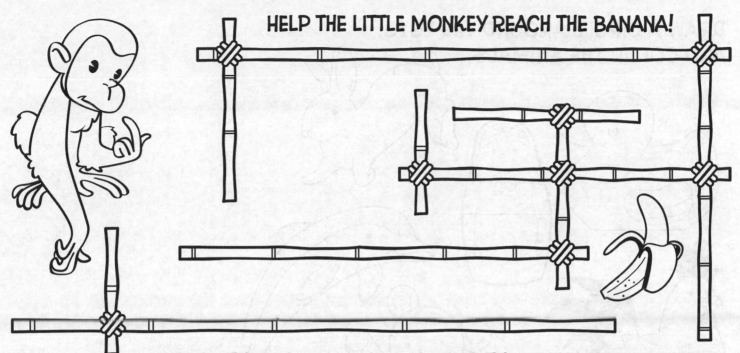

COLOR THE BIG BALLS ORANGE AND THE SMALL ONES PURPLE.

FILL THE OTHER COMPARTMENTS WITH OTHER CREATURES FROM YOUR GARDEN!

DRAW A CIRCLE AROUND THE TOYS, AND COLOR THE ANIMALS.

COLOR THE COLD THINGS BLUE AND THE HOT ONES RED.

CONTINUE DRAWING UPWARD, AS MANY BLOCKS AS YOU NEED, TO REACH THE TOP OF THIS PAGE!

DRAW EIGHT LEGS ON EACH BABY SPIDER, AND THEN COLOR THEM AND THEIR MOM.

HOW MANY SPIDERS DO YOU COUNT?

COLOR THE PIGEONS GREY, BROWN, AND WHITE, AS YOU PLEASE.

65

COLOR THE TALLEST GNOME HAT RED, THE MIDDLE SIZED HAT YELLOW, AND THE SMALL ONE BLUE.

COLOR THE FIRST GNOME'S JACKET RED, THE SECOND ONE BLUE, AND THE LAST ONE YELLOW.

IF YOU MIX THE COLORS ON EACH GNOME'S HAT AND JACKET AND USE IT TO COLOR THEIR PANTS, WHAT COLOR WOULD EACH GNOME'S PANTS BE?

FIND THE ONE THAT'S DIFFERENT.

WHAT DOES THE ELEPHANT EAT?

MATCH THE ROOSTER TO THE APPROPRIATE OUTLINE.

67

DRAW THE OTHER HALF.

HOW CAN THIS LITTLE DRAGONFLY ESCAPE THE MOSQUITO NET?

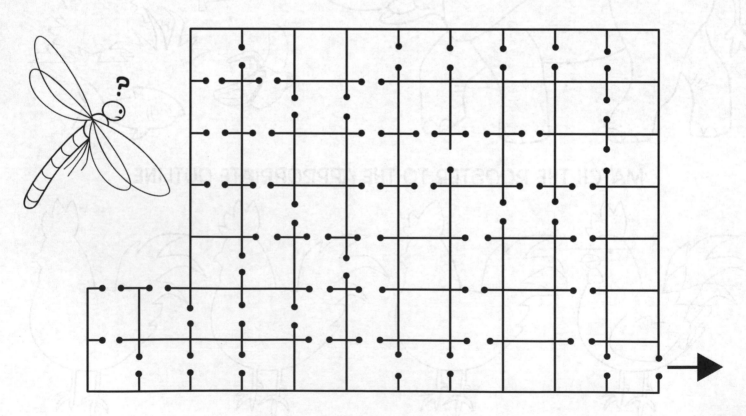

WHICH PINEAPPLE DOES NOT LOOK LIKE THE OTHERS?

WHAT PIECE DOES NOT MATCH THE DRAWING?

TRACE A LINE OVER THE DOTS WITHOUT LIFTING YOUR HAND.

WHAT IS IT?

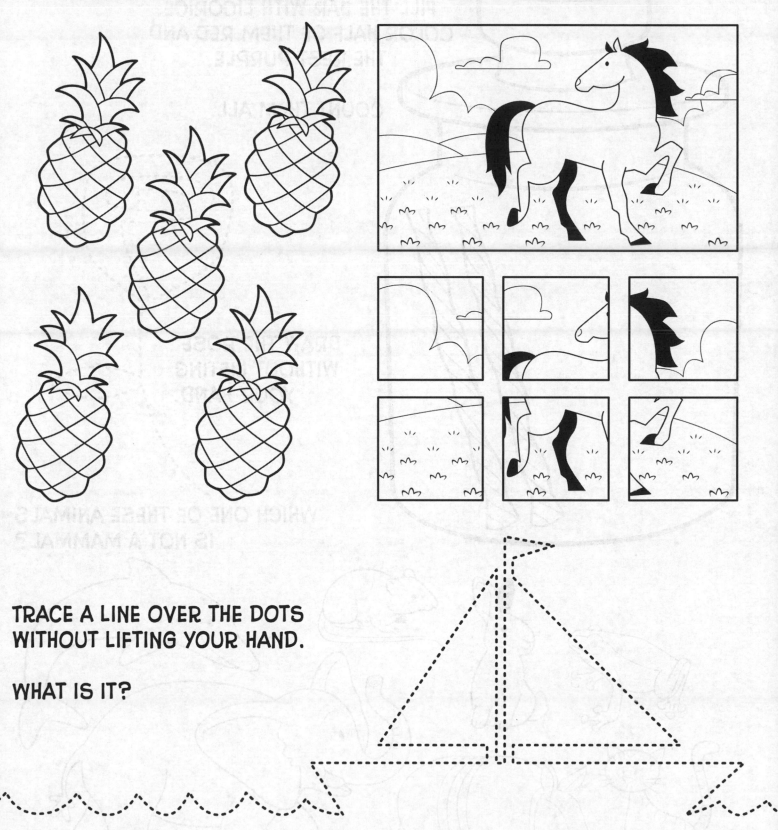

FILL THE JAR WITH LICORICE.
COLOR HALF OF THEM RED AND
THE REST PURPLE.

COUNT THEM ALL.

DRAW THE ROSE
WITHOUT LIFTING
YOUR HAND.

WHICH ONE OF THESE ANIMALS
IS NOT A MAMMAL?

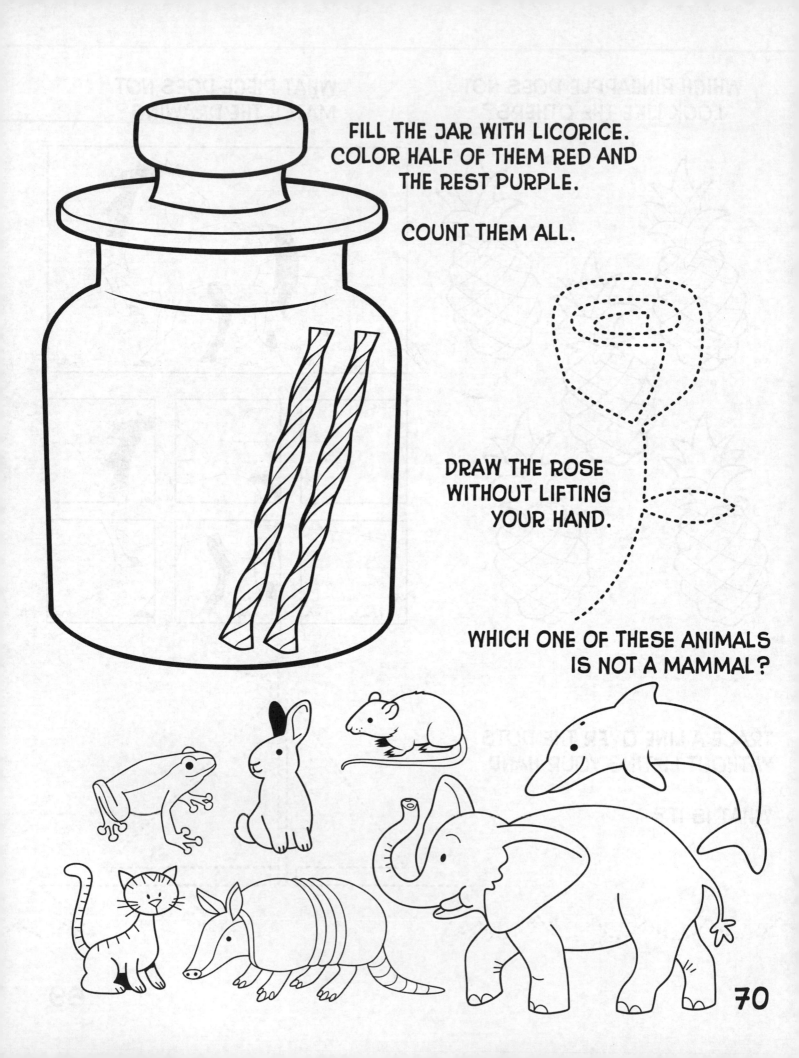

70

WHAT'S MISSING FROM
MR. SCARECROW'S HEAD?

WHAT DO WE CALL THE
BLACK BIRD PERCHED ON
HIS ARM?

C _ _ _

DECORATE THE SHIRT,
AND COLOR THE BIB BLUE.

CHOOSE A FACE
TO DRAW ON IT'S HEAD.

WHAT ARE THESE CALLED?
COLOR THEM!

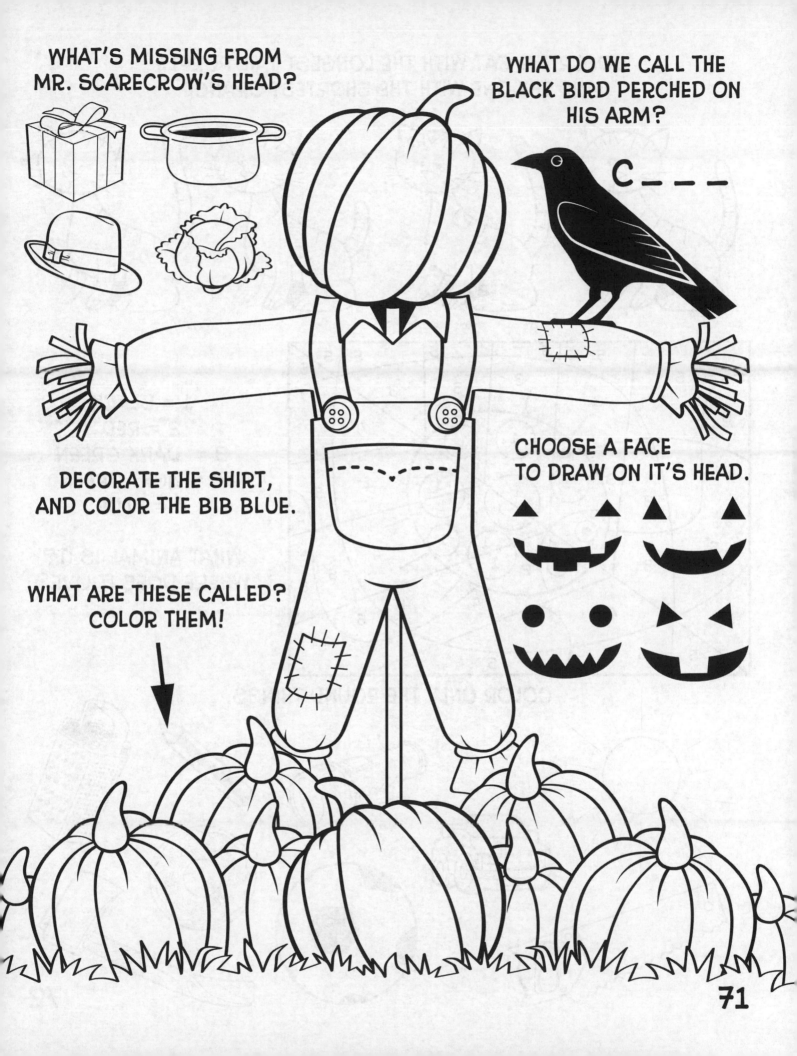

71

COLOR THE CAT WITH THE LONGEST TAIL PURPLE AND THE ONE WITH THE SHORTEST ORANGE.

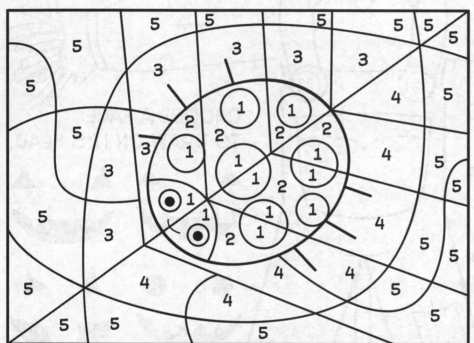

1 = BLACK
2 = RED
3 = DARK GREEN
4 = LIGHT GREEN
5 = BLUE

WHAT ANIMAL IS IT?
WHERE DOES IT LIVE?

COLOR ONLY THE ROUND THINGS.

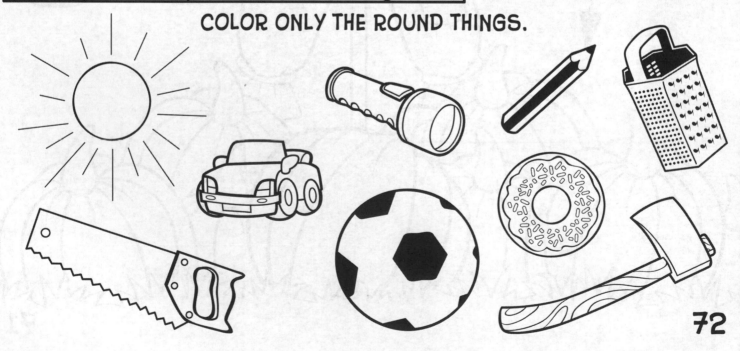

HOW MANY
TRIANGLES
DO YOU SEE?
COLOR THEM
YELLOW.

FIND THE SIX DIFFERENCES.

COLOR THE BROKEN LOLLIPOPS GREEN AND THE STRAIGHT ONES RED.
WHICH ONE ISN'T A LOLLIPOP? WHAT IS IT? COLOR IT PINK.

HELP ICHA'S KISS FIND ITS WAY TO DIEGO'S CHEEK!

FILL THE PAGE WITH HEARTS! →

74

COLOR ONLY THE THINGS PEOPLE WEAR.

COLOR THE BASKET WITH THE MOST APPLES IN IT.

COLOR THE BIG PEARS YELLOW AND THE SMALL ONES GREEN. COLOR ALL CHERRIES RED.

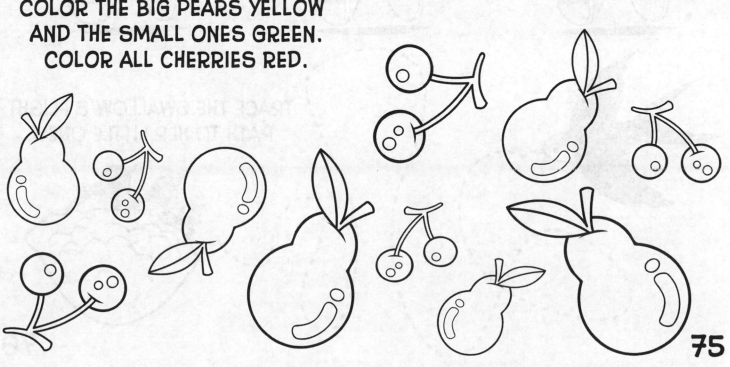

FIND THE ONE THAT'S DIFFERENT.

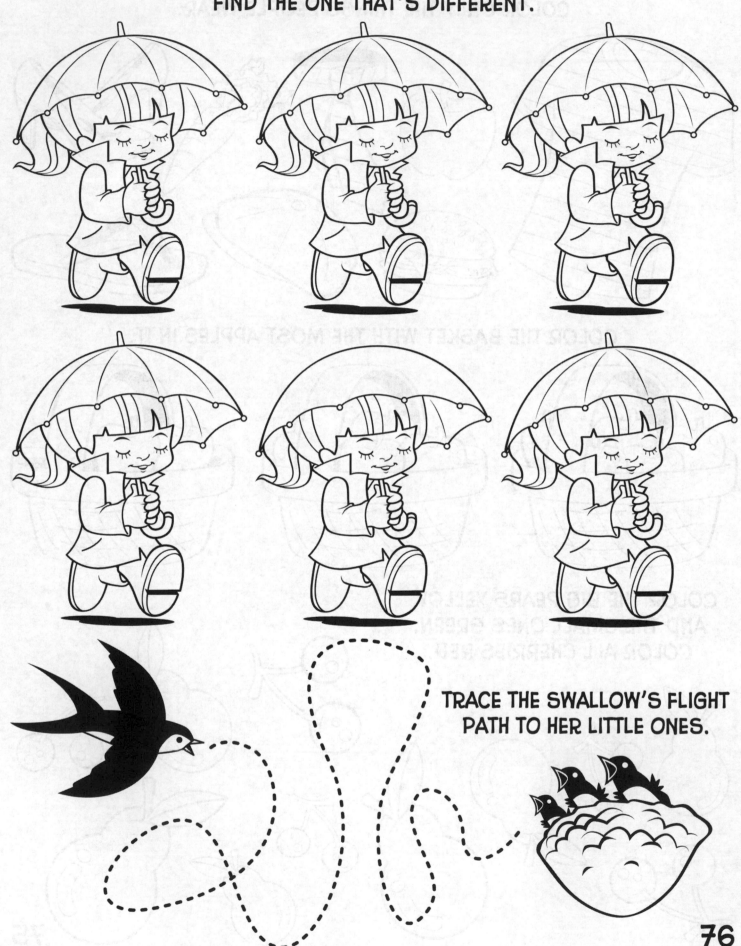

TRACE THE SWALLOW'S FLIGHT PATH TO HER LITTLE ONES.

WHICH ONE DOESN'T BELONG?

WHY?

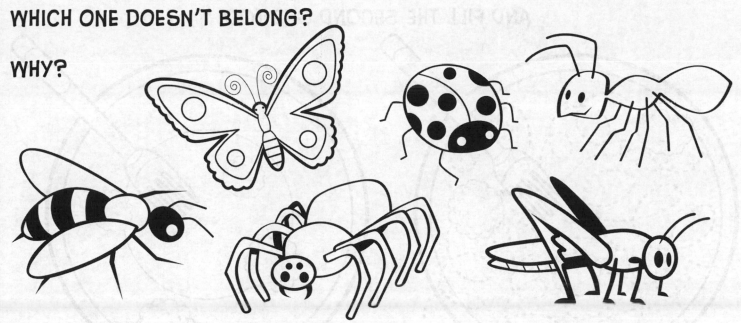

DRAW THE OTHER HALF, AND PAINT FRECKLES ON HIS FACE.

WHAT IS THE NAME OF THIS TOOL?

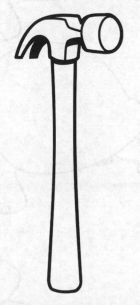

WHAT IS IT FOR?

FINISH DRAWING THE SPAGHETTI ON THE FIRST PLATE, AND FILL THE SECOND ONE TOO!

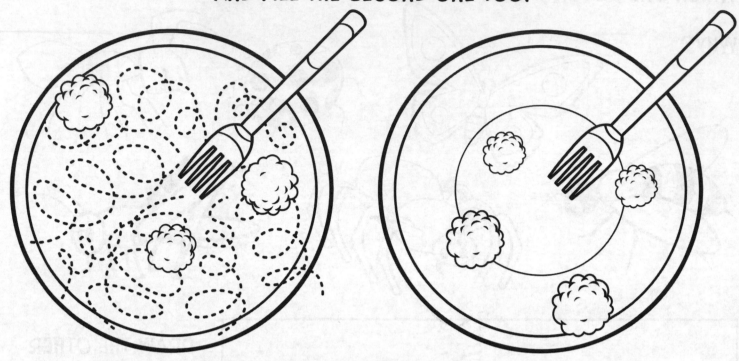

DECORATE EACH TORTOISE SHELL THE WAY SHE WANTS.

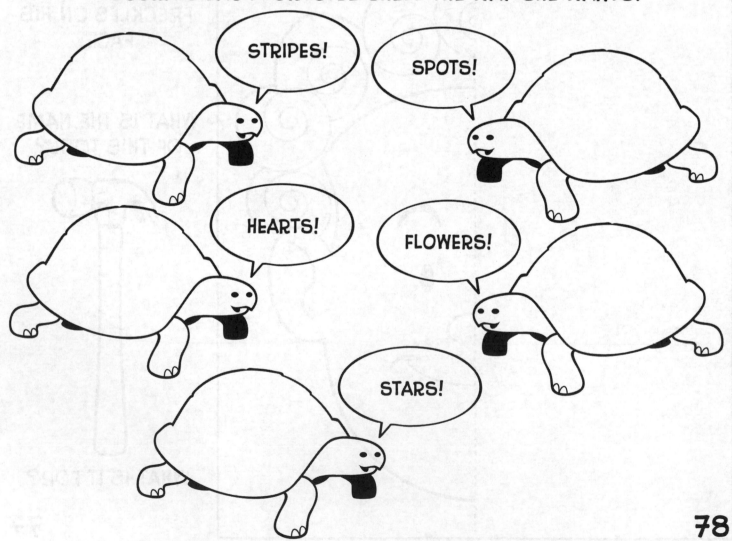

78

WHICH ONE OF THESE BIRDS DOES NOT FLY?

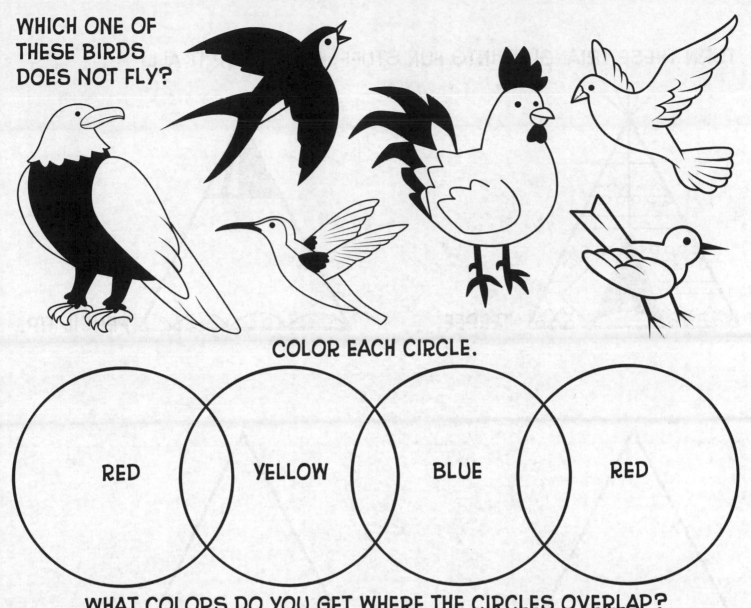

COLOR EACH CIRCLE.

RED   YELLOW   BLUE   RED

WHAT COLORS DO YOU GET WHERE THE CIRCLES OVERLAP?

HOW MANY HEARTS DO YOU COUNT?

TURN THESE TRIANGLES INTO FUN STUFF, AND COLOR IT ALL!

 TEEPEE.

 PENCIL TIP.

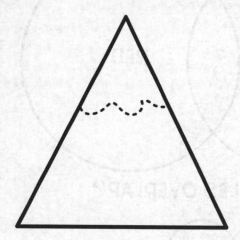 MOUNTAIN.

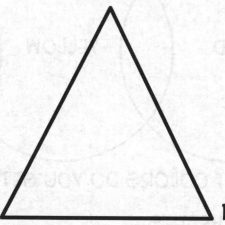 PARTY HAT.

 PAPER PLANE.

 PYRAMID.

HELP THE LITTLE PIRATE FIND THE TREASURE!

COLOR THE DOUBLOONS YELLOW AND THE CHEST BROWN!

HOW MANY ICEBERGS DOES THE PENGUIN HOP ON TO REACH HIS FRIEND?

FIND THE
MATCHING KITES
AND
COLOR THEM
ALIKE!

CAN YOU COUNT THE NUMBER OF SPOTS ON THE DALMATIAN ON THE LEFT, AND MIRROR THEM ON THE SPOTLESS ONE?

COLOR THE TALLEST ONE PURPLE AND THE SMALLEST YELLOW.

83

DO YOU LIKE THIS PUPPY?
DRAW ANOTHER ONE JUST LIKE IT,
AND COLOR THE FRISBEE RED!

FOLLOW EACH THREAD TO FIND OUT
WHICH BALLOON IS SHE HOLDING,
AND COLOR IT BLUE!

84

FIND THE TRUE SHADOW OF THE HAMBURGER.

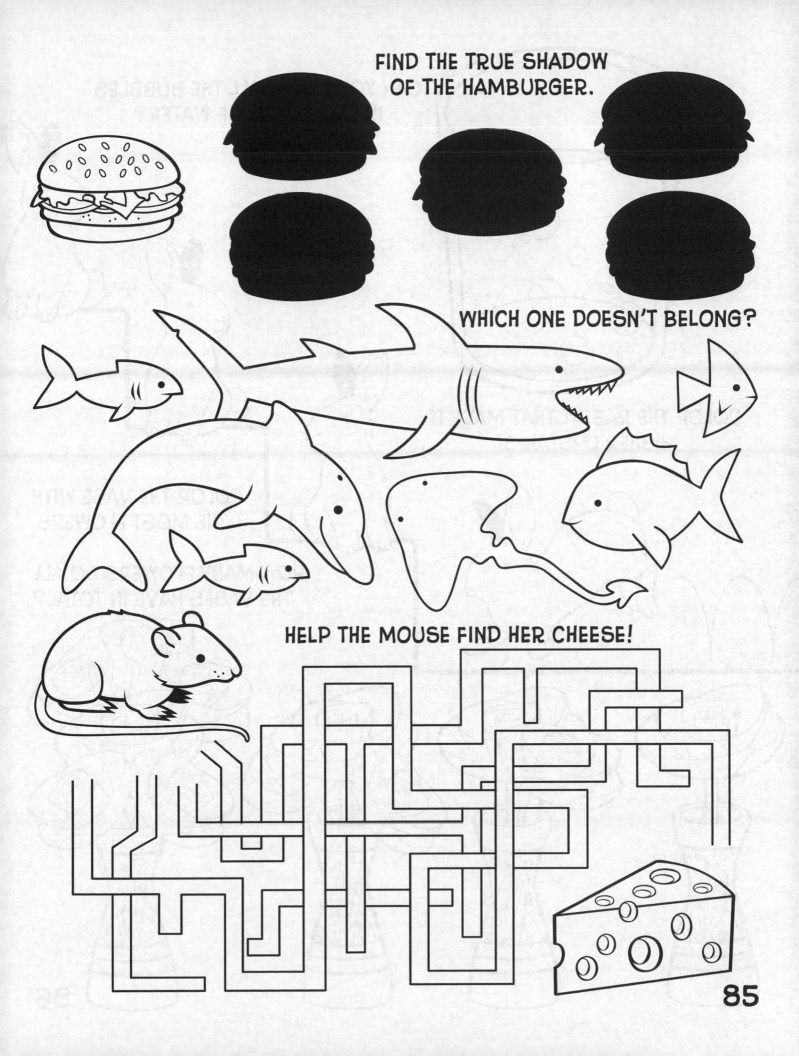

WHICH ONE DOESN'T BELONG?

HELP THE MOUSE FIND HER CHEESE!

CAN YOU COUNT ALL THE BUBBLES
IN THIS GLASS OF WATER?

COLOR THE RABBIT THAT MADE IT
HIGHER UPSTAIRS!

COLOR THE VASE WITH
THE MOST FLOWERS.

HOW MANY FLOWERS DO ALL
THE VASES HAVE IN TOTAL?

COLOR ONLY THE THINGS THAT FLY.

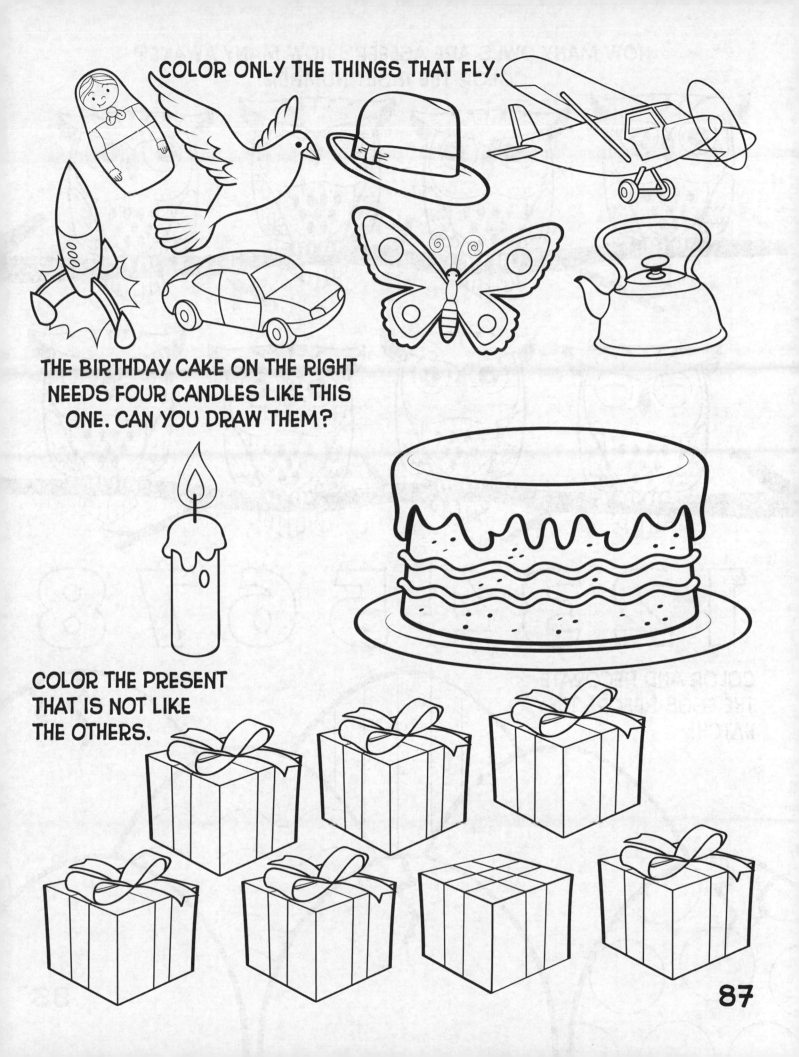

THE BIRTHDAY CAKE ON THE RIGHT NEEDS FOUR CANDLES LIKE THIS ONE. CAN YOU DRAW THEM?

COLOR THE PRESENT THAT IS NOT LIKE THE OTHERS.

HOW MANY OWLS ARE ASLEEP? HOW MANY AWAKE? COLOR THE RIGHT NUMBER.

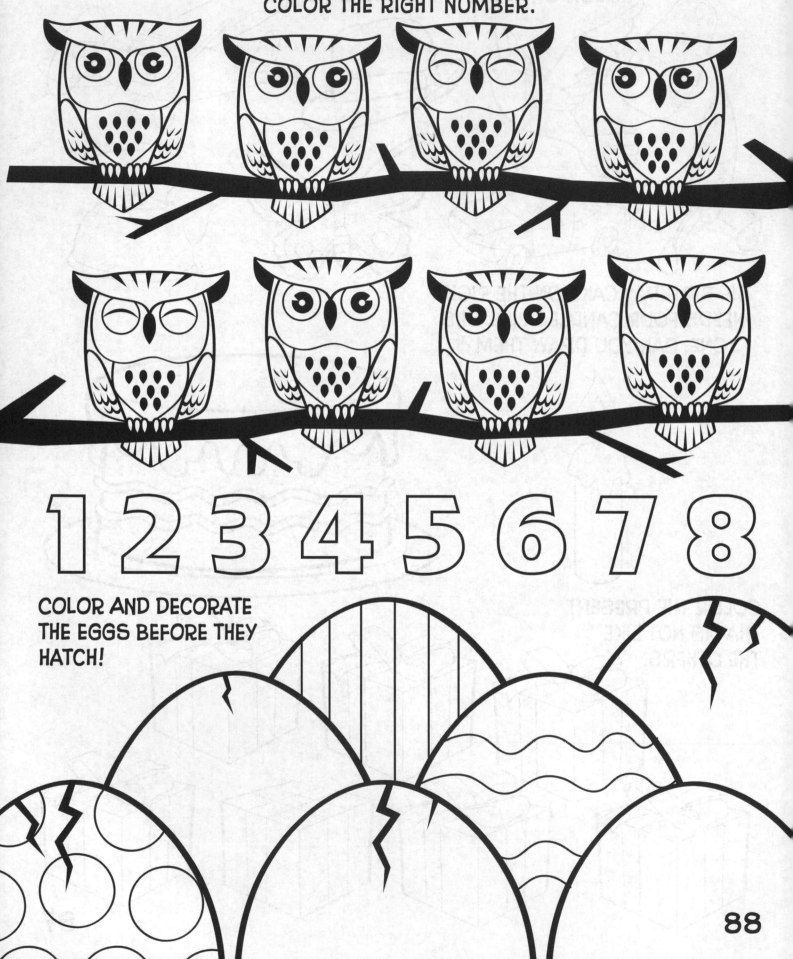

1 2 3 4 5 6 7 8

COLOR AND DECORATE THE EGGS BEFORE THEY HATCH!

CAN YOU DRAW WHAT'S ON AMY'S MIND?

WHICH TOOL DO PAINTERS NOT USE?

CONNECT THE DOTS TO SEE WHAT SHE'S PAINTING!

HELP MISSY FIND HER LUNCH.

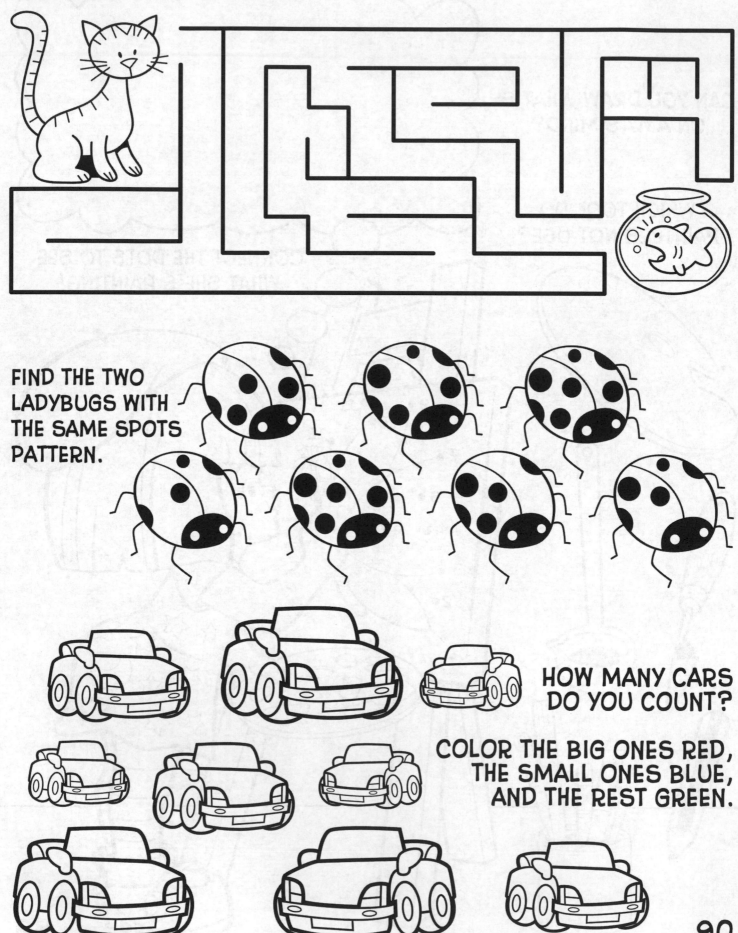

FIND THE TWO
LADYBUGS WITH
THE SAME SPOTS
PATTERN.

HOW MANY CARS
DO YOU COUNT?

COLOR THE BIG ONES RED,
THE SMALL ONES BLUE,
AND THE REST GREEN.

90

COLOR THE BUTTERFLY ON THE LEFT, AND DRAW ANOTHER JUST LIKE IT.

CAN YOU DRAW THE LOVE LETTER ENVELOPE WITHOUT LIFTING YOUR HAND?

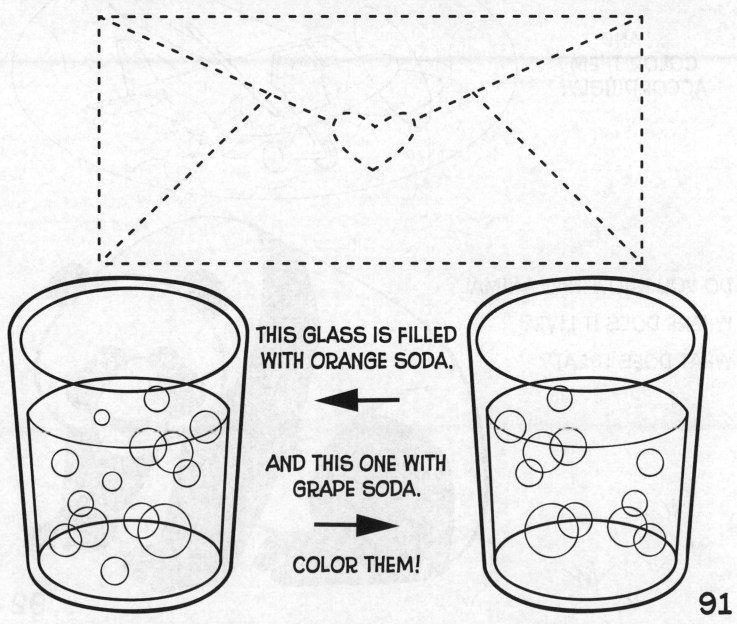

THIS GLASS IS FILLED WITH ORANGE SODA.

AND THIS ONE WITH GRAPE SODA.

COLOR THEM!

91

FIND THE
DIFFERENCES
BETWEEN
THESE TWO
SCENES...

... AND
COLOR THEM
ACCORDINGLY!

DO YOU KNOW THIS ANIMAL?

WHERE DOES IT LIVE?

WHAT DOES IT EAT?

92

1 = LIGHT BROWN
2 = DARK BROWN
3 = YELLOW
4 = GREEN

WHAT IS IT?

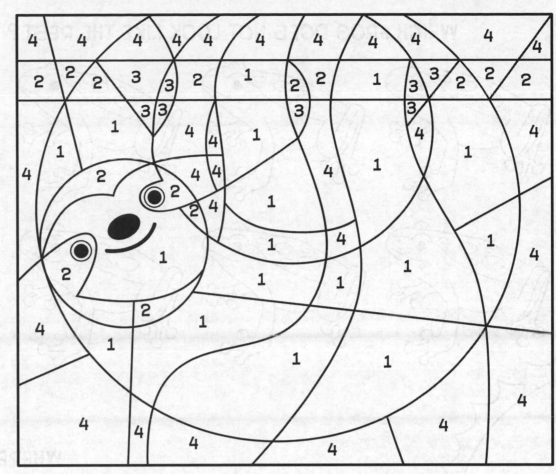

CONNECT EACH
ANIMAL TO ITS
FAVORITE FOOD.

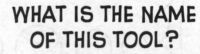

WHAT IS THE NAME
OF THIS TOOL?

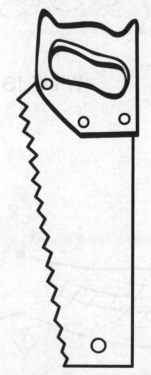

WHAT IS IT FOR?

93

WHICH FROG DOES NOT LOOK LIKE THE REST?

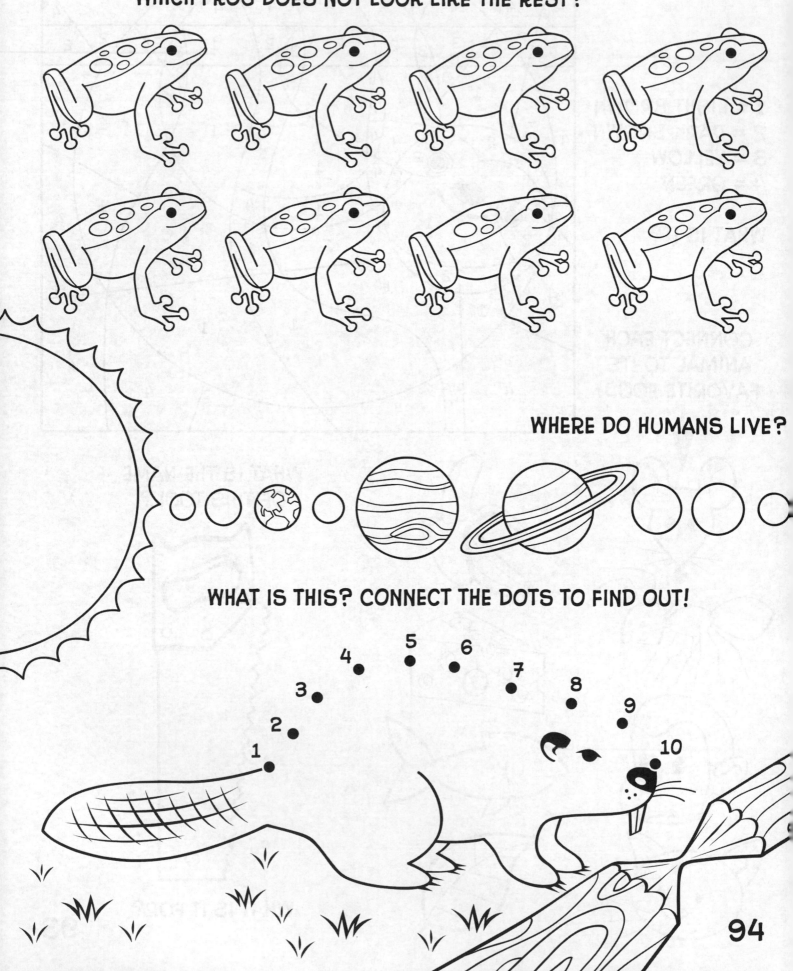

WHERE DO HUMANS LIVE?

WHAT IS THIS? CONNECT THE DOTS TO FIND OUT!

94

FIND THE MISSING PIECE.

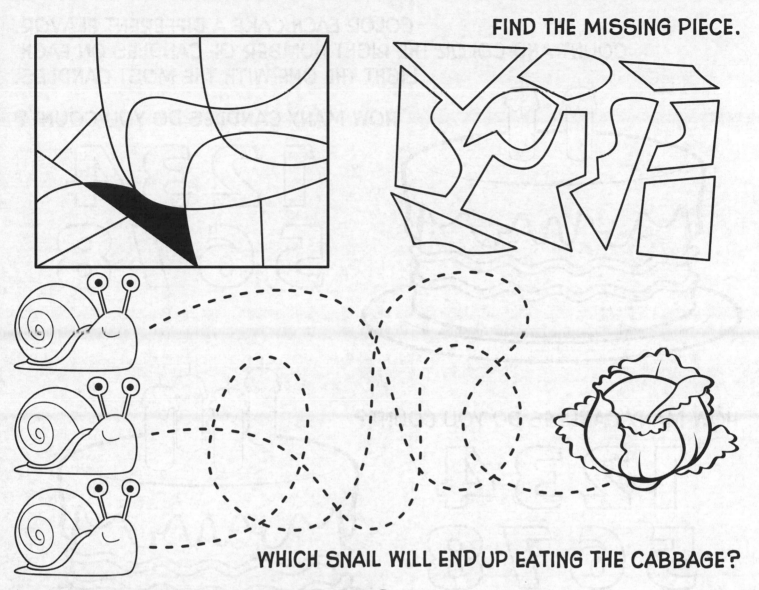

WHICH SNAIL WILL END UP EATING THE CABBAGE?

DO YOU RECOGNIZE THESE OUTLINES?
WHICH ONES CAN FLY?

COLOR EACH CAKE A DIFFERENT FLAVOR.
COUNT AND COLOR THE RIGHT NUMBER OF CANDLES ON EACH.
LIGHT THE ONE WITH THE MOST CANDLES.

HOW MANY CANDLES DO YOU COUNT?

1 2 3 4
5 6 7 8

HOW MANY CANDLES DO YOU COUNT?

1 2 3 4
5 6 7 8

HOW MANY CANDLES DO YOU COUNT?

1 2 3 4
5 6 7 8

ONE OF THESE OUTLINES DOES NOT MATCH THE ELEPHANT ON THE LEFT.

THIS FISH HAS A THREE LETTER NAME. WHAT IS IT?

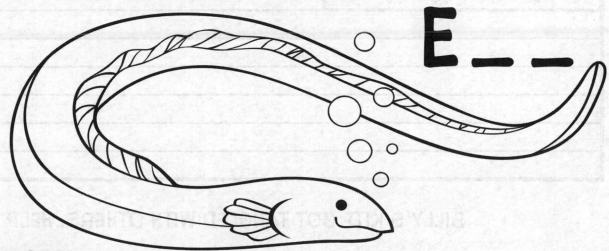

E _ _

FIDO WANTS BONES. IF HE TAKES TWO, HOW MANY ARE LEFT?

COLOR THE TWO IDENTICAL MICE.

COUNT THE NUMBER OF STARS AND STRIPES, AND THEN COLOR THE FLAG.

BILLY'S KITE GOT TANGLED WITH OTHERS. HELP HIM FIND IT!

WHAT IS SALLY KNITTING?
FOLLOW THE WOOL THREAD TO THE RIGHT
PIECE OF CLOTHING, AND COLOR EACH
ACCORDING TO THE LIST BELOW.

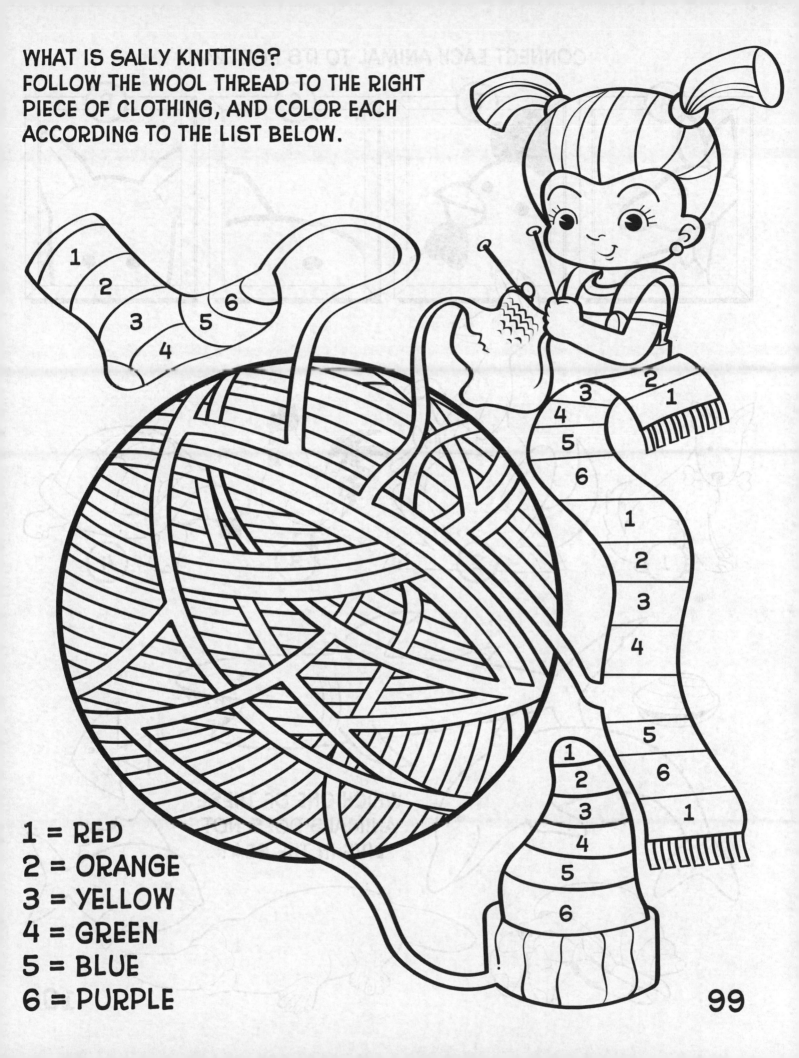

1 = RED
2 = ORANGE
3 = YELLOW
4 = GREEN
5 = BLUE
6 = PURPLE

99

CONNECT EACH ANIMAL TO ITS PORTRAIT

WHICH ONE OF THESE ANIMALS DOES NOT LIVE IN THE SEA?

100

WRITE THE FIRST LETTER OF YOUR NAME, AND TURN IT INTO A BIRD!

IT'S COLD AND THESE HANDS NEED GLOVES. CAN YOU DESIGN THEM?

LEFT

RIGHT

GIVE HER DIFFERENT HAIRCUTS.

DRAW FEATHERS FOR EACH ONE! ➡️

WHAT SONG IS THE BIRD SINGING? WRITE IT DOWN.

DRAW AND COLOR YOUR OWN SUNSET.

DRAW THE HEADS AND FACES OF THE PEOPLE WEARING THESE HATS.

12 11
13
14
10
9
8
15
7 6 5 4
23
24
16 22 25 3
35 33 34 2
36 17 26 1
32 27
31 30 29 18 19 20 21 28 42 43

37
38 39 40 41

CONNECT THE DOTS!

WHAT DOES THIS ANIMAL EAT? DRAW IT!

WHICH ITEM DOES A DOCTOR NOT USE?

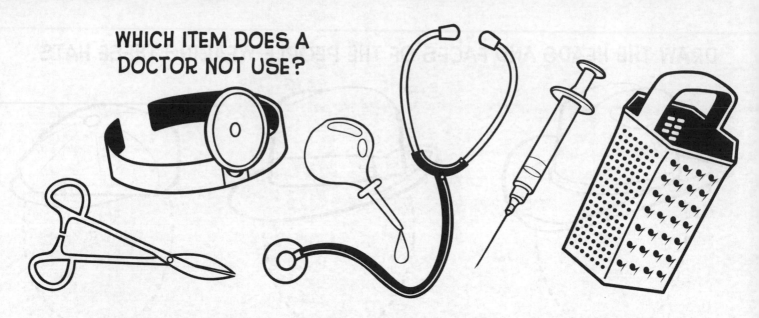

WHAT COUNTRY DOES THE FLAG BELONG TO? COLOR IT!

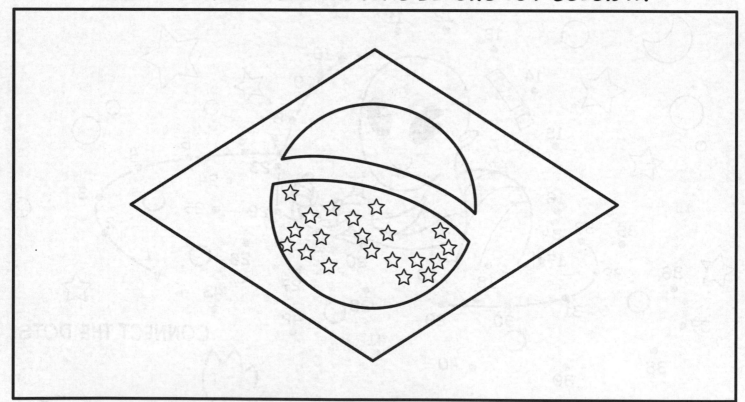

CONNECT THE SQUID TO THE RIGHT SILHOUETTE.

FILL THIS PAGE WITH MUSIC NOTES! →

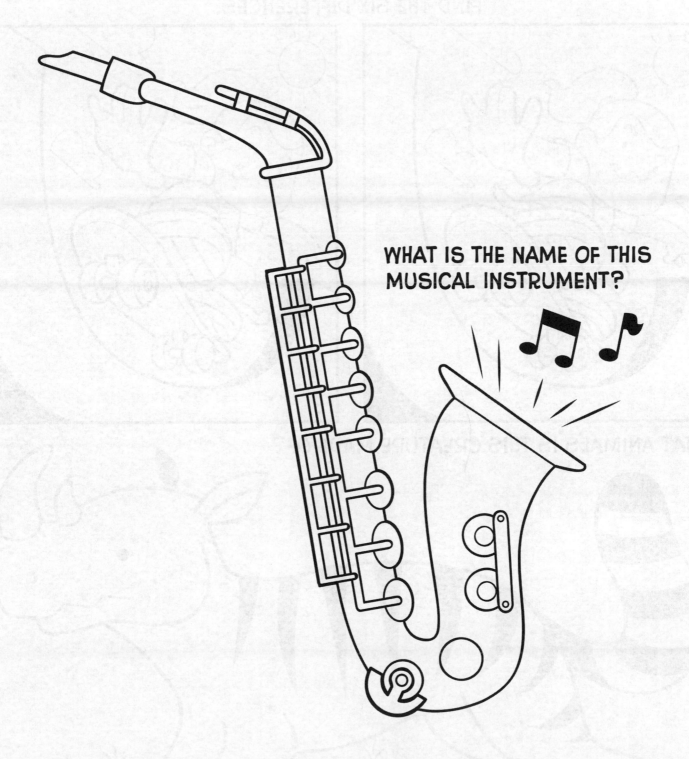

WHAT IS THE NAME OF THIS MUSICAL INSTRUMENT?

TRACE THE DOTS TO DRAW THE FISH IN A SINGLE STROKE.

FIND THE SIX DIFFERENCES.

WHAT ANIMALS IS THIS CREATURE MADE OF?

DRAW THE OTHER HALF AND COLOR IT!

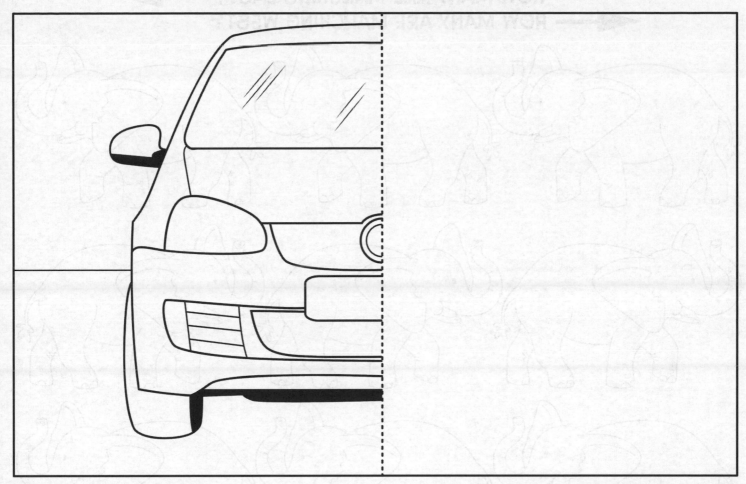

ONE OF THESE DOESN'T BELONG IN THE GROUP. WHY?

109

COLOR AND DECORATE THE ELEPHANTS ANYWAY YOU LIKE!
HOW MANY ARE MARCHING EAST? ➡
⬅ HOW MANY ARE MARCHING WEST?

110

THE LITTLE MONKEY LOVES BANANAS. WHAT OTHER FRUITS DOES HE LIKE TO EAT?

DRAW THEM HERE!

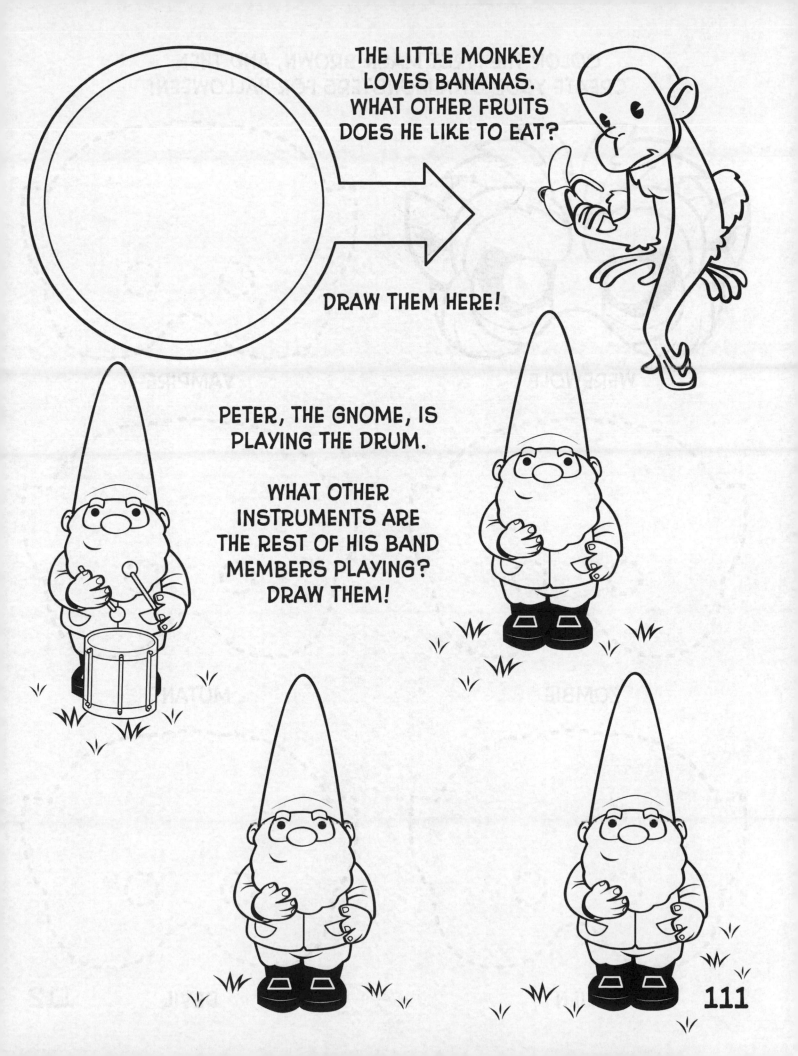

PETER, THE GNOME, IS PLAYING THE DRUM.

WHAT OTHER INSTRUMENTS ARE THE REST OF HIS BAND MEMBERS PLAYING? DRAW THEM!

COLOR THE FIRST MASK BROWN, AND THEN CREATE YOUR OWN MONSTERS FOR HALLOWEEN!

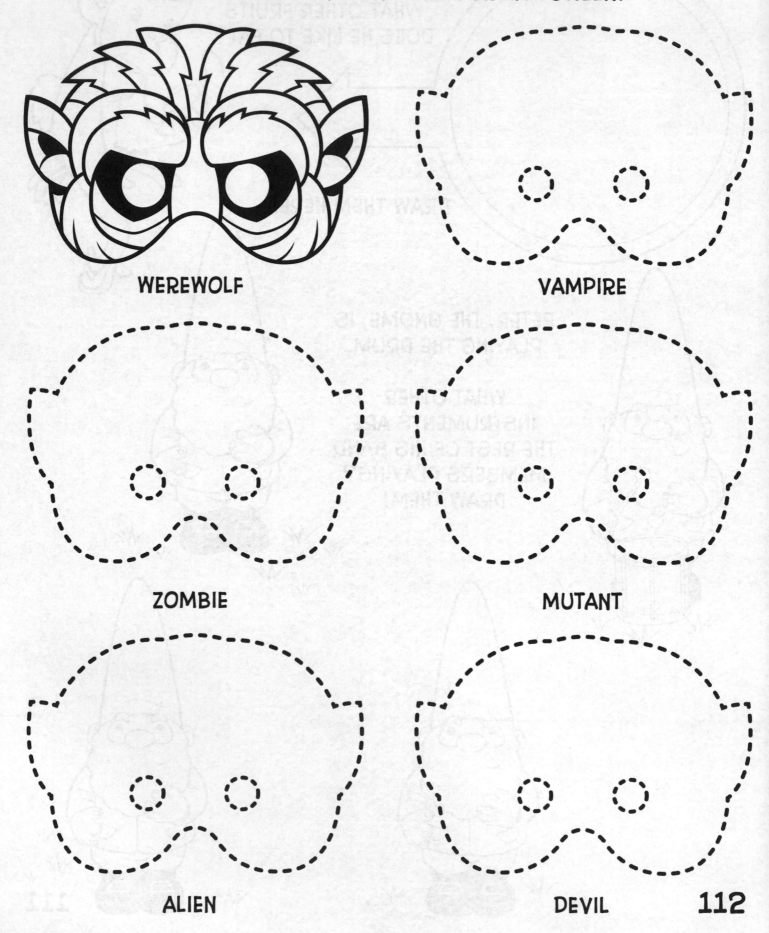

WEREWOLF

VAMPIRE

ZOMBIE

MUTANT

ALIEN

DEVIL

COUNT THE NUMBER
OF ORANGES.
WHICH TREE HAS
MORE OF THEM?

COLOR THE ONES THAT CAN'T FLY.

113

WHAT IS THE NAME OF THIS BIRD?
WHAT COLOR SHOULD
YOU PAINT IT?

WHAT DOES IT EAT?

WHAT'S MISSING FROM
THIS JET PLANE?
FINISH DRAWING IT.

HELP THE ANT FIND ITS LEAF.

COLOR THE TWO IDENTICAL CATS.

DECORATE YOUR DAD'S TIE ANYWAY YOU LIKE!

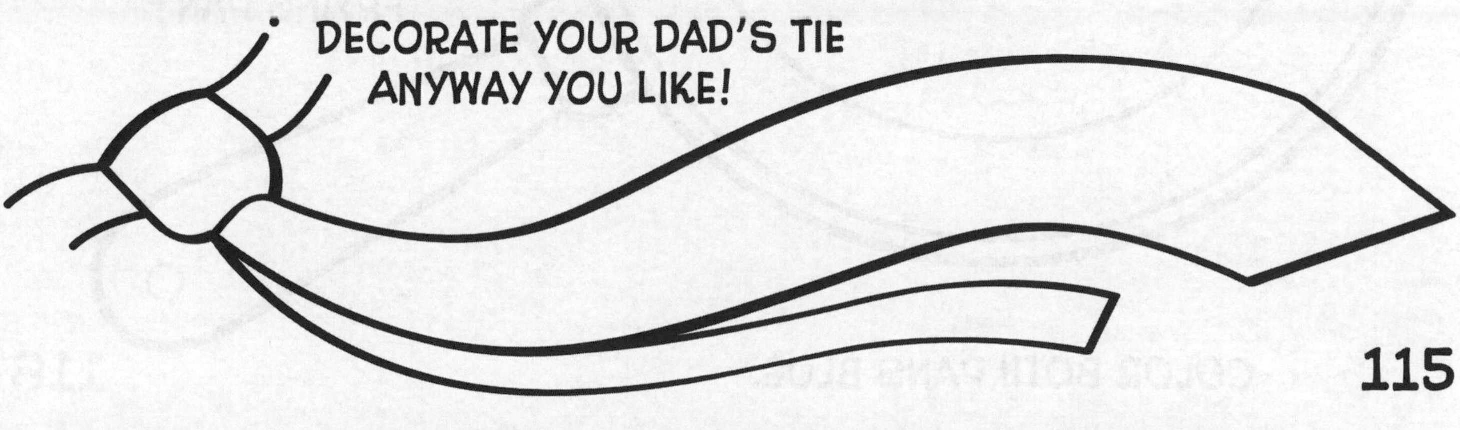

BREAKFAST IS THE MOST IMPORTANT MEAL OF THE DAY.

TRACE THE DOTTED LINES
TO DRAW THE FRIED EGGS.

WHICH ONE IS THE YOLK?
WHAT COLOR IS IT?

WHAT DO WE CALL THE AREA
AROUND IT?

CAN YOU DRAW SAUSAGES
AND BACON IN THIS EMPTY
FRYING PAN?

COLOR BOTH PANS BLUE.

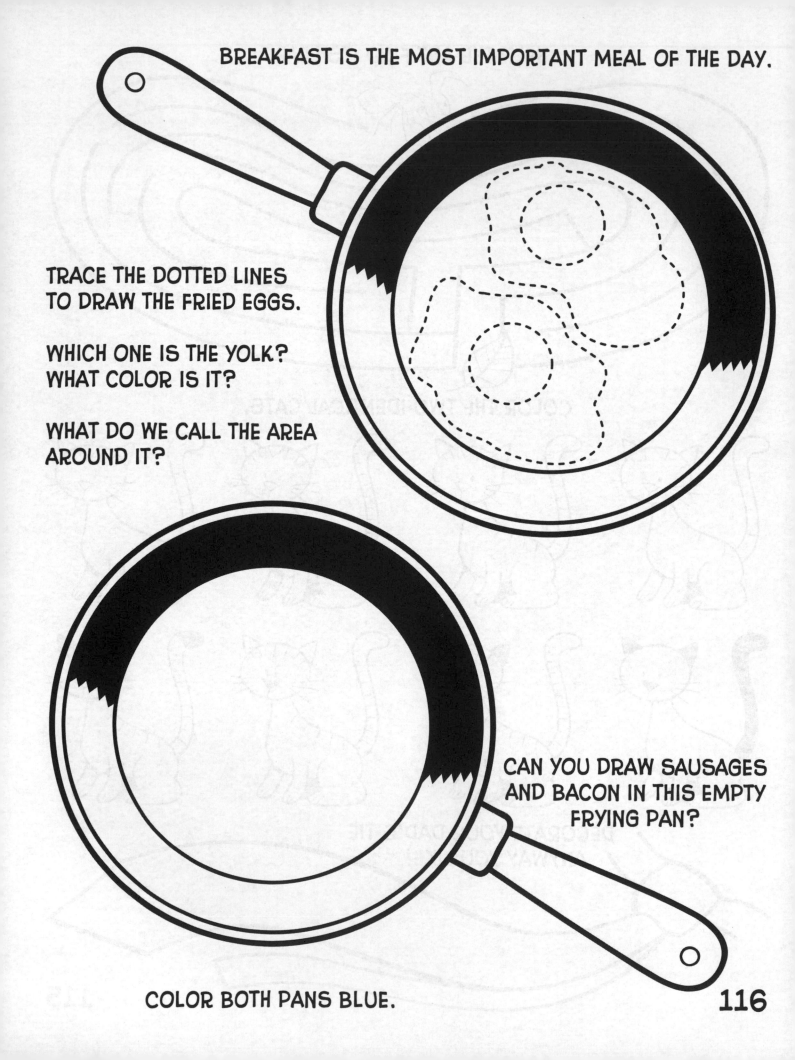

116

CONNECT EACH PERSON TO THE RIGHT TOOL.

WHAT ANIMALS IS THIS STRANGE CREATURE MADE OF?

WHAT DOES THE SHARK EAT?

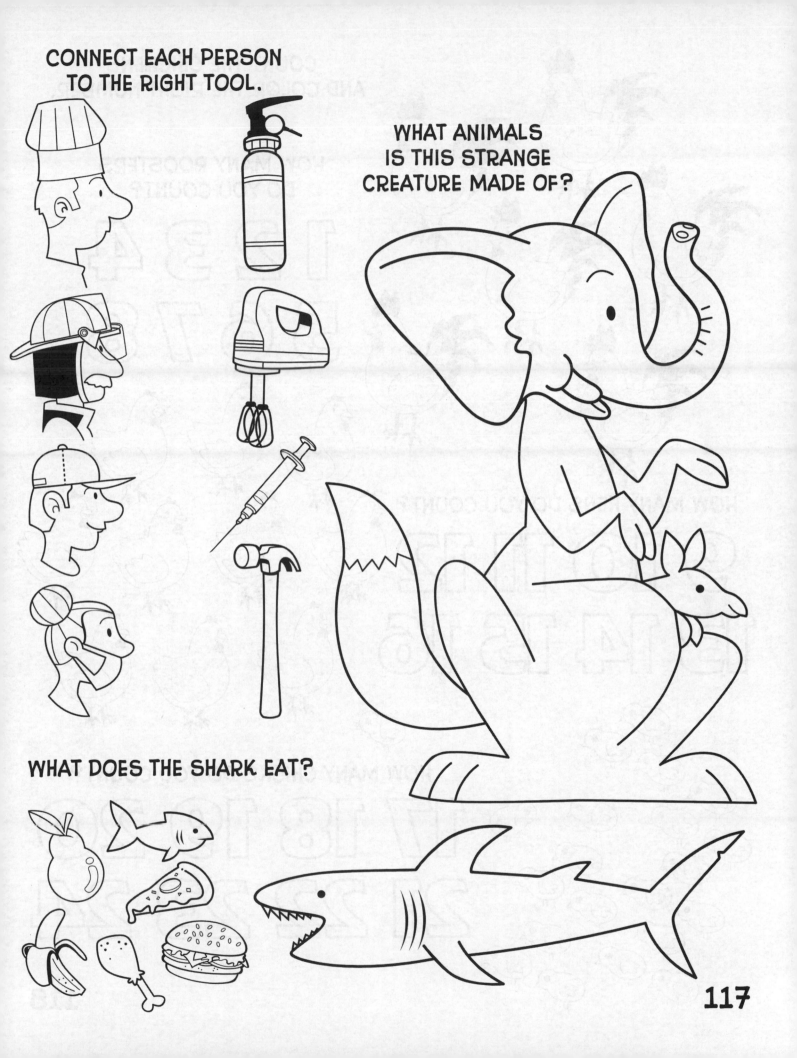

COUNT THE CHICKENS
AND COLOR THE RIGHT NUMBER.

HOW MANY ROOSTERS
DO YOU COUNT?

1 2 3 4
5 6 7 8

HOW MANY HENS DO YOU COUNT?

9 10 11 12
13 14 15 16

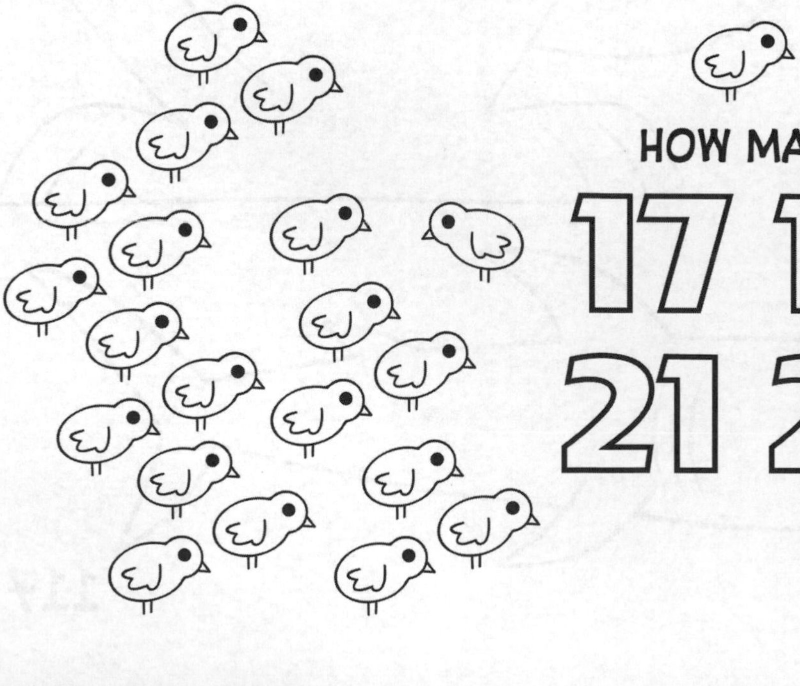

HOW MANY CHICKS DO YOU COUNT?

17 18 19 20
21 22 23 24

118

TRACE THE DOTTED LINES TO FINISH DRAWING THE TRAIN.

FIND THE PIECE OF THE DRAWING ON THE RIGHT THAT DOESN'T BELONG TO THE ONE ON THE LEFT.

WHICH COW DOES NOT LOOK LIKE THE OTHERS?

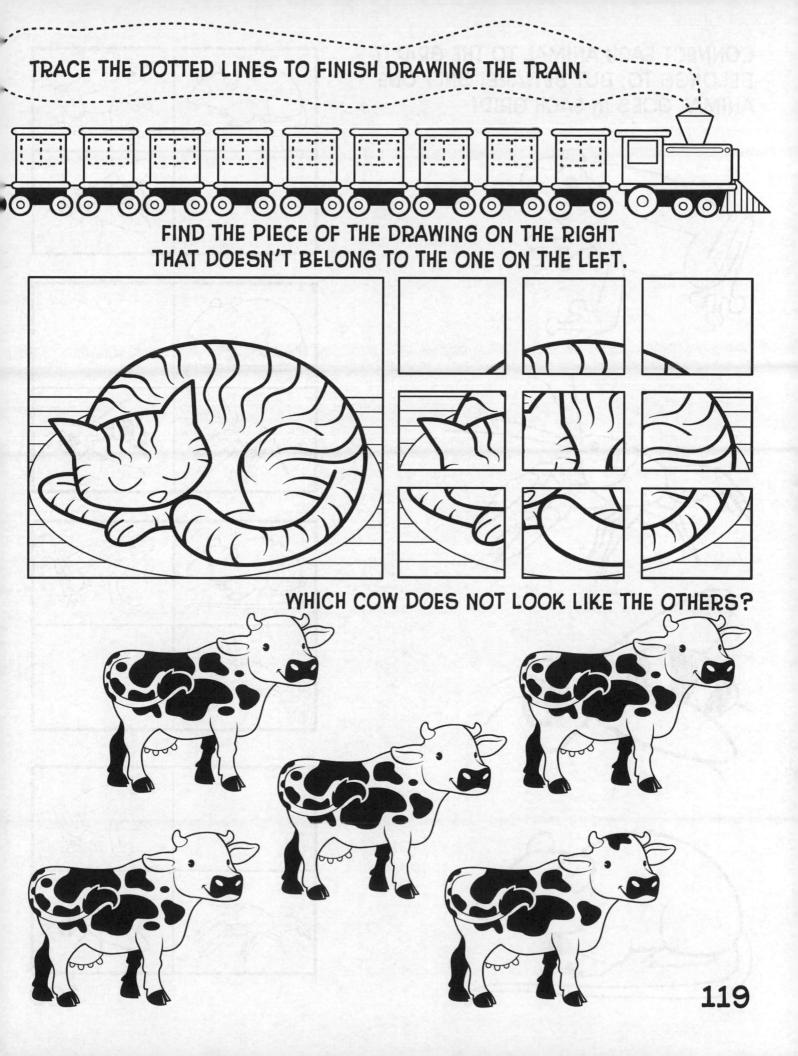

CONNECT EACH ANIMAL TO THE GRID IT
BELONGS TO, BUT BEWARE, ONLY ONE
ANIMAL GOES IN EACH GRID!

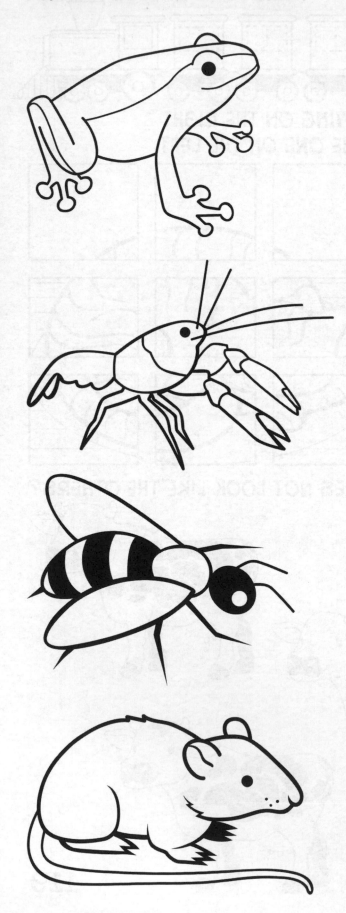

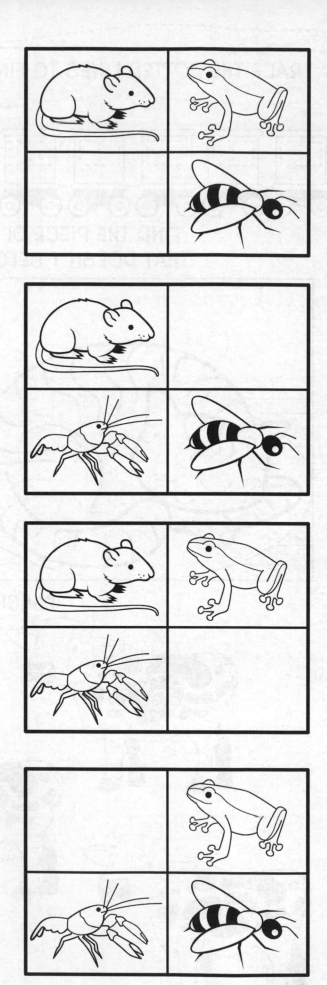

COLOR ONLY THE RED FOODS.

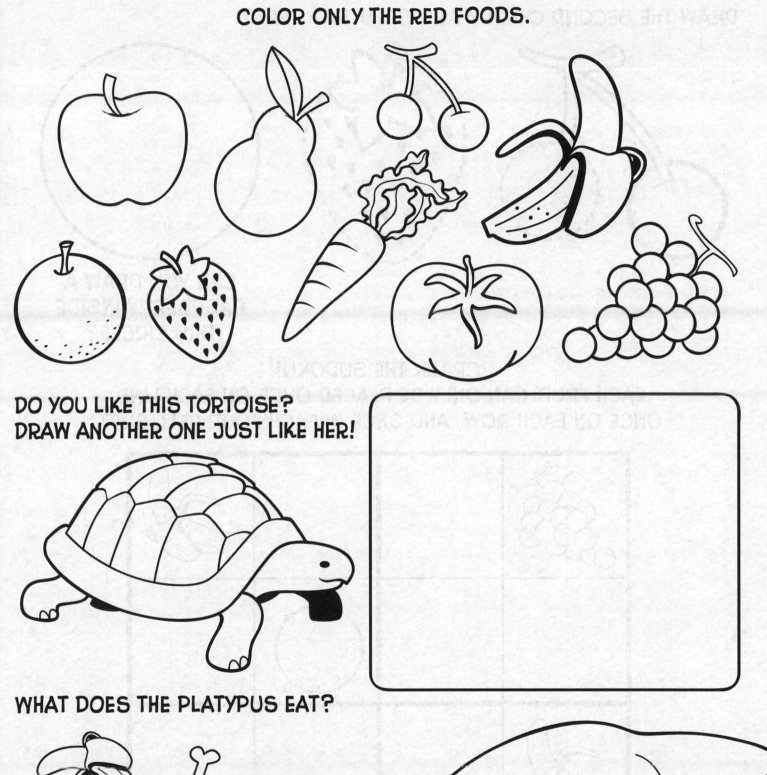

DO YOU LIKE THIS TORTOISE?
DRAW ANOTHER ONE JUST LIKE HER!

WHAT DOES THE PLATYPUS EAT?

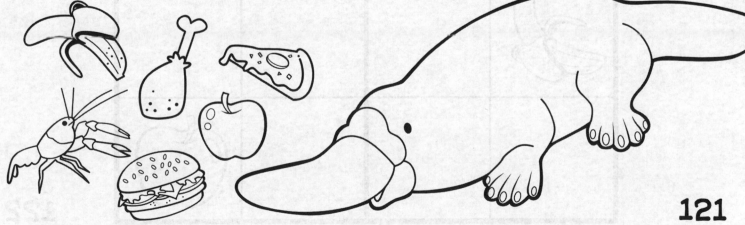

DRAW THE SECOND CHERRY AND THE STRAWBERRY.

CAN YOU DRAW A
RASPBERRY INSIDE
THIS CIRCLE?

CRACK THE SUDOKU!
EACH FRUIT CAN ONLY BE PLACED ONCE ON EACH LINE,
ONCE ON EACH ROW, AND ONCE IN EACH FOUR CELL GRID.

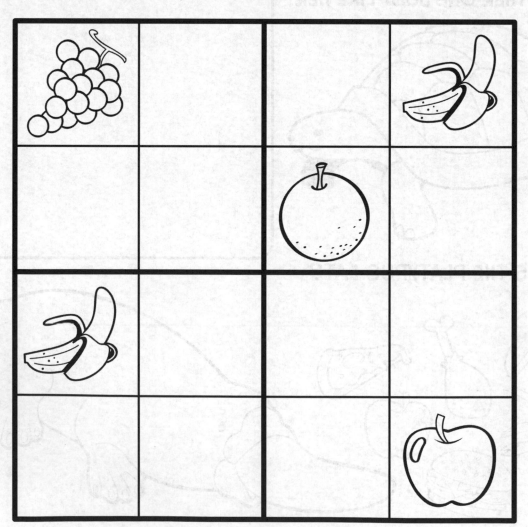

WHICH RABBIT WILL GET THE CARROT?
FOLLOW THE DOTTED LINES TO FIND OUT.

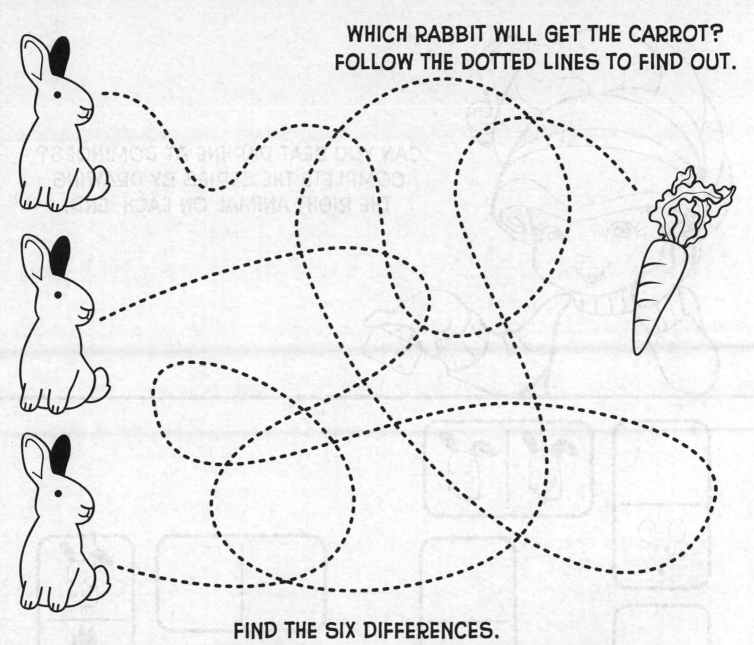

FIND THE SIX DIFFERENCES.

CAN YOU BEAT DAPHNE AT DOMINOES?
COMPLETE THE SERIES BY DRAWING
THE RIGHT ANIMAL ON EACH END.

IF YOU PUT ALL THESE CHERRIES INSIDE THE JAR, HOW MANY CHERRIES WILL IT CONTAIN IN TOTAL?

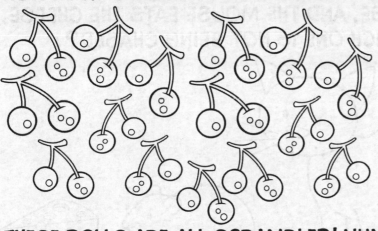

THESE DOLLS ARE ALL SCRAMBLED! NUMBER EACH ONE FROM THE SMALLEST TO THE BIGGEST, IN THE ORDER THEY'D BE NESTED INSIDE ONE ANOTHER.

NAME ALL PLANETS. WHICH ONE IS CLOSEST TO THE SUN?

IF THE DOG CHASES THE CAT, THE CAT CHASES THE MOUSE, AND THE MOUSE EATS THE CHEESE, WHICH ONE IS NOT BEING CHASED?

HELP THE DOLPHIN FIND THE TUNA!

CAN YOU FIND THE SMALLER COMBINATIONS IN THE BIG GRID BELOW? COLOR THEM WHEN YOU DO!

COMPLETE EACH LINE IN THE CORRECT SEQUENCE.

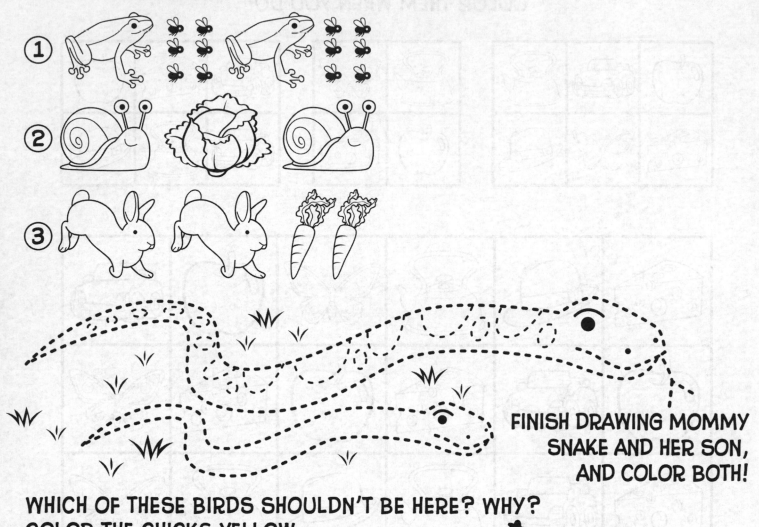

①
②
③

FINISH DRAWING MOMMY
SNAKE AND HER SON,
AND COLOR BOTH!

WHICH OF THESE BIRDS SHOULDN'T BE HERE? WHY?
COLOR THE CHICKS YELLOW.

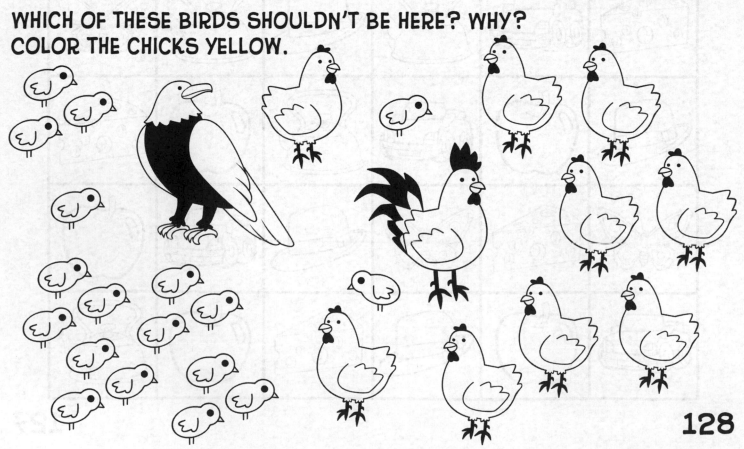

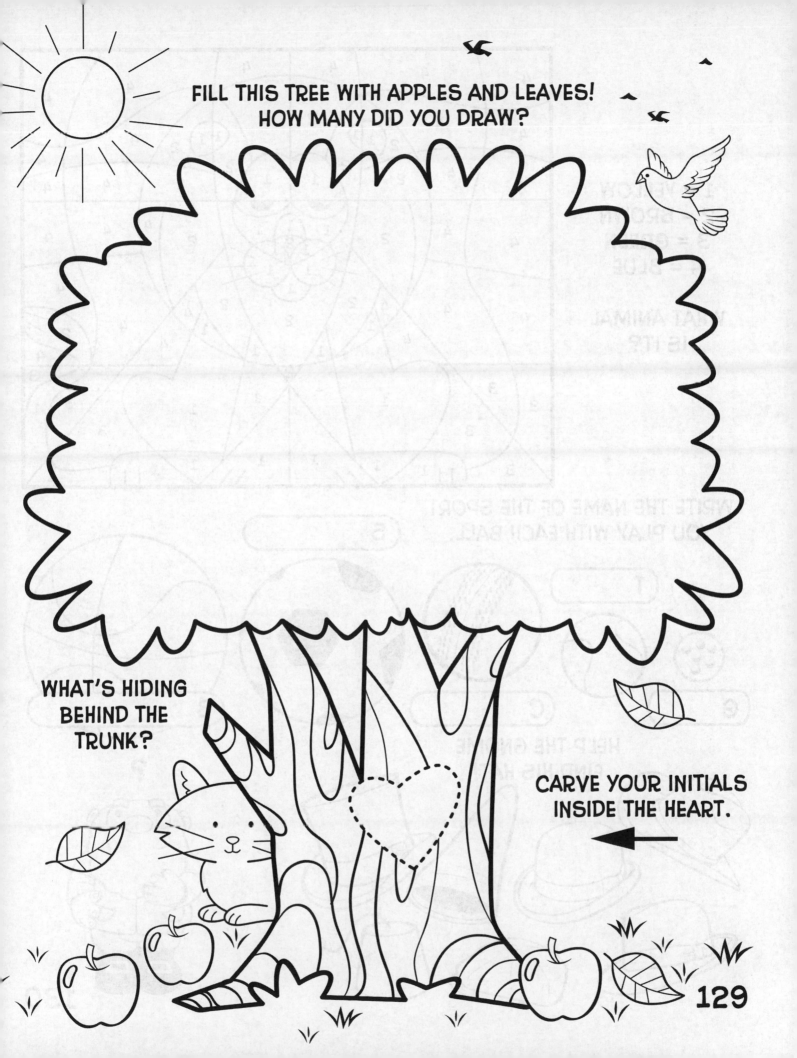

FILL THIS TREE WITH APPLES AND LEAVES!
HOW MANY DID YOU DRAW?

WHAT'S HIDING
BEHIND THE
TRUNK?

CARVE YOUR INITIALS
INSIDE THE HEART.

1 = YELLOW
2 = BROWN
3 = GREEN
4 = BLUE

WHAT ANIMAL
IS IT?

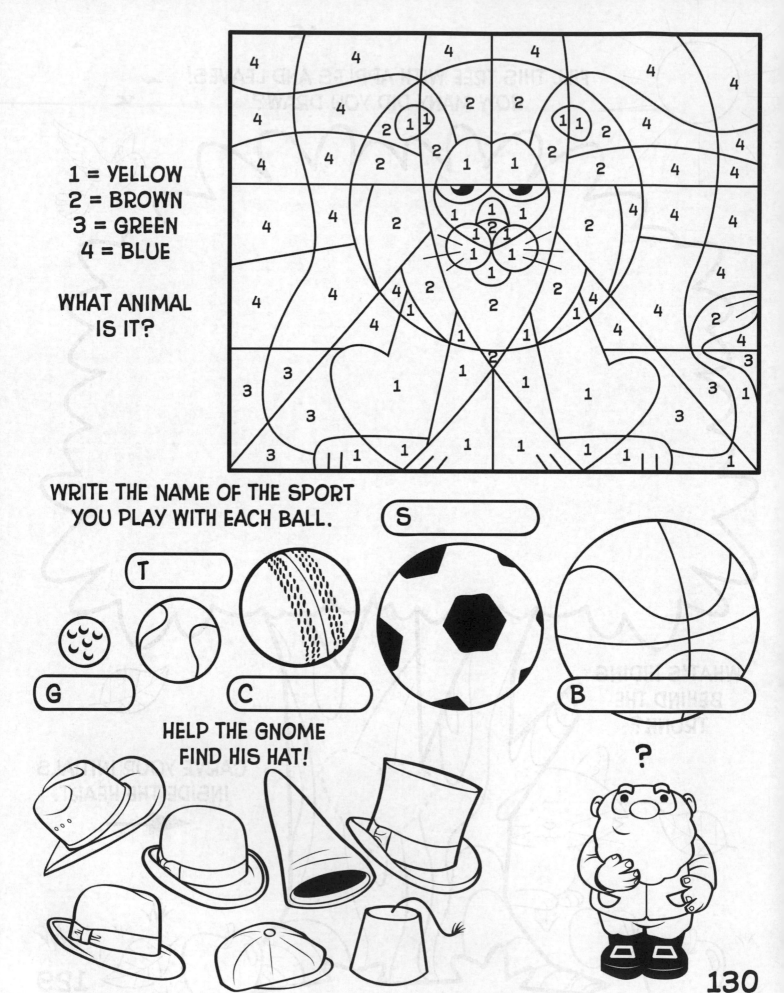

WRITE THE NAME OF THE SPORT
YOU PLAY WITH EACH BALL.

S

T

G

C

B

?

HELP THE GNOME
FIND HIS HAT!

130

COLOR THE TWO THAT LOOK ALIKE.

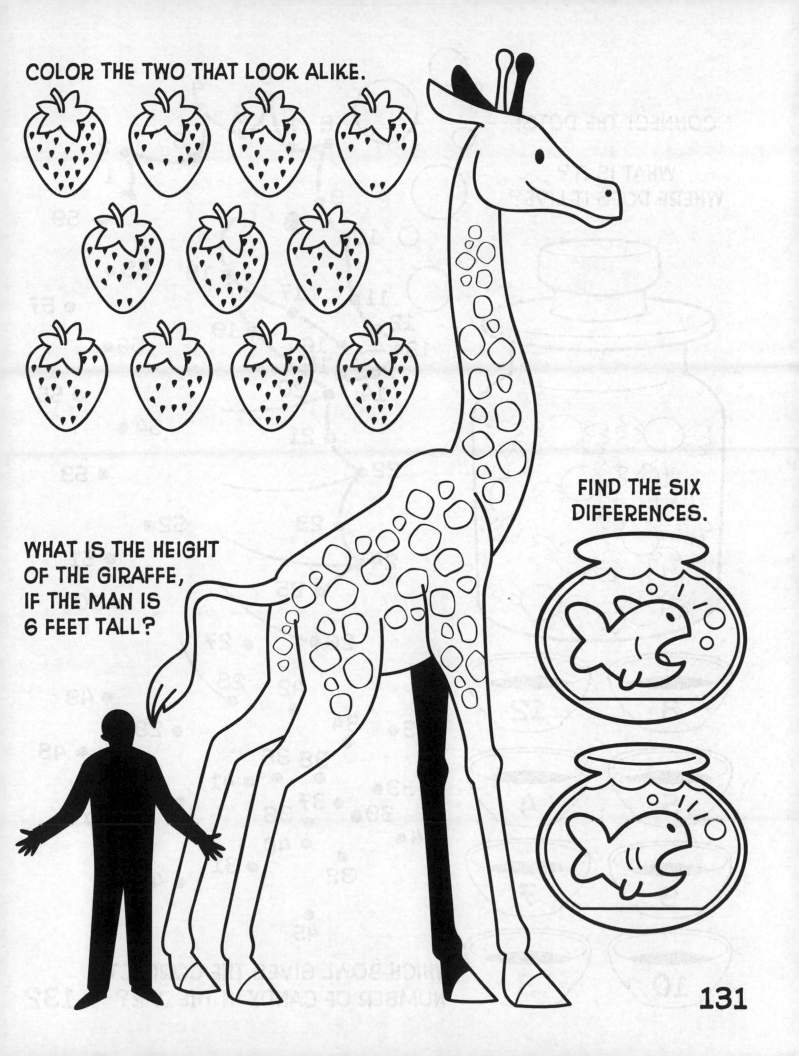

WHAT IS THE HEIGHT
OF THE GIRAFFE,
IF THE MAN IS
6 FEET TALL?

FIND THE SIX
DIFFERENCES.

131

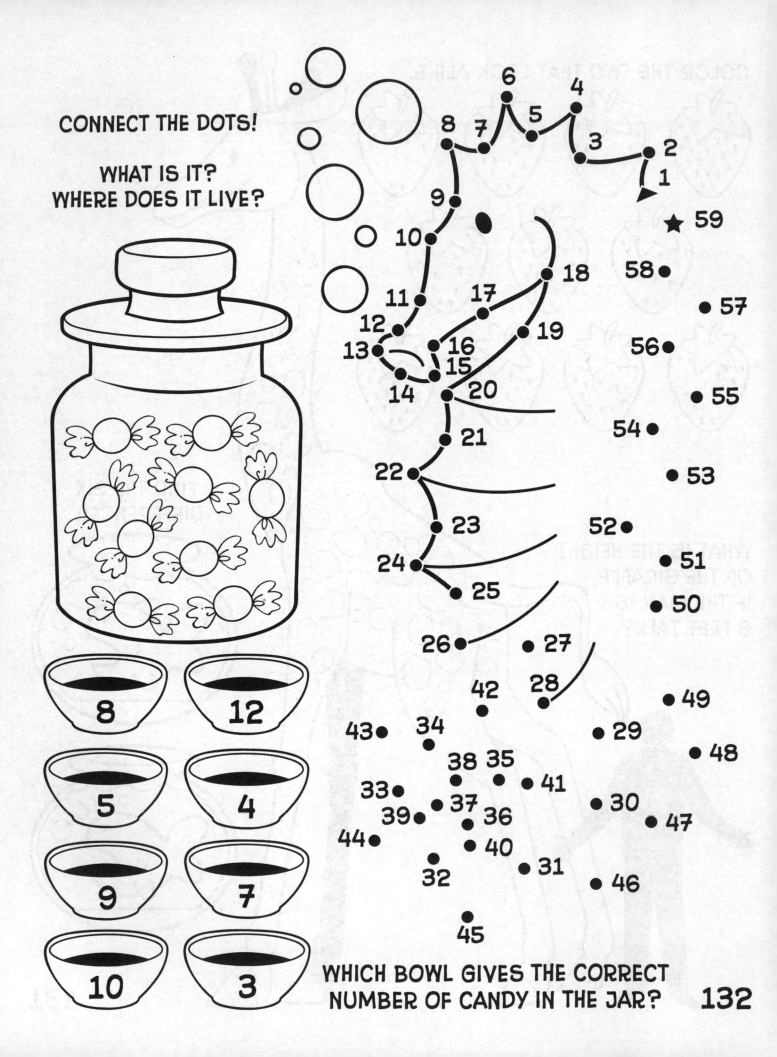

CONNECT THE DOTS!

WHAT IS IT?
WHERE DOES IT LIVE?

8

12

5

4

9

7

10

3

WHICH BOWL GIVES THE CORRECT
NUMBER OF CANDY IN THE JAR? 132

HOW MANY CIRCLES ARE IN THIS TABLE?
HOW MANY STARS? AND SQUARES?

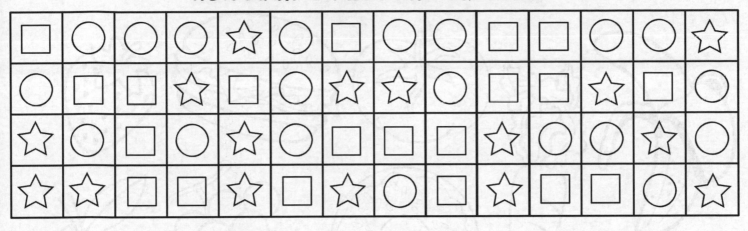

 WRITE FOUR ANIMALS THAT START WITH THE LETTER "O".

O
O
O
O

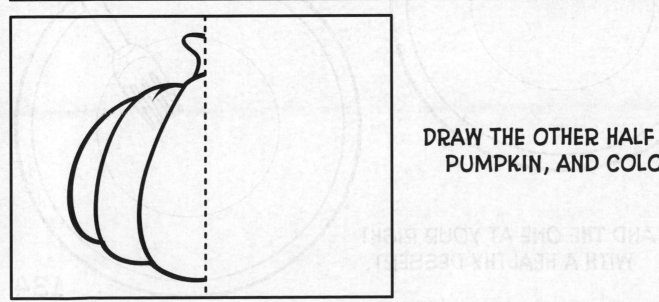

DRAW THE OTHER HALF OF THE
PUMPKIN, AND COLOR IT.

DRAW A CIRCLE AROUND THE FOODS THAT AREN'T GOOD FOR YOU, AND COLOR THE HEALTHY ONES.

DRAW YOURSELF A HEALTHY MEAL!

FILL THE PLATE ON THE LEFT WITH THE MAIN COURSE.

AND THE ONE AT YOUR RIGHT WITH A HEALTHY DESSERT.

ADD THE NUMBERS WRITTEN ON THE SAILS.
WHAT RESULTS DO YOU GET?

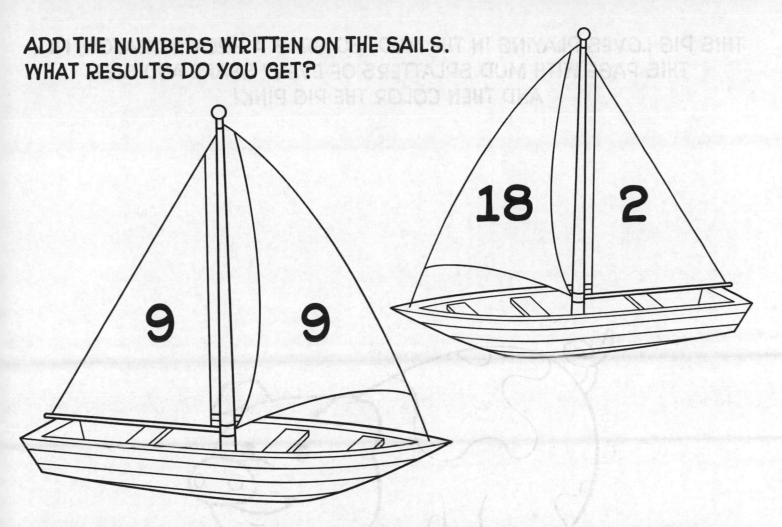

ONLY TWO HENS ARE MOMS. THREE CHICKS BELONG TO ONE, AND ONLY
ONE TO THE OTHER. CAN YOU GUESS WHICH CHICKS BELONG
TO EACH HEN?

THIS PIG LOVES PLAYING IN THE MUD, SO GRAB A BROWN CRAYON, FILL THIS PAGE WITH MUD SPLATTERS OF EVERY SHAPE AND SIZE, AND THEN COLOR THE PIG PINK!

FIND THE 10 DIFFERENCES.

WHAT IS INSIDE THIS BOTTLE?

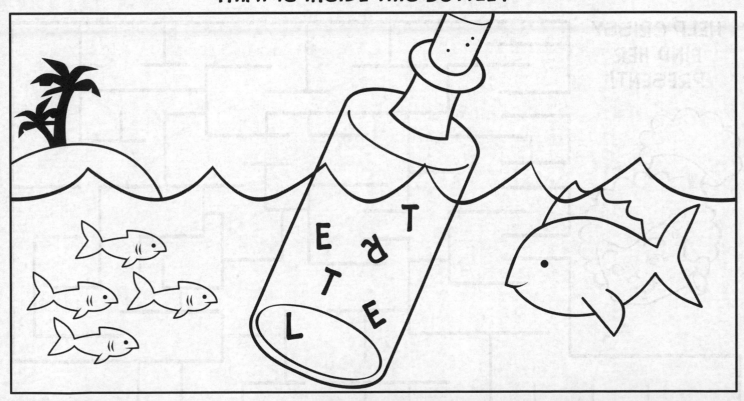

IN WHAT BOX WILL CAR #1 AND CAR #2 MEET,
KNOWING THAT #2 GOES TWO TIMES FASTER
THAN #1? COLOR #1 BLUE AND #2 RED.

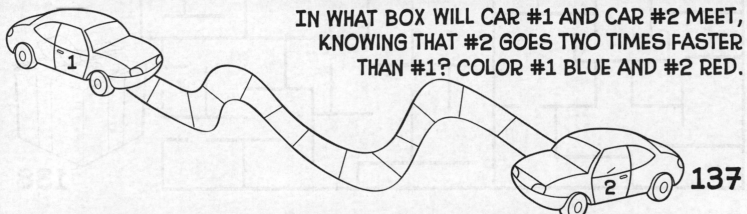

COLOR ONLY THE THINGS THAT GIVE LIGHT.

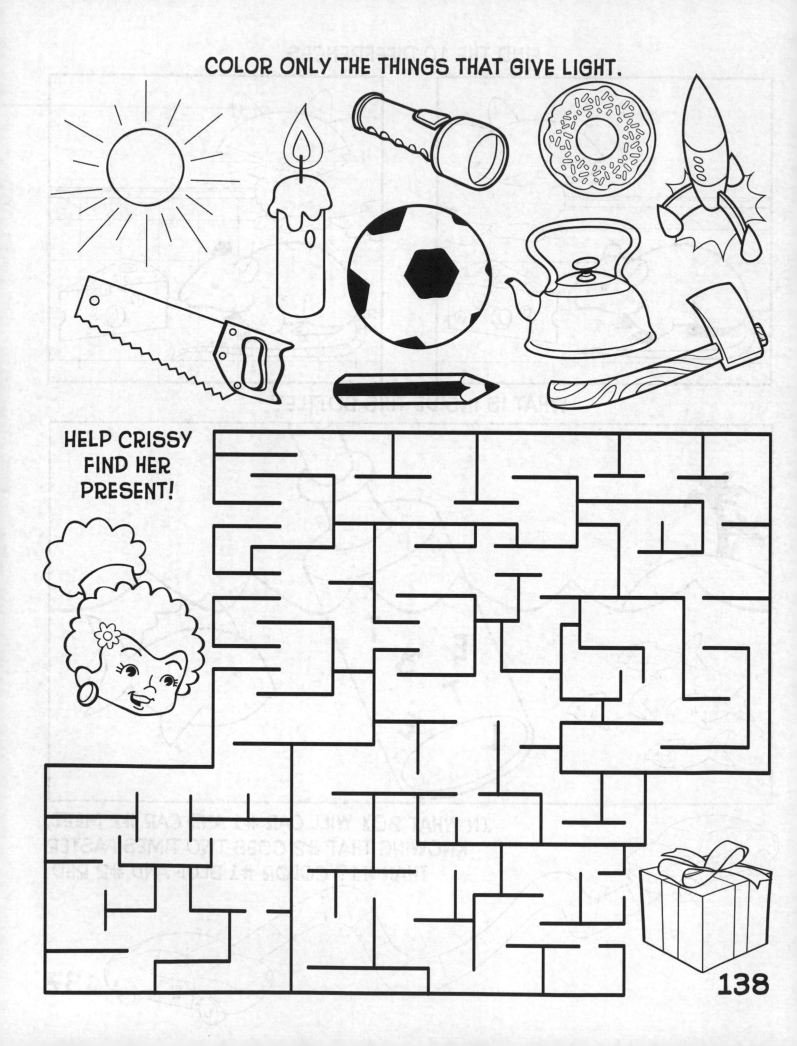

HELP CRISSY FIND HER PRESENT!

138

WHICH DRAWING ON THE RIGHT IS IDENTICAL TO THE ONE IN THE LEFT COLUMN?

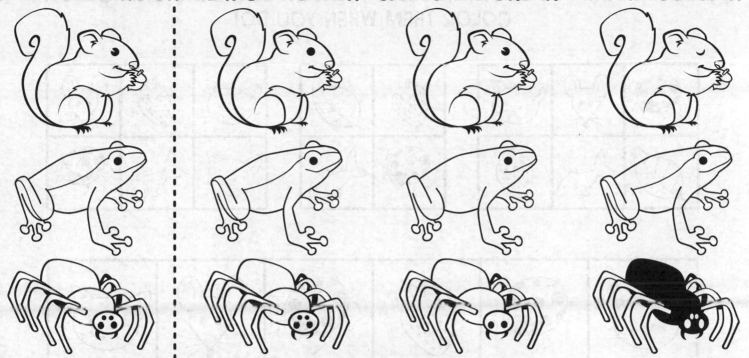

CRACK THE SUDOKU!
EACH ELEMENT CAN ONLY BE PLACED ONCE ON EACH LINE,
ONCE ON EACH ROW, AND ONCE IN EACH FOUR CELL GRID.

CAN YOU FIND THE SMALLER COMBINATIONS IN THE BIG GRID BELOW? COLOR THEM WHEN YOU DO!

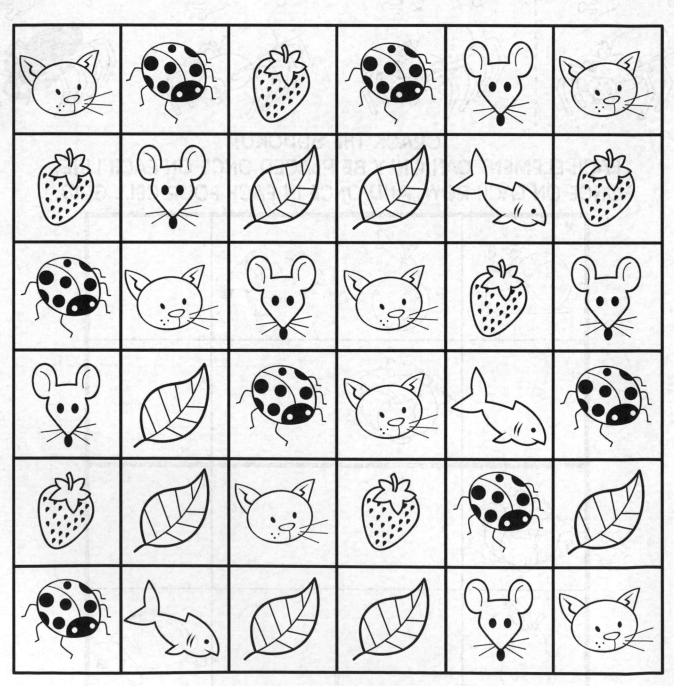

140

WHICH ELEPHANT WEIGHS MORE?

WHAT DO WE CALL THIS STRANGE CREATURE?

WHERE DOES IT LIVE?

WHICH OF THESE KEYS IS MADE FOR THAT LOCK?

IF THE GORILLA EATS TWO BANANAS PER DAY,
HOW MANY DAYS WILL IT TAKE HIM TO EAT THEM ALL?

HOW MANY WATERLILIES DOES THE
FROG JUMP ON IF IT GOES AROUND
THE POND THREE TIMES?

WHICH ONE IS NOT A TOY?

142

HOW MANY POUNDS OF COAL DOES THE TRAIN TRANSPORT?

| 10 | 20 | 7 | 8 | 15 |

GIVE NUMBERS TO THE ANIMALS FROM THE SMALLEST (1) TO THE BIGGEST (6) IN REAL LIFE.

HOW OLD IS THIS FELLED TREE?
COUNT THE TRUNK RINGS TO FIND OUT!

143

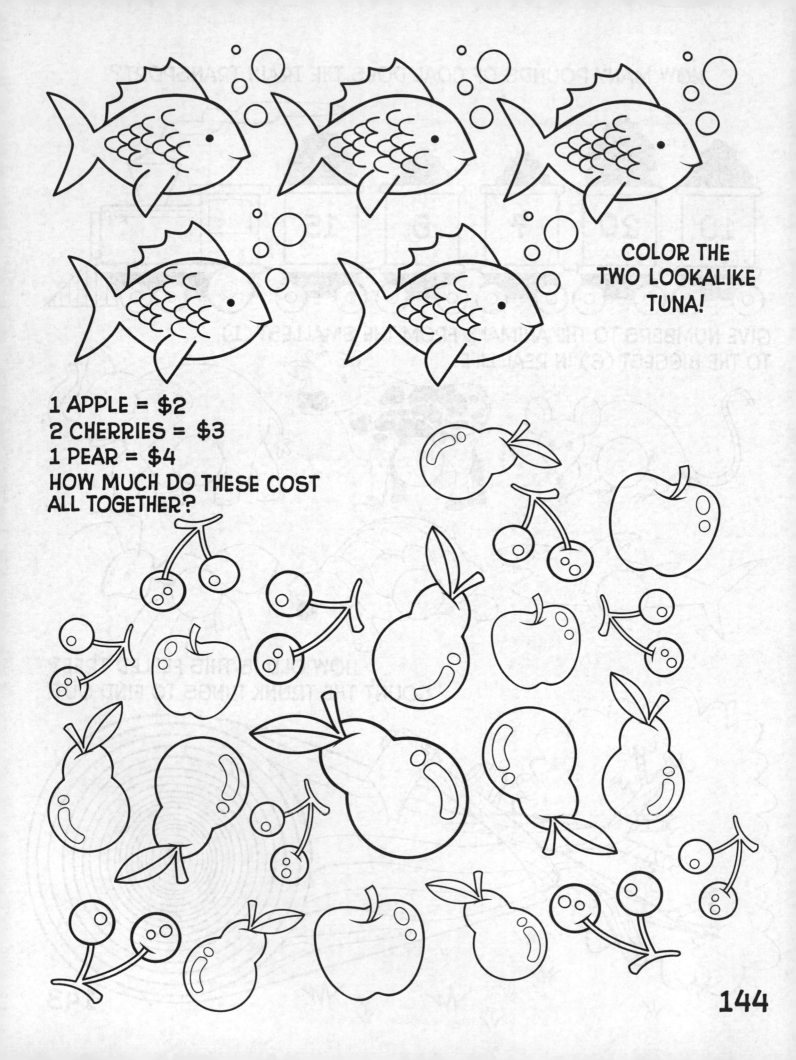

COLOR THE
TWO LOOKALIKE
TUNA!

1 APPLE = $2
2 CHERRIES = $3
1 PEAR = $4
HOW MUCH DO THESE COST
ALL TOGETHER?

144

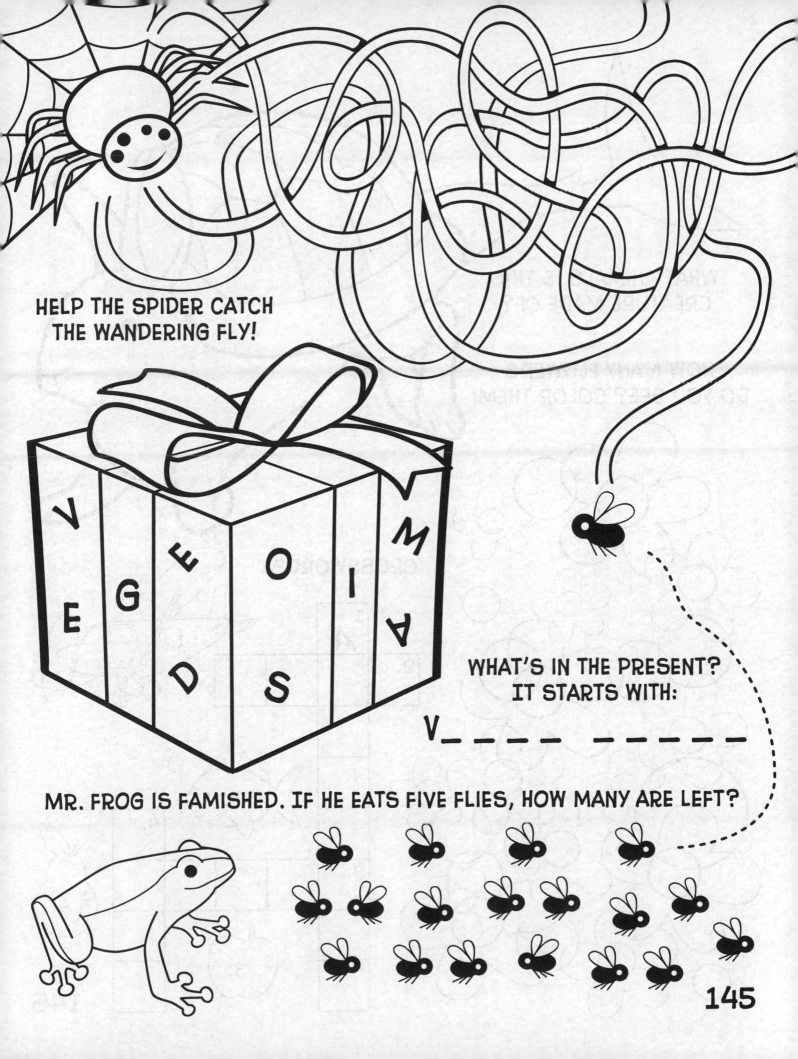

HELP THE SPIDER CATCH
THE WANDERING FLY!

WHAT'S IN THE PRESENT?
IT STARTS WITH:

V_ _ _ _ _ _ _ _ _ _

MR. FROG IS FAMISHED. IF HE EATS FIVE FLIES, HOW MANY ARE LEFT?

145

WHAT ANIMALS IS THIS
CREATURE MADE OF?

HOW MANY FLOWERS
DO YOU SEE? COLOR THEM!

CROSSWORDS.

1.
A

2.

3.

4.

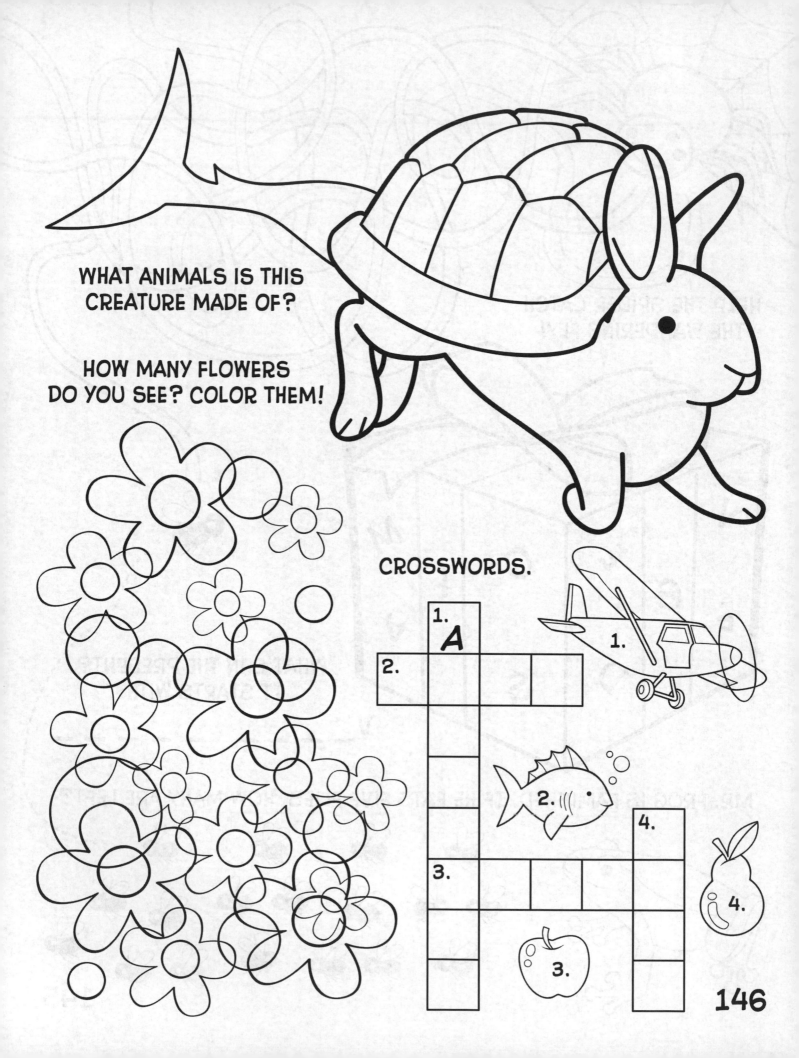

CREATE YOUR OWN FLAG!

MATCH THESE ANIMALS TO THEIR PROPER FEET!

ONE OF THESE ANIMALS HAS HAS NO LUNGS... WHICH ONE?

IF YOU ADD ALL THE NUMBERS IN THE SQUARES AND SUBTRACT ALL THE NUMBERS IN THE CIRCLES, WHAT WILL THE RESULT BE?

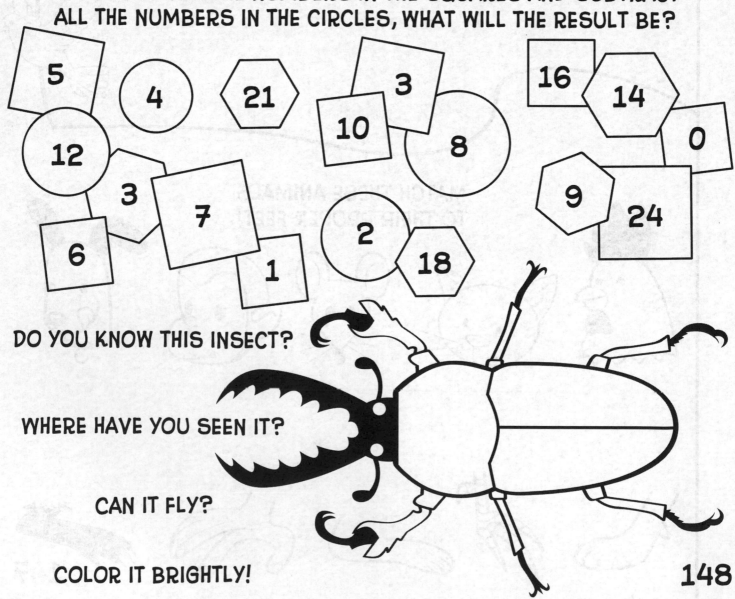

DO YOU KNOW THIS INSECT?

WHERE HAVE YOU SEEN IT?

CAN IT FLY?

COLOR IT BRIGHTLY!

THE KIDS HAVE GONE OUTSIDE TO PLAY!

TRACE THE DOTTED LINE TO FINISH THE SWINGS.

FOLLOW THE THREAD TO FIND OUT WHICH TOP SALLY IS REALLY THROWING FOR A SPIN.

CREATE AN ORIGINAL DESIGN TO DECORATE BILLY'S CAP.

COLOR THE BIG MARBLES GREEN AND THE SMALL ONES BLUE.

CROSSWORDS.

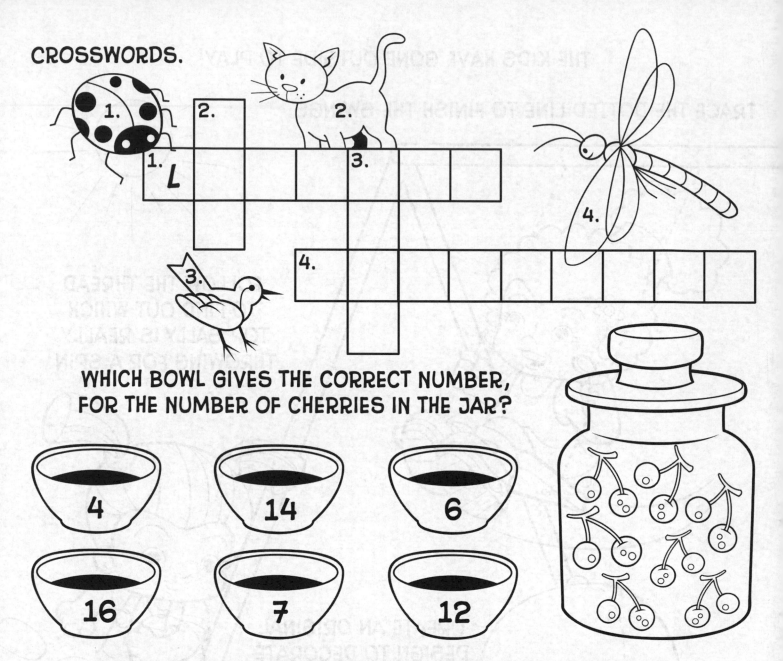

1. **L**

WHICH BOWL GIVES THE CORRECT NUMBER, FOR THE NUMBER OF CHERRIES IN THE JAR?

4

14

6

16

7

12

WHICH ANIMALS HERE EAT THE NECTAR FROM FLOWERS?

WHICH BALL DOES NOT LOOK LIKE THE OTHERS?

HOW MANY CAN YOU COUNT IN EACH SERIES? COLOR THE RIGHT NUMBER.

1 2 3 4 5 6 7 8

1 2 3 4 5 6 7 8

1 2 3 4 5 6 7 8

FIND THE STALLION'S CORRESPONDING SHADOW.

WHICH RABBIT GOT THE MOST CARROTS? COLOR HIS STASH!

152

FIDO FORGOT WHERE HE BURIED HIS TREASURE TROVE OF BONES. CAN YOU HELP HIM FIND IT?

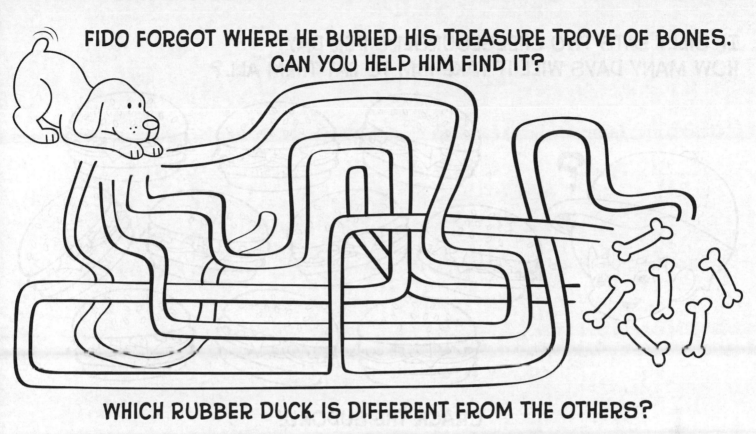

WHICH RUBBER DUCK IS DIFFERENT FROM THE OTHERS?

COLOR THE TREE WITH MORE PEARS.

IF BILLY EATS TWO CHEESEBURGERS PER DAY,
HOW MANY DAYS WILL IT TAKE HIM TO EAT THEM ALL?

CRACK THE SUDOKU!
EACH DRAWING CAN ONLY BE PLACED ONCE ON EACH LINE,
ONCE ON EACH ROW, AND ONCE IN EACH FOUR CELL GRID.

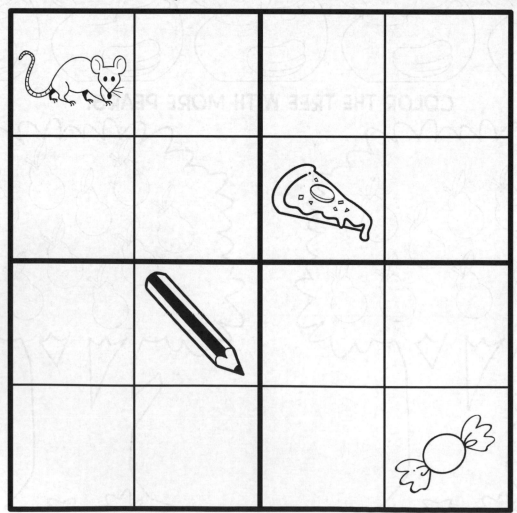

154

WRITE FOUR ANIMALS THAT START WITH THE LETTER "B".

B
B
B
B

WHAT COLOR IS THE LIGHT?

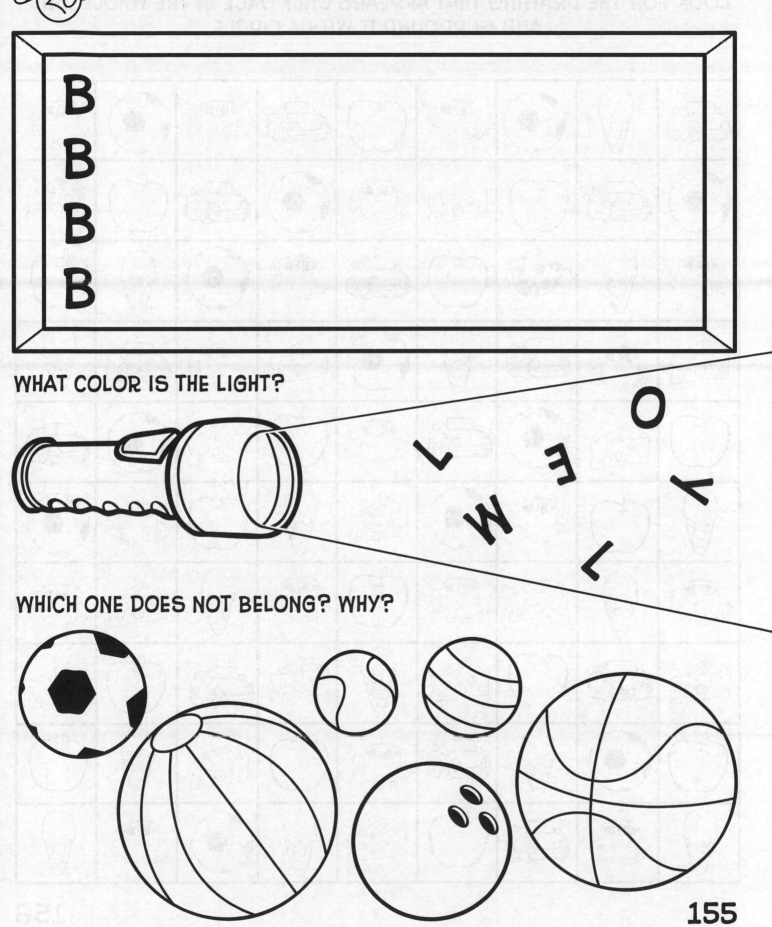

YELLOW

WHICH ONE DOES NOT BELONG? WHY?

155

LOOK FOR THE DRAWING THAT APPEARS ONLY ONCE IN THE WHOLE GRID AND SURROUND IT WITH A CIRCLE.

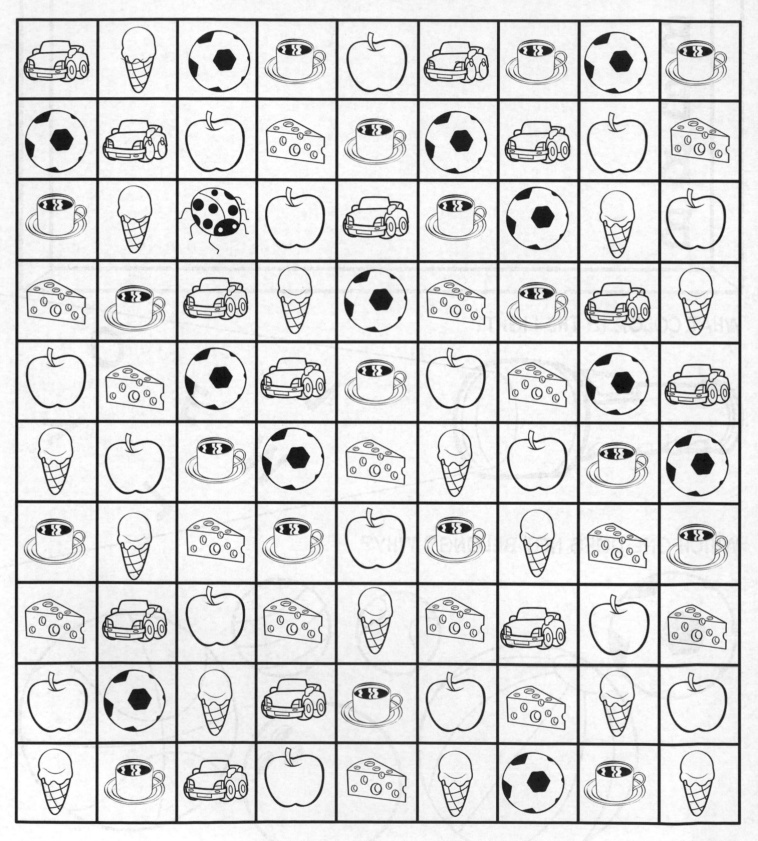

156

WHICH DRAWING ON EACH LINE LOOKS JUST LIKE THE ONE IN THE LEFT COLUMN?

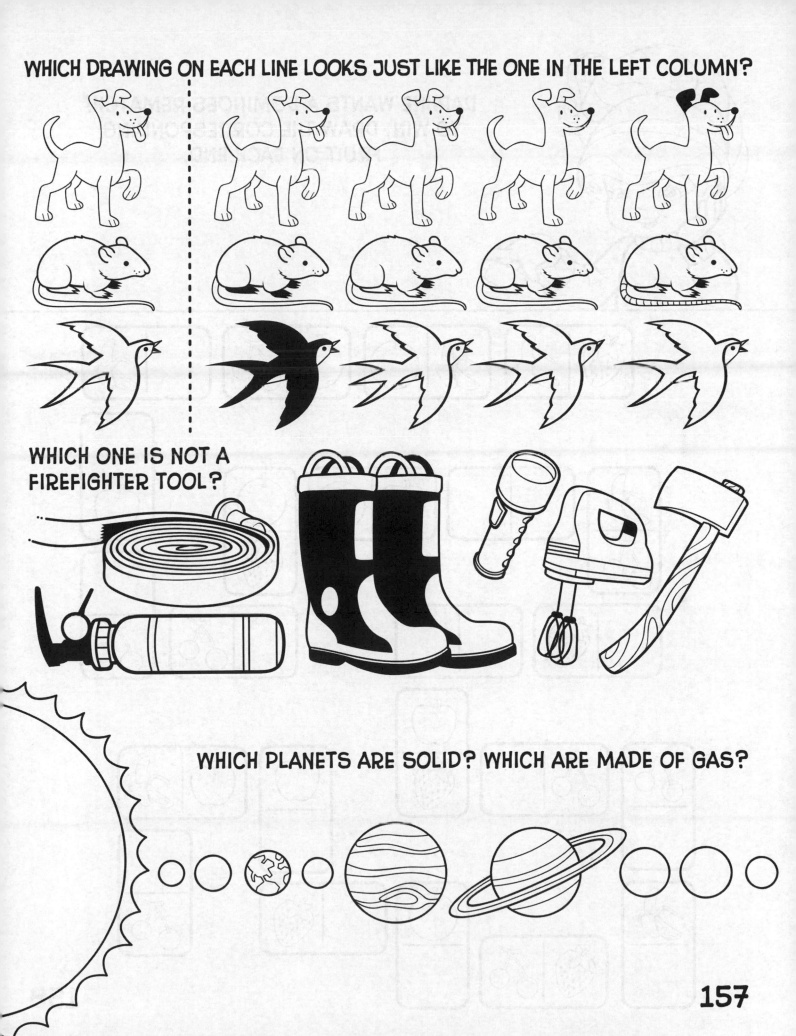

WHICH ONE IS NOT A FIREFIGHTER TOOL?

WHICH PLANETS ARE SOLID? WHICH ARE MADE OF GAS?

DAPHNE WANTS A DOMINOES REMATCH! TO WIN, DRAW THE CORRESPONDING FRUIT ON EACH END.

CROSSWORDS.

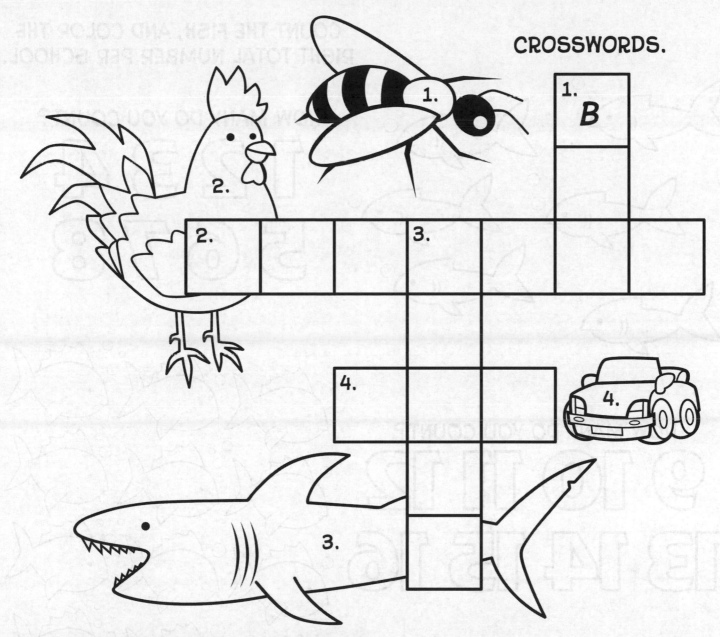

1.
B

2.

3.

4.

4.

3.

IF MIMI EATS THREE TREATS PER DAY,
HOW MANY DAYS WILL IT TAKE HER TO EAT THEM ALL?

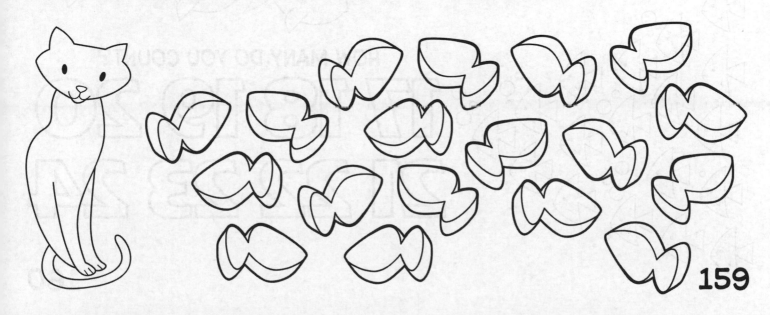

COUNT THE FISH, AND COLOR THE RIGHT TOTAL NUMBER PER SCHOOL.

HOW MANY DO YOU COUNT?

1 2 3 4
5 6 7 8

HOW MANY DO YOU COUNT?

9 10 11 12
13 14 15 16

HOW MANY DO YOU COUNT?

17 18 19 20
21 22 23 24

160

CROSS OUT THE PIG THAT APPEARS IN THE IMAGE ONLY ONCE.

EVERY ANIMAL HAS A SHADOW. WHICH ONE HAS NONE?

CAN YOU FIND THE SMALLER COMBINATIONS IN THE BIG GRID BELOW?
COLOR THEM WHEN YOU DO!

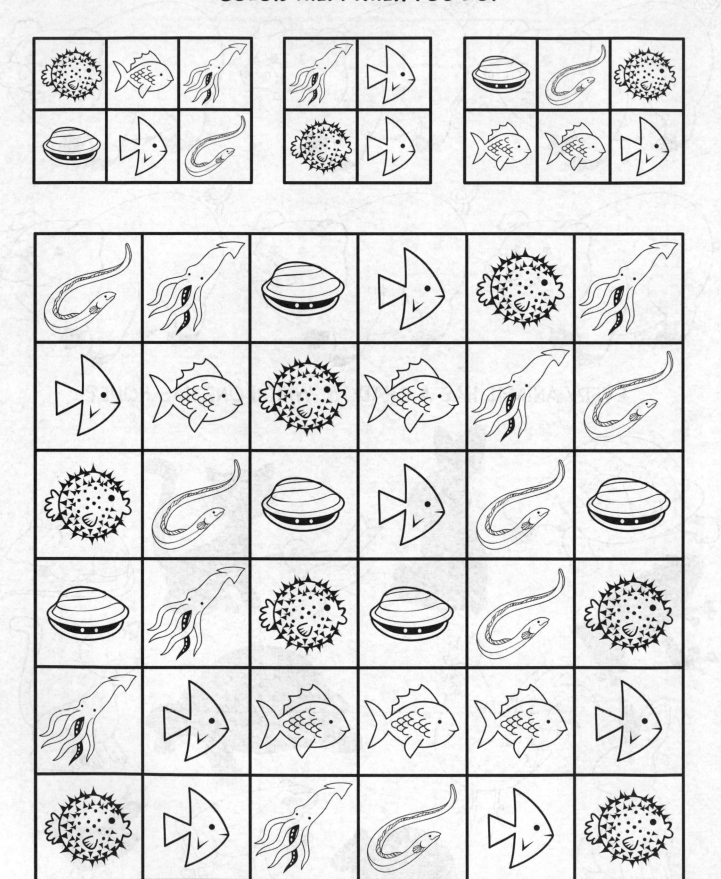

COMPLETE THE UNDERWATER VIEW WITH FISH AND OTHER MARINE LIFE!

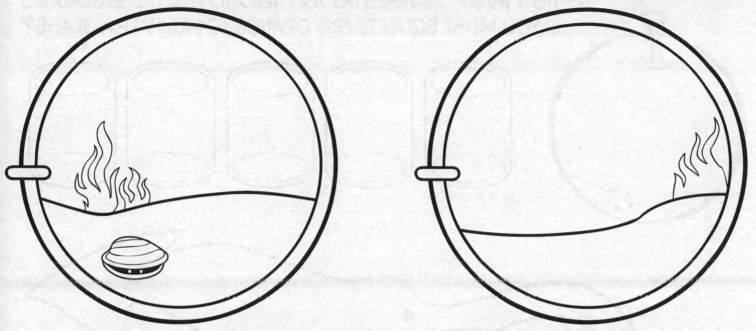

WHICH OUTLINE DOES NOT MATCH THE FROG'S DRAWING?

DRAW DIFFERENT FLOWER BOUQUETS ACCORDING TO THE FLOWERS NAMED ON EACH VASE.

ROSES

DAISIES

BEGONIAS

MARIGOLDS

HOW MANY ORANGES DO YOU NEED TO FILL THESE GLASSES
IF YOU MUST SQUEEZE ONE ORANGE TO FILL HALF A GLASS?

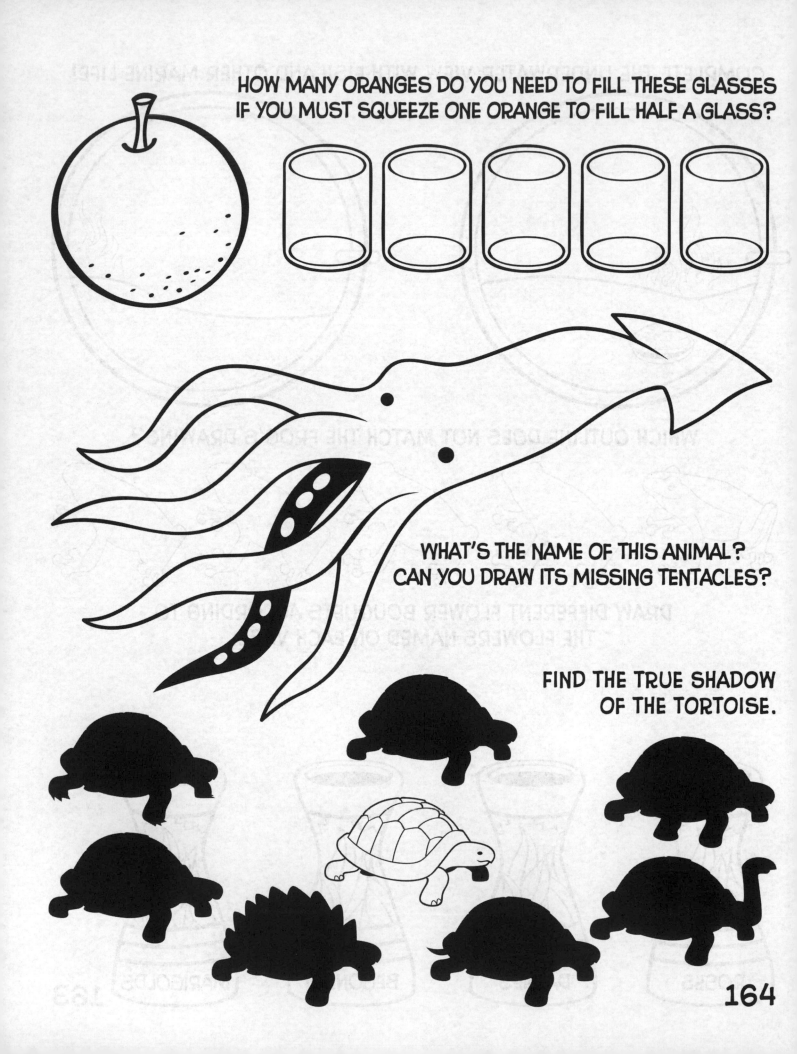

WHAT'S THE NAME OF THIS ANIMAL?
CAN YOU DRAW ITS MISSING TENTACLES?

FIND THE TRUE SHADOW
OF THE TORTOISE.

164

CONNECT EACH FRUIT AND VEGGIE TO THE GRID IT BELONGS TO, BUT BEWARE, ONLY ONE OF EACH BELONGS IN EACH GRID!

FIND THE TEN DIFFERENCES.

WHICH DRAWING ON EACH LINE IS IDENTICAL TO THE ONE IN THE LEFT COLUMN?

CONNECT THE DOTS!

ALL THESE FLAGS ARE RED, WHITE, AND BLUE.
COLOR THEM ACCORDING TO THEIR COUNTRY.

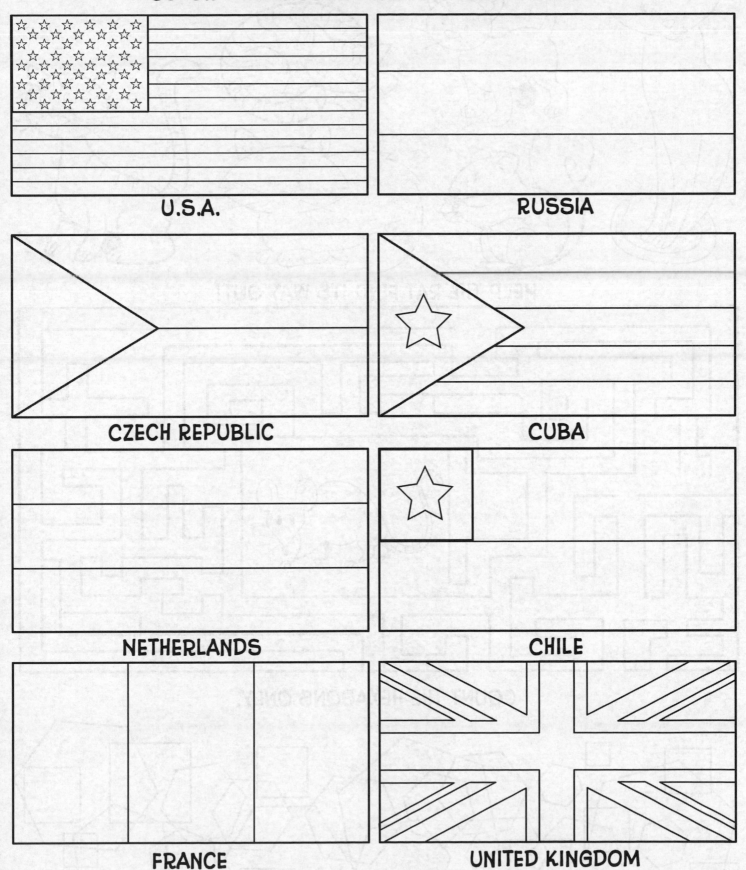

U.S.A.

RUSSIA

CZECH REPUBLIC

CUBA

NETHERLANDS

CHILE

FRANCE

UNITED KINGDOM

FIND THE ONE THAT DOESN'T BELONG.

HELP THE RAT FIND ITS WAY OUT!

COUNT THE HEXAGONS ONLY.

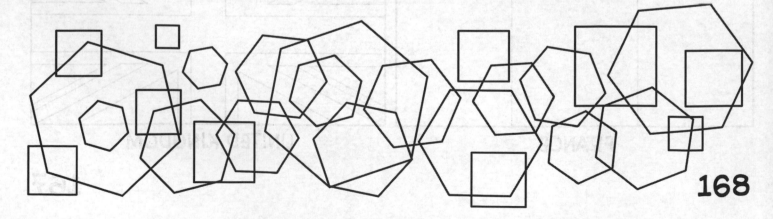

WHAT DOES THE BEE EAT?

FILL THE OTHER COMPARTMENTS WITH MORE TOYS YOU LIKE.

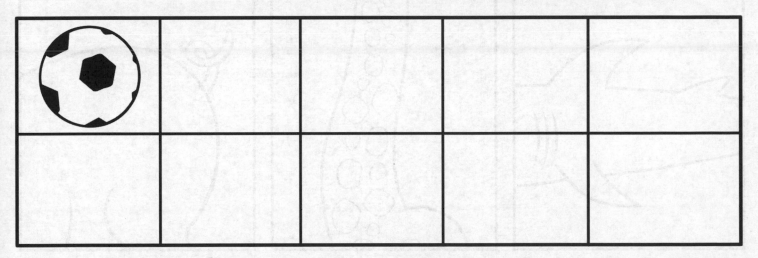

WHICH ONE DOES NOT EAT OTHER ANIMALS?

169

CAN YOU DRAW THE SAILBOAT IN THE RIGHT PANEL?

DO YOU RECOGNIZE THE ANIMALS IN THESE INCOMPLETE DRAWINGS?

FIND THE MATCHING BUTTERFLIES
AND COLOR THEM ALIKE.

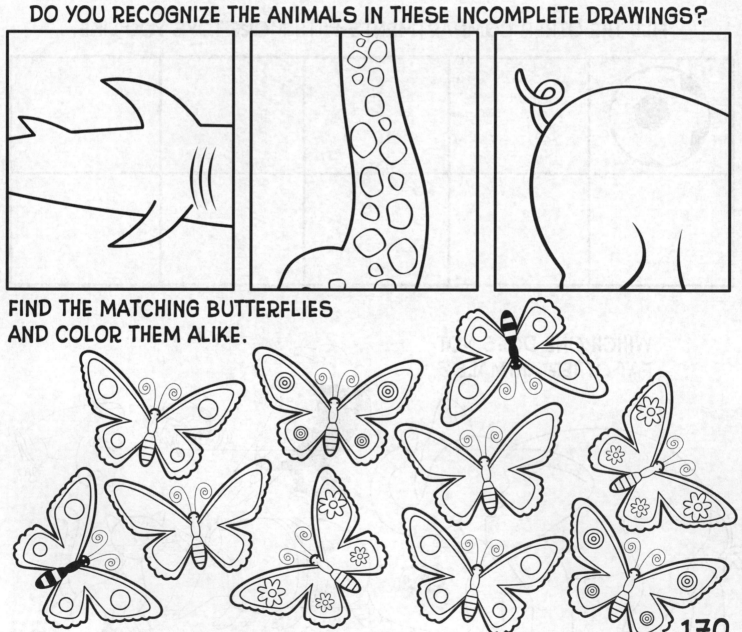

DO YOU RECOGNIZE THESE SILHOUETTES? WHICH ONE DOES NOT BELONG?

WHAT'S MISSING FROM THIS PICTURE? DRAW IT BY TRACING THE DOTTED LINE.

HOW MANY APPLES DO YOU NEED TO FILL THESE GLASSES IF YOU MUST SQUEEZE TWO APPLES TO FILL A GLASS?

FILL THIS PAGE WITH FALLING LEAVES FOR SALLY TO RAKE! →

IF YOU CONTINUE THE PROGRESSION OF SYMBOLS FROM LEFT TO RIGHT, WHICH ONE WOULD SUBSTITUTE THE QUESTION MARK?

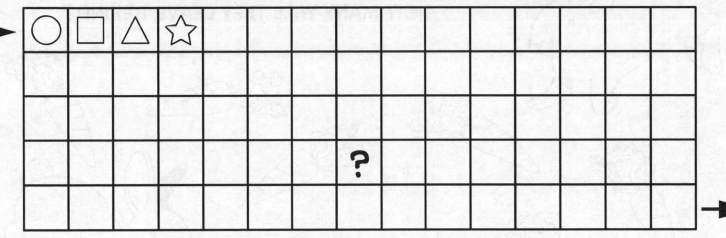

WHAT BIRDS ARE HIDING IN THE TREES?

COLOR ONLY THE ONES THAT ARE MAN-MADE.

173

EACH RABBIT CAN ONLY TAKE ONE CARROT.
HOW MANY WILL THEY LEAVE BEHIND?

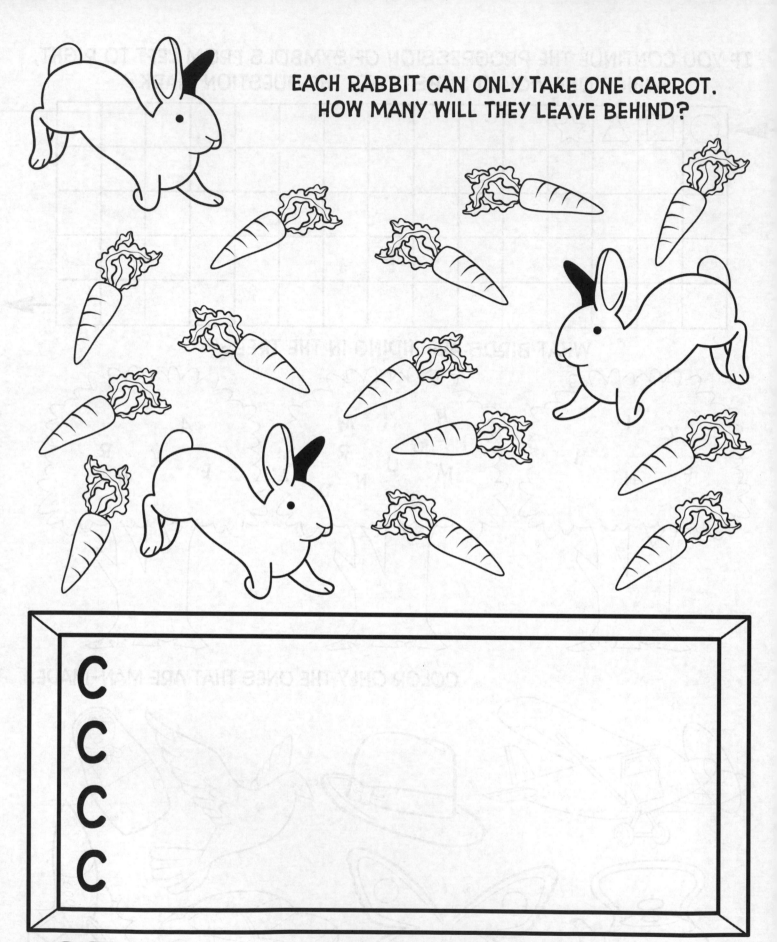

C
  C
    C
      C

 WRITE FOUR ANIMALS THAT START WITH THE LETTER "C" .

174

CAN YOU SEE THE TWO IDENTICAL LEAVES?

HOPPING ONLY ON THE WATERLILY PATH,
AND AVOIDING THE INSECTS, HELP THE FROG REACH HIS GIRLFRIEND.
HOW MANY JUMPS WILL IT TAKE?

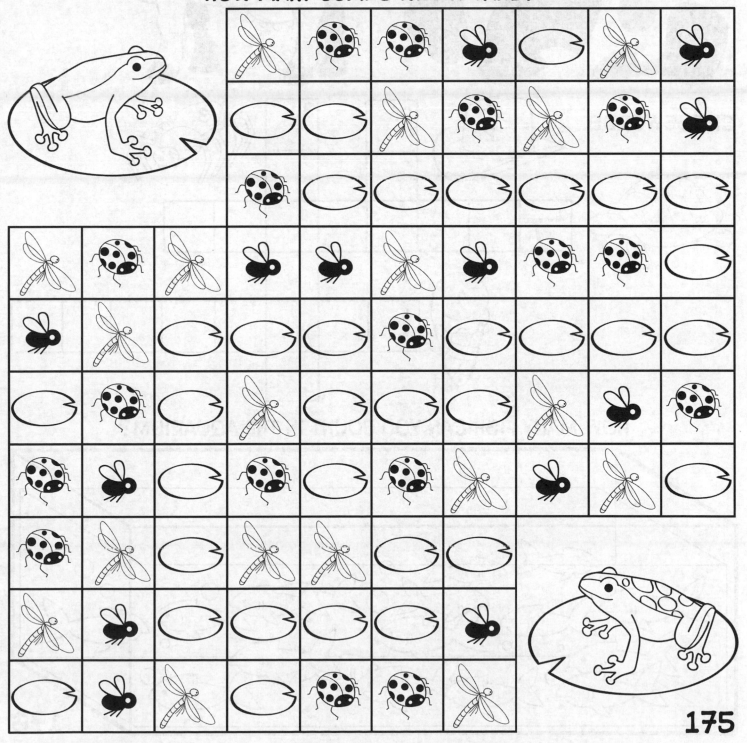

MATCH THE IDENTICALLY SHAPED SPOT.

CROSSWORDS.

1. T

HOW MANY FISH CAN YOU COUNT IN THE AQUARIUM?

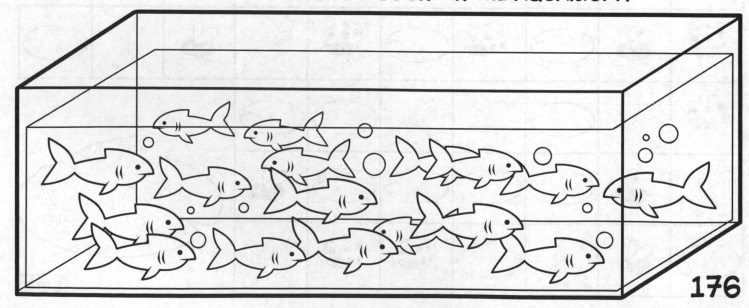

MATCH THE ANIMAL TO ITS TAIL.

TO GET TO THE APPLE, YOU CAN GO VERTICALLY OR HORIZONTALLY, BUT CANNOT CROSS OVER THE SAME SYMBOL TWICE!

IDENTIFY THE TEEPEE THAT BELONGS TO ANOTHER TRIBE.

WHAT CLASSIC FAIRY TALE DO ALL THESE ELEMENTS BELONG TO?

C _ _ _ _ _ _ _ _ _ _ _

WHAT DOES THE ARMADILLO EAT?

DRAW YOUR FAVORITE TV SHOW!

WHAT IS IT CALLED?

IF YOU FOLLOW THE PATTERN, WHAT SYMBOL DOES THE RABBIT ARRIVE AT?

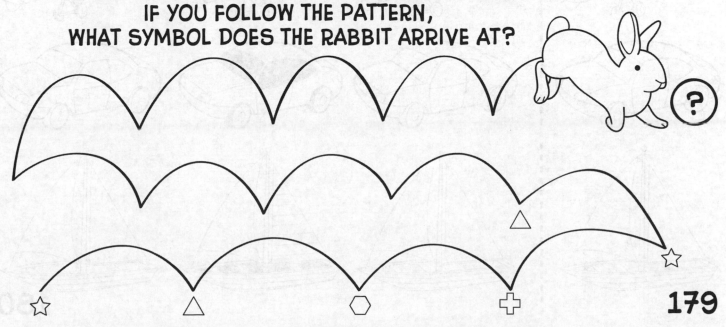

ALL THESE FLAGS ARE RED, GREEN, AND WHITE.
COLOR THEM ACCORDING TO THEIR COUNTRY.

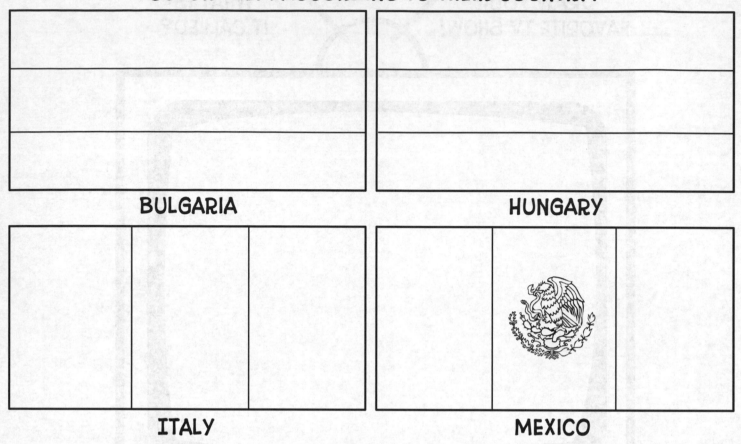

BULGARIA

HUNGARY

ITALY

MEXICO

WHICH DRAWING ON EACH LINE IS IDENTICAL TO THE ONE IN THE LEFT COLUMN?

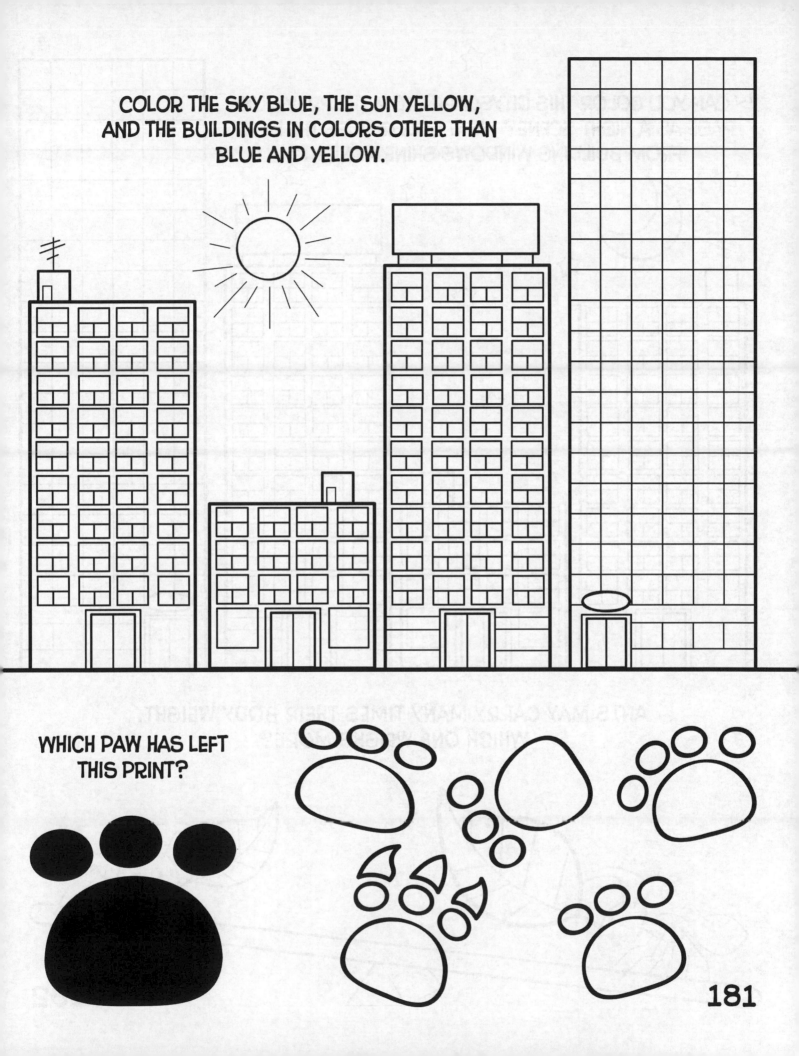

COLOR THE SKY BLUE, THE SUN YELLOW,
AND THE BUILDINGS IN COLORS OTHER THAN
BLUE AND YELLOW.

WHICH PAW HAS LEFT
THIS PRINT?

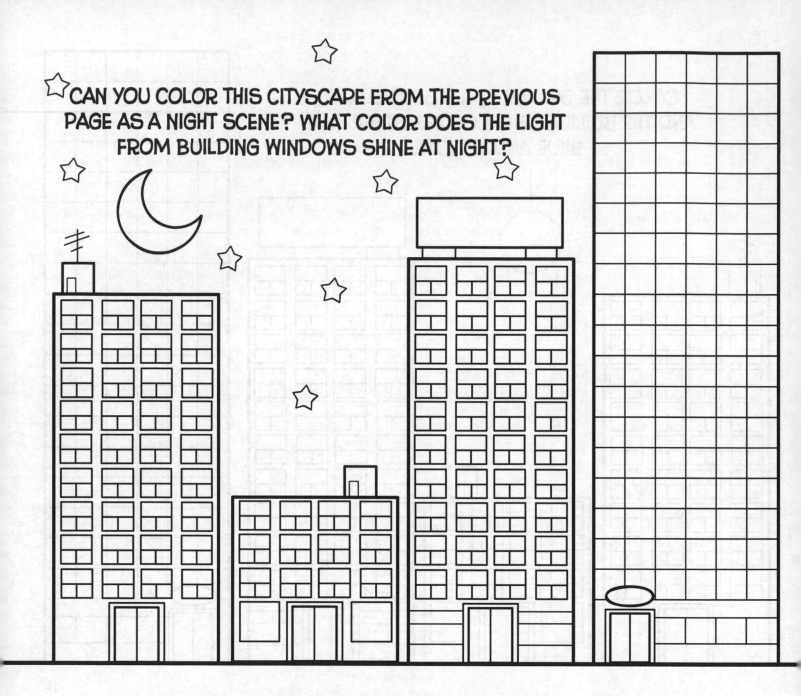

CAN YOU COLOR THIS CITYSCAPE FROM THE PREVIOUS PAGE AS A NIGHT SCENE? WHAT COLOR DOES THE LIGHT FROM BUILDING WINDOWS SHINE AT NIGHT?

ANTS MAY CARRY MANY TIMES THEIR BODY WEIGHT. WHICH ONE WEIGHS MORE?

WHICH ONE DOES NOT LOOK LIKE THE REST?

HOW MANY DIFFERENCES CAN YOU FIND?

WHAT ANIMAL LIVES HERE?

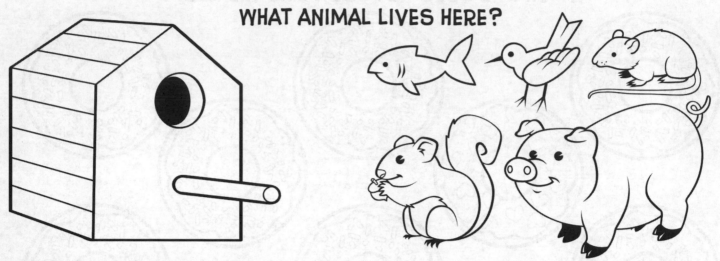

SOMETHING IN THIS PICTURE IS IMPOSSIBLE. CAN YOU GUESS WHAT?

IDENTIFY THE MATCHING OWL COUPLES AND COLOR THEM ALIKE.

184

THESE TWO ARE RELATED. CAN YOU GUESS THE NAME OF THEIR FAMILY?

C_ _ _ _ _ _ _ _ _

WRITE FOUR ANIMALS THAT START WITH THE LETTER "S".

```
S

S

S

S
```

DECORATE AND COLOR THIS CAKE TO MATCH YOUR FAVORITE FLAVORS.

185

EACH APE CAN ONLY TAKE TWO BANANAS.
HOW MANY WILL THEY LEAVE BEHIND?

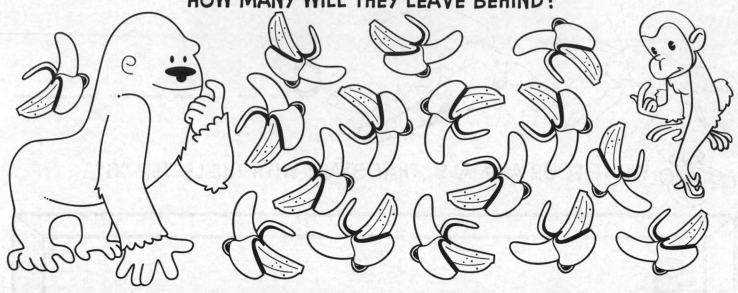

COMPLETE THIS BY CREATING YOUR OWN SYMBOLS MOVING FORWARD.

HELP THE SWALLOWS MEET!

CONNECT EACH ANIMAL TO THE GRID IT BELONGS TO, BUT BEWARE, ONLY ONE ANIMAL BELONGS IN EACH GRID!

HOW MANY PLANES DO YOU COUNT?

COLOR THE BIG ONES RED, THE SMALL ONES YELLOW, AND THE REST GREEN.

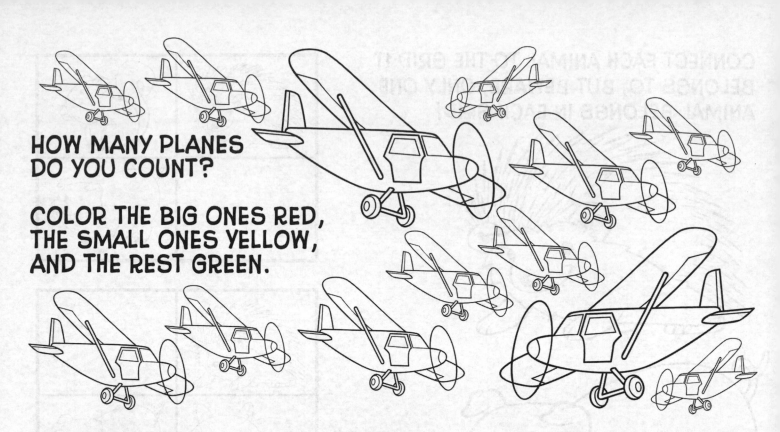

IF THE BOWLING BALL KNOCKS SEVEN PINS, HOW MANY ARE LEFT STANDING?

WHAT ANIMALS IS THIS WEIRD CREATURE MADE OF?

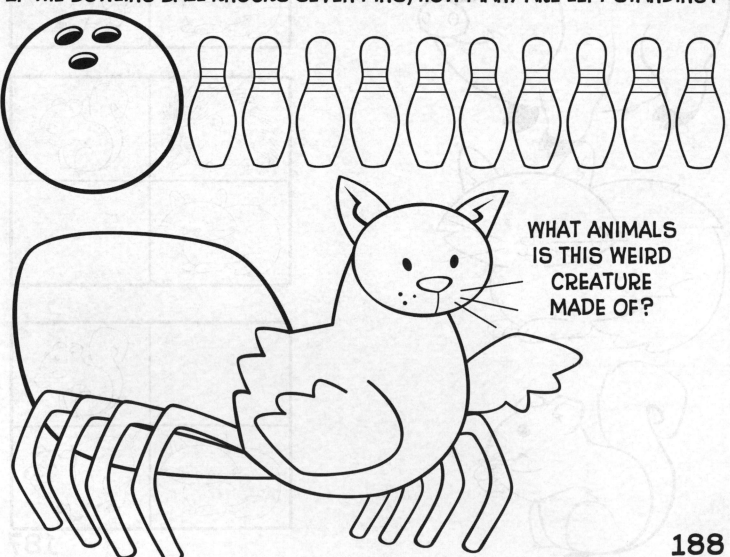

188

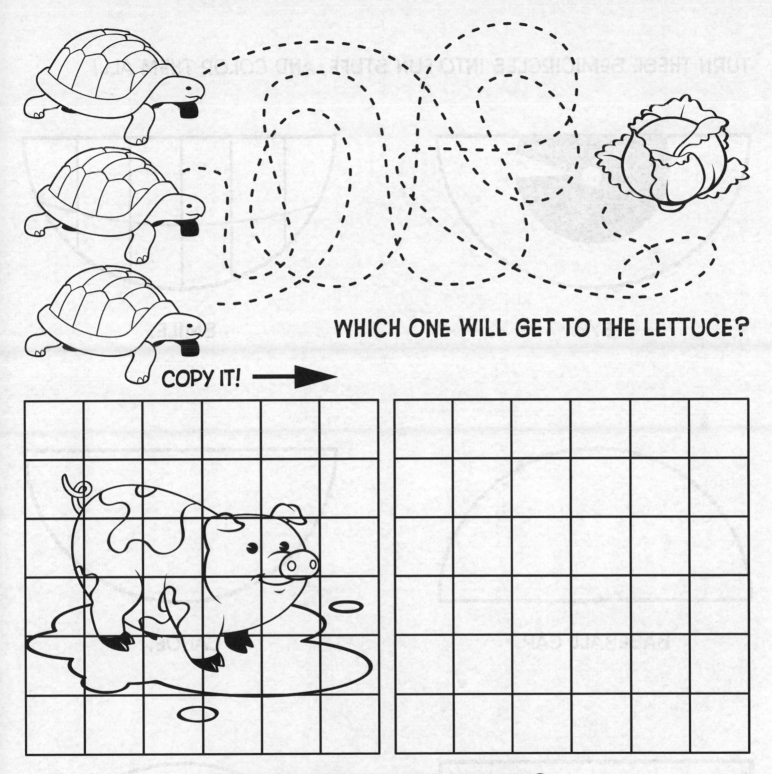

WHICH ONE WILL GET TO THE LETTUCE?

COPY IT! ➡️

WHAT DO THESE HAVE IN COMMON?

189

TURN THESE SEMICIRCLES INTO FUN STUFF, AND COLOR THEM ALL!

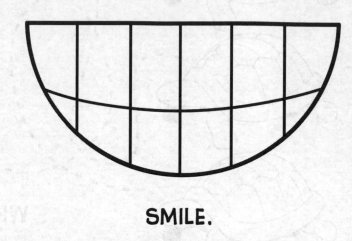

EYE.

SMILE.

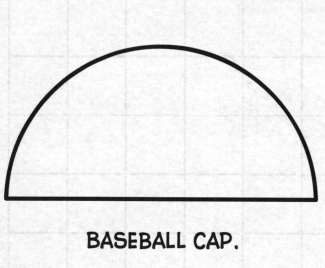

BASEBALL CAP.

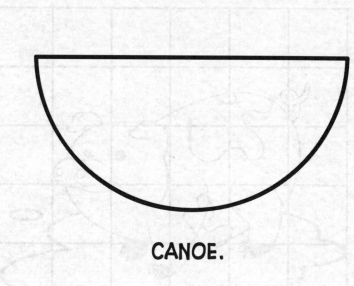

CANOE.

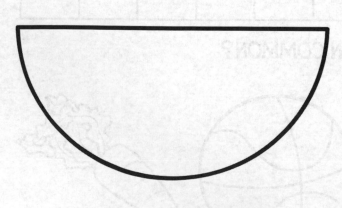

WATERMELON SLICE.

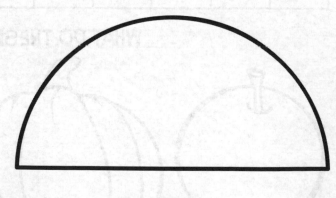

RAINBOW.

DRAW THE OTHER HALF.

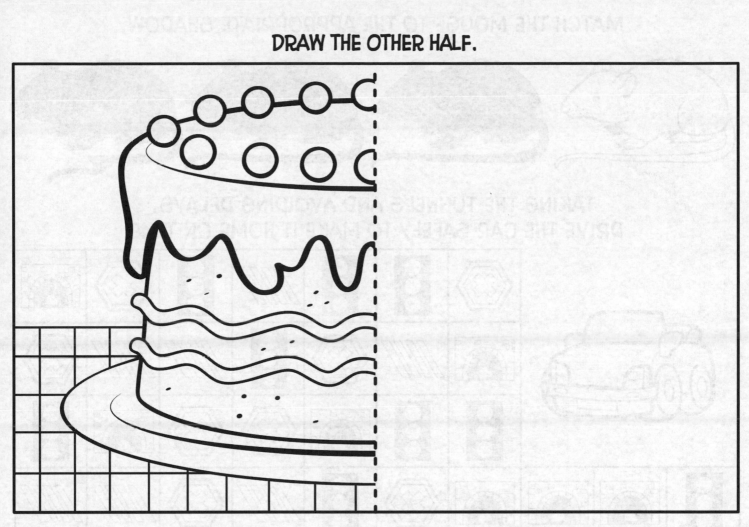

HOW MANY CARROTS DO YOU NEED TO FILL THESE GLASSES IF YOU MUST GRIND THREE TO FILL A GLASS?

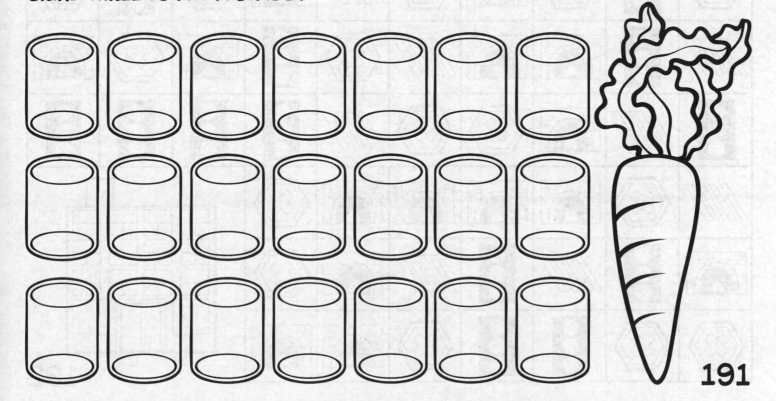

MATCH THE MOUSE TO THE APPROPRIATE SHADOW.

TAKING THE TUNNELS AND AVOIDING DELAYS, DRIVE THE CAR SAFELY TO MAKE IT HOME ON TIME.

192

HORSES CAN ONLY WEAR FOUR HORSESHOES EACH. HOW MANY WILL THEY LEAVE BEHIND?

COMPLETE EACH LOGICAL SEQUENCE.

DRAW A CIRCLE AROUND THE GIRAFFE WITH MOST SPOTS.

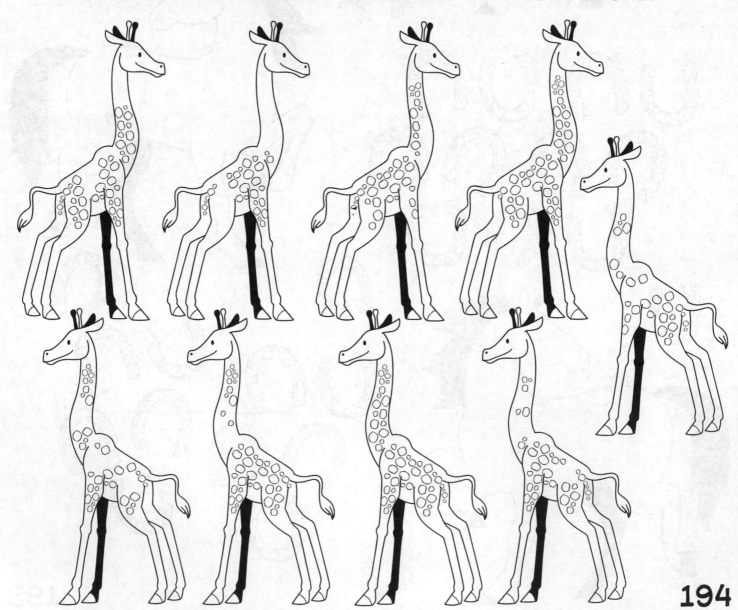

194

FILL THE WATER WITH FRIENDLY FISH,
AND COLOR IT ALL!

195

WHERE DO YOU FIND THESE PIECES
IN THE DRAWING?

WHO LIVES
IN HERE?

196

HOW DOES THE FLY GET TO THE ICE CREAM?

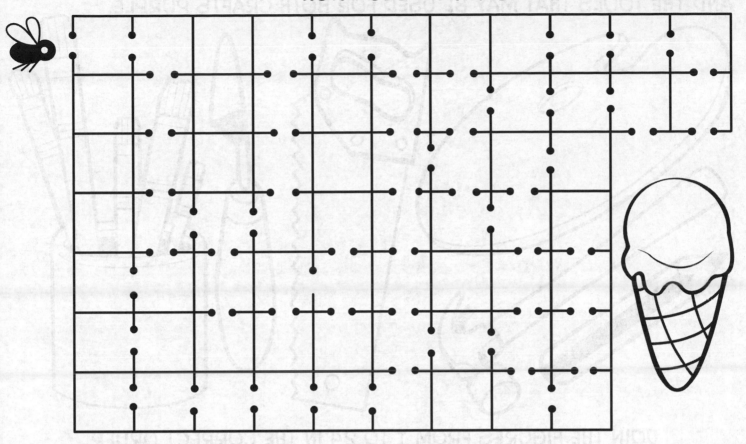

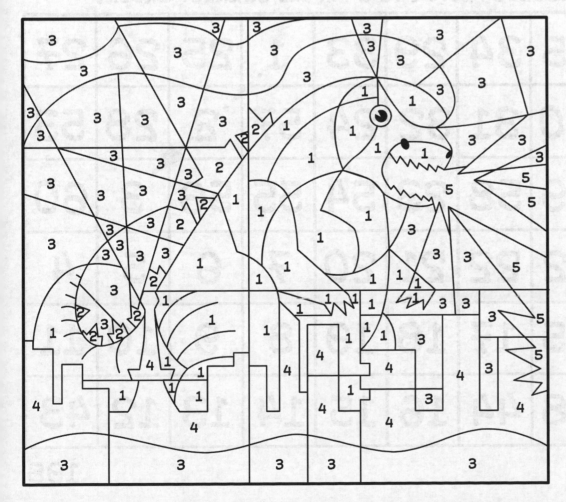

1 = GREEN
2 = PURPLE
3 = BLUE
4 = GRAY
5 = YELLOW

WHAT IS IT?

COLOR THE PAINTING TOOLS RED, THE CARPENTRY TOOLS BLUE, AND THE TOOLS THAT MAY BE USED FOR BOTH CRAFTS PURPLE.

JOIN THE FIGURES FROM 1 TO 24 IN THE CORRECT ORDER.

37	36	35	34	29	33	1	25	26	27
38	39	30	31	32	24	57	2	28	53
40	41	59	58	23	54	55	56	3	60
49	50	42	22	21	20	7	6	5	4
51	46	45	17	18	19	8	9	10	11
52	47	48	44	16	15	14	13	12	43

IF EACH HAMBURGER COSTS TWO DOLLARS, HOW MUCH DO THEY COST ALL TOGETHER?

WHAT CHANGED IN THE SECOND AND THIRD IMAGES, COMPARED TO THE FIRST?

WHAT COUNTRY IS IT?
DO YOU REMEMBER THE COLORS OF ITS FLAG?
COLOR THE MAP THE SAME WAY.

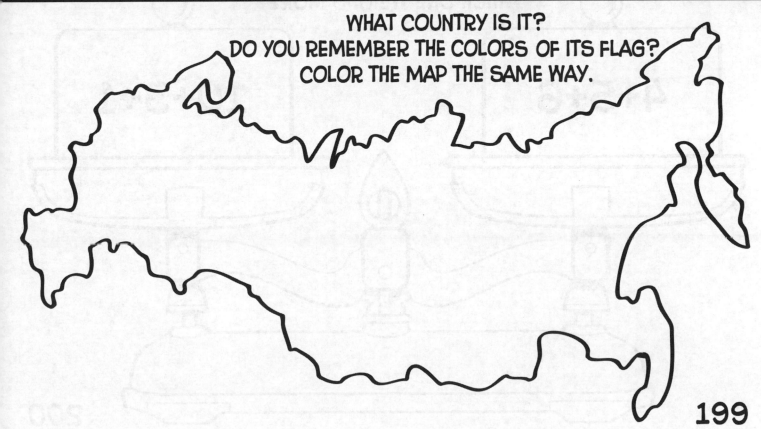

REMEMBER THESE INSECTS' NAMES? CAN YOU SPELL THEM?

A _ _

S _ _ _ _ _ _

B _ _ _

L _ _ _ _ _ _ _

G _ _ _ _ _ _ _ _ _

THE PACK HAS BEEN INFILTRATED! CAN YOU TELL WHO THE OUTSIDER IS?

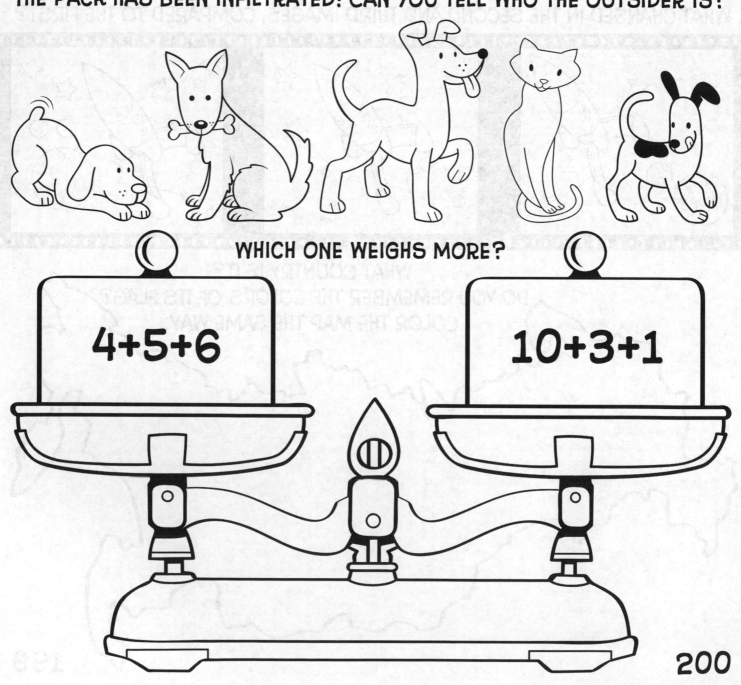

WHICH ONE WEIGHS MORE?

4+5+6

10+3+1

IF MAYA EATS FOUR SLICES OF PIZZA PER DAY,
HOW MANY DAYS WILL IT TAKE HER TO EAT THEM ALL?

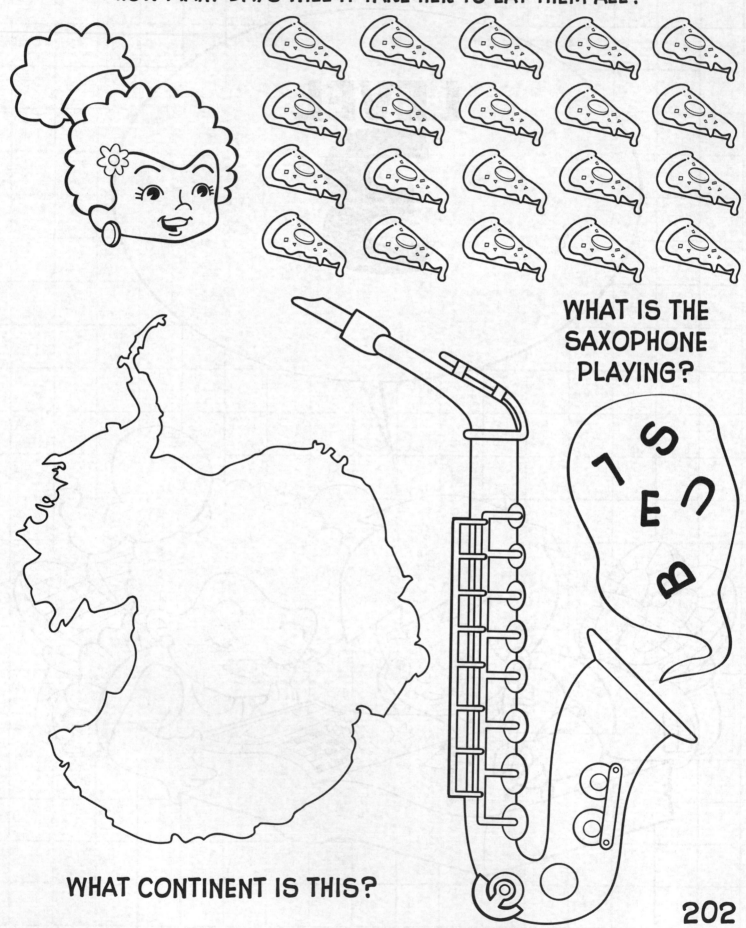

WHAT IS THE
SAXOPHONE
PLAYING?

WHAT CONTINENT IS THIS?

WHAT IS THE AVERAGE NUMBER OF APPLES IN THESE BASKETS?

WHICH DRAWING ON EACH LINE IS IDENTICAL TO THE ONE IN THE LEFT COLUMN?

TO CATCH THE MOUSE, THE CAT NEEDS TO GO THROUGH THE ODD NUMBERS.

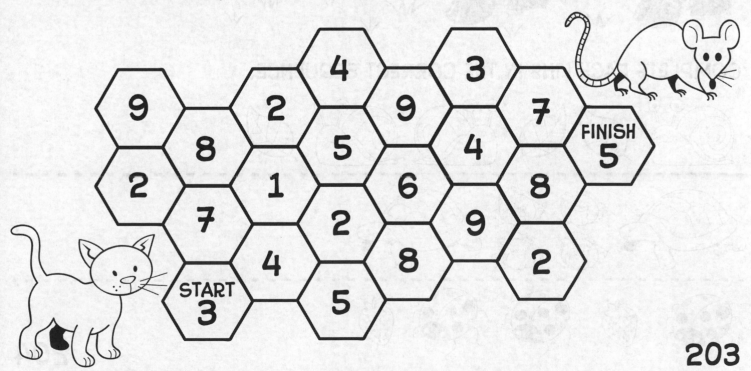

DRAW A CIRCLE AROUND THE ITEMS YOU PUT ON YOUR FEET.
COLOR THE ONES THAT COVER YOUR HEAD.

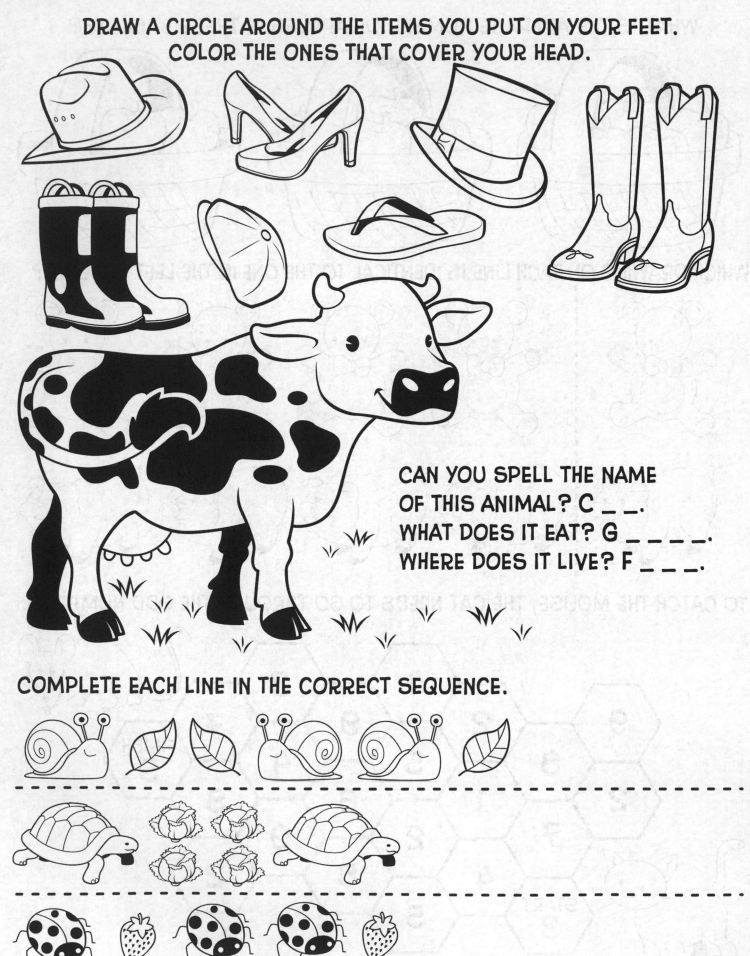

CAN YOU SPELL THE NAME
OF THIS ANIMAL? C _ _.
WHAT DOES IT EAT? G _ _ _ _.
WHERE DOES IT LIVE? F _ _ _.

COMPLETE EACH LINE IN THE CORRECT SEQUENCE.

WHICH ONE OF THESE ANIMALS IS BEST CAPABLE OF WITHSTANDING FREEZING TEMPERATURES?

HOW MANY SWALLOWS ARE FLYING EAST? COLOR THEM BLUE.
HOW MANY FLY WEST? COLOR THEM PURPLE.

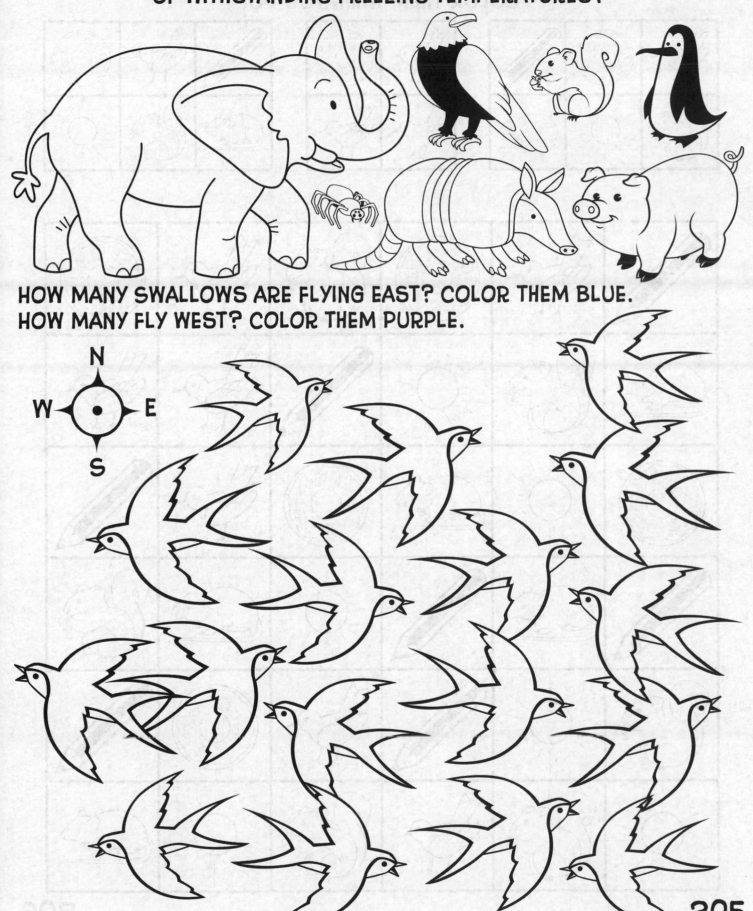

CAN YOU FIND THE SMALLER COMBINATIONS IN THE BIG GRID BELOW?
COLOR THEM WHEN YOU DO!

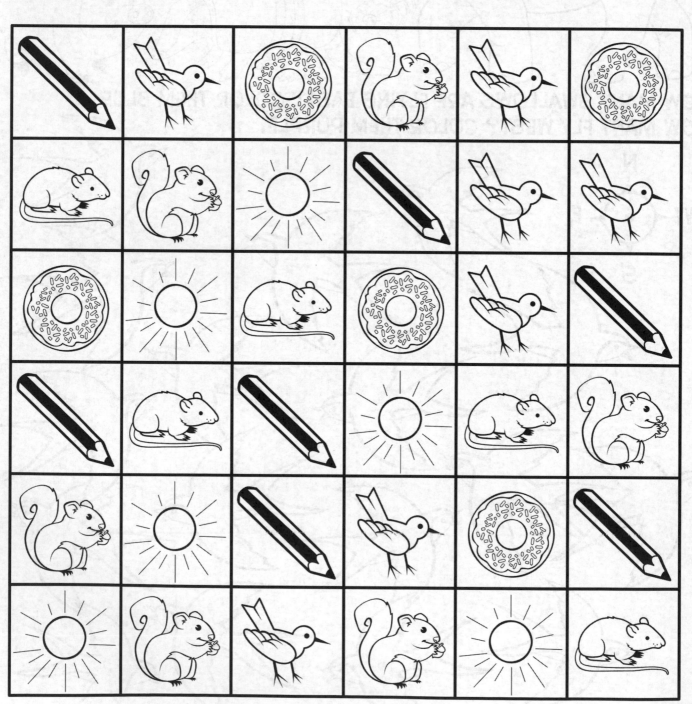

206

IF YOU CONTINUE THE PROGRESSION OF SYMBOLS FROM LEFT TO RIGHT, WHICH ONE WOULD SUBSTITUTE THE QUESTION MARK?

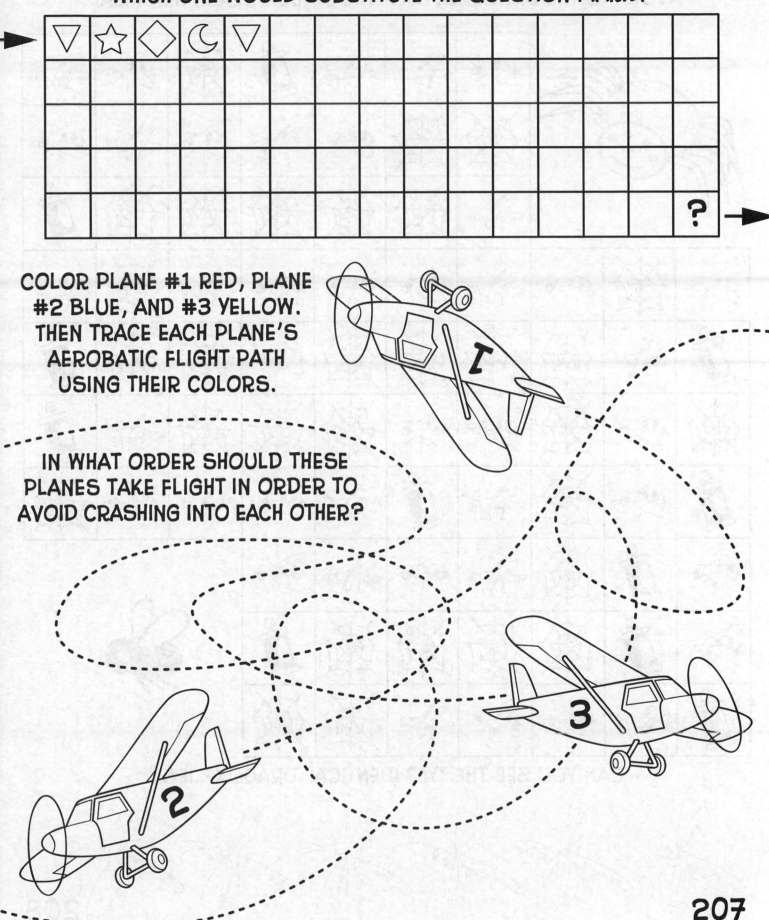

COLOR PLANE #1 RED, PLANE #2 BLUE, AND #3 YELLOW. THEN TRACE EACH PLANE'S AEROBATIC FLIGHT PATH USING THEIR COLORS.

IN WHAT ORDER SHOULD THESE PLANES TAKE FLIGHT IN ORDER TO AVOID CRASHING INTO EACH OTHER?

207

JUMPING ONLY FROM ONE WEBBING TO THE OTHER, WHILE AVOIDING THE DANGERS, HELP THE SPIDER REACH HER MEAL.

CAN YOU SEE THE TWO IDENTICAL DRAGONFLIES?

IT'S GETTING LATE, AND THE KIDS NEED TO BE BACK HOME BEFORE THE SUN SETS. TRACE THE DOTTED PATHS TO FIND OUT WHERE EACH ONE LIVES.

CONNECT EACH SHOE TO ITS APPROPIATE FOOTPRINT.

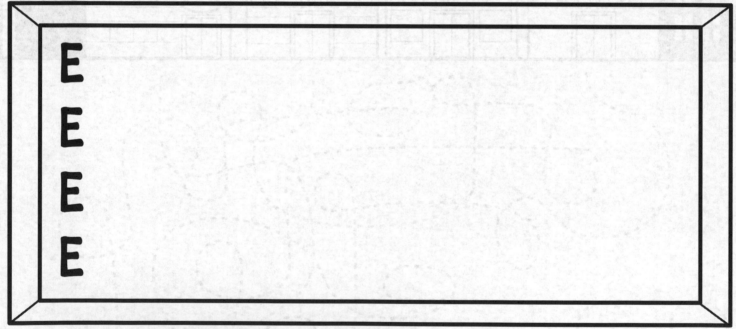

WRITE FOUR ANIMALS THAT START WITH THE LETTER "E".

E
E
E
E

DRAW THE HANDS OF THE CLOCKS.

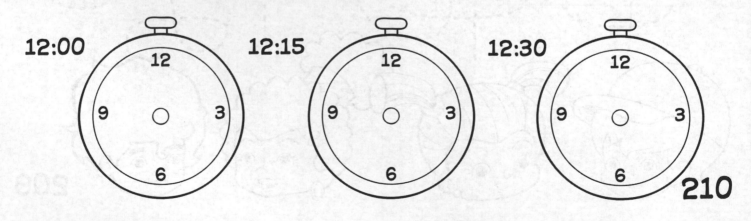

12:00

12:15

12:30

THE MORE LEAVES A CATERPILLAR EATS, THE MORE IT GROWS. COUNT THE LEAVES ON EACH PLANT AND DRAW AN EQUAL NUMBER OF CIRCLES FOR EACH CATERPILLAR.

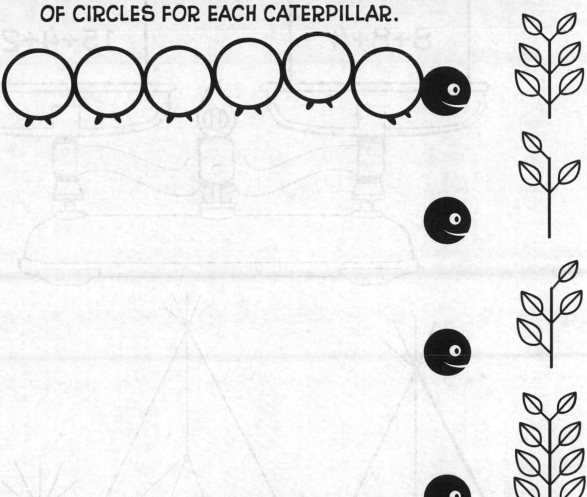

WHICH OF THE ANIMALS BELOW DO CATERPILLARS TURN INTO? COLOR IT. WHAT IS THE TRANSFORMATION CALLED?

M _ _ _ _ _ _ _ _ _ _ _ _ _ _ _ _ _ _

WHICH ONE WEIGHS MORE?

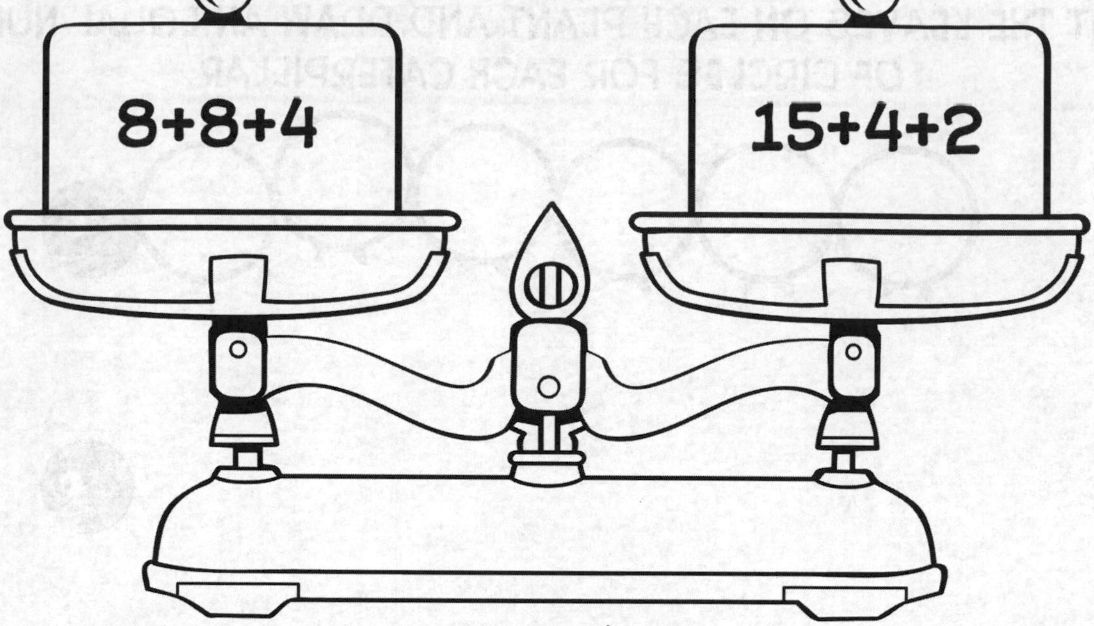

8+8+4

15+4+2

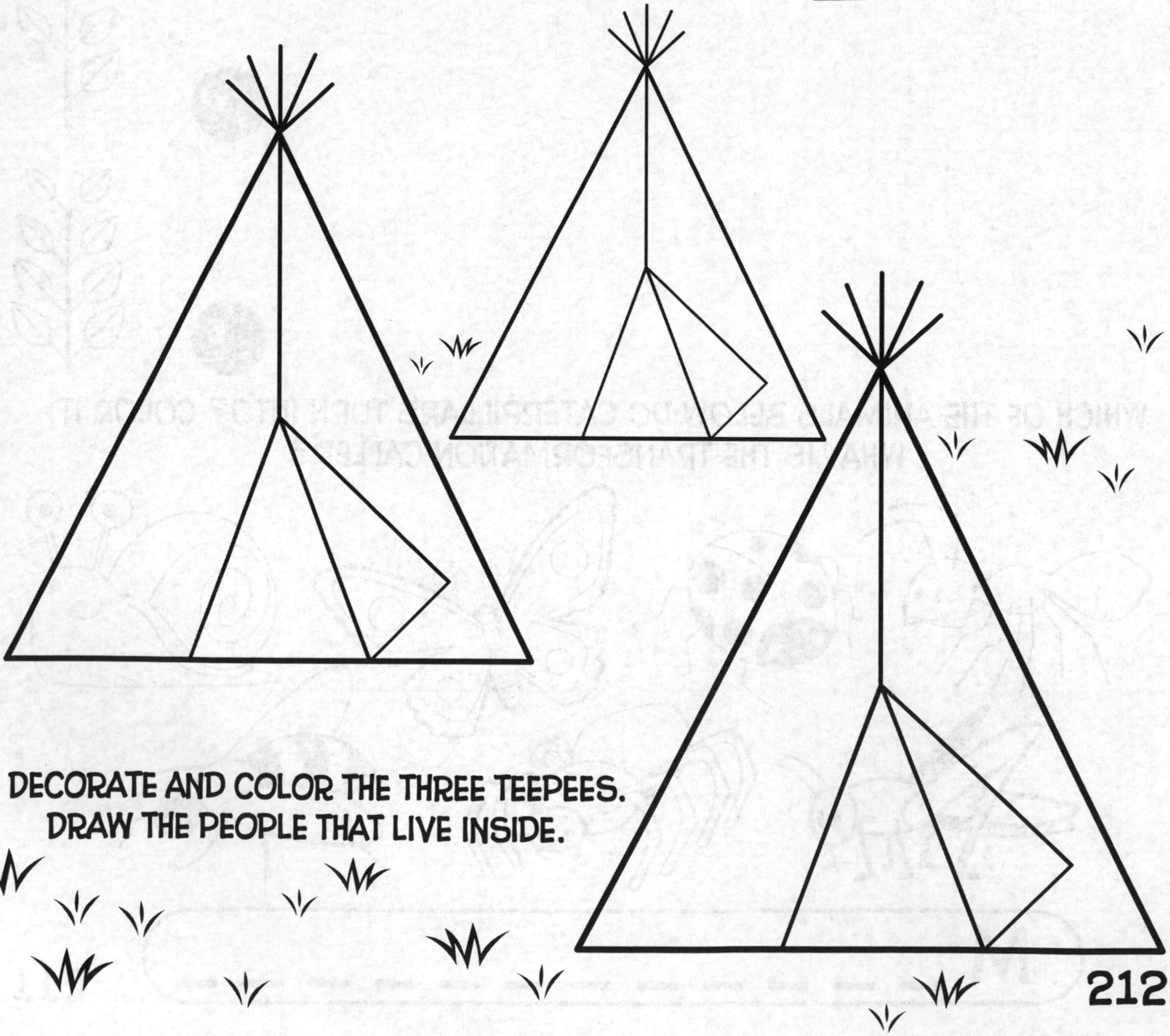

DECORATE AND COLOR THE THREE TEEPEES.
DRAW THE PEOPLE THAT LIVE INSIDE.

SOLVE THE ADDITIONS, AND WRITE YOUR RESULTS BELOW.

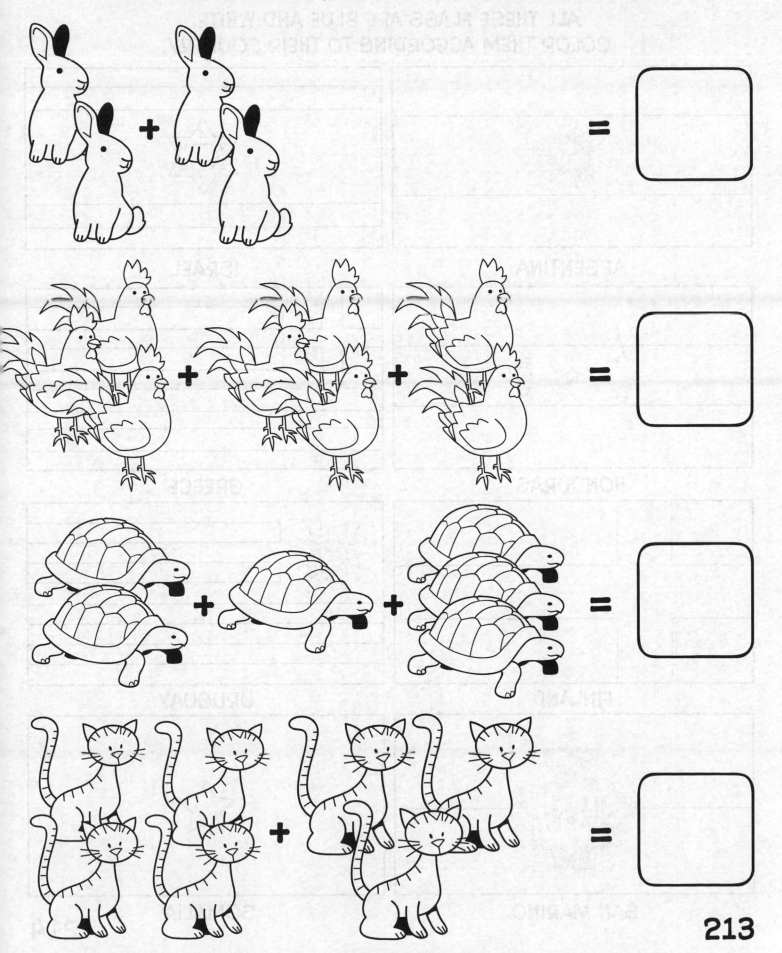

ALL THESE FLAGS ARE BLUE AND WHITE.
COLOR THEM ACCORDING TO THEIR COUNTRY.

ARGENTINA

ISRAEL

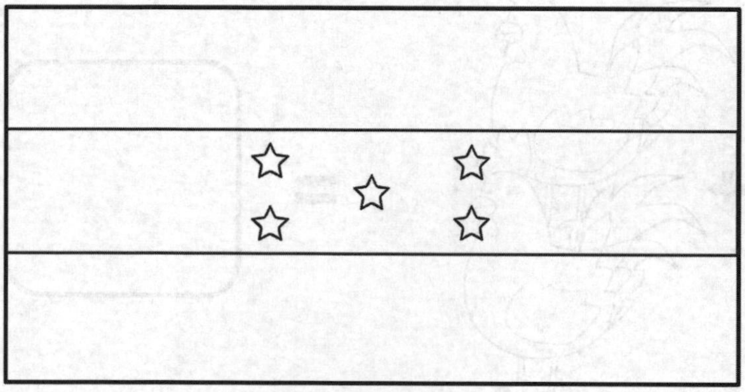

HONDURAS

GREECE

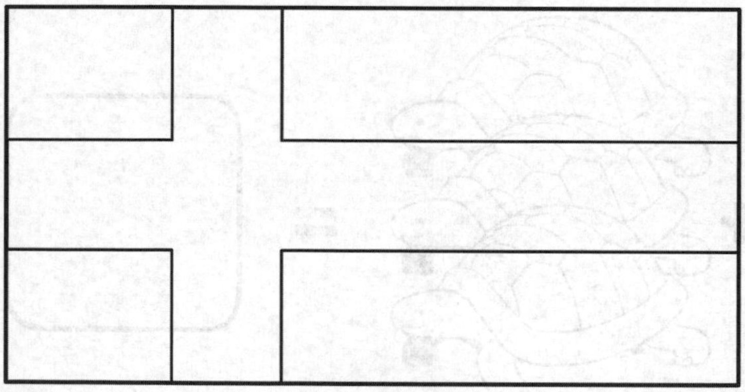

FINLAND

URUGUAY

SAN MARINO

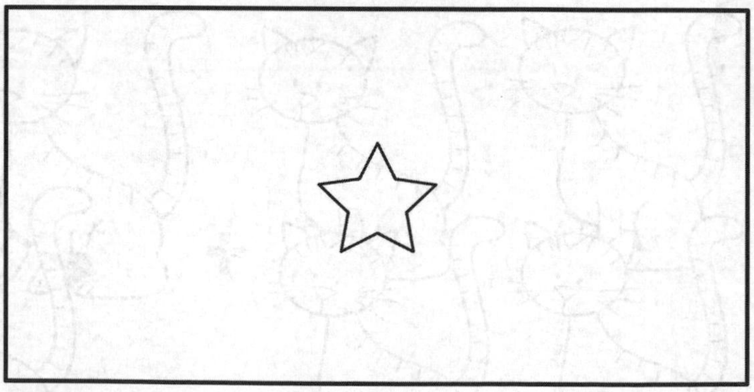

LIBERTAS

SOMALIA

FIND THE SILHOUETTE THAT DOESN'T BELONG TO THIS AIRPLANE.

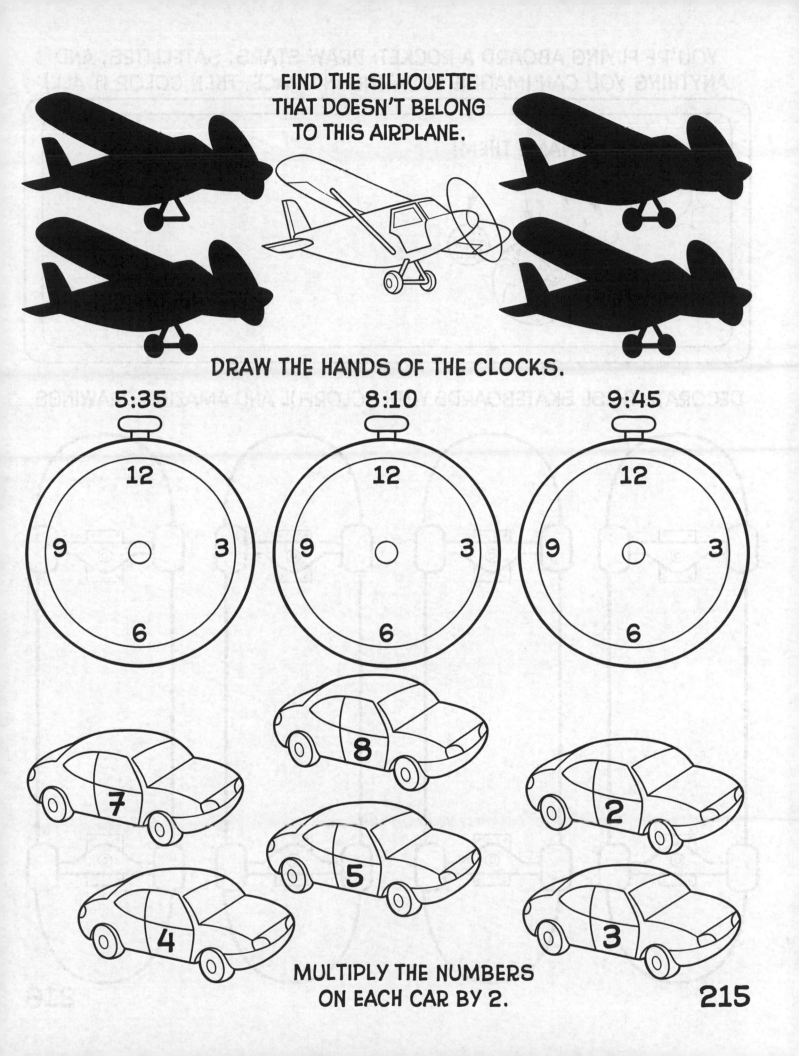

DRAW THE HANDS OF THE CLOCKS.

5:35

8:10

9:45

MULTIPLY THE NUMBERS ON EACH CAR BY 2.

7

8

2

5

4

3

YOU'RE FLYING ABOARD A ROCKET: DRAW STARS, SATELLITES, AND ANYTHING YOU CAN IMAGINE FLOATING IN SPACE, THEN COLOR IT ALL!

NAME THEM!

DECORATE THESE SKATEBOARDS WITH COLORFUL AND AMAZING DRAWINGS.

LOOK FOR THE DRAWINGS THAT APPEAR TWICE IN THE WHOLE GRID AND SURROUND THEM WITH A CIRCLE.

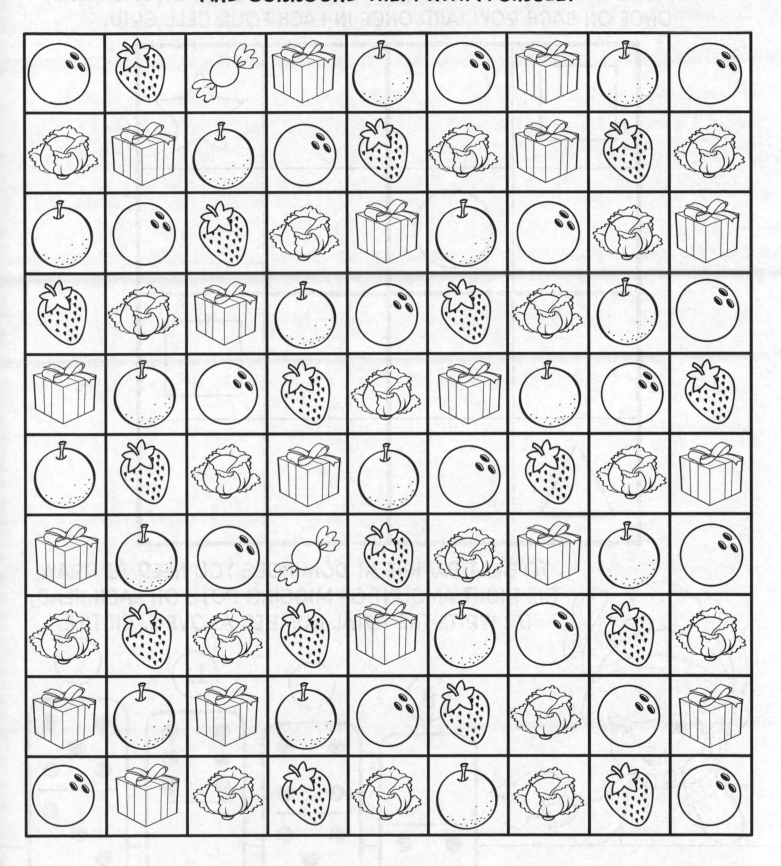

CRACK THE SUDOKU!
REMEMBER EACH SYMBOL CAN ONLY BE PLACED ONCE ON EACH LINE, ONCE ON EACH ROW, AND ONCE IN EACH FOUR CELL GRID.

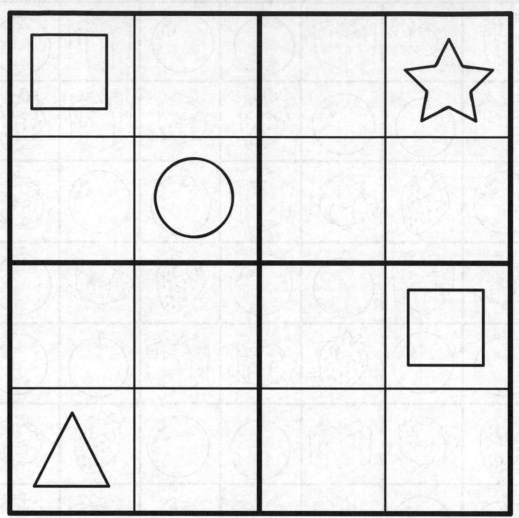

TO BEAT DAPHNE AT DOMINOES YOU NEED TO DRAW THE RIGHT AMOUNT OF MISSING DOTS ON EACH HEAD, OR WRITE THE TOTAL NUMBER ABOVE EACH TILE.

218

DRAW YOUR OWN COMIC-BOOK COVER.

DESIGN THE COVER TITLE.

DRAW THE CITY THEY PROTECT IN THE BACKGROUND.

GIVE THESE HEROES CAPES, MASKS, AND OTHER GEAR!

AND COLOR IT ALL!

WHICH ONE WEIGHS MORE?

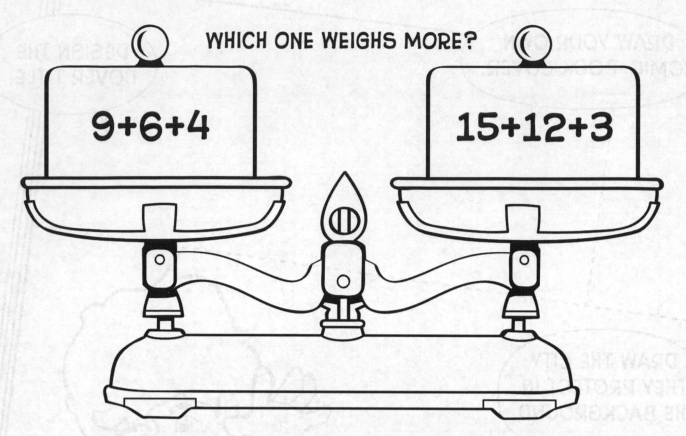

9+6+4

15+12+3

THERE'S AN INTRUDER AND THE ANTS ARE SLEEPING!
CAN YOU DRAW THE ONES MISSING FROM THE NEST AND WAKE THEM
UP? CAN YOU COUNT THEM ALL? WHERE IS THE QUEEN?

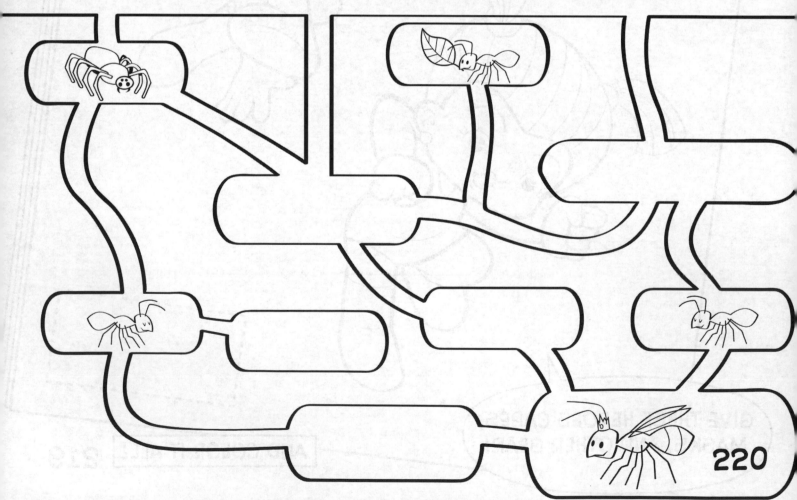

THERE ARE TEN
MAMMALS
TO BE FOUND
IN THIS
WORDSEARCH.

CLUE: ONE OF
THEM IS PICTURED
BELOW!

```
G D O L P H I N H S E
E O G D S P P T O A W
B A R B E A V E R Z B
F N F I G E D F S J Z
R T N I L R T W E I F
M E P B I L Q C O W B
F A V L U K A Z Q W E
X T A D B L J S H L V
C E Q M A E L G A L I
B R E H I U A H E A O
V J I W V H W R P B M
```

WHAT'S ITS NAME?
WHERE DOES IT LIVE?
WHAT DOES IT EAT?

221

WRITE THE FIRST LETTER OF EACH OBJECT.

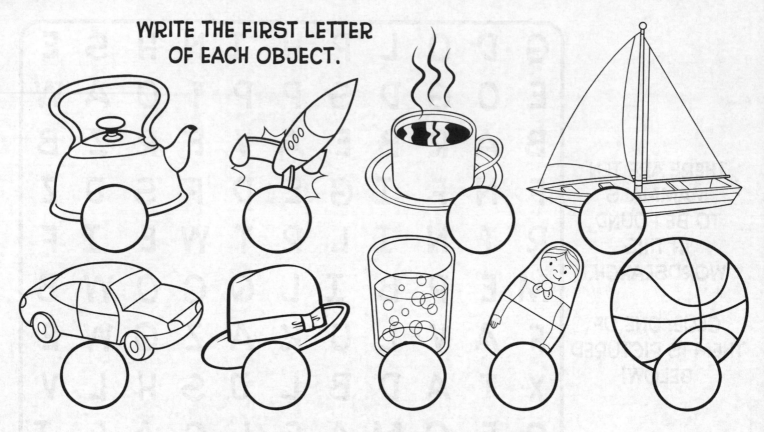

DRAW THE CAT IN THREE EASY STEPS!

DIVIDE THIS PATCH OF LAND SO THAT EACH VEGGIE WILL GET AN EQUAL SIZE AREA.

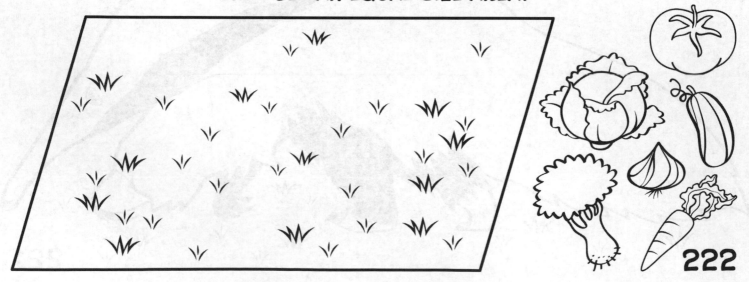

222

HAVE YOU EVER SEEN A PIG FLY?
GIVE EACH PIG ITS OWN PARACHUTE!

COLOR THE SKY BLUE AND ADD MORE WHITE CLOUDS.

DRAW A CIRCLE AROUND THE THINGS THAT FLY AND A SQUARE AROUND THE ONES THAT FLOAT.

223

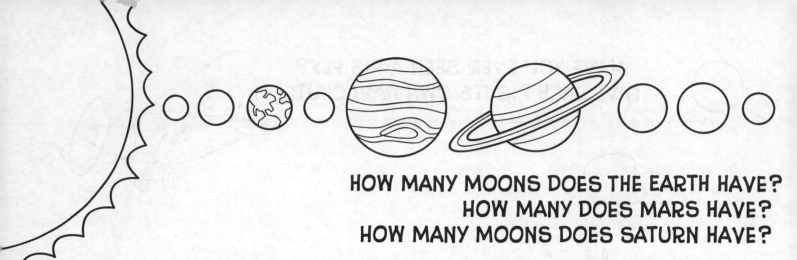

HOW MANY MOONS DOES THE EARTH HAVE?
HOW MANY DOES MARS HAVE?
HOW MANY MOONS DOES SATURN HAVE?

WHICH ONE DOES NOT BELONG IN THIS GROUP?

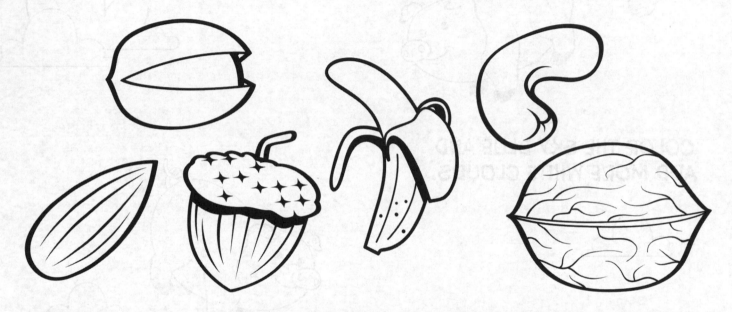

HOW MANY TIMES DOES THE BALL SPIN BEFORE HITTING THE FIRST PIN?
TRACE THE DOTTED LINE TO FIND OUT!

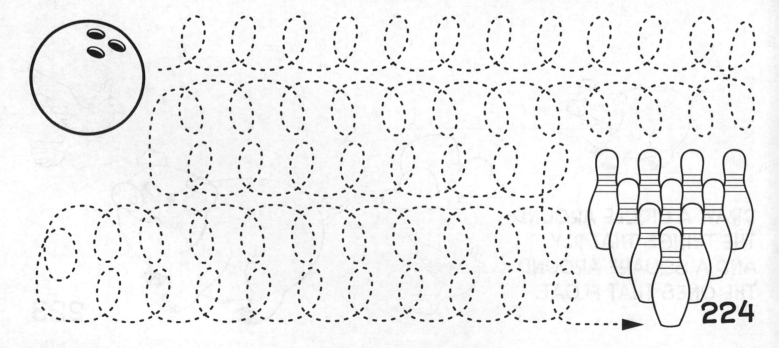

EACH CAR CONSUMES 1 GALLON PER BOX. CAR #1 HAS 12 GALLONS IN ITS TANK. CAR #2 HAS 38 GALLONS, AND #3 HAS 28 GALLONS, WHICH ONE GETS STOPPED BY TRAFFIC LIGHTS?

1

2

3

WHICH ONE STOPS AT THE "X" SIGN?

WHICH ONE MAKES IT HOME?

COMPLETE EACH COLUMN SO THE SUM OF THESE NUMBERS IS ALWAYS 27.

↓	9	7	14	11	5	18	3	20	18	13	4	15
9												
5												
4												

C
C
C
C

 WRITE FOUR COUNTRIES THAT START WITH THE LETTER "C".

ADD THE MISSING NUMBER TO LEVEL THE WEIGHT.

80

35
+
?

COLOR THE
STRONGMAN'S
LEOTARD!

COMPLETE AND COLOR THE
FELINES TO TURN ONE INTO
A TIGER AND THE OTHER
A PANTHER.

COLOR THE BALL, ALTERNATING
RED, WHITE, AND BLUE.

DRAW A CIRCLE AROUND THE FOOD THAT DOESN'T BELONG.

IF FOUR APPLES FROM THE TREE ON THE LEFT WILL FILL A BASKET,
HOW MANY BASKETS WILL YOU NEED?
KEEP IN MIND THE APPLES ON THE SECOND TREE
ARE TWICE AS BIG.

227

FILL THE CIRCLES TO MAKE LETTERS, SUCH AS THE "A" ABOVE.
CAN YOU WRITE YOUR NAME VERTICALLY OR HORIZONTALLY?

SALLY HAS SENT BILLY A CODED MESSAGE.
CAN YOU DECIPHER IT?

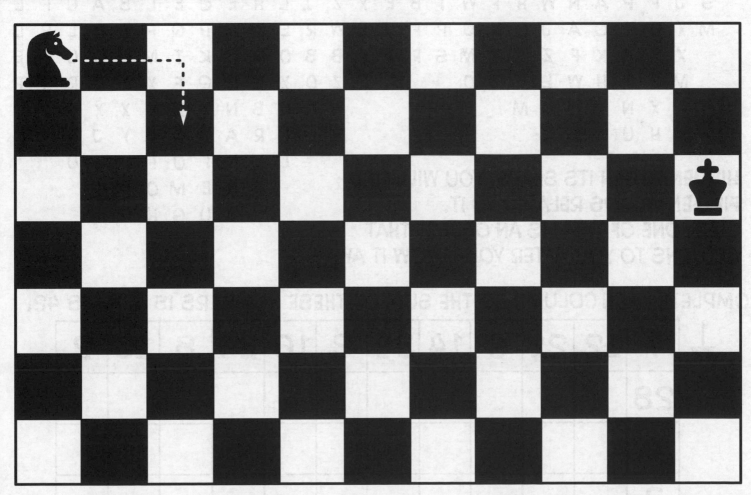

HOW MANY MOVES DOES THE HORSE NEED TO CHECK THE KING?

OLLIE LIVES IN A COUNTRY SURROUNDED BY SEA. CAN YOU GUESS WHICH COUNTRY IT IS?

```
            E B X                    V
           N V A H A                 W
       X    I H T J E             Y  R
         S T A S M A N I A        M  G S
         G U T I W S Y D N E Y    B  P E R
         S O R A C M K A U E A Y  K Z T H H F
         K X F E C V T U C C K B N Q  J B Y W
       L C V C S E A H C A P M R  I O Y O A R M U
   H Y Q W O U Y B L T T S M E W O Q R L Z G P Z J
 D K Y X O O L H L Q A B F E S O E C A I G N G K A
 L I T B Z U N I X G B Y D A A E F L O O X G N A A G S
 F B B D I T W U M M K J O W R H B K U F D A I U N K S
 Q O K V B B X H O B Z I M T Z R V M V  J R I H N G P F I
 S J F P A N W H F W T B E X Z I L H E C E L B A U F L
 M X S T C A J G V U P F I L W R E M W P Q F E R L R L
   X T B K F Z I Y M S F X R B B O R B K T M B O U F E
   M Z T H W L Z J O      E Z O X K R Q F X E O R X F
     X N J W U M         B H U B N E R V X X U F
     H U   S I           P  L R A U E J Y J U
                            L K N F O F M U U
                            A B E M O D S
                            B U G H Q
```

HIDDEN WITHIN ITS SHAPE, YOU WILL FIND FIFTEEN WORDS RELATED TO IT.
CLUE: ONE OF THEM IS AN OBJECT THAT RETURNS TO YOU AFTER YOU THROW IT AWAY!

COMPLETE EACH COLUMN SO THE SUM OF THESE NUMBERS IS ALWAYS 42.

↓	7	12	21	6	14	39	3	16	24	8	18	2
28												
4												
3												

DRAW THE NUMBER OF BALLS AND HATS AS INDICATED BY EACH TILE.

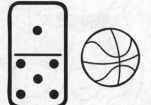

DRAW THE HANDS OF THE CLOCKS.

6:55   8:30   4:15

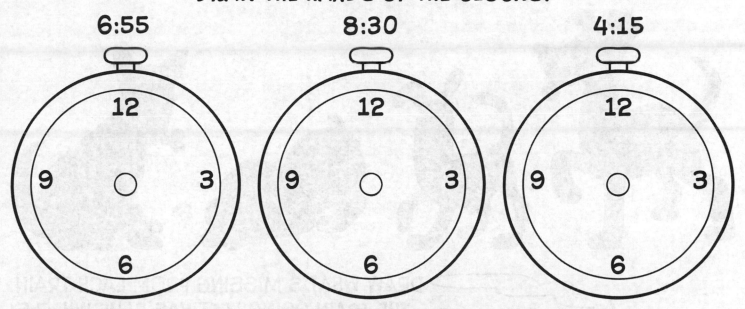

TO FIND THE WAY OUT, CONNECT THE NUMBERS DIVISIBLE BY TWO.

9	4	8	6	5	3	7	5	2	◀	
3	2	5	9	2	8	6	4	3		
6	5	3	1	7	5	3	9	5	4	7
6	3	1	4	6	8	2	4	7	5	3
8	2	4	2	3	4	1	4	6	8	▶

CONNECT EACH DOG TO ITS
CORRESPONDING SHADOW.

DRAW WHAT'S MISSING FROM EACH TRAIN.
THE TRAIN GOING LEFT HAS BLUE WHEELS
AND THE TRAIN GOING RIGHT RED WHEELS.

CRACK THE SUDOKU!
EACH DRAWING CAN ONLY BE PLACED ONCE ON EACH LINE, ONCE ON EACH ROW, AND ONCE IN EACH FOUR CELL GRID.

THE ROOSTER AND THE HEN HAD MANY CHICKS.
FIGURE OUT HOW MANY BY COUNTING ALL THE
BROKEN EGG SHELLS.
DRAW THE MISSING CHICKS.

SOLVE THE EQUATIONS AND WRITE YOUR RESULTS BELOW.

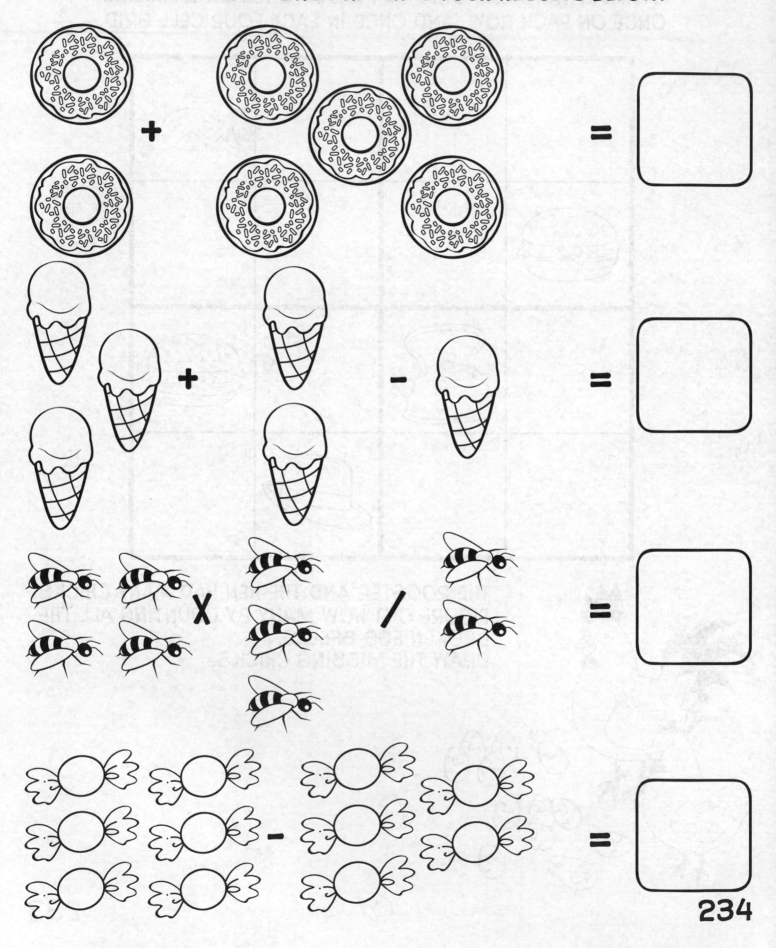

234

WHAT DO YOU GET WHEN YOU BLOW THROUGH THIS RING?

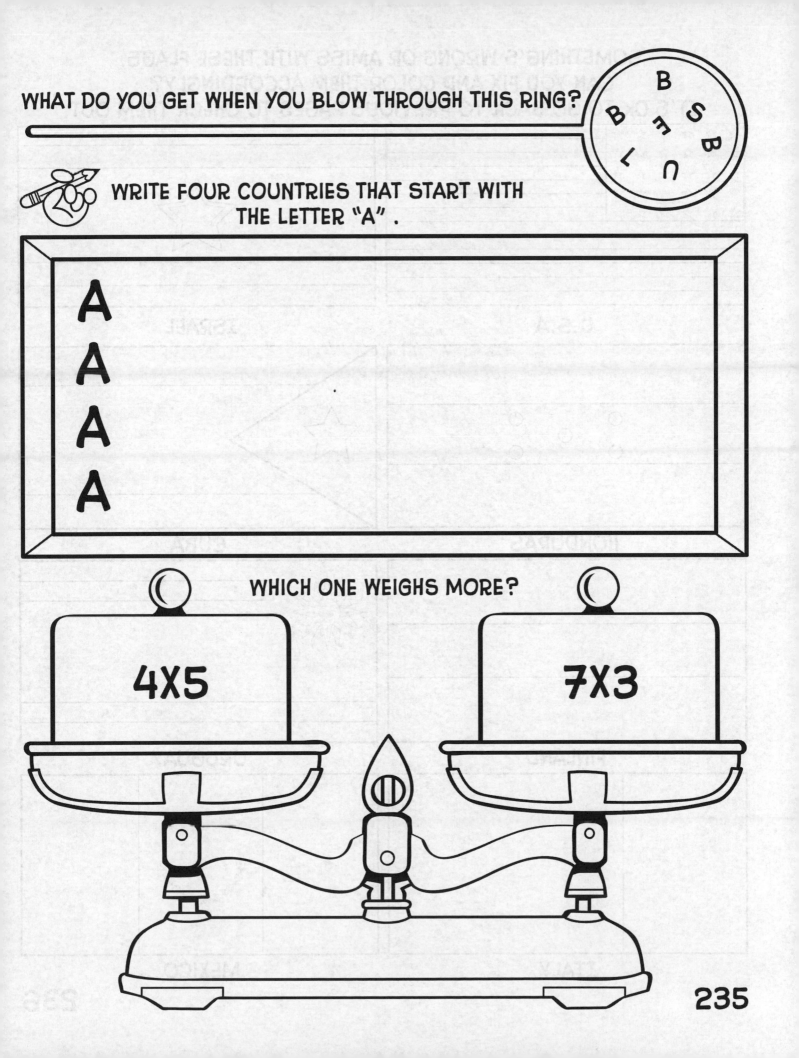

WRITE FOUR COUNTRIES THAT START WITH THE LETTER "A".

A
A
A
A
A

WHICH ONE WEIGHS MORE?

4X5   7X3

SOMETHING'S WRONG OR AMISS WITH THESE FLAGS.
CAN YOU FIX AND COLOR THEM ACCORDINGLY?
IT'S OK TO GO BACK TO PREVIOUS PAGES TO CHECK THEM OUT.

U.S.A

ISRAEL

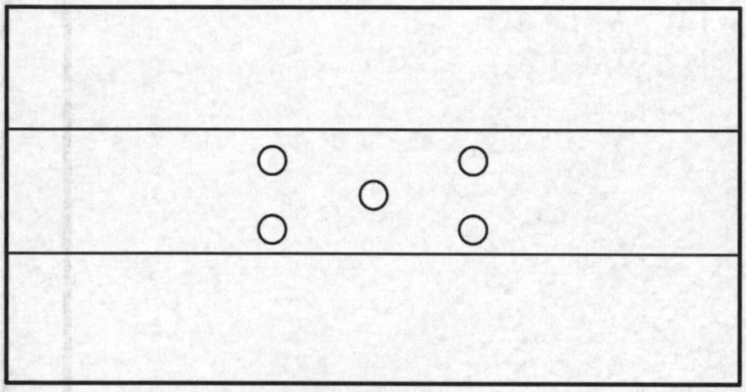

HONDURAS

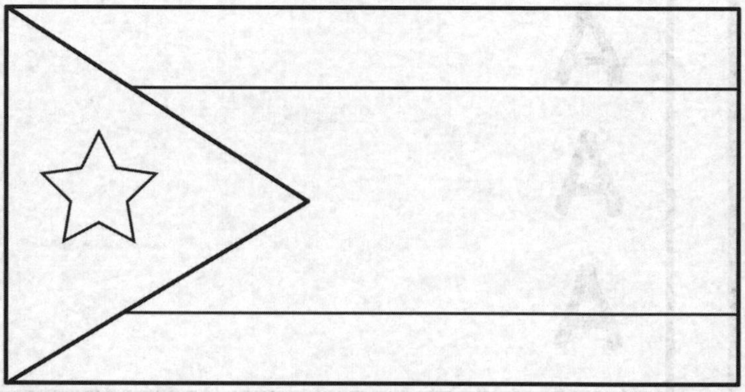

CUBA

FINLAND

URUGUAY

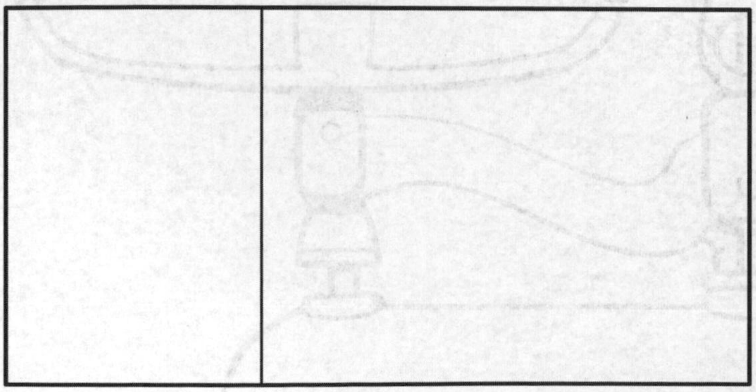

ITALY

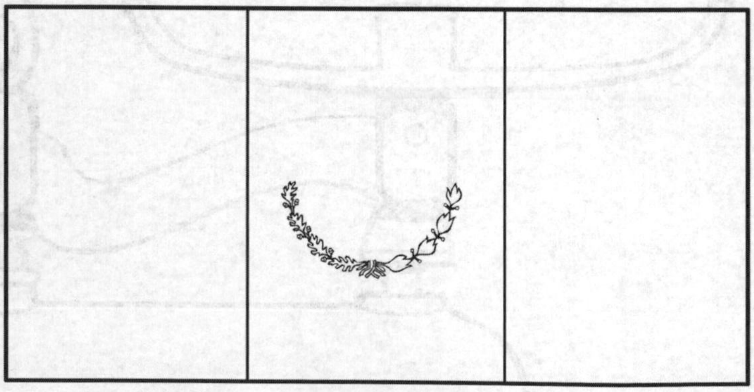

MEXICO

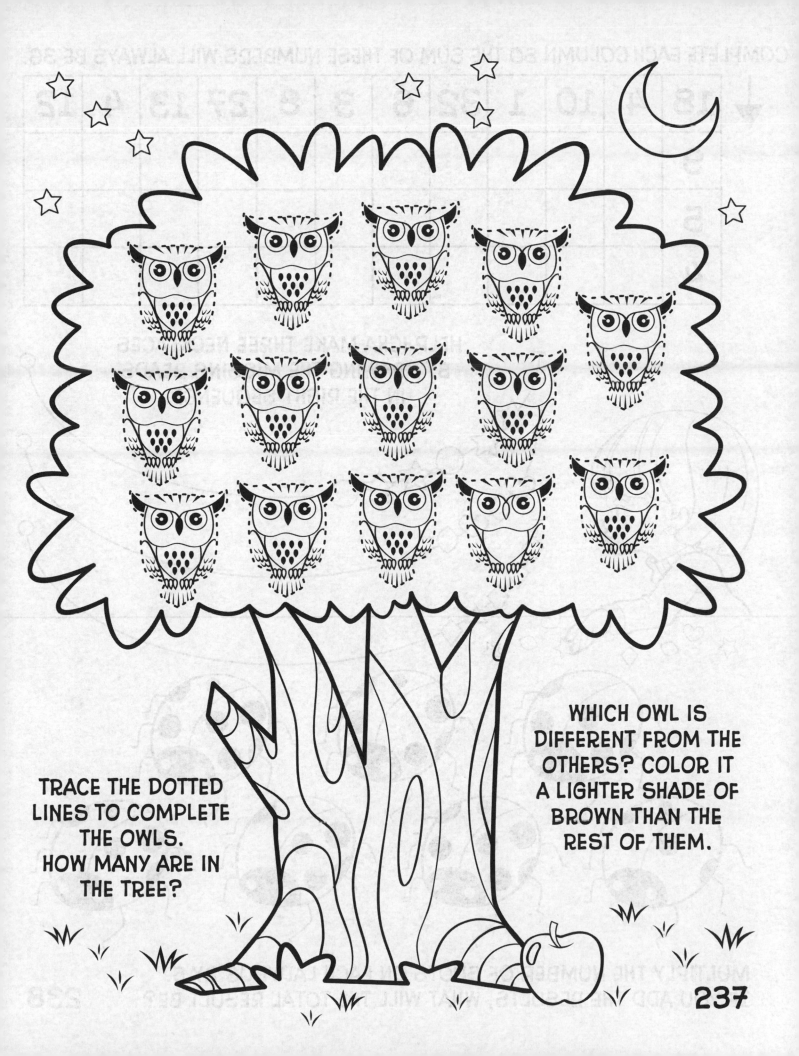

TRACE THE DOTTED
LINES TO COMPLETE
THE OWLS.
HOW MANY ARE IN
THE TREE?

WHICH OWL IS
DIFFERENT FROM THE
OTHERS? COLOR IT
A LIGHTER SHADE OF
BROWN THAN THE
REST OF THEM.

COMPLETE EACH COLUMN SO THE SUM OF THESE NUMBERS WILL ALWAYS BE 36.

↓	18	4	10	1	32	6	3	8	27	13	4	12
9												
5												
4												

HELP ICHA MAKE THREE NECKLACES BY DRAWING THE MISSING BEADS IN THE RIGHT SEQUENCE.

MULTIPLY THE NUMBER OF SPOTS ON EACH LADYBUG BY 5. IF YOU ADD THE RESULTS, WHAT WILL THE TOTAL RESULT BE?

238

SUROUND THE DUCKIES WITH A LINE IN GROUPS OF THREE, BUT BE CAREFUL NOT TO INCLUDE THE FROGS IN ANY OF THE GROUPS!

DRAW AS MANY PRESENTS AND ICE CREAM CONES AS INDICATED BY EACH TILE.

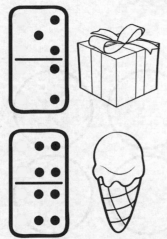

THESE SILHOUETTES CORRESPOND TO IMPORTANT MONUMENTS. CAN YOU NAME THEM?

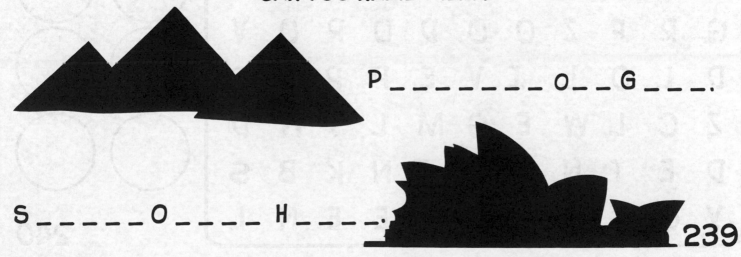

P _ _ _ _ _ _ _ O _ _ G _ _ _.

S _ _ _ _ _ O _ _ _ H _ _ _ _.

SPELL THE NAME OF EACH ANIMAL ALOUD, AND WRITE IT DOWN.

FIND THE NAMES OF TEN DIFFERENT COLORS,
AND FILL THE CIRCLES WITH EACH ONE AS YOU DO.

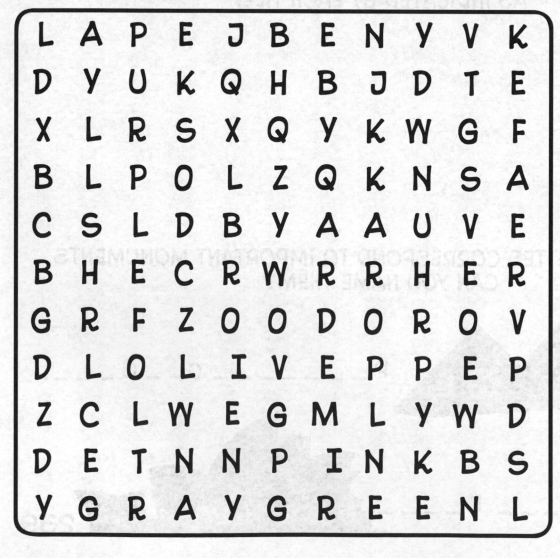

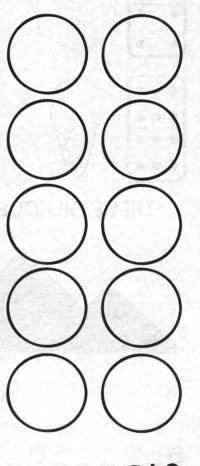

240

FILL THE CIRCLES TO MAKE LETTERS, SUCH AS THE "S" ABOVE.
CAN YOU WRITE THE NAME OF YOUR FAVORITE SUPERHERO?

HOW MANY MOVES DOES THE BISHOP NEED TO CHECK THE KING?

IDENTIFY THE FIGURE THAT LOOKS LIKE THE FIRST ON EACH ROW, AND COLOR BOTH THE SAME.

WHERE IS THE BUNGEE JUMPER? DRAW YOURSELF DANGLING FROM THE ROPE!

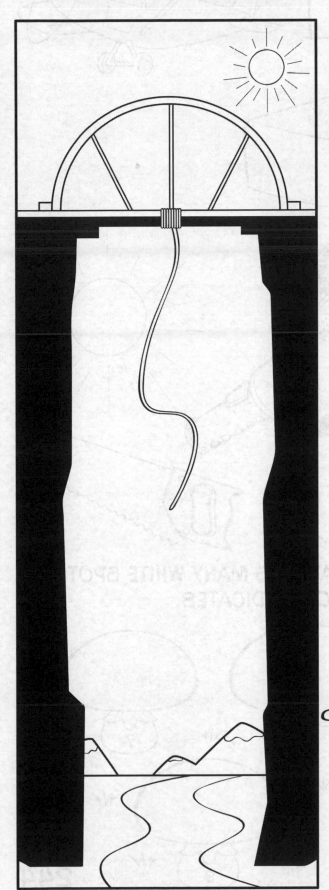

COLOR ONLY THE EVEN NUMBERS.

1 2 3 4 5
6 7 8 9 10
11 12 13 14
15 16 17 18

```
            C
        E   O   V
    H   U T O M         T
    O J C T A X T
    C   A O K
    M   L N P B
    L A Y W N I S
    E C H P O N R N R
  Q G Y O T O L C I E C
    P G U D J H Y
    O R A S X A Q M T
    C K E N A L E R C E T
  Q E R S Y C A M O R E W L
  V Q D H S L J A C A R A N D A
        H   B D
        R   E R C
        C   F F
```

HIDDEN WITHIN THIS PINE (CLUE!)
YOU WILL FIND ELEVEN OTHER TREE NAMES.

243

WRITE ANYTHING YOU LIKE ON THE BANNER.

WHICH ONE REQUIRES BATTERIES?

WHICH ONE IS NOT MAN-MADE?

COLOR THE MUSHROOMS RED, BUT LEAVE AS MANY WHITE SPOTS AS THE NUMBER ON EACH ONE INDICATES.

244

FIND THE TEN DIFFERENCES.

FILL THE OTHER COMPARTMENTS WITH OTHER ART SUPPLIES YOU USE!

COLOR THE DOTTED SKIRT ONLY.

DECORATE THE ONE IN THE MIDDLE ANY WAY YOU LIKE!

WHAT COUNTRY IS IT? WHERE IS IT LOCATED?
DO YOU REMEMBER THE COLOR OF ITS FLAG?
COLOR THE MAP THE SAME WAY.

THESE SILHOUETTES CORRESPOND
TO IMPORTANT MONUMENTS.
CAN YOU NAME THEM?

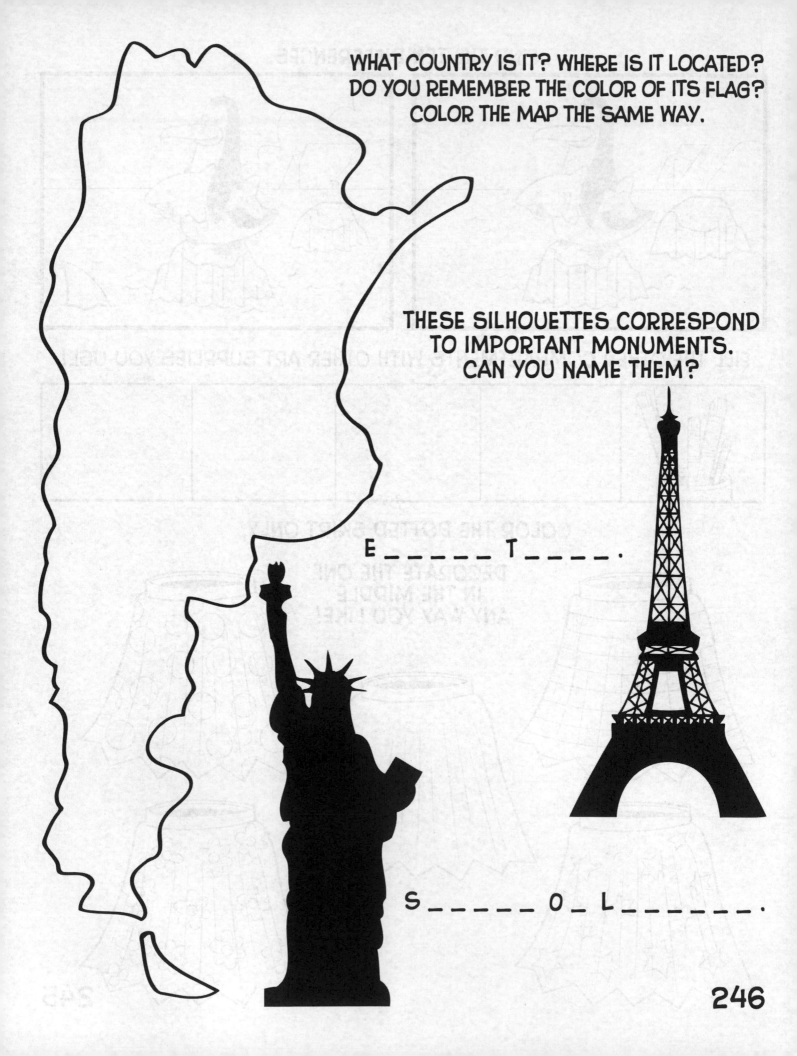

E _ _ _ _ _ T _ _ _ _ _ .

S _ _ _ _ _ _ O _ L _ _ _ _ _ _ .

246

WRITE FOUR COUNTRIES THAT START WITH THE LETTER "U".

U

U

U

U

IF EACH ICE CREAM COSTS FOUR DOLLARS, HOW MUCH DO THESE COST ALL TOGETHER?

DRAW AS MANY FRUITS ON EACH TREE AS INDICATED BY THE RESPECTIVE TILE.

HOW MANY CUPCAKES
CAN YOU COUNT?
COLOR THE RIGHT
NUMBER.

HOW MANY HAVE
SPRINKLED HEARTS?
COLOR THE RIGHT
NUMBER.

1 2 3
4 5 6
7 8 9
10 11
12 13
14 15
16 17
18 19
20

HOW MANY HAVE A
CHERRY ON TOP?
COLOR THE RIGHT
NUMBER.

HOW MANY
HAVE SPRINKLES?
COLOR THE
NUMBER.

COLOR ALL
CUPCAKES IN
DIFFERENT
FLAVORS!

248

HELP THE DOG FIND THE FRISBEE!

COMPLETE EACH COLUMN SO THE SUM OF THESE NUMBERS IS ALWAYS 57.

↓ 9	18	21	10	13	7	3	48	24	8	34	2
19											
19											
10											

WHAT IS THE NAME OF THIS ANIMAL?
WHERE DOES IT LIVE?

FILL THE EMPTY JARS WITH ALL THE ICKY, YUCKY, GOOEY,
AND HALLOWEENY STUFF YOU CAN IMAGINE!
THEN WRITE THEIR NAMES ON EACH LABEL, AND COLOR IT ALL. 250

CROSSWORDS.

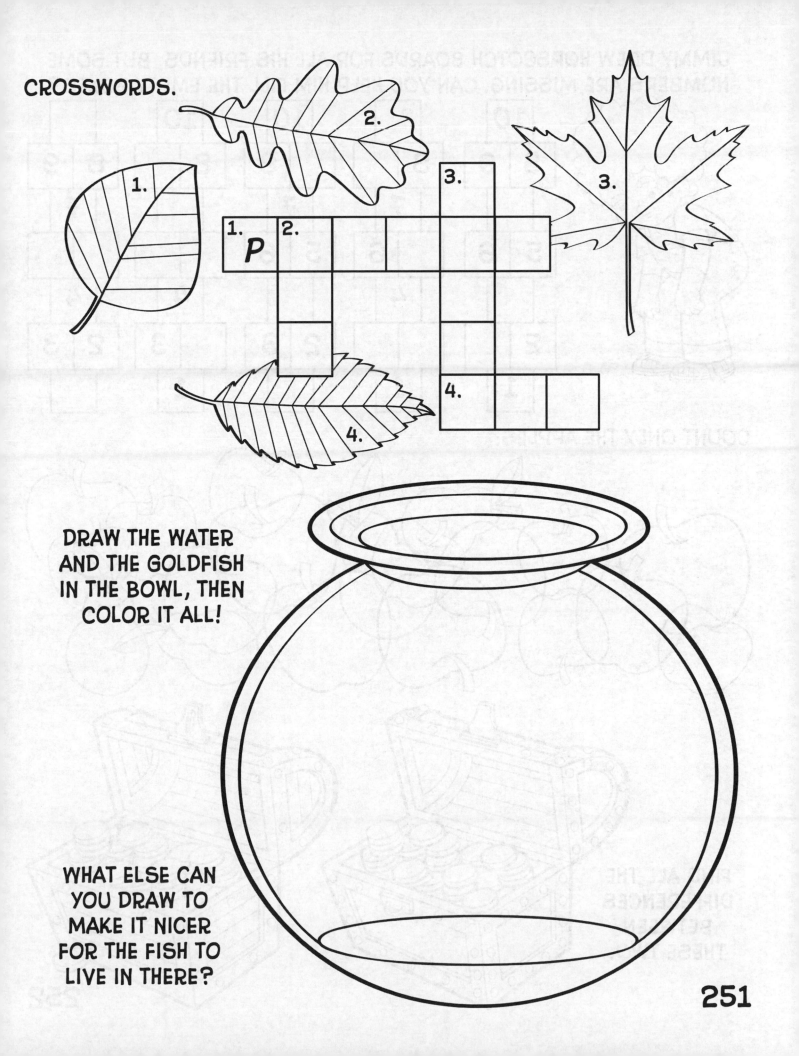

1.

2.

3.

1. **P** 2.

4.

3.

4.

DRAW THE WATER AND THE GOLDFISH IN THE BOWL, THEN COLOR IT ALL!

WHAT ELSE CAN YOU DRAW TO MAKE IT NICER FOR THE FISH TO LIVE IN THERE?

JIMMY DREW HOPSCOTCH BOARDS FOR ALL HIS FRIENDS, BUT SOME NUMBERS ARE MISSING. CAN YOU HELP HIM FILL THE EMPTY BOXES?

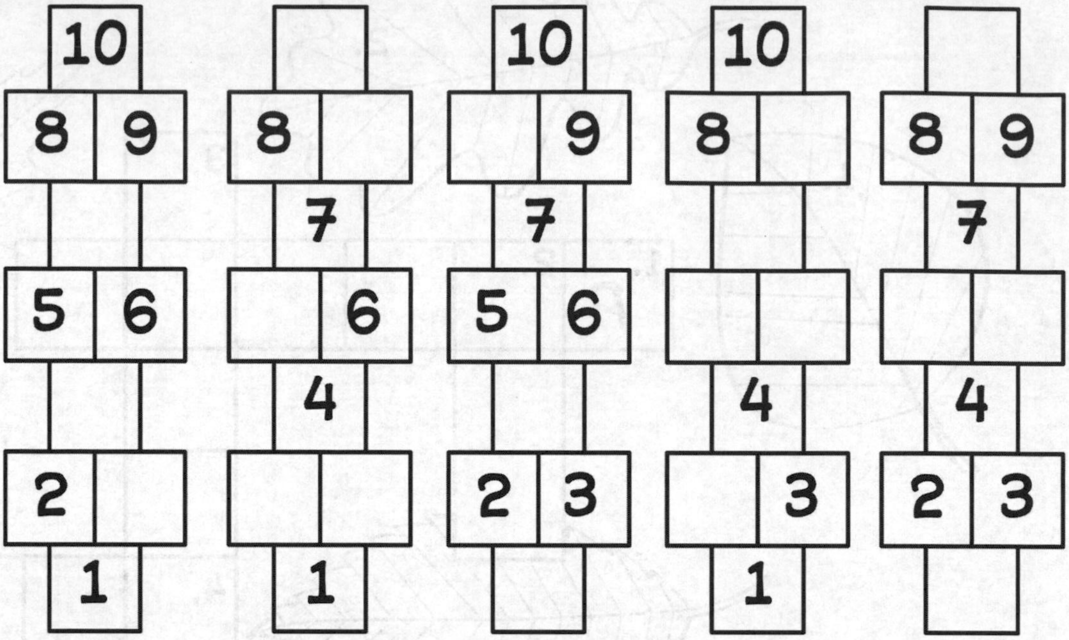

COUNT ONLY THE APPLES.

FIND ALL THE DIFFERENCES BETWEEN THESE TWO.

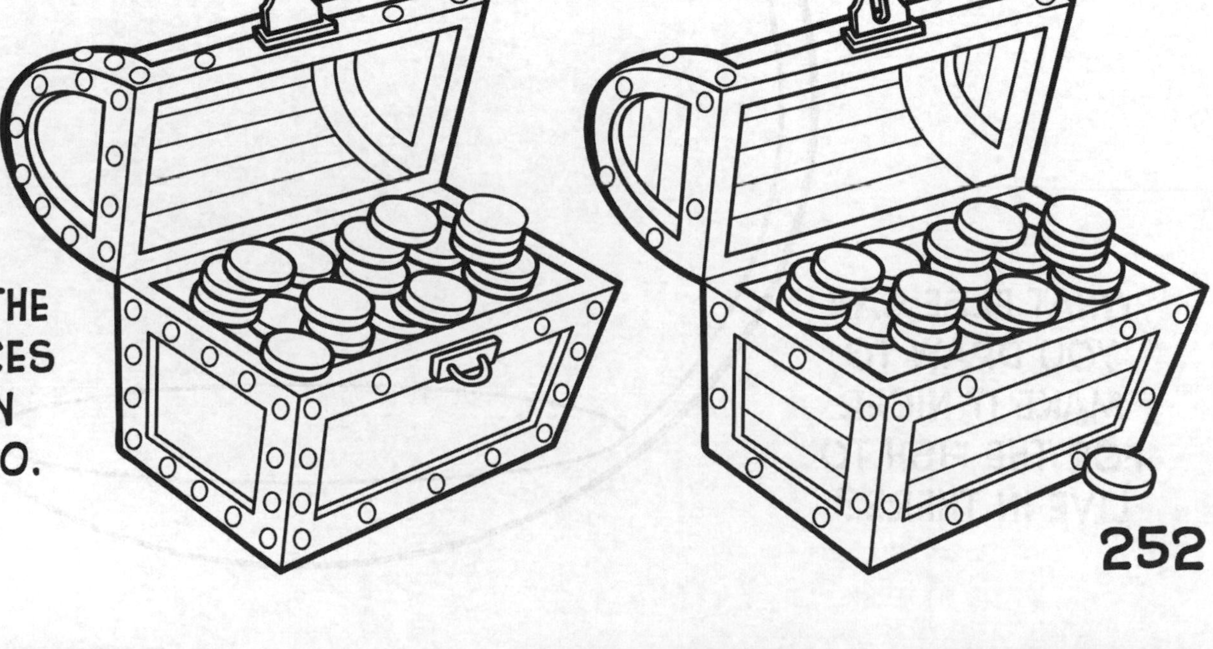

DESIGN YOUR OWN KITE, ANYWAY YOU LIKE.

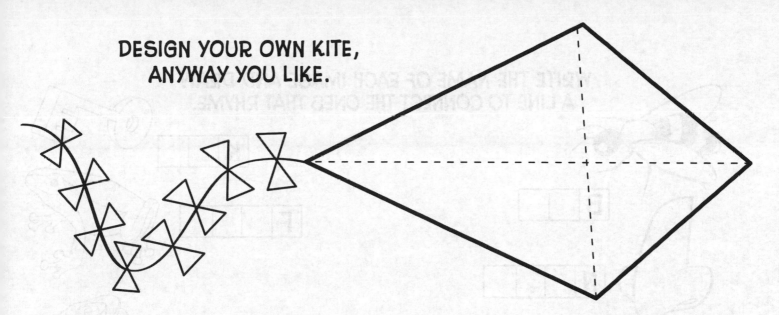

COMPLETE THIS BY CREATING YOUR OWN SYMBOLS MOVING FORWARD.

WRITE THE NAME OF EACH IMAGE AND DRAW A LINE TO CONNECT THE ONES THAT RHYME.

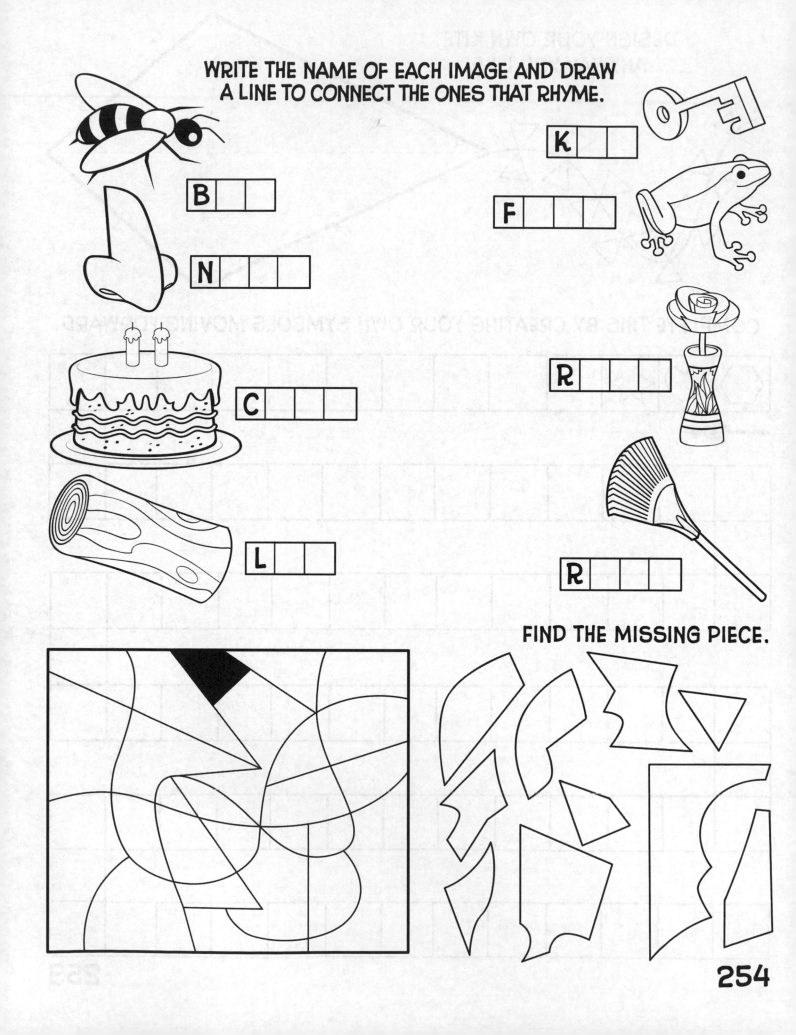

B ☐ ☐

N ☐ ☐ ☐

C ☐ ☐ ☐

L ☐ ☐

K ☐ ☐

F ☐ ☐ ☐ ☐

R ☐ ☐ ☐

R ☐ ☐ ☐ ☐

FIND THE MISSING PIECE.

COLOR THE FIRST MASK, AND THEN CREATE YOUR OWN CHARACTERS FOR HALLOWEEN!

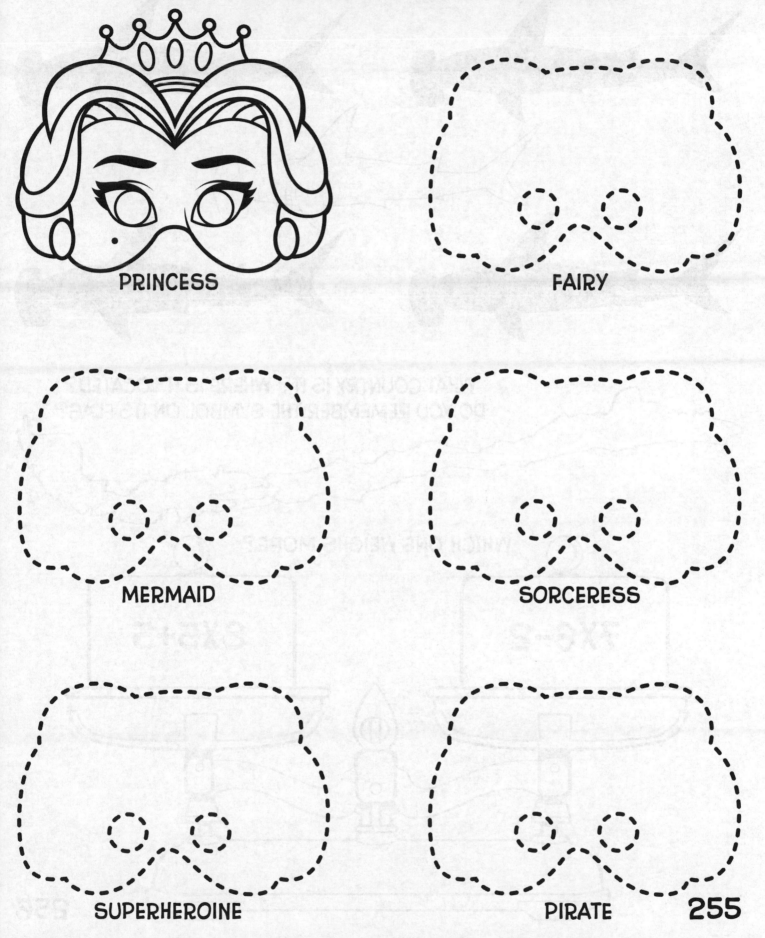

PRINCESS

FAIRY

MERMAID

SORCERESS

SUPERHEROINE

PIRATE

255

FIND THE HAMMERHEAD SHARK'S NON-CORRESPONDING SHADOW.

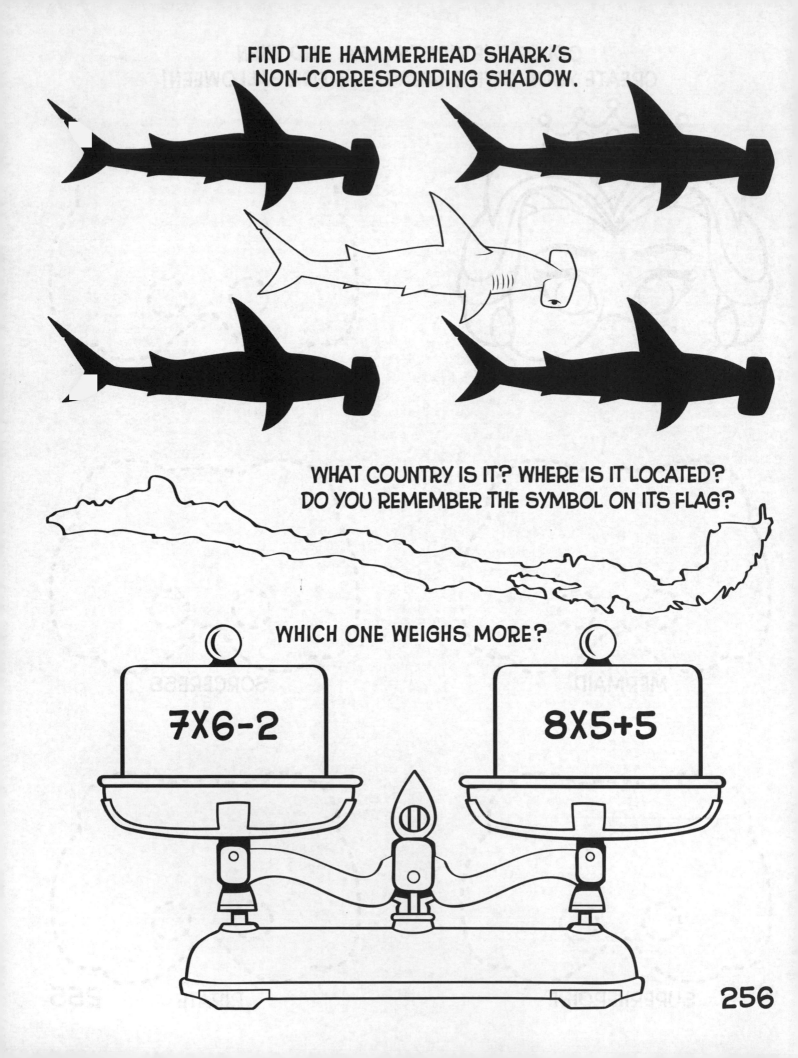

WHAT COUNTRY IS IT? WHERE IS IT LOCATED? DO YOU REMEMBER THE SYMBOL ON ITS FLAG?

WHICH ONE WEIGHS MORE?

7X6-2

8X5+5

CAN YOU HELP THE SQUIRREL FIND HER TREE?

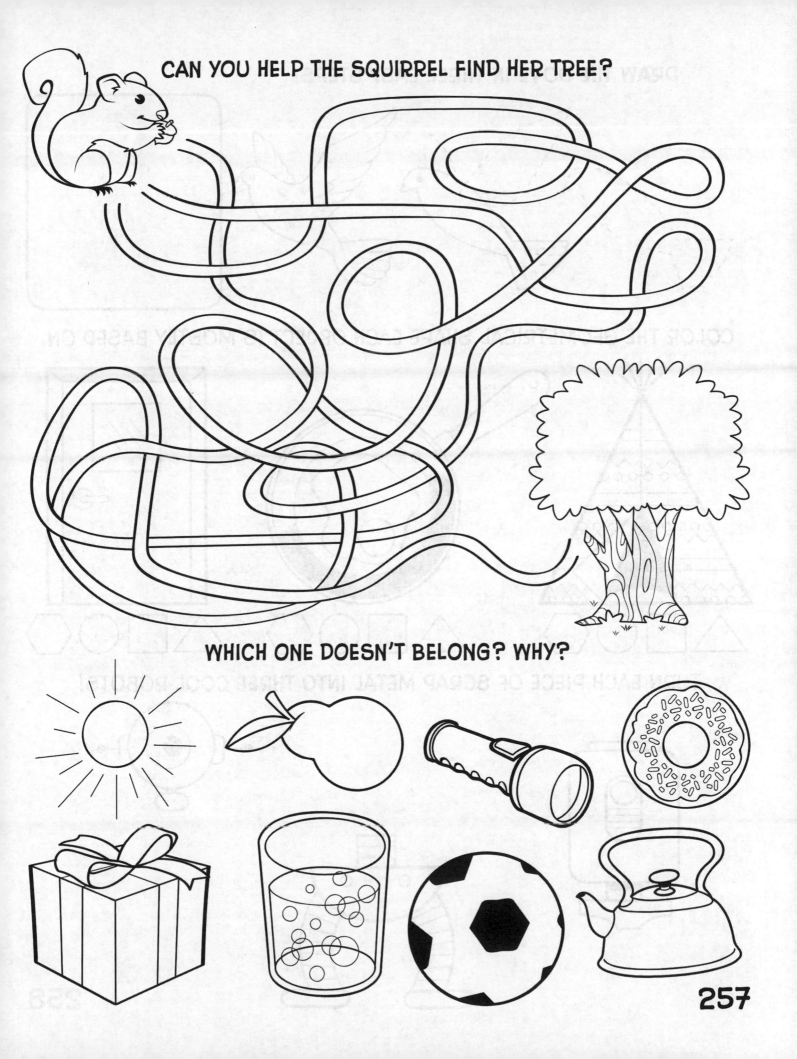

WHICH ONE DOESN'T BELONG? WHY?

DRAW THE DOVE IN THREE EASY STEPS!

COLOR THE GEOMETRICAL SHAPE EACH OBJECT IS MOSTLY BASED ON.

TURN EACH PIECE OF SCRAP METAL INTO THREE COOL ROBOTS!

HELP OLLIE FIND THE TREASURE CHESTS HIDDEN ON THE ISLAND!

COLOR THE ISLAND'S MAP TO MAKE IT LOOK REAL,
AND GIVE NAMES TO ALL THE PLACES IN IT!

SALLY HAS SENT BILLY ANOTHER SECRET MESSAGE. CAN YOU BREAK THE CODE?

A B C D E F G H I J K L M

N O P Q R S T U V W X Y Z

DRAW YOURSELF AND YOUR BEST FRIEND AS THE MEANEST COWBOY OR COWGIRL OF THE OLD WEST!

WRITE BOTH YOUR NAMES BELOW THE PICTURES.

FIND THE BIRTHDAY CAKE
THAT DOESN'T MATCH ALL OTHERS,
AND COLOR THE REST.

THERE ARE TWENTY HOME-RELATED ITEMS TO BE FOUND IN THIS WORDSEARCH.

CLUE: START AT THE DOOR.

```
              Z
L  J  J      T  G  V
O  I  O      A  T  V  E  J
   I  D  G  V  C  J  R  S  C  Z
   P  F  S  H  K  U  W  U  E  L  T
   B  A  T  H  T  U  B  H  E  T  O  A
   H  P  F  I  V  S  N  M  N  D  R  S  B
   H  D  L  N  I  Y  C  O  F  R  I  D  G  E  L
D  O  O  R  S  R  O  O  M  S  A  N  I  S  Y  T  E
H  F  U  A  B  E  R  C  N  H  D  M  S  W  I  X  P
C  F  V  H  G  G  X  E  C  S  M  R  H  I  T  N  L
F  A  B  A  N  W  H  I  E              W  N  C  T  K
E  E  R  I  A  C  N  L  L              A  D  O  O  T
J  A  V  P  T  K  I  I  L              S  O  U  I  E
G  I  P  I  E  B  D  N  A              H  W  C  L  P
L  X  K  Q  N  T  B  G  R              E  S  H  E  H
C  U  P  B  O  A  R  D  P              R  O  U  T  Y
```

261

ILLUSTRATE YOUR OWN POSTAGE STAMPS!

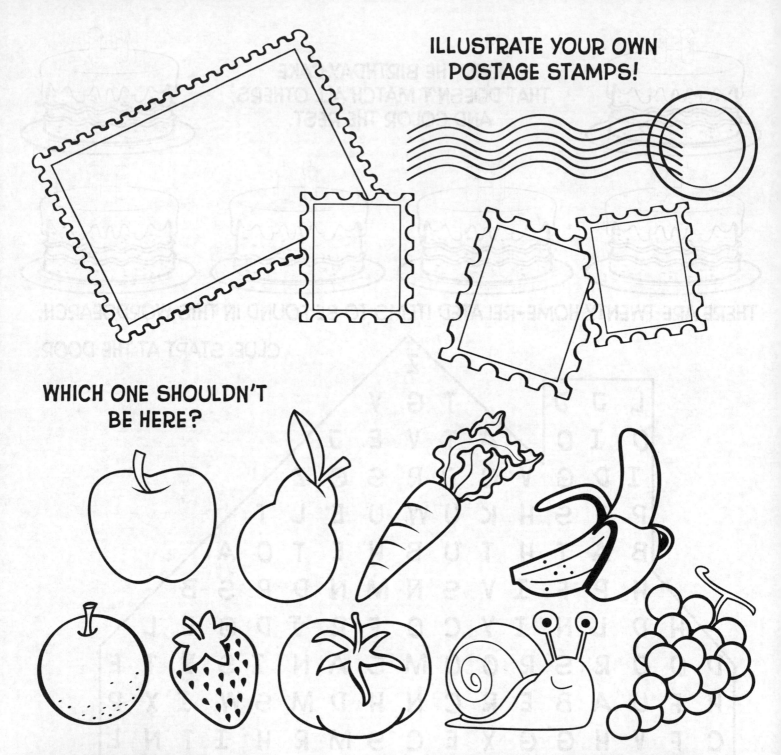

WHICH ONE SHOULDN'T BE HERE?

COMPLETE EACH COLUMN SO THE SUM OF THESE NUMBERS IS ALWAYS 74.

↓ 30	28	11	13	18	7	3	40	26	8	64	9
8											
6											
30											

FILL THE CIRCLES TO MAKE LETTERS, SUCH AS THE "U" ABOVE.
CAN YOU WRITE THE NAME OF YOUR TOWN AND COUNTRY?

DRAW MORE CUPCAKES, OR CROSS THEM OUT UNTIL THERE'S 15 ON EACH TRAY.

CAN YOU ALSO HELP HER FINISH BAKING HER COOKIES?

DRAW THE MISSING GINGERBREAD MEN IN EACH ROW.

COLOR THIS ENTIRE FLAG GREEN.

CAN YOU GUESS THE NAME OF THE COUNTRY IT BELONGS TO?

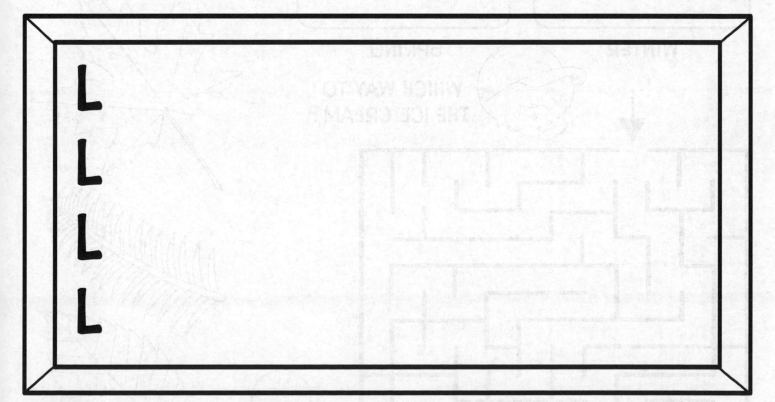

L
L
L
L

 WRITE FOUR OTHER COUNTRIES THAT START WITH THE LETTER "L"!

IF THE SUN MEANS SUMMER, WHAT OTHER SYMBOLS CAN YOU DRAW TO REPRESENT THE OTHER SEASONS?

WHICH LEAF IS COMPLETELY DIFFERENT FROM THE REST?

SUMMER

FALL

WINTER

SPRING

WHICH WAY TO THE ICE CREAM?

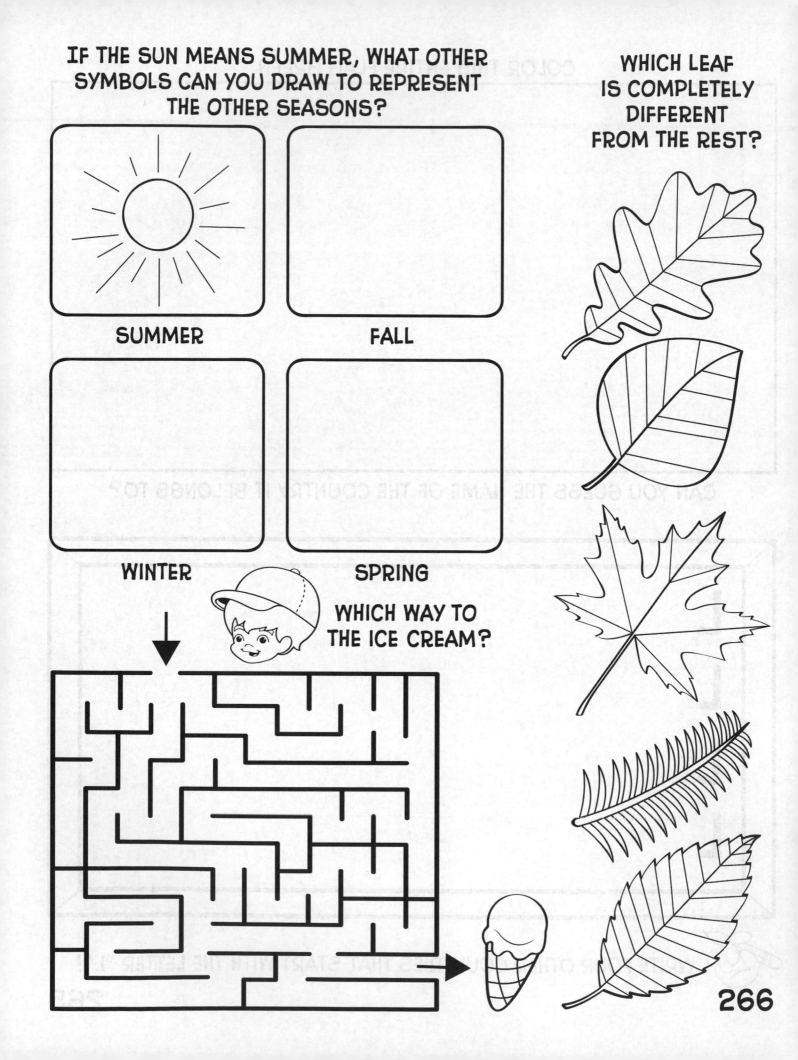

266

WHAT ARE THE NAMES
OF THESE TWO ANIMALS?

COLOR THEM BOTH
GRAY AND WHITE.

WHAT MAKES THEM SIMILAR?

WHAT MAKES THEM DIFFERENT?

DRAW THE HANDS OF THE CLOCKS.

12:30   10:45   3:15

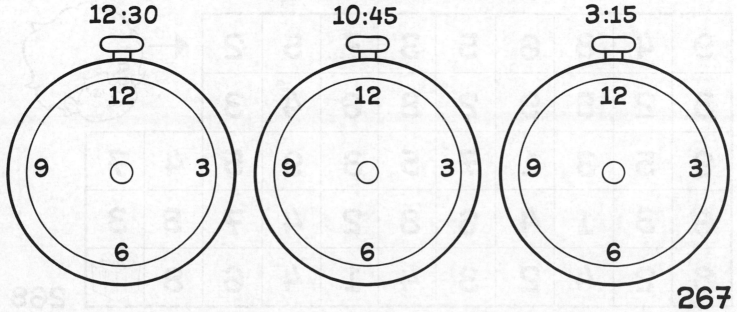

THAT IS ONE BIG SNAKE!
CAN YOU GUESS ITS NAME?

IF IT TAKES THE BEE A DAY TO POLLINATE THREE FLOWERS, HOW MANY
DAYS WILL IT TAKE HER TO POLLINATE ALL THE ONES IN THIS FIELD?

CONNECT THE NUMBERS DIVISIBLE BY 2.

9	4	8	6	5	3	7	5	2		
3	2	5	9	2	8	6	4	3		
6	5	3	1	7	5	3	9	5	4	7
6	3	1	4	6	8	2	4	7	5	3
8	2	4	2	3	4	1	4	6	8	

FIND THE SIX DIFFERENCES.

THE FORTUNE COOKIE HAS A MESSAGE FOR YOU.
CAN YOU GUESS WHAT IT SAYS?

COMPLETE THE SERIES.

$$5 = \bigcirc + \star$$
$$2 = \square + \square$$
$$? = \square + \bigcirc$$
$$4 = \square + \star$$

FIND THE ONE SHADOW THAT DOESN'T MATCH THE SQUIRREL.

HOW MANY CHERRIES ARE HIDING IN THESE TWO TREES? DRAW THEM. IF 16 FROM THE TREE ON THE LEFT WILL FILL A BASKET, HOW MANY BASKETS WILL YOU NEED IF THE CHERRIES ON THE OTHER TREE ARE HALF AS BIG?

Left tree:
$$4 \times 2$$
$$+ 10 \times 2$$
$$+ 6 \times 2$$
$$=$$

Right tree:
$$6 \times 3$$
$$+ 30 / 2$$
$$- 16 / 2$$
$$=$$

EACH ONE OF
THESE TWO CAMELS
IS CALLED BY A
DIFFERENT NAME.
DO YOU KNOW THEM?

TO PAINT A DOOR YOU
NEED A WHOLE CAN
OF PAINT.

TO PAINT A WINDOW
FRAME YOU NEED TWO.

TO PAINT THE WALL ON
EACH FLOOR THREE.

HOW MANY CANS WILL
YOU NEED TO PAINT
ALL THESE BUILDINGS?

```
      R Y K M C
      E W B E A C O    B J
      G R A Q N D A T M E O E L
    I H I N T Y A M A Y O T T E
    N L A T D T A G E N W A R H S R
    E I N R A O Y A R Z P E N O I W
    E B A E O G S S O A C G B G S O A
    Z Y O A C O J C O N O Y E H O N P N
    A L G E R I A N I N P N M O L S I A F
    R O F   R B A G T I I J S A K A M
            Q U O U N M A L A W I
            Z J R U I N C H A D
            I E U A N A T Z
            R M D N I E F C
            O U B B D W A A
            S O M A L I A N
            N A M I B I A
            G U G M E W X
            U G A N D A E
            Z B S L I
            Z O X X
            H N Q
```

THIS WORDSEARCH IS SHAPED LIKE
A CONTINENT, AND CONTAINS
THE NAMES OF SOME OF ITS MORE
THAN FIFTY BEAUTIFUL COUNTRIES.
CAN YOU GUESS WHICH ONE?

CLUE: ITS NAME STARTS WITH "A".

WHICH ONE OF THE FOLLOWING ANIMALS
DOES NOT LIVE THERE?

272

DRAW AND COLOR YOUR FAVORITE FLAGS FROM SOME OF THE COUNTRIES ON THE PREVIOUS PAGE'S WORDSEARCH.

WRITE THE NAME OF EACH COUNTRY BELOW THE CORRESPONDING FLAG.

COMPLETE THE PATTERN AS BEST YOU CAN.

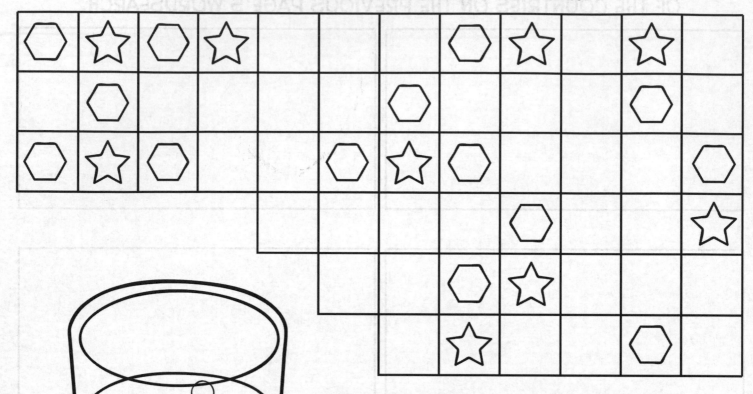

WHAT ARE SODA BUBBLES MADE OF?

HOW ARE THEY DIFFERENT FROM THE ONES
WE MAKE WITH SOAP AND WATER?

WHY DO THEY FLOAT UPWARD?

ONLY ONE OF THESE IS WORN AROUND THE NECK. COLOR IT!

TURN EACH PIECE OF SCRAP METAL INTO THREE COOL ROBOTS!

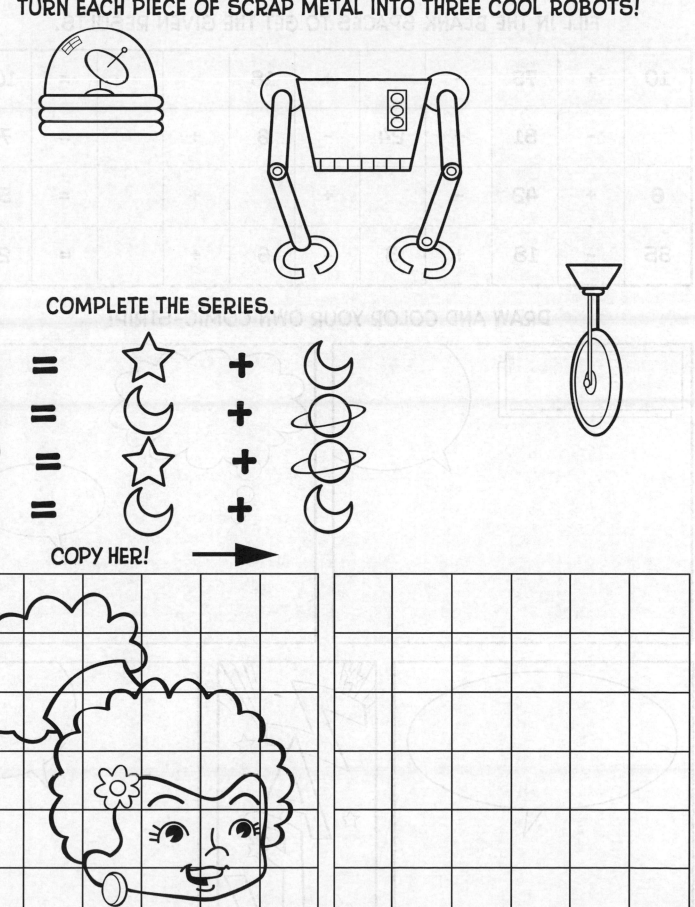

COMPLETE THE SERIES.

$3 = $ ⭐ $+$ 🌙

$5 = $ 🌙 $+$ 🪐

$? = $ ⭐ $+$ 🪐

$4 = $ 🌙 $+$ 🌙

COPY HER! →

FILL IN THE BLANK SPACES TO GET THE GIVEN RESULTS.

10	+	75	-		+	18	-		=	100
	-	81	+	24	-	6	+		=	78
6	+	42	-		+		+		=	56
35	-	18	+	3	-	6	+		=	21

DRAW AND COLOR YOUR OWN COMIC-STRIP!

HELP THE DONKEY FIND ITS LUNCH!

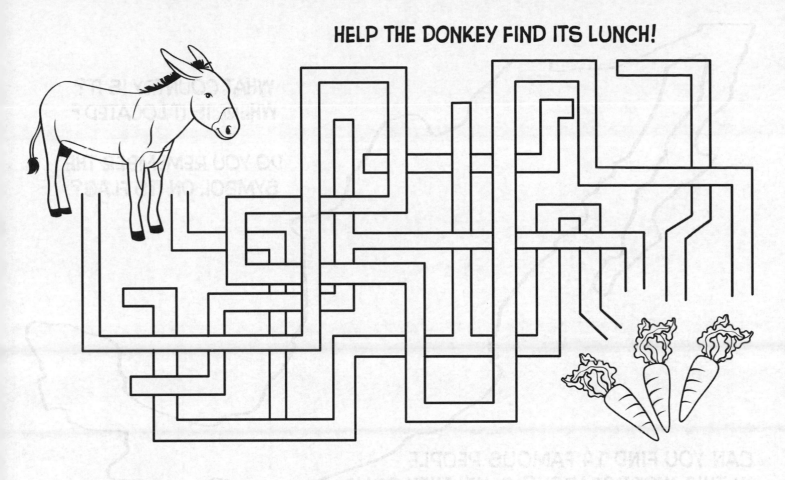

ADD THE NUMBERS WRITTEN ON THE SAILS.
WHICH SAILBOAT CARRIES THE HEAVIER LOAD?

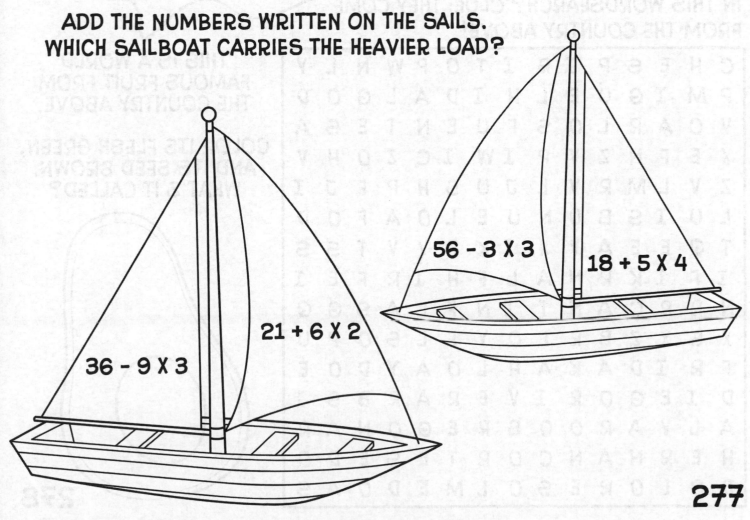

36 - 9 X 3

21 + 6 X 2

56 - 3 X 3

18 + 5 X 4

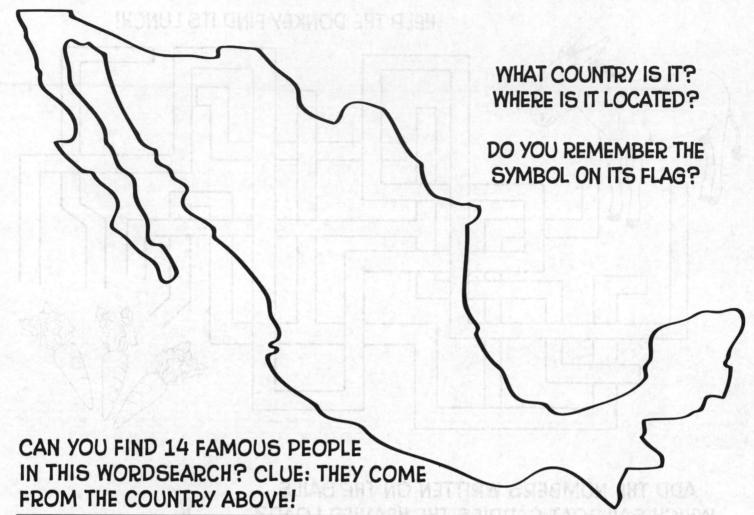

WHAT COUNTRY IS IT?
WHERE IS IT LOCATED?

DO YOU REMEMBER THE SYMBOL ON ITS FLAG?

CAN YOU FIND 14 FAMOUS PEOPLE IN THIS WORDSEARCH? CLUE: THEY COME FROM THE COUNTRY ABOVE!

THIS IS A WORLD FAMOUS FRUIT FROM THE COUNTRY ABOVE.

COLOR ITS FLESH GREEN, AND ITS SEED BROWN. WHAT'S IT CALLED?

```
C H E S P I R I T O P W N L Y
P M I G U E L H I D A L G O D
V C A R L O S F U E N T E S A
X E F N Z V P I W I C Z O H V
Z V L M R V L J U S H P F J I
L U I S B U N U E L O A F O D
T Q E E A V X I K P V V T S S
I F I K R N A L F H I R F E I
N R R C A N T I N F L A S G Q
X S X Z B R L O Y F L S O P U
F R I D A K A H L O A Y D O E
D I E G O R I V E R A R B S I
A L V A R O O B R E G O N A R
H E R N A N C O R T E S E D O
D O L O R E S O L M E D O A S
```

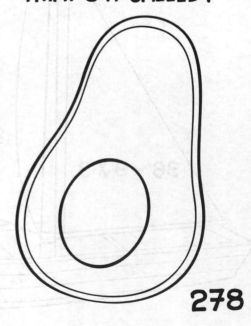

278

CRACK THE SUDOKU!
EACH DRAWING CAN ONLY BE PLACED ONCE ON EACH LINE, ONCE ON EACH ROW, AND ONCE IN EACH FOUR CELL GRID.

CAN YOU GUESS EACH DOUGHNUT'S FLAVOR? COLOR THEM ACCORDINGLY!

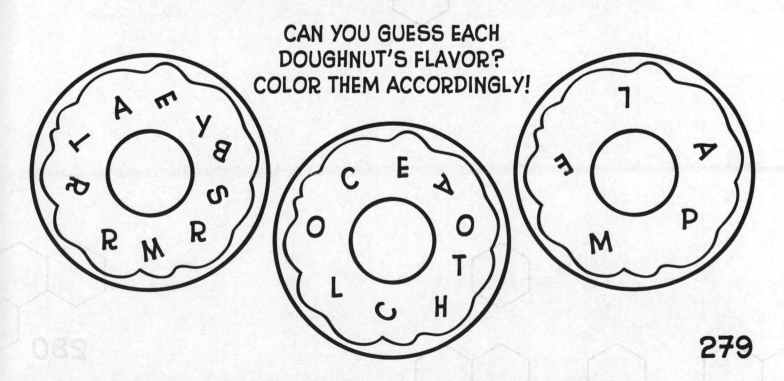

279

FILL THE PAGE WITH HEXAGONS UNTIL THE HONEYCOMB IS FINISHED.

THEN DRAW CUTE BEES LIVING IN IT. ➡️

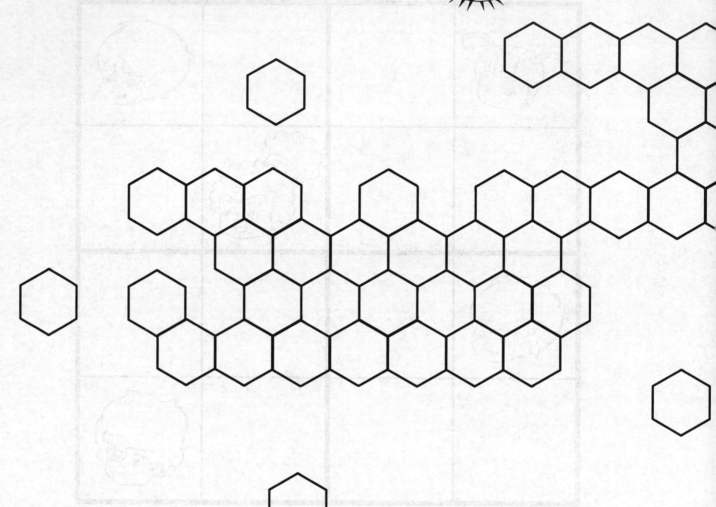

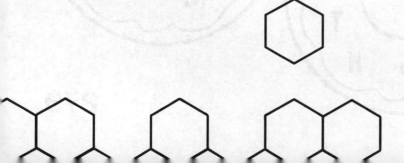

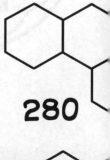

WHICH ONE WEIGHS MORE?

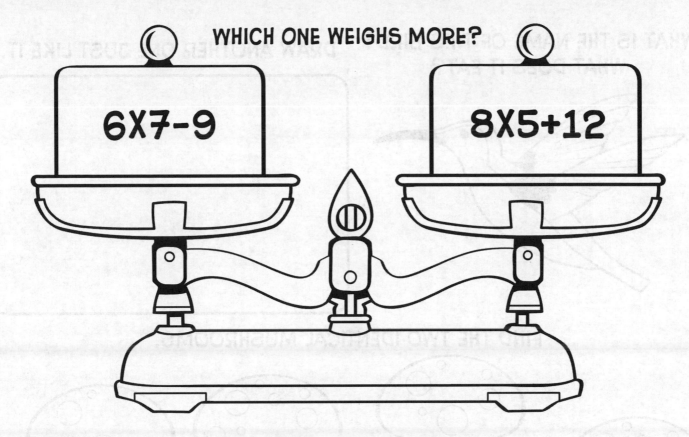

6X7-9

8X5+12

HOW LONG IS THE LADDER?

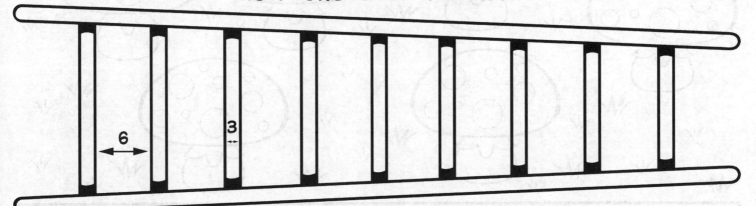

6

3

DRAW AS MANY BUTTERFLIES AND SNAILS AS INDICATED BY EACH TILE.

WHAT IS THE NAME OF THIS BIRD? WHAT DOES IT EAT?

DRAW ANOTHER ONE JUST LIKE IT.

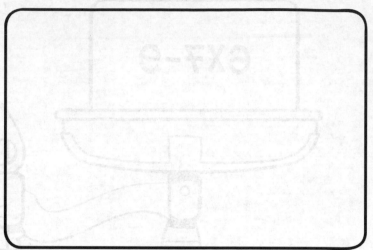

FIND THE TWO IDENTICAL MUSHROOMS.

5	2		3	6		5	27
4		1	2	1	8	9	
9	3	4		7	11		

FILL THE BLANKS SO THE RESULTS OF ADDING THE NUMBERS
MATCH HORIZONTALLY.

HOW MANY OF EACH TYPE OF
ICE CREAM CAN YOU COUNT?
WRITE THE CORRECT NUMBER.

CAN YOU GUESS THE NAME
OF THIS COUNTRY?
WHAT IS IT FAMOUS FOR?

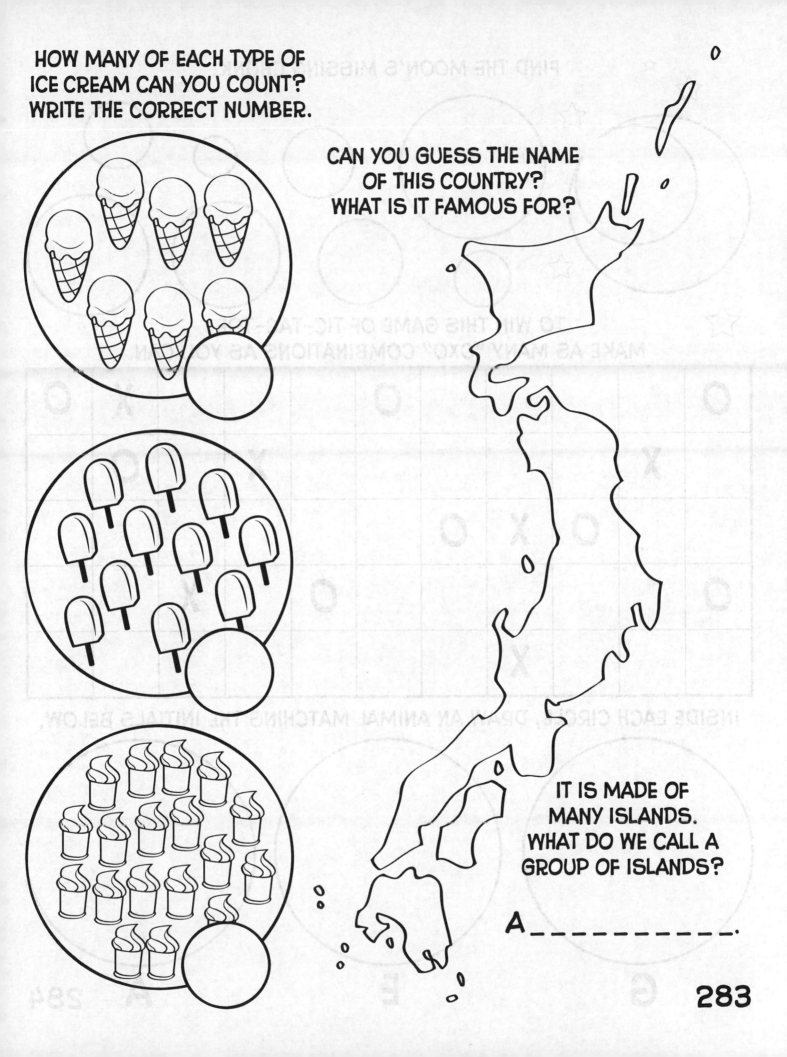

IT IS MADE OF
MANY ISLANDS.
WHAT DO WE CALL A
GROUP OF ISLANDS?

A_____.

283

FIND THE MOON'S MISSING CHUNK.

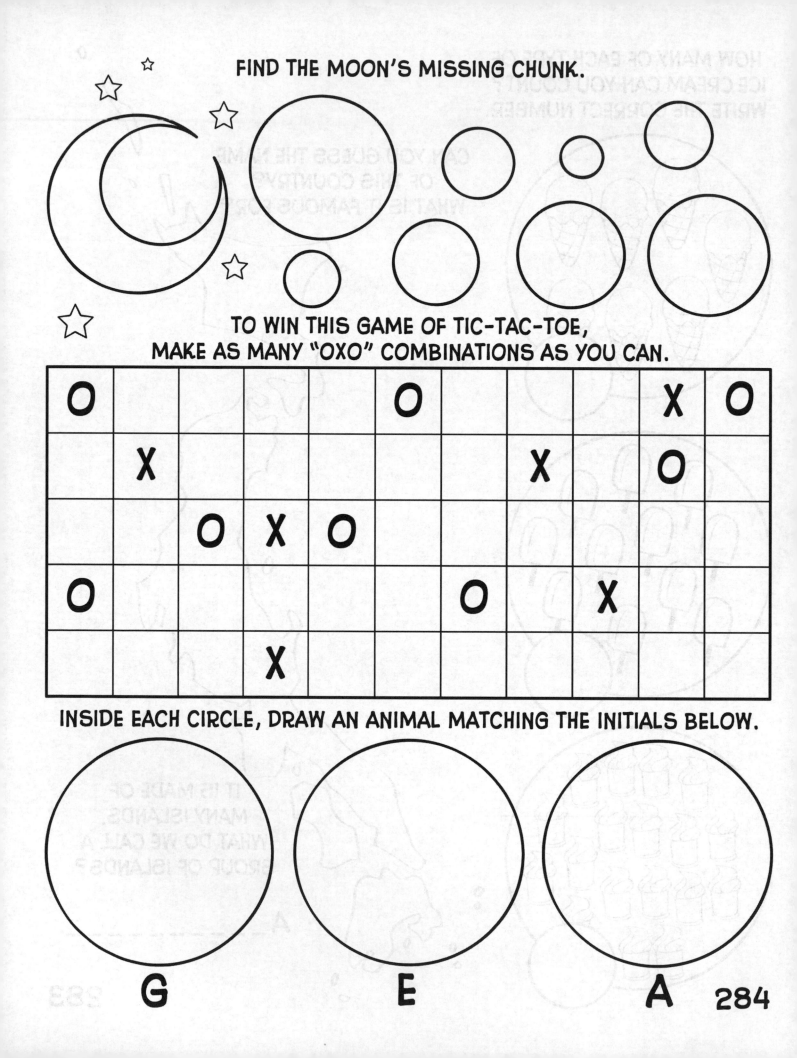

TO WIN THIS GAME OF TIC-TAC-TOE,
MAKE AS MANY "OXO" COMBINATIONS AS YOU CAN.

O					O			X	O
	X					X		O	
	O	X	O						
O						O		X	
			X						

INSIDE EACH CIRCLE, DRAW AN ANIMAL MATCHING THE INITIALS BELOW.

G   E   A

284

THIS BEACH LOOKS EMPTY!
CAN YOU FILL IT WITH CHILDREN HAVING FUN?

SOME MAY BE SWIMMING.
SOME MAY BE PLAYING IN THE SAND.

CAN YOU DRAW MORE
BRIGHTLY COLORED
UMBRELLAS?

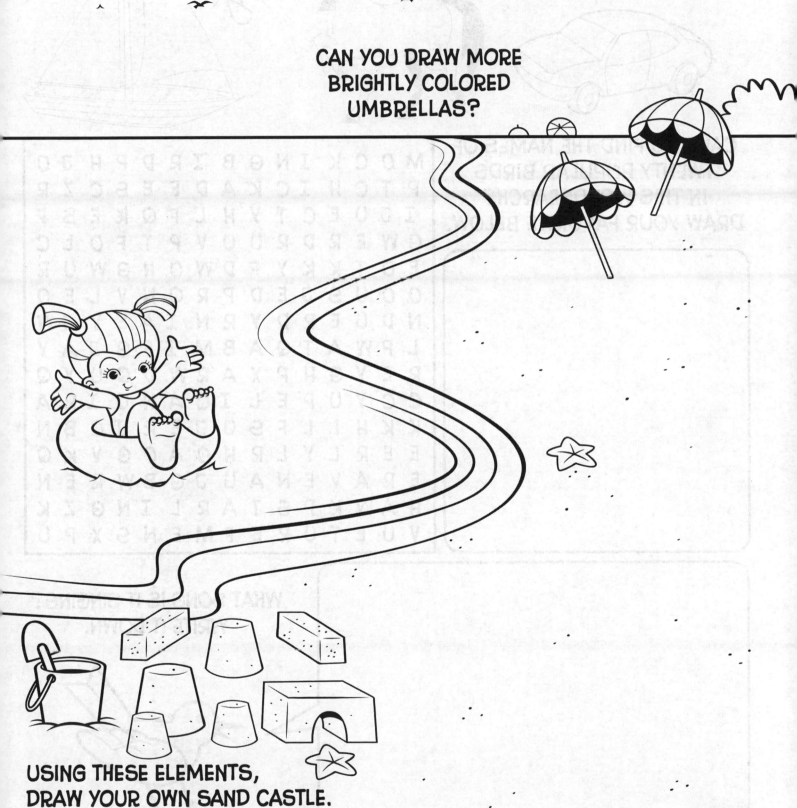

USING THESE ELEMENTS,
DRAW YOUR OWN SAND CASTLE.

WHICH ONE DOESN'T BELONG?

CAN YOU FIND THE NAMES OF
TWENTY POPULAR BIRDS
IN THIS WORDSEARCH?
DRAW YOUR FAVORITE BELOW.

```
M O C K I N G B I R D P H J O
P T C H I C K A D E E S C Z R
I J U E C T Y H L F Q K E B F
G W E R D R U U V P T F O L C
E O T K K Y F D W O H G W U R
O O U S J E D P R Q N V L E O
N D U E R D Y R N I A E V J W
L P W A T Q A B M I F G J A V
R E Y G H P X A R W D Q U Y Q
C C Y U P E L I C A N U I R A
K K H L L F S U J E R I C B N
E E R L Y L R H O A O G V K Q
E R A V E N A U J G B W R E N
H A W K P S T A R L I N G Z K
V U L T U R E F M E N S X P U
```

WHAT SONG IS IT SINGING?
WRITE IT DOWN.

286

FILL WITH ALL POSSIBLE COMBINATIONS OF THE FOUR SYMBOLS.

⬡ ☆ ▢ △		

COLOR THIS CATERPILLAR IN SEVEN COLORS AND CONTINUE THE SERIES. WHAT COLOR WILL THE LAST CIRCLE BE?

IF THE LITTLE FISH DOUBLES ITS CURRENT SIZE EVERY DAY, HOW LONG WILL IT TAKE IT TO BE BIGGER THAN IT'S MOM?

30 IN

9 FT

287

FILL THE SHELVES WITH AS MANY BOOKS AS YOU CAN.

CAN YOU ILLUSTRATE
THE COVER OF HIS BOOK?

WHAT IS IT ABOUT?

HELP THE BEE GO FROM FLOWER #1 TO FLOWER #10, IN THE RIGHT ORDER. THERE IS ONLY ONE CORRECT PATH, GOING THROUGH EACH NUMBER ONCE.

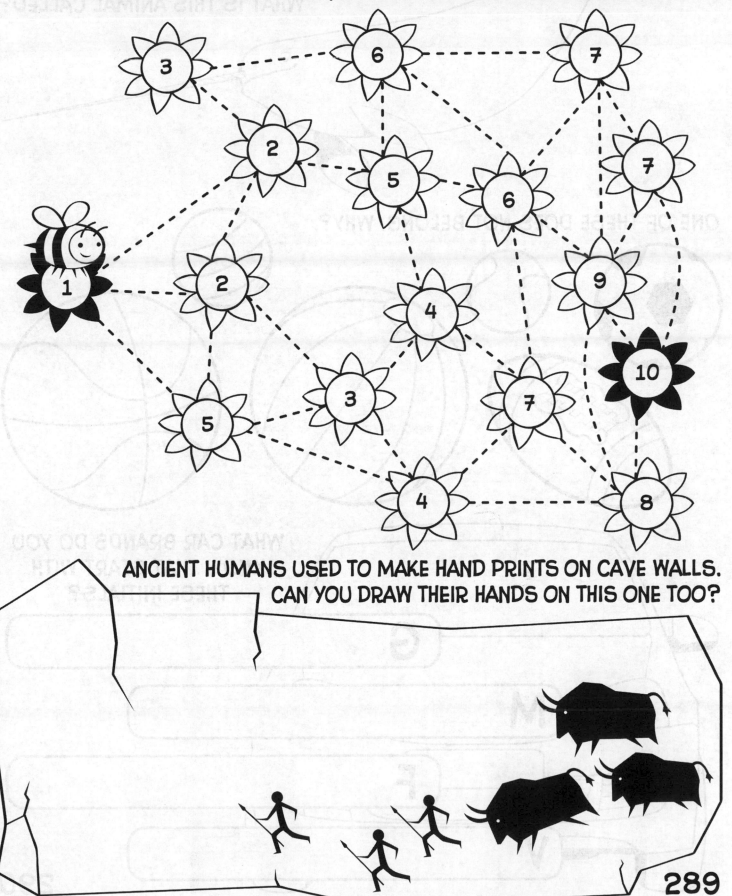

ANCIENT HUMANS USED TO MAKE HAND PRINTS ON CAVE WALLS. CAN YOU DRAW THEIR HANDS ON THIS ONE TOO?

WHAT IS THIS ANIMAL CALLED?

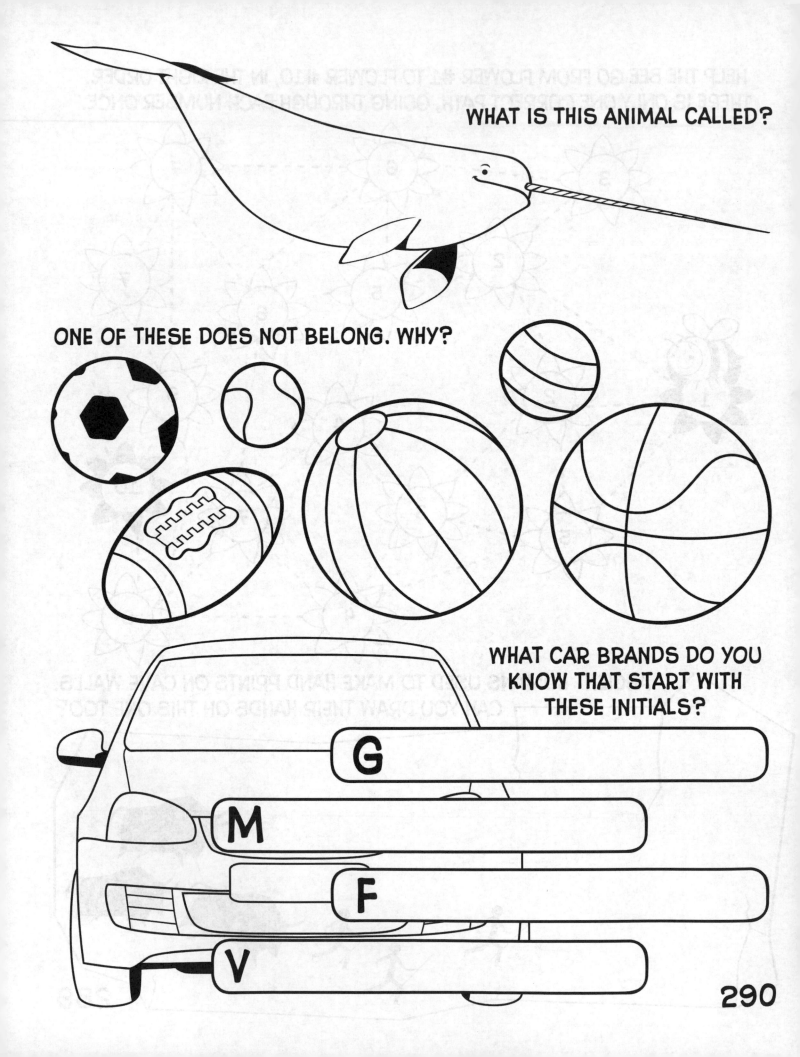

ONE OF THESE DOES NOT BELONG. WHY?

WHAT CAR BRANDS DO YOU KNOW THAT START WITH THESE INITIALS?

G

M

F

V

HOW LONG IS THE BRIDGE IF ALL ITS
STONES ARE OF THE SAME LENGTH,
AND THE TRAIN HAS COVERED
SIXTY FEET ALREADY?

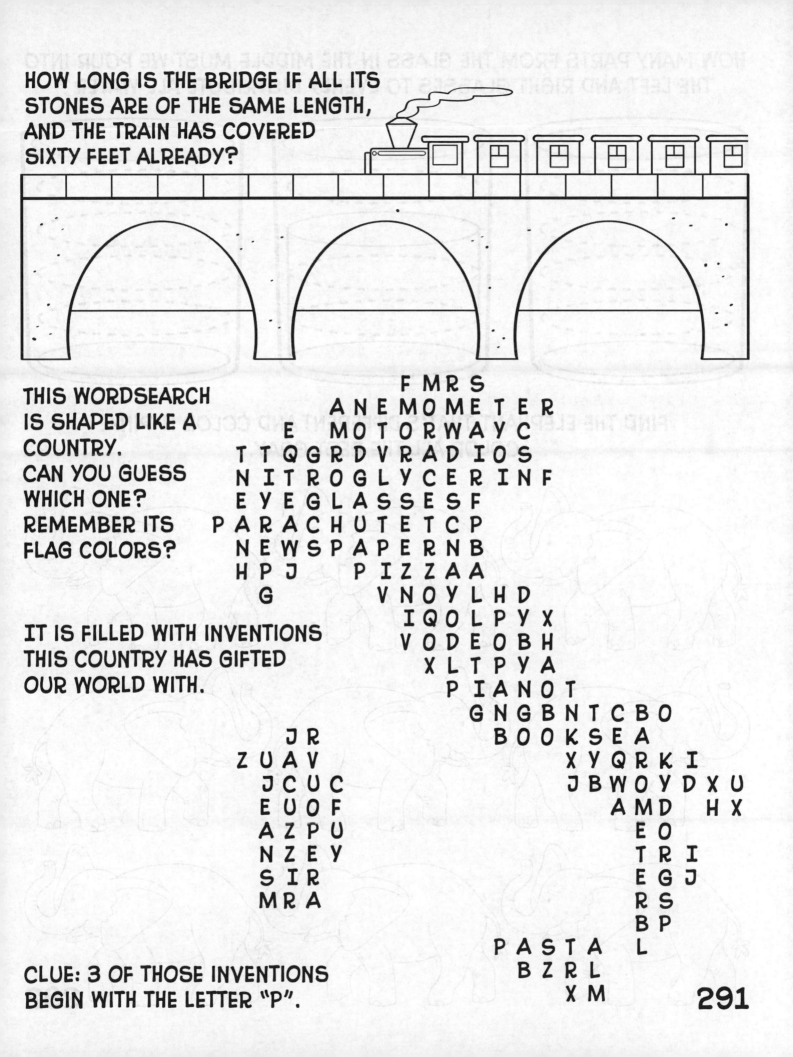

THIS WORDSEARCH
IS SHAPED LIKE A
COUNTRY.
CAN YOU GUESS
WHICH ONE?
REMEMBER ITS
FLAG COLORS?

IT IS FILLED WITH INVENTIONS
THIS COUNTRY HAS GIFTED
OUR WORLD WITH.

```
                    F M R S
          A N E M O M E T E R
        E   M O T O R W A Y C
    T T Q G R D V R A D I O S
    N I T R O G L Y C E R I N F
    E Y E G L A S S E S F
  P A R A C H U T E T C P
  N E W S P A P E R N B
  H P J   P I Z Z A A
    G       V N O Y L H D
            I Q O L P Y X
            V O D E O B H
            X L T P Y H A
            P   I A N O T
              G N G B N T C B O
              B O O K S E A
                  X Y Q R K I
          J R         J B W O Y D X U
      Z U A V           A M D   H X
        J C U C           E O R   I
        E U O F U           T R G J
        A Z P F Y           E R G S P
        N Z E Y             R B L
        S I R               B L
        M R A
                        P A S T A   L
                        B Z R L
                        X M
```

CLUE: 3 OF THOSE INVENTIONS
BEGIN WITH THE LETTER "P".

291

HOW MANY PARTS FROM THE GLASS IN THE MIDDLE MUST WE POUR INTO THE LEFT AND RIGHT GLASSES TO EVENLY DISTRIBUTE ALL WATER?

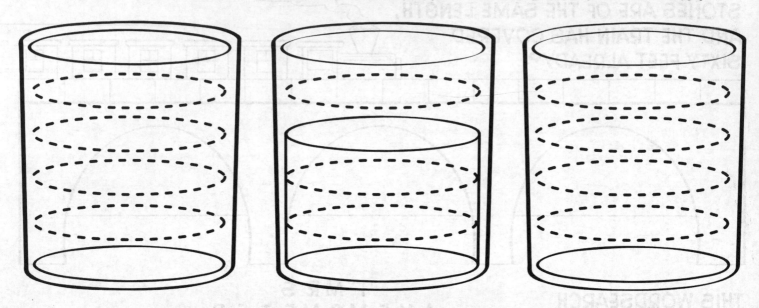

FIND THE ELEPHANT THAT'S DIFFERENT AND COLOR IT PINK. COLOR ALL THE REST GRAY.

WHAT TIME IS IT?

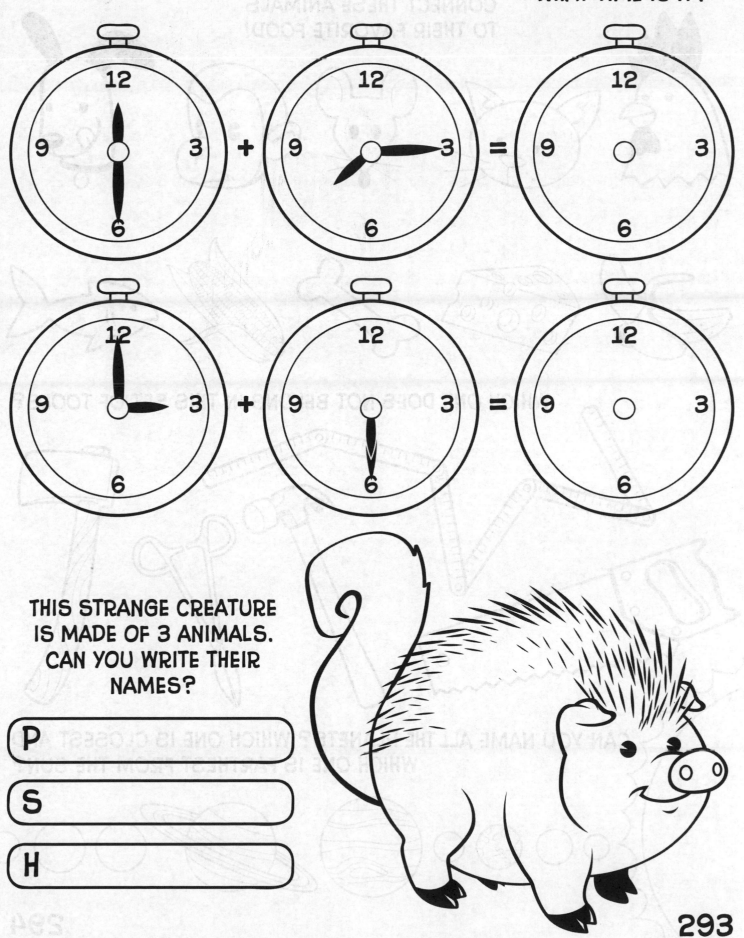

THIS STRANGE CREATURE IS MADE OF 3 ANIMALS. CAN YOU WRITE THEIR NAMES?

P
S
H

CONNECT THESE ANIMALS TO THEIR FAVORITE FOOD!

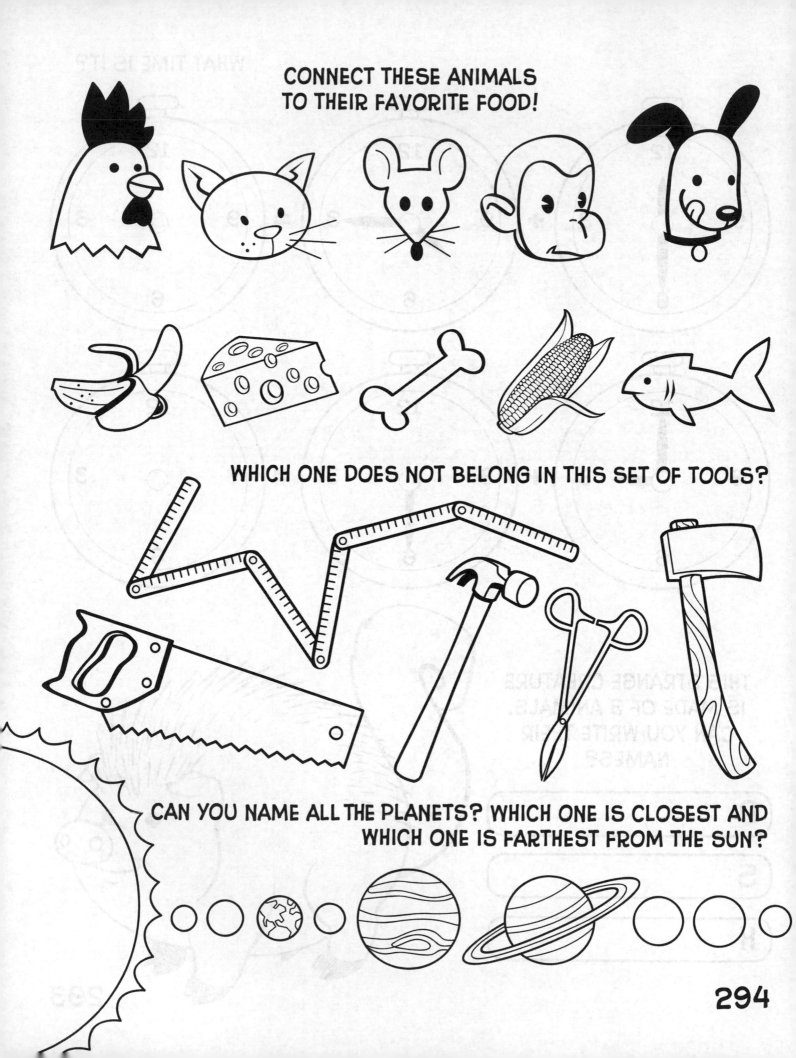

WHICH ONE DOES NOT BELONG IN THIS SET OF TOOLS?

CAN YOU NAME ALL THE PLANETS? WHICH ONE IS CLOSEST AND WHICH ONE IS FARTHEST FROM THE SUN?

294

INSIDE EACH CIRCLE, DRAW AN INSECT MATCHING THE INITIALS BELOW.

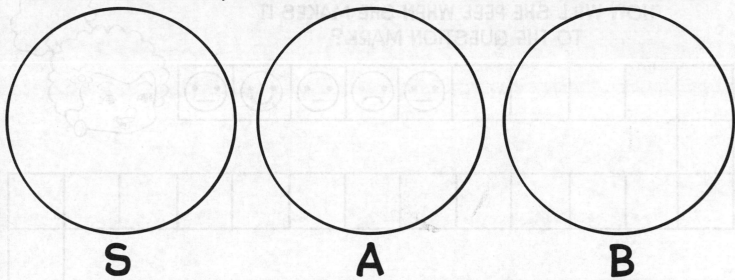

S   A   B

FILL IN THE BLANK SPACES TO GET THE GIVEN RESULTS.

1	+	85	+		+	8	+		=	98
	-	27	+	44	-		+		=	128
7	+	62	-		+		+		=	86
10	-	5	+	8	-	4	+		=	49

WHICH DIRECTION WILL THE FIFTH WHEEL TURN ?

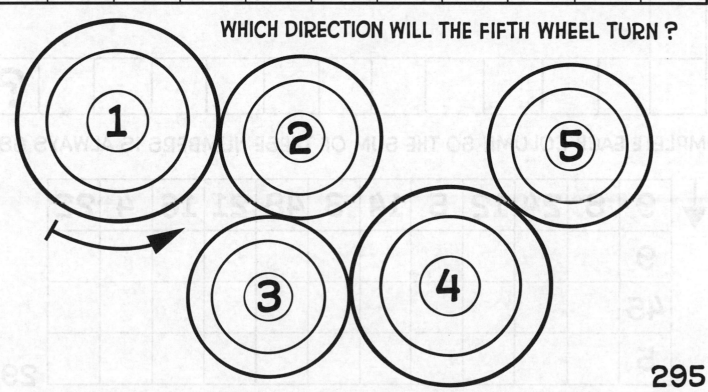

HOW WILL SHE FEEL WHEN SHE MAKES IT TO THE QUESTION MARK?

COMPLETE EACH COLUMN SO THE SUM OF THESE NUMBERS IS ALWAYS 68.

↓	9	8	24	12	5	14	3	48	21	16	4	22
	9											
	45											
	5											

296

SUBTRACT THE NUMBER OF BEES FROM THE TOTAL OF BUTTERFLIES YOU COUNT.

WHAT ROAD MUST THE CAR TAKE TO GET HOME IN EXACTLY 180 SECONDS?

15	8	18
▲		9
		23
	▶	15	24

| 30 | 15 | 12 | 9 | 1 | 8 | 5 | 36 | 7 | 6 | 1 |

▼					7
15					
8	4	1	5	8	9	23

HOW TALL IS THE LADDER?

3 +6 -7 x2 +8 -4 x2 +8 ÷8 x3 =?

297

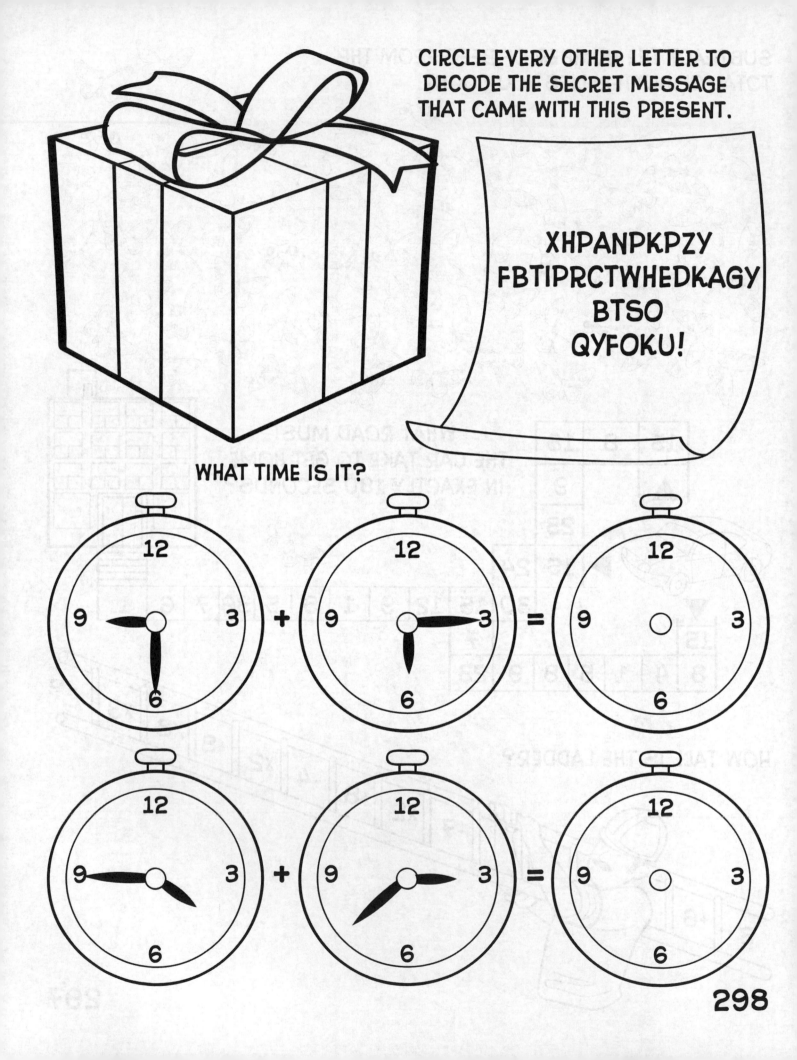

CIRCLE EVERY OTHER LETTER TO DECODE THE SECRET MESSAGE THAT CAME WITH THIS PRESENT.

XHPANPKPZY
FBTIPRCTWHEDKAGY
BTSO
QYFOKU!

WHAT TIME IS IT?

298

HELP THE ALIEN FIND
THE SHORTEST WAY
BACK TO ITS HOME PLANET,
PASSING THROUGH
ONLY TEN STARS.

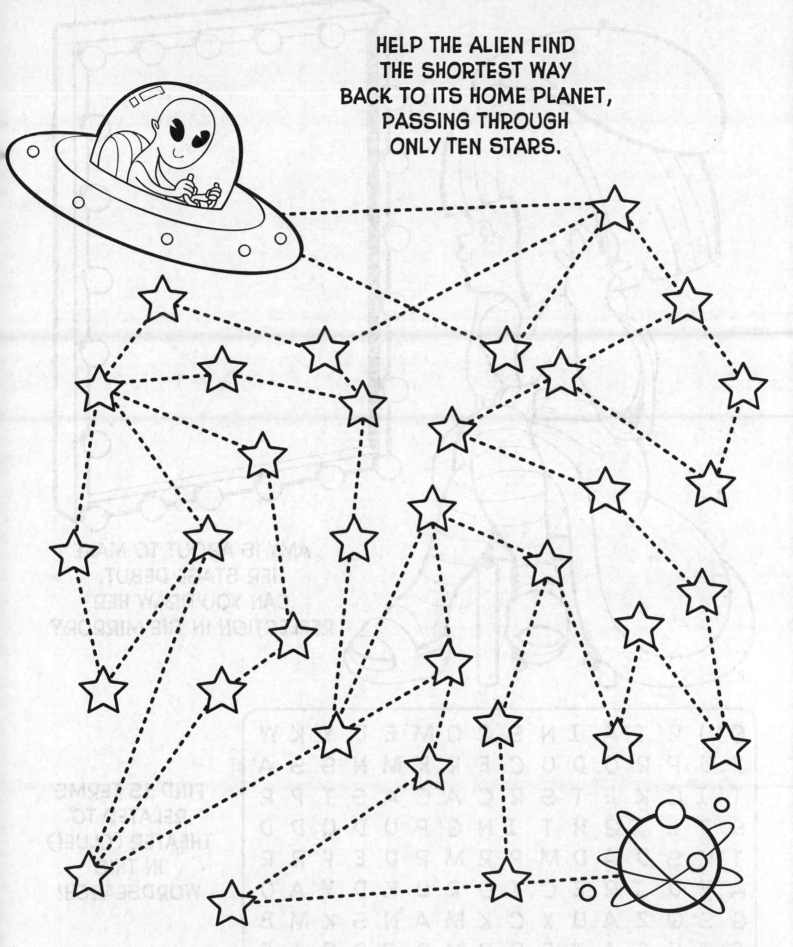

AMY IS ABOUT TO MAKE
HER STAGE DEBUT.
CAN YOU DRAW HER
REFLECTION IN THE MIRROR?

FIND 15 TERMS
RELATED TO
THEATER (CLUE!)
IN THIS
WORDSEARCH!

```
C U R T A I N S C O M E D Y K W
X U P R O D U C E R K M N S S A
T I C K E T S R C A C A S T P R
S F L I G H T I N G P U D U D D
T K S D A D M P R M P D E F R R
A Y D I R E C T O R U K D Y A O
G S Q Z A U X C K M A N S K M B
E T H E A T E R R M R J O Q A E
```

300

HOW IS THE GANG GOING TO MAKE IT OUT OF THE MAZE?

TO WIN THIS GAME OF TIC-TAC-TOE, MAKE AS MANY "OXO" COMBINATIONS AS YOU CAN.

O	X									O
									X	
X					X	O	X	O		
		X			O		O			

INSIDE EACH CIRCLE, DRAW A VEGGIE MATCHING THE INITIALS BELOW.

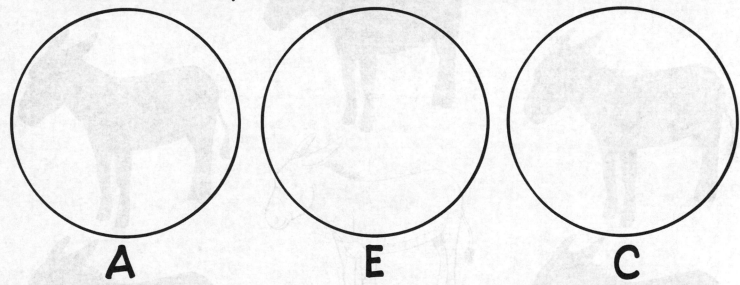

A   E   C

OMPLETE EACH COLUMN SO THE SUM OF THESE NUMBERS IS ALWAYS 124.

↓	22	7	64	11	5	8	3	20	18	40	4	15
	60											
	2											
	40											

303

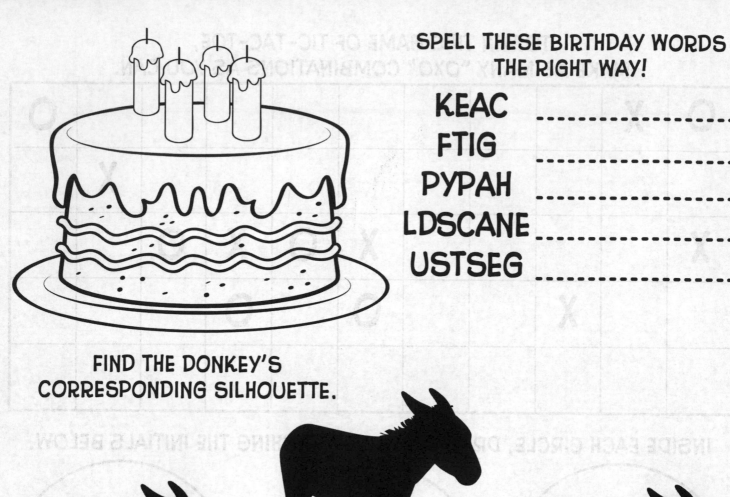

SPELL THESE BIRTHDAY WORDS THE RIGHT WAY!

KEAC ....

FTIG ....

PYPAH ....

LDSCANE ....

USTSEG ....

FIND THE DONKEY'S CORRESPONDING SILHOUETTE.

COMPLETE.

3	− 2	−	+ 5	+ 4	−	+ 6	−	+ 2	= 15

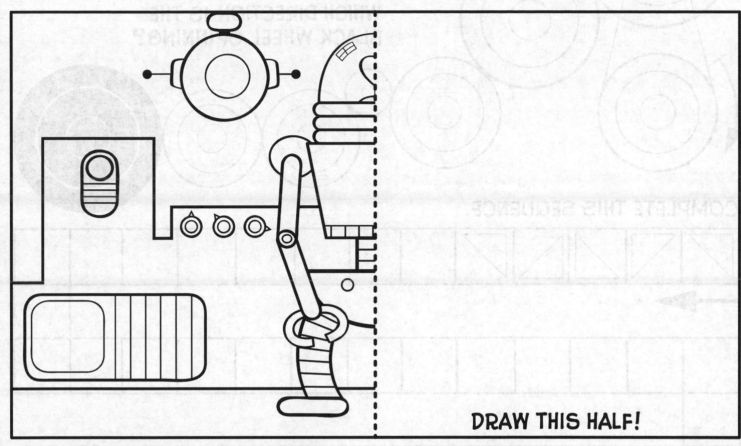

DRAW THIS HALF!

IN ORDER TO BUILD THE MAYAN PYRAMID, MAKE IT SO THE ADDITION OF EACH NUMBER ON THE LEFT TO THE NUMBER ON THE RIGHT EQUALS THE NUMBER OF THE BRICK ON TOP OF BOTH.

22

14

4   10

305

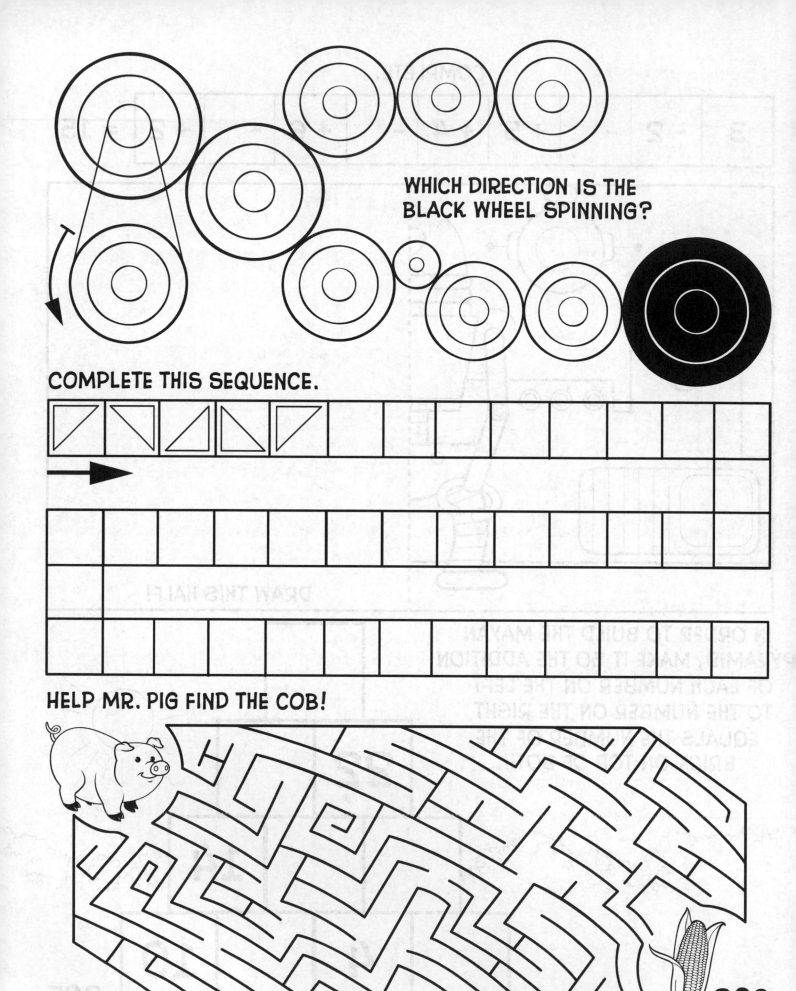

WHICH DIRECTION IS THE BLACK WHEEL SPINNING?

COMPLETE THIS SEQUENCE.

HELP MR. PIG FIND THE COB!

CAN YOU FIND THE FRUIT COMBINATIONS ON THE RIGHT WITHIN THE MAIN GRID?

+5	**+7**	**-2**	**+3**	**-4**	**-6**	**-9**	**-8**	**-2**	**+1**	**=**
+9	**+2**	**-3**	**-**	**-4**	**+5**	**-4**	**+6**	**-2**	**+4**	**= 11**
+	**+2**	**-1**	**+6**	**+2**	**+4**	**-5**	**-2**	**+9**	**-3**	**=**
+6	**+3**	**-2**	**+4**	**-1**	**+3**	**+5**	**-6**	**+5**	**-1**	**=**
= 25	**=**	**=**	**=**	**=**	**=**	**=**	**=**	**=**	**=**	**29**

DO THE MATH BOTH VERTICALLY AND HORIZONTALLY!   307

HOW MUCH DO YOU KNOW ABOUT OUR PLANET? TEST YOUR KNOWLEDGE BY CRACKING THIS WORDSEARCH!

1. WHAT IS THE BIGGEST CONTINENT?
2. WHAT IS THE LARGEST OCEAN?
3. WHAT IS ITS LONGEST RIVER?
4. WHAT IS ITS BIGGEST DESERT?
5. WHAT IS ITS BIGGEST INLAND SEA?
6. WHAT IS THE COLDEST CONTINENT?
7. WHAT IS THE BIGGEST ISLAND?
8. WHAT IS ITS HIGHEST MOUNTAIN?
9. WHAT ABOUT THE SECOND HIGHEST?

```
T P C N G E V E R E S T
K I D E F Z S Y I M H N
W J J U B K Q U Z E O P
Z X V S K V L E D D N R
A H N I H V G N H I O K
R Z N U P I A J A T W K
T O I G H L A O C E R M
R D Q I N C K N O R W M
U S A E V R T Z N R V W
I U E X E C B O C A I I
I R J H U Q B N A N Q X
G Y Z W R B D C G E F V
Y G Z R A F I J U A Z V
K U B O S F I F A N S U
N B O G I S A H A R A Z
N Z C C A Z N B D M O Q
H Y A J V O N K Z I H R
D P V L Z U X I N V D U
A N T A R C T I C A I B
M H M A G W J F Y C T G
I A N S A Z J Q T B W A
```

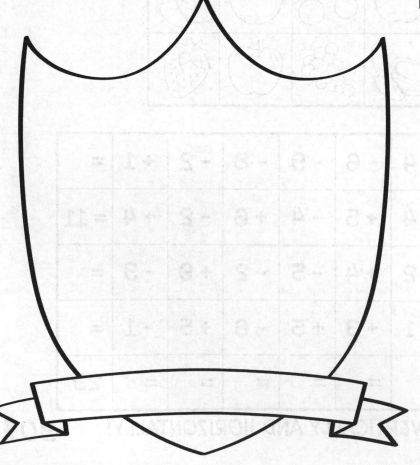

DESIGN AND COLOR
YOUR OWN
COAT OF ARMS.

THINK AND WRITE A
GOOD MOTTO TOO!

DRAW PATHS CONNECTING NUMBERS 1 TO 9 TO FORM A CONSTELLATION.

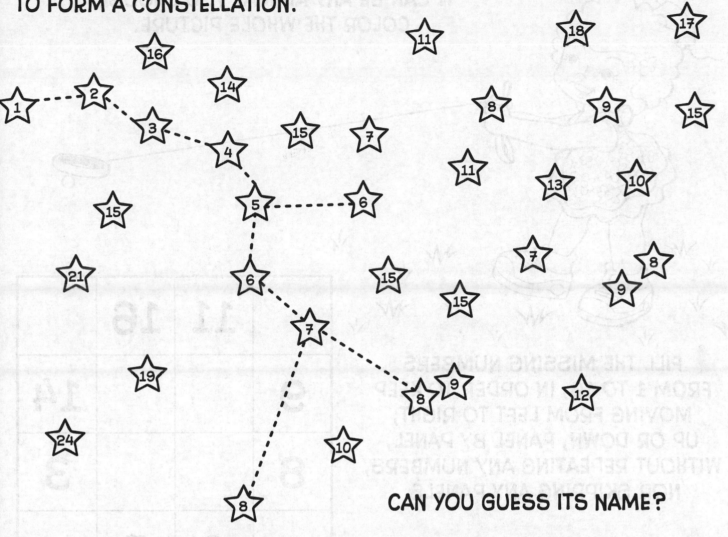

CAN YOU GUESS ITS NAME?

CONNECT ALL THE TOTALS THAT EQUAL 9!

8 + 1	6 + 3	11 − 2	7 + 3	4 + 5	6 + 3	2 + 7	8 + 7	3 + 6	1 X 9
6 + 5	4 + 5	3 X 3	2 X 5	3 X 3	5 − 2	7 + 2	5 + 6	4 + 5	5 + 5
9 − 3	12 + 5	5 X 2	3 X 6	13 − 4	1 + 3	9 X 1	12 − 6	9 X 1	1 + 5
4 + 8	7 + 2	13 + 4	8 + 1	9 − 0	4 X 3	14 + 6	13 − 4	16 − 7	8 − 2

DRAW MAYA'S PET.
IT CAN BE ANY ANIMAL YOU CHOOSE!
COLOR THE WHOLE PICTURE.

FILL THE MISSING NUMBERS
FROM 1 TO 16, IN ORDER TO KEEP
MOVING FROM LEFT TO RIGHT,
UP OR DOWN, PANEL BY PANEL,
WITHOUT REPEATING ANY NUMBERS,
NOR SKIPPING ANY PANELS.

	11	16	
9			14
8			3
	6	5	

IF THE FIRST WHEEL OF CHEESE WEIGHS 12 POUNDS,
WHAT IS THE SECOND WHEEL'S WEIGHT?

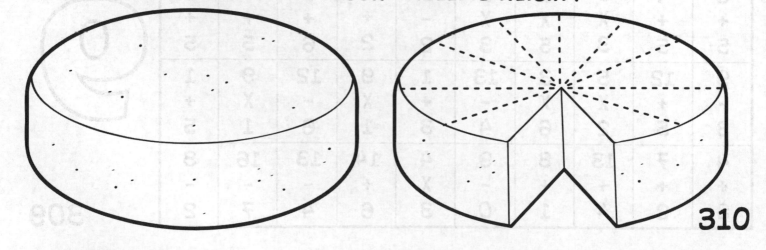

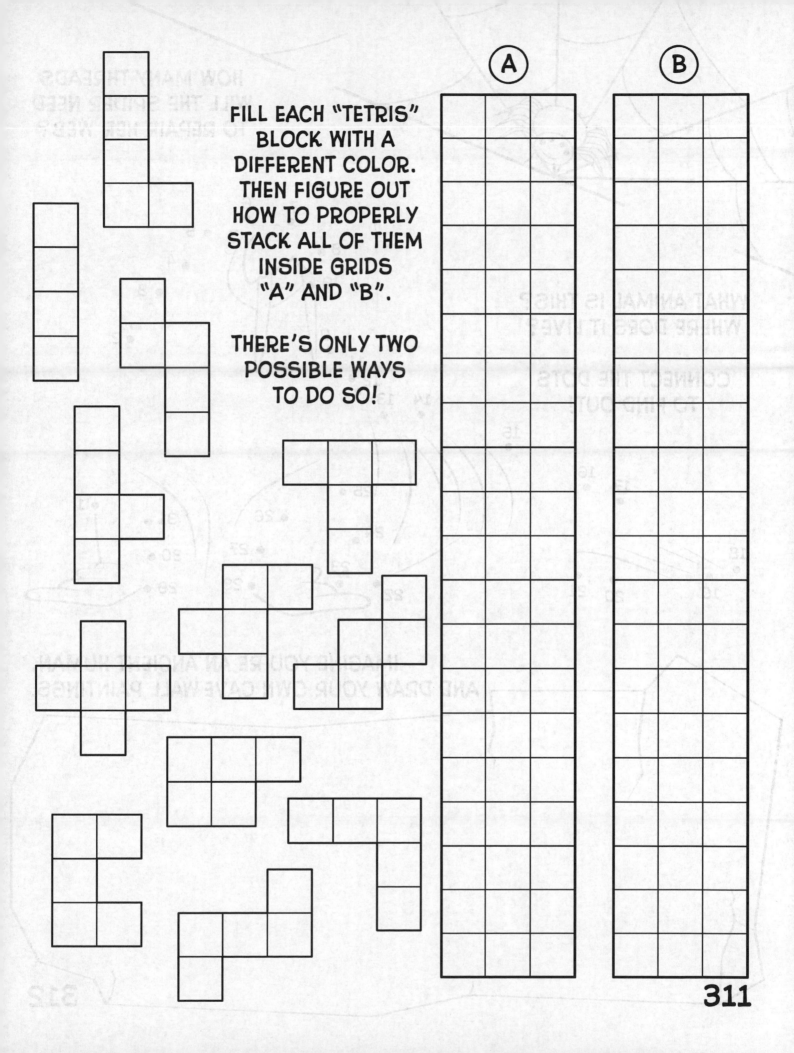

FILL EACH "TETRIS" BLOCK WITH A DIFFERENT COLOR. THEN FIGURE OUT HOW TO PROPERLY STACK ALL OF THEM INSIDE GRIDS "A" AND "B".

THERE'S ONLY TWO POSSIBLE WAYS TO DO SO!

HOW MANY THREADS
WILL THE SPIDER NEED
TO REPAIR HER WEB?

WHAT ANIMAL IS THIS?
WHERE DOES IT LIVE?

CONNECT THE DOTS
TO FIND OUT!

7 6
8 5
9 4
    3
10 2
11
12
14 13
15
17 16
18
19 20 21
25
26
24 27
23 31 1
22 28 30 29

IMAGINE YOU'RE AN ANCIENT HUMAN,
AND DRAW YOUR OWN CAVE WALL PAINTINGS.

21		9		3	5		15
	10	8		2		8	10	16
	6		2	0	2			8

THIS MONUMENT IS A COMMON SIGHT AROUND THE WORLD. WHAT IS IT CALLED? WHERE WAS IT ORIGINALLY INVENTED? NAME THREE CAPITAL CITIES WHERE YOU KNOW IT CAN BE FOUND.

② ③ ②

①

①

② ②

② ①

CONNECT EACH NUMBERED CIRCLE WITH ONLY VERTICAL OR HORIZONTAL, NON OVERLAPPING LINES. THE NUMBER ON EACH CIRCLE INDICATES THE NUMBER OF LINES EACH ONE IS ALLOWED.

HOW MANY PENCILS WOULD THE OCTOPUS NEED TO FINISH WRITING THE LETTER SOONER?

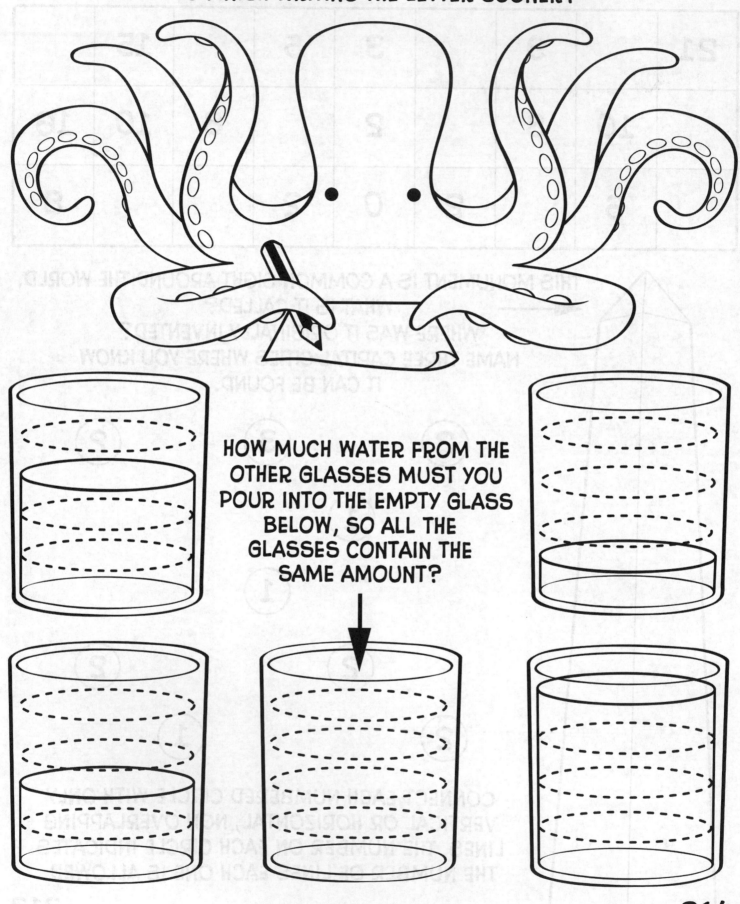

HOW MUCH WATER FROM THE OTHER GLASSES MUST YOU POUR INTO THE EMPTY GLASS BELOW, SO ALL THE GLASSES CONTAIN THE SAME AMOUNT?

COMPLETE THIS SEQUENCE
TO FIND OUT WHICH INSECTS
WILL REPLACE THE QUESTION MARKS.

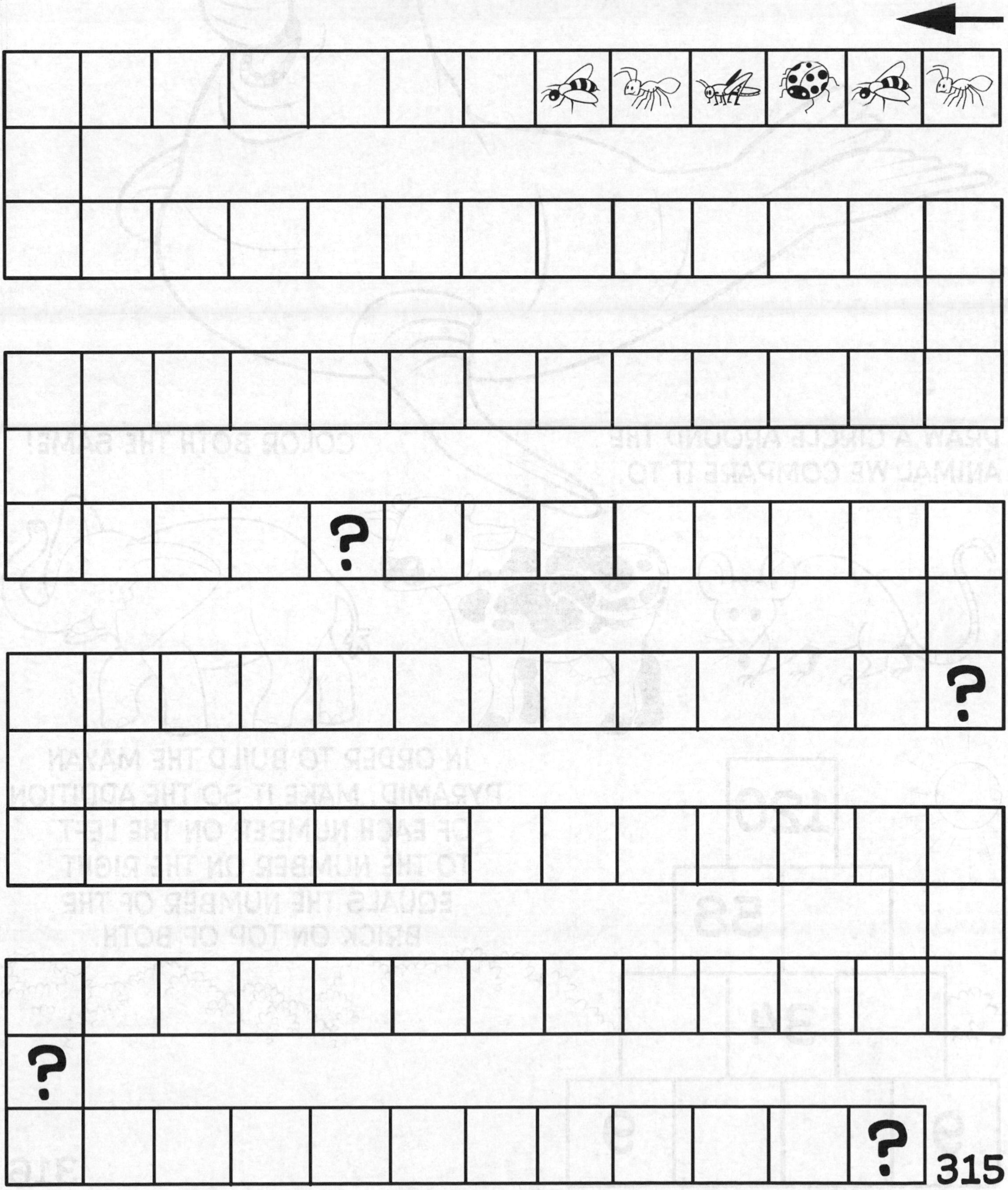

315

WHAT STRANGE ANIMAL IS THIS?
WHERE DOES IT LIVE?
WHAT DOES IT EAT?

DRAW A CIRCLE AROUND THE
ANIMAL WE COMPARE IT TO.

COLOR BOTH THE SAME!

IN ORDER TO BUILD THE MAYAN
PYRAMID, MAKE IT SO THE ADDITION
OF EACH NUMBER ON THE LEFT
TO THE NUMBER ON THE RIGHT
EQUALS THE NUMBER OF THE
BRICK ON TOP OF BOTH.

120

58

34

9   9

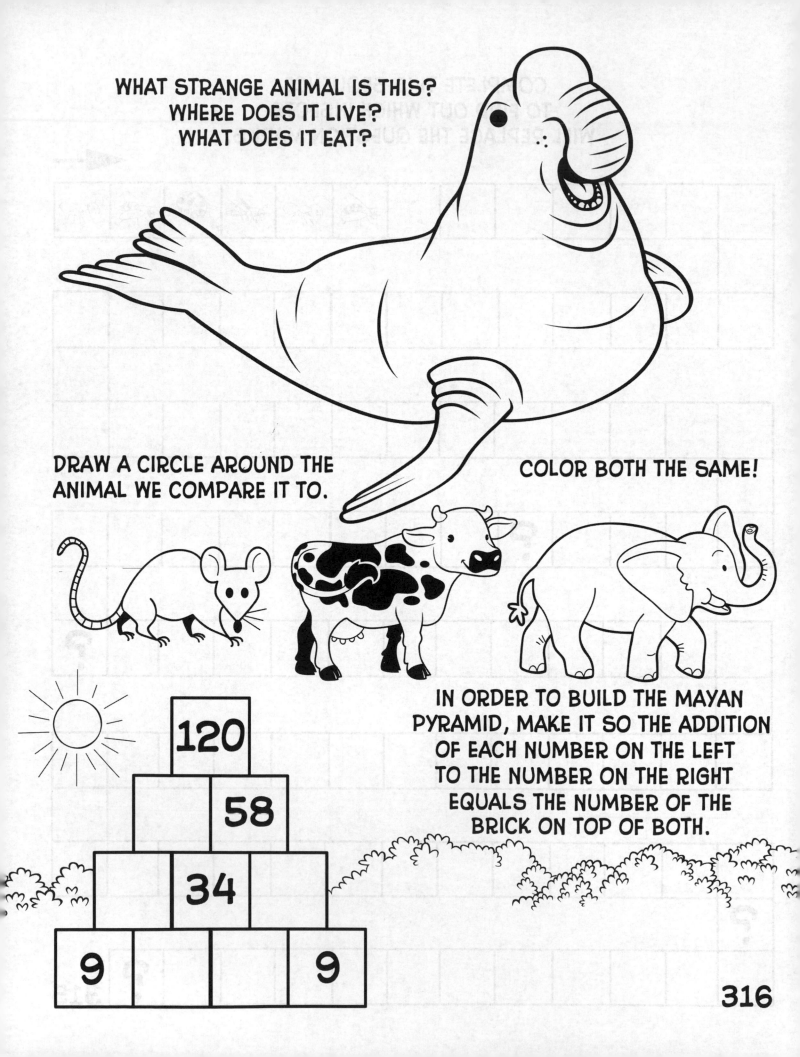

HELP AMY COLOR THIS PICTURE IN THE STYLE OF DUTCH PAINTER, PIET MONDRIAN! TO DO SO, FILL EACH PANEL USING ONLY PRIMARY COLORS, BUT NEVER PAINT JOINT PANELS USING THE SAME COLOR (YOU MAY CHEAT BY NOT COLORING A FEW).

NOW DRAW AND PAINT YOUR OWN "MONDRIAN" USING ONLY STRAIGHT LINES AND THREE COLORS!

DID YOU KNOW YOU CAN FILL ANY SHAPE WITH AN INFINITE NUMBER OF CIRCLES? WHAT'S THE BIGGEST CIRCLE YOU CAN DRAW IN THIS RECTANGLE? GO AHEAD AN FILL EVERY AVAILABLE SPACE WITH SMALLER ONES!

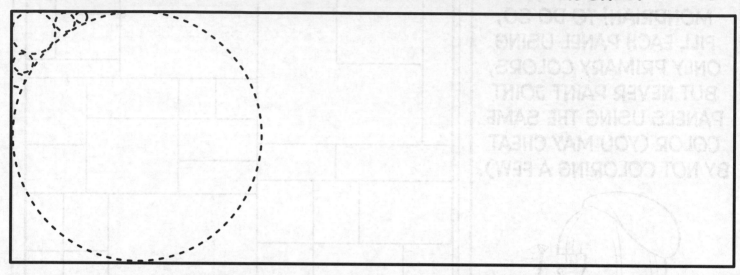

CAN YOU FIND THE NEW FOUR FRUIT COMBINATIONS AT THE RIGHT?

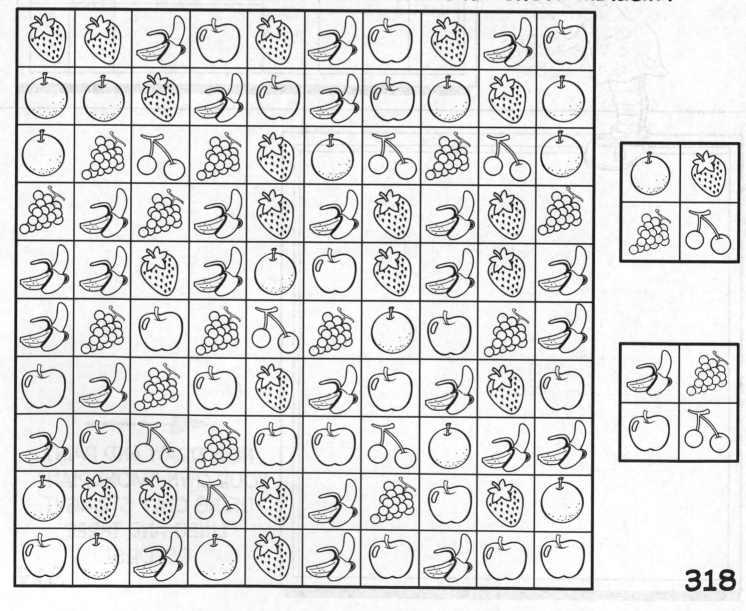

318

WHAT TIME IS IT?

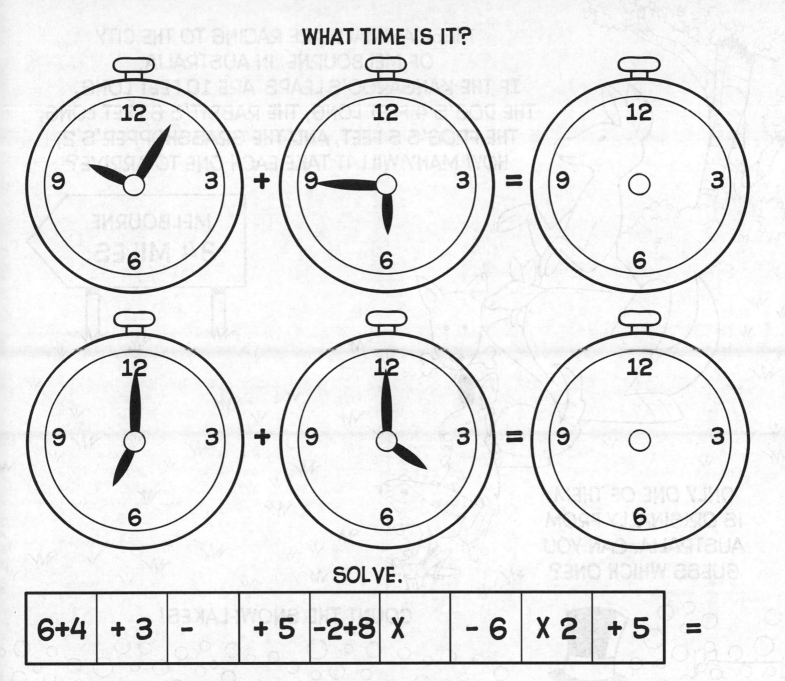

+ = + =

SOLVE.

6+4	+ 3	-		+ 5	-2+8	X		- 6	X 2	+ 5	=

CAN YOU FIND ALL 14 FELINE SPECIES IN THIS WORDSEARCH?

CLUE: "FELINE" MEANS CAT!

```
T H L A D O M E S T I C C A T F
P P Y E J A G U A R B T V R P D
O A I D Y O L Y N X O O E J U Z
B E N C A R A C A L T G B Z M L
E V O T L Y M F E W I L D C A T
Y I M R H I G C J T S E R V A L
S N O W L E O P A R D M J C F T
V B N L T N R N C H E E T A H H
```

319

THESE ANIMALS ARE RACING TO THE CITY
OF MELBOURNE, IN AUSTRALIA.
IF THE KANGAROO'S LEAPS ARE 10 FEET LONG,
THE DOG'S 4 FEET LONG, THE RABBIT'S 6 FEET LONG,
THE FROG'S 5 FEET, AND THE GRASSHOPPER'S 2,
HOW MANY WILL IT TAKE EACH ONE TO ARRIVE?

MELBOURNE
34 MILES.

ONLY ONE OF THEM
IS ORIGINALLY FROM
AUSTRALIA. CAN YOU
GUESS WHICH ONE?

COUNT THE SNOWFLAKES!

IF SNOWMAN IS 5 FEET TALL, AND IT'S SNOWING 7 INCHES PER HOUR,
HOW LONG WILL IT TAKE FOR IT TO COMPLETELY COVER HIM UP?

320

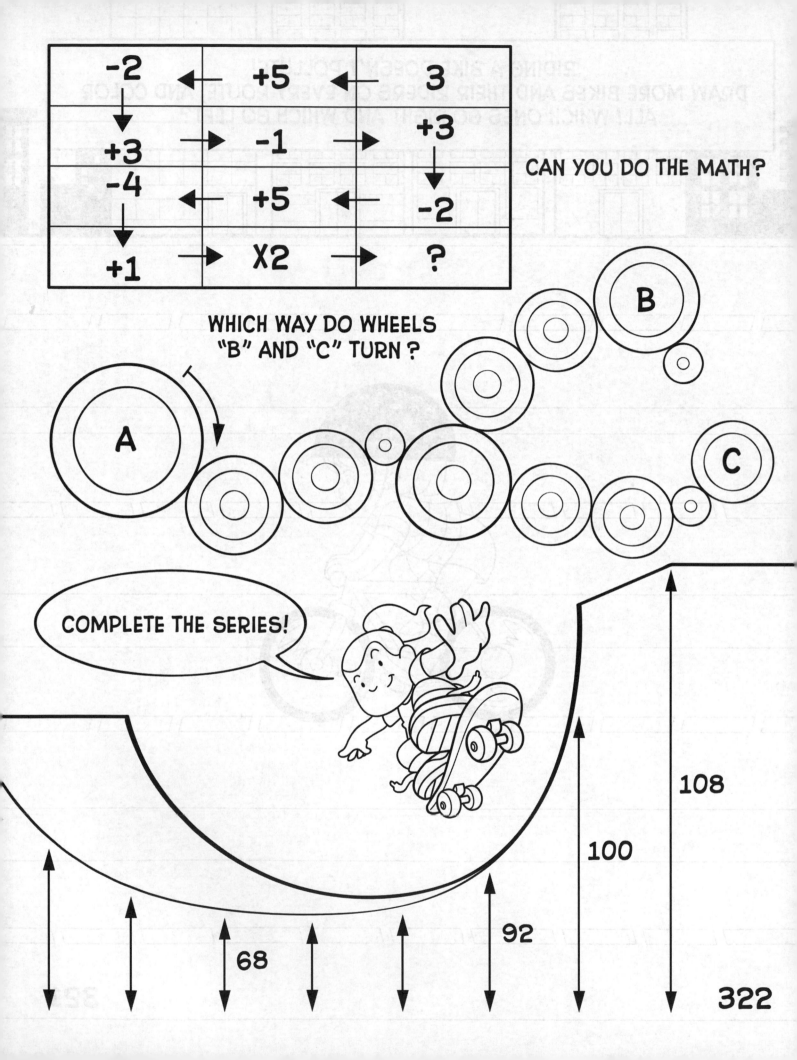

-2	←	+5	←	3
↓				↓
+3	→	-1	→	+3
				↓
-4	←	+5	←	-2
↓				↓
+1	→	X2	→	?

CAN YOU DO THE MATH?

WHICH WAY DO WHEELS "B" AND "C" TURN?

A

B

C

COMPLETE THE SERIES!

108

100

92

68

322

CONNECT EACH NUMBERED CIRCLE WITH ONLY VERTICAL OR HORIZONTAL, NON OVERLAPPING LINES. THE NUMBER ON EACH CIRCLE INDICATES THE NUMBER OF LINES EACH ONE IS ALLOWED.

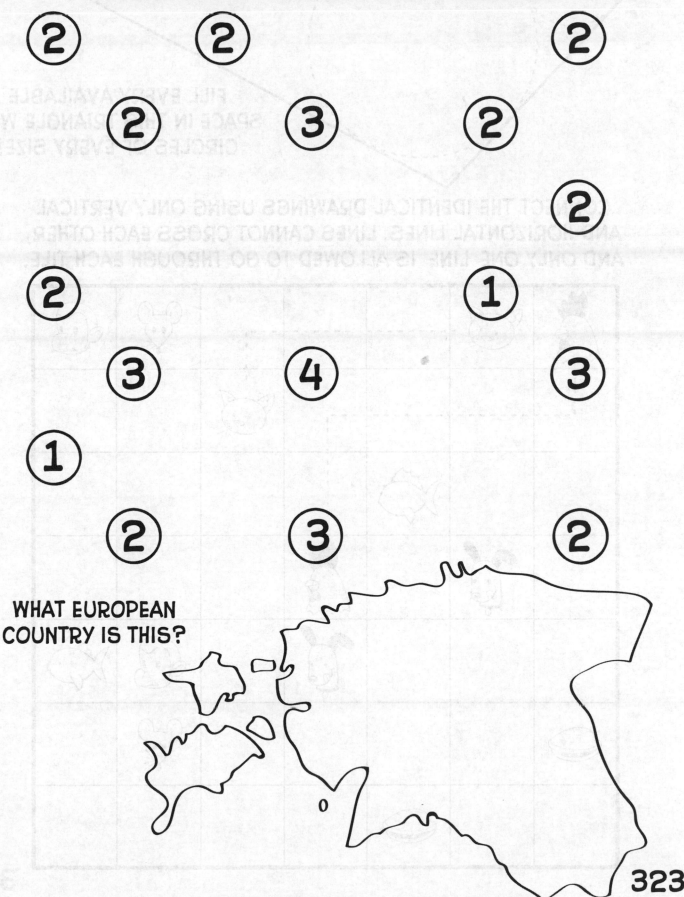

WHAT EUROPEAN
COUNTRY IS THIS?

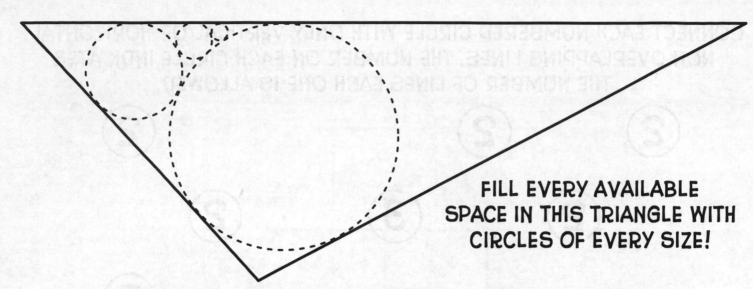

FILL EVERY AVAILABLE
SPACE IN THIS TRIANGLE WITH
CIRCLES OF EVERY SIZE!

CONNECT THE IDENTICAL DRAWINGS USING ONLY VERTICAL
AND HORIZONTAL LINES. LINES CANNOT CROSS EACH OTHER,
AND ONLY ONE LINE IS ALLOWED TO GO THROUGH EACH TILE.

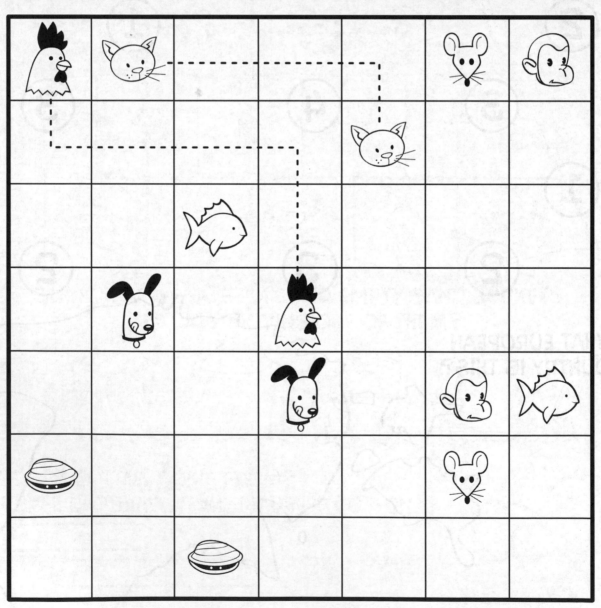

324

COMPLETE THIS TABLE WITH + AND − SIGNS.

3	5	2	5	6	9	= 30
8	3	6	5	2	1	= 3
4	5	9	6	8	7	= 25
6	3	5	9	8	2	= 7

FILL EACH EMPTY CIRCLE SO THE SUM OF EACH LINE IS ALWAYS 10.

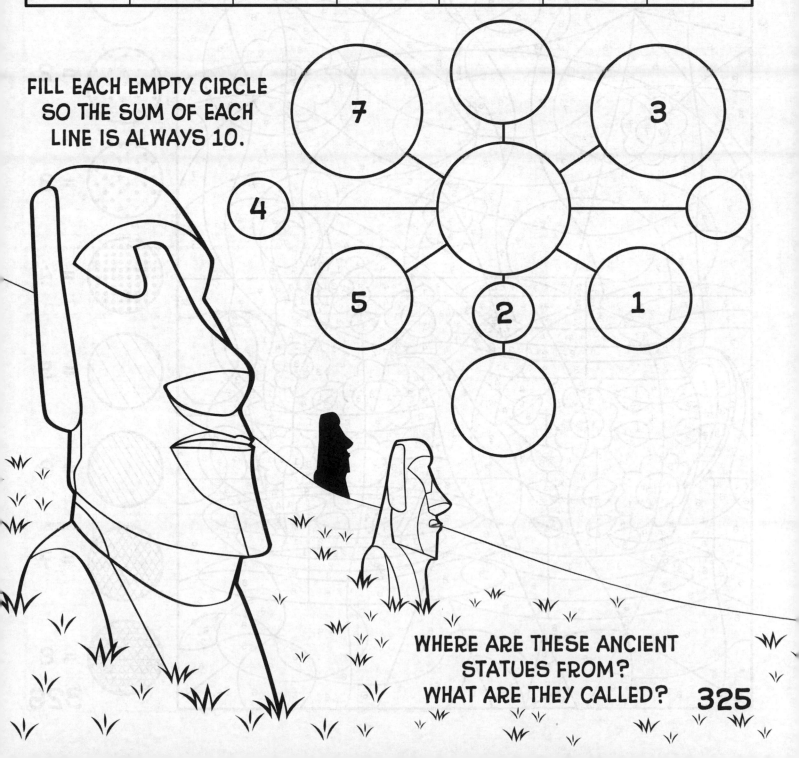

WHERE ARE THESE ANCIENT STATUES FROM? WHAT ARE THEY CALLED?

SOLVE.

8-3	+ 3	–	X 2	– 6	X	+ 12	/ 2	X 5	=

TO FIGURE OUT WHAT THE MYSTERY PICTURE IS, FILL EACH NUMBERED AREA AS INSTRUCTED.

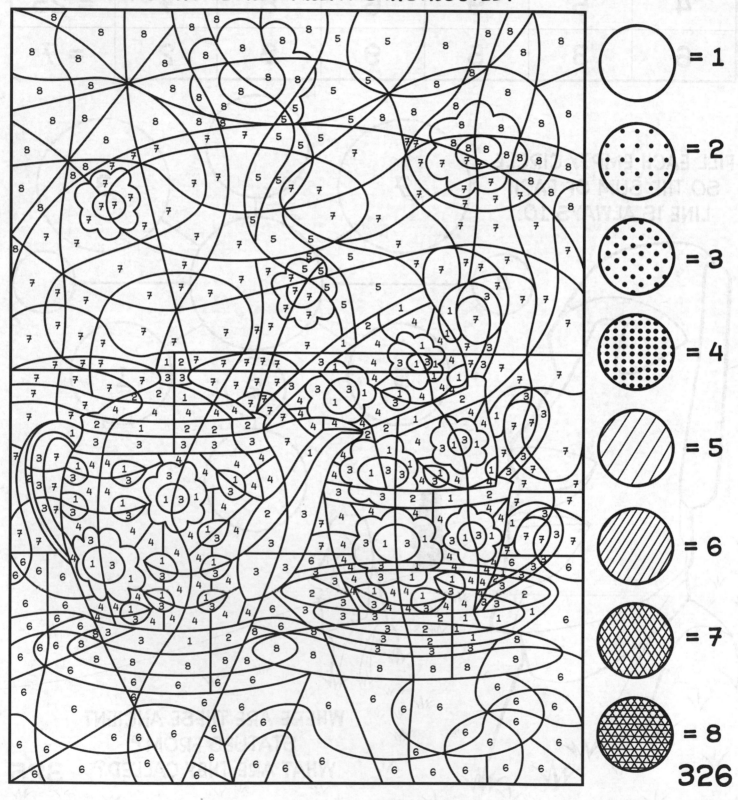

= 1

= 2

= 3

= 4

= 5

= 6

= 7

= 8

326

OLLIE IS A VEGETARIAN: DRAW A CIRCLE AROUND THE FOODS HE CAN EAT, AND COLOR IT.

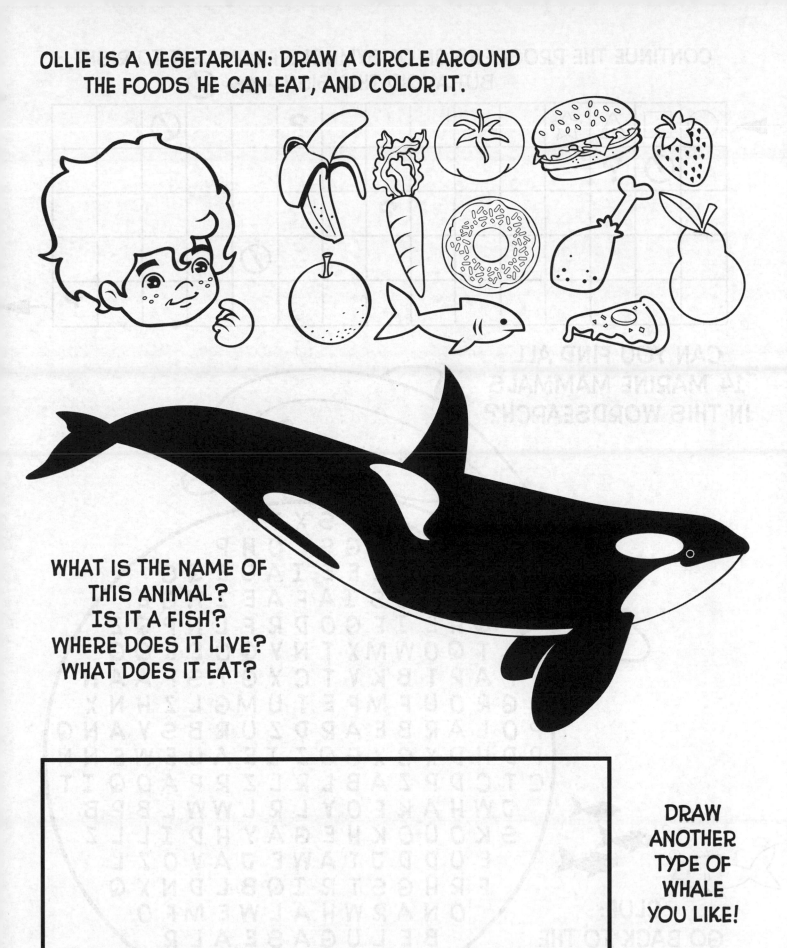

WHAT IS THE NAME OF
THIS ANIMAL?
IS IT A FISH?
WHERE DOES IT LIVE?
WHAT DOES IT EAT?

DRAW
ANOTHER
TYPE OF
WHALE
YOU LIKE!

CONTINUE THE PROGRESSION OF SYMBOLS FROM LEFT TO RIGHT, BUT AVOID THIS SIGN ⟶ ⊘

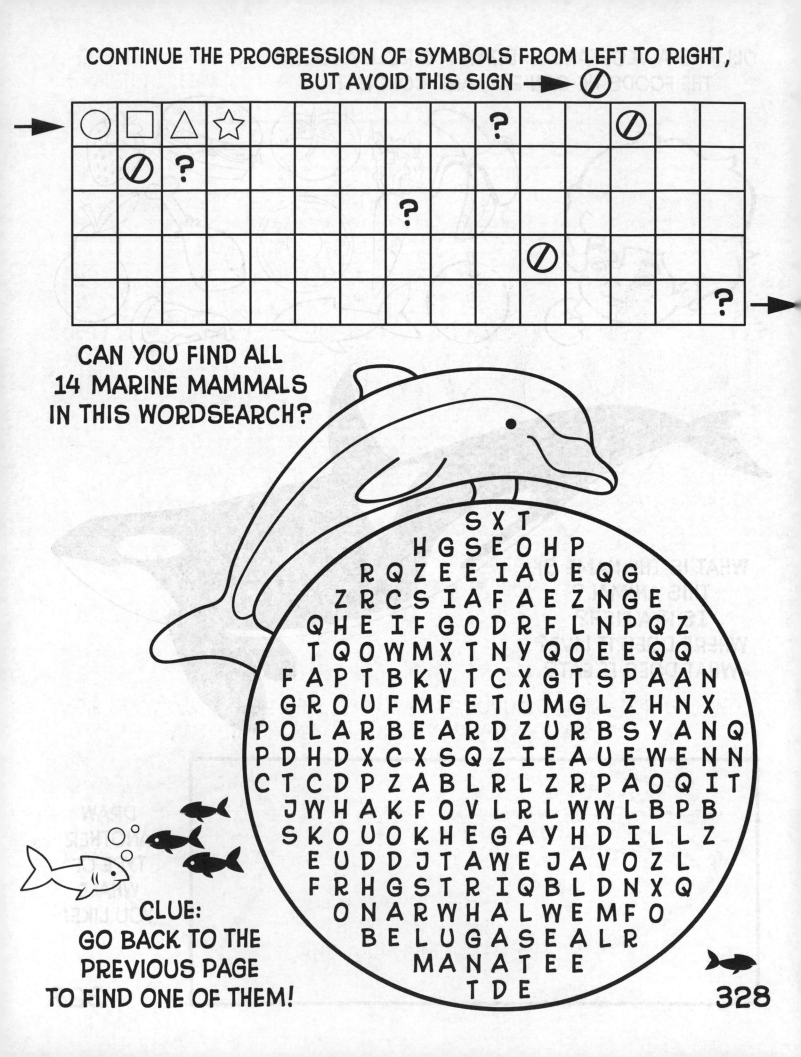

CAN YOU FIND ALL 14 MARINE MAMMALS IN THIS WORDSEARCH?

```
          S X T
        H G S E O H P
      R Q Z E E I A U E Q G
    Z R C S I A F A E Z N G E
    Q H E I F G O D R F L N P Q Z
    T Q O W M X T N Y Q O E E Q Q
  F A P T B K V T C X G T S P A A N
  G R O U F M F E T U M G L Z H N X
  P O L A R B E A R D Z U R B S Y A N Q
  P D H D X C X S Q Z I E A U E W E N N
  C T C D P Z A B L R L Z R P A O Q I T
  J W H A K F O V L R L W W L B P B
  S K O U O K H E G A Y H D I L L Z
    E U D D J T A W E J A V O Z L
    F R H G S T R I Q B L D N X Q
    O N A R W H A L W E M F O
      B E L U G A S E A L R
        M A N A T E E
          T D E
```

CLUE:
GO BACK TO THE
PREVIOUS PAGE
TO FIND ONE OF THEM!

328

EARTH HAS ONE MOON, MARS HAS TWO.
DO YOU KNOW THEIR NAMES?

P _ _ _ _ _ _ AND D _ _ _ _ _.

WHICH ONE OF THESE
INSECTS LIVES HERE? →

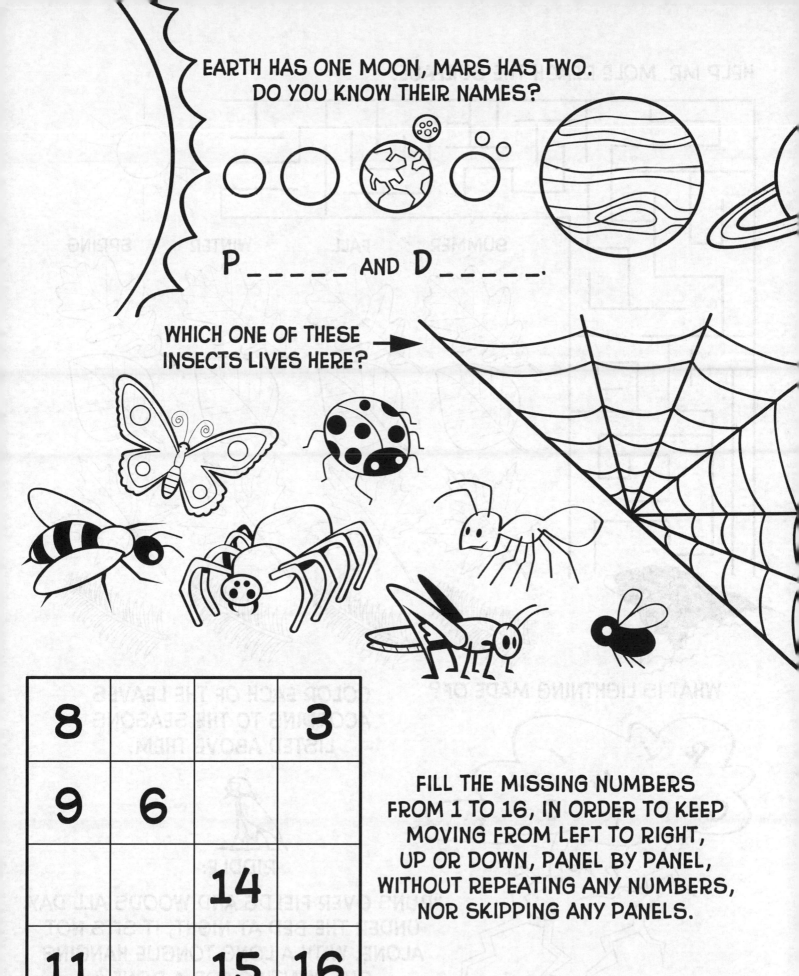

8		3
9	6	
	14	
11		15	16

FILL THE MISSING NUMBERS
FROM 1 TO 16, IN ORDER TO KEEP
MOVING FROM LEFT TO RIGHT,
UP OR DOWN, PANEL BY PANEL,
WITHOUT REPEATING ANY NUMBERS,
NOR SKIPPING ANY PANELS.

HELP MR. MOLE REACH THE SURFACE!

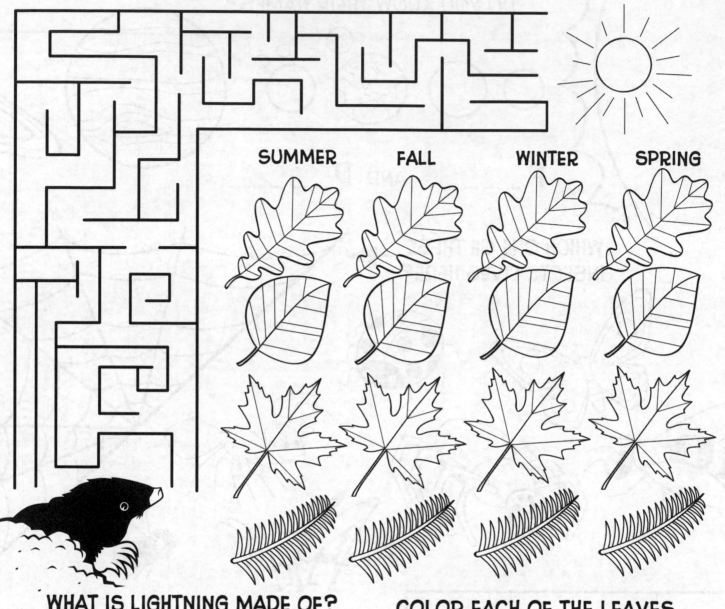

SUMMER   FALL   WINTER   SPRING

WHAT IS LIGHTNING MADE OF?

COLOR EACH OF THE LEAVES
ACORDING TO THE SEASONS
LISTED ABOVE THEM.

RIDDLE:

"RUNS OVER FIELDS AND WOODS ALL DAY.
UNDER THE BED AT NIGHT, IT SITS NOT
ALONE, WITH A LONG TONGUE HANGING
OUT, WAITING FOR A BONE."

DESIGN BOTH SIDES OF YOUR OWN COIN!

↔

REMEMBER: ONE SIDE MUST FEATURE YOUR PORTRAIT, AND THE OTHER, THE VALUE OF THE COIN.

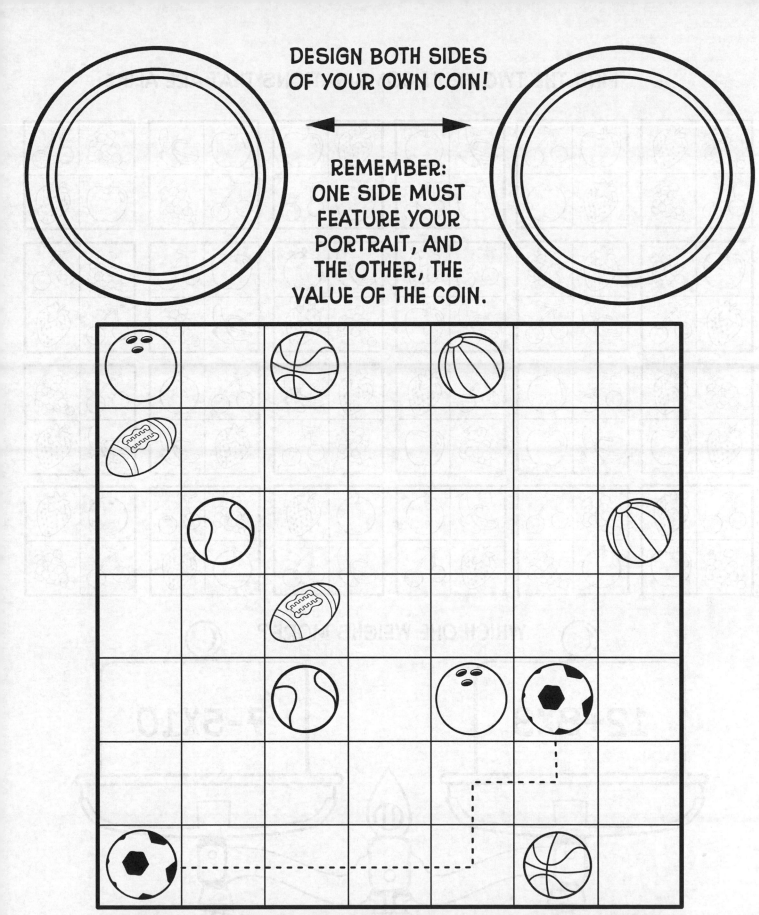

CONNECT THE IDENTICAL DRAWINGS USING ONLY VERTICAL AND HORIZONTAL LINES. LINES CANNOT CROSS EACH OTHER, AND ONLY ONE LINE IS ALLOWED TO GO THROUGH EACH TILE.

FIND THE TWO FRUIT COMBINATIONS THAT ARE ALIKE.

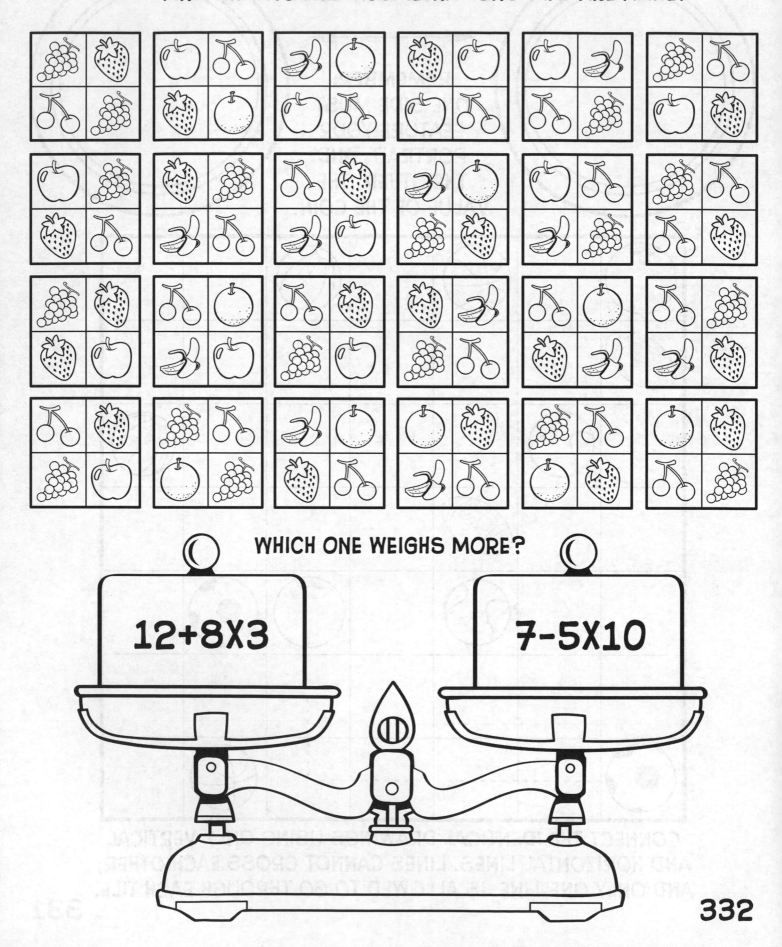

WHICH ONE WEIGHS MORE?

12+8X3

7-5X10

WOULD YOU HELP SALLY DESIGN HER BLANKET? BY DIVIDING A SQUARE DIAGONALLY, AND FILLING ONE HALF BLACK, YOU MAKE A TRIANGLE. IF YOU DO THAT TO OTHER SQUARES YOU CAN CREATE ANY PATTERN YOU CAN IMAGINE!

ONE OF THESE DOES NOT BELONG IN THIS GROUP.

CAN YOU THINK OF ANOTHER ANIMAL THAT'S BLACK AND WHITE? DRAW IT HERE! ➔

WHICH PATH DOES THE RABBIT NEED TO FOLLOW TO PICK ALL THE EGGS?

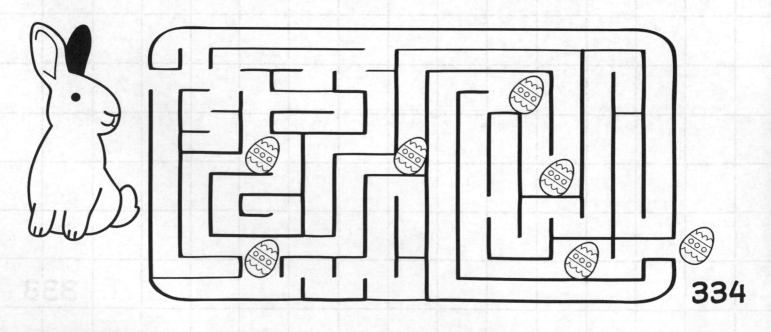

IDENTIFY AND COLOR ONLY THE TRIANGLES!

WHICH OF THE THREE BELLS IS SHE GOING TO RING?

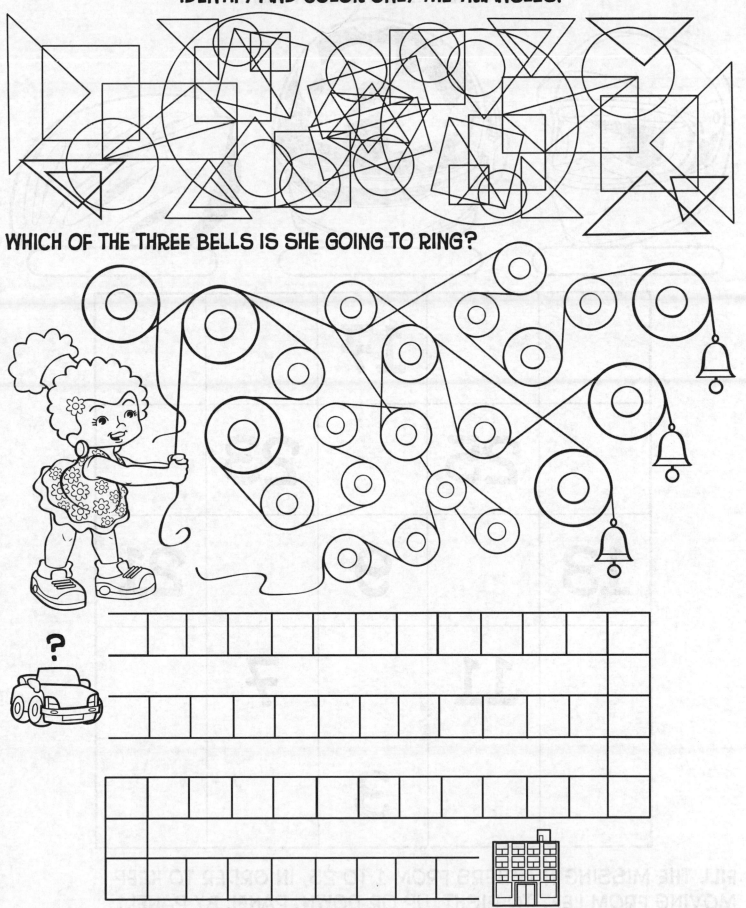

WHICH ROAD IS THE SHORTEST IF EACH TILE IS 10 FEET?

WHO WEARS THESE MODERN HELMETS?

FILL THE MISSING NUMBERS FROM 1 TO 25, IN ORDER TO KEEP
MOVING FROM LEFT TO RIGHT, UP OR DOWN, PANEL BY PANEL,
WITHOUT REPEATING ANY NUMBERS, NOR SKIPPING ANY PANELS.

WHICH ONE OF THESE FOOTPRINTS BELONGS TO THE BOOT ON THE LEFT?

HOW TALL IS THIS BRIDGE, IF ITS LENGTH IS 4 TIMES ITS HEIGHT?

3 FT.

?

IN ORDER TO BUILD THE MAYAN PYRAMID, MAKE IT SO THE ADDITION OF EACH NUMBER ON THE LEFT TO THE NUMBER ON THE RIGHT EQUALS THE NUMBER OF THE BRICK ON TOP OF BOTH.

224

93 109

57

30

COMPLETE THE LOGICAL LEFT TO RIGHT PROGRESSION PER ROW.

1	2	4		8			16	18		
1	4		13		22					
2	6	10			34					
5		20	25		45	55				
1	3	5		13						

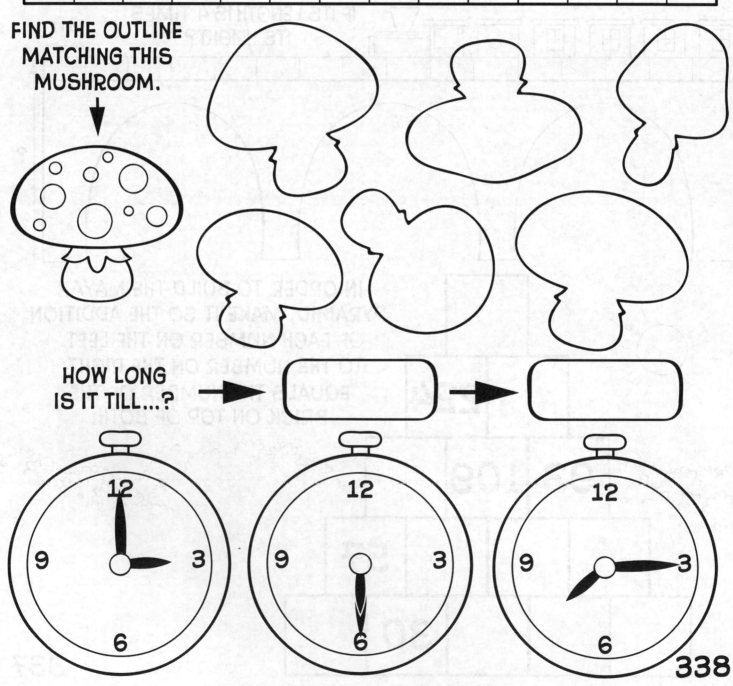

FIND THE OUTLINE MATCHING THIS MUSHROOM.

HOW LONG IS IT TILL...?

338

HELP BILLY FIND HIS FOOTBALL, AND WHILE YOU'RE AT IT, SEE HOW MANY WORDS RELATED TO THE KING OF SPORTS CAN YOU FIND BELOW! CLUE: ONE OF THEM IS ALSO AN AFRICAN EQUID.

```
E N C R O A C H M E N T
N E U T R A L Z O N E K
I B U T T O N H O O K I
C P N A K S Q U I B E C
K E S C R I M M A G E K
E U A K B O O T L E G G
L J B L I T Z J G W D D
B Z L E Y N J B U L D O
A E O F F E N C E K E W
C B C N A U D I B L E N
K R K W D E F E N C E C
L A T E R A L C A T C H
```

FILL THE CIRCLES SO A=B

2 (A) → X3 → ( ) X2 → ( ) -2 → X3 → ( ) -6 → ( ) -22 → ( ) X4 → ( ) -22 → ( ) B
339

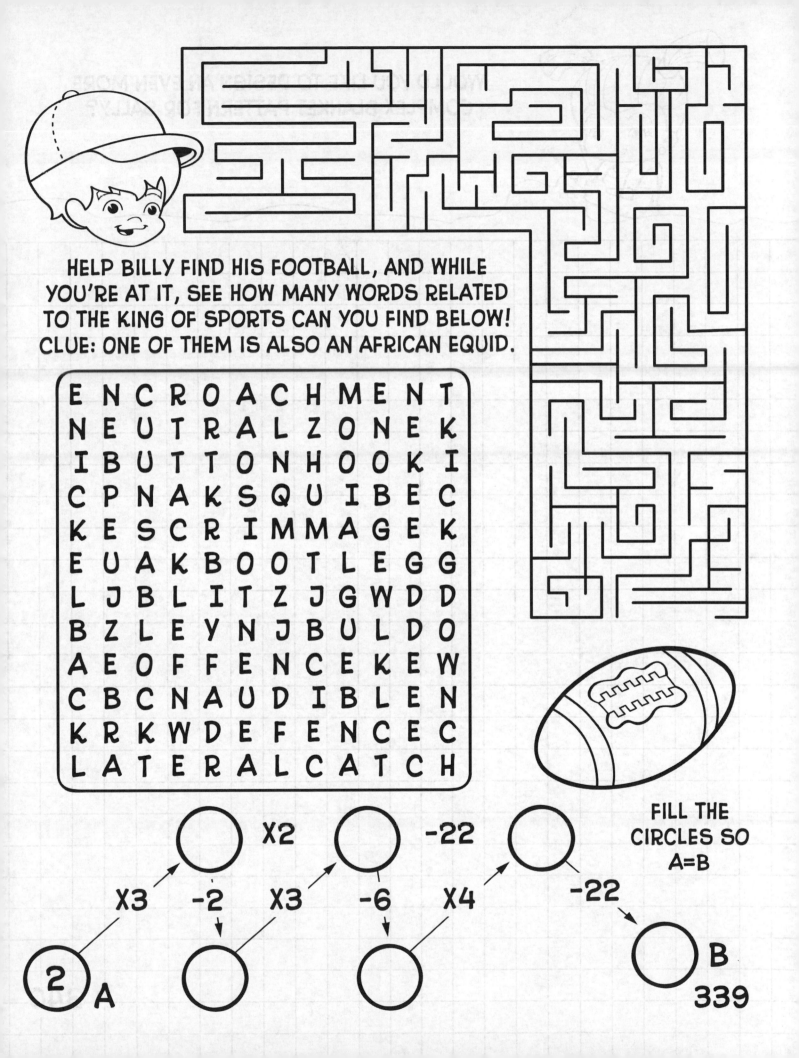

WOULD YOU LIKE TO DESIGN AN EVEN MORE
COMPLEX BLANKET PATTERN FOR SALLY?

CAN YOU GUESS WHAT THE PHOTOGRAPHER WAS SHOOTING AT?

HOW LONG IS IT TILL...?

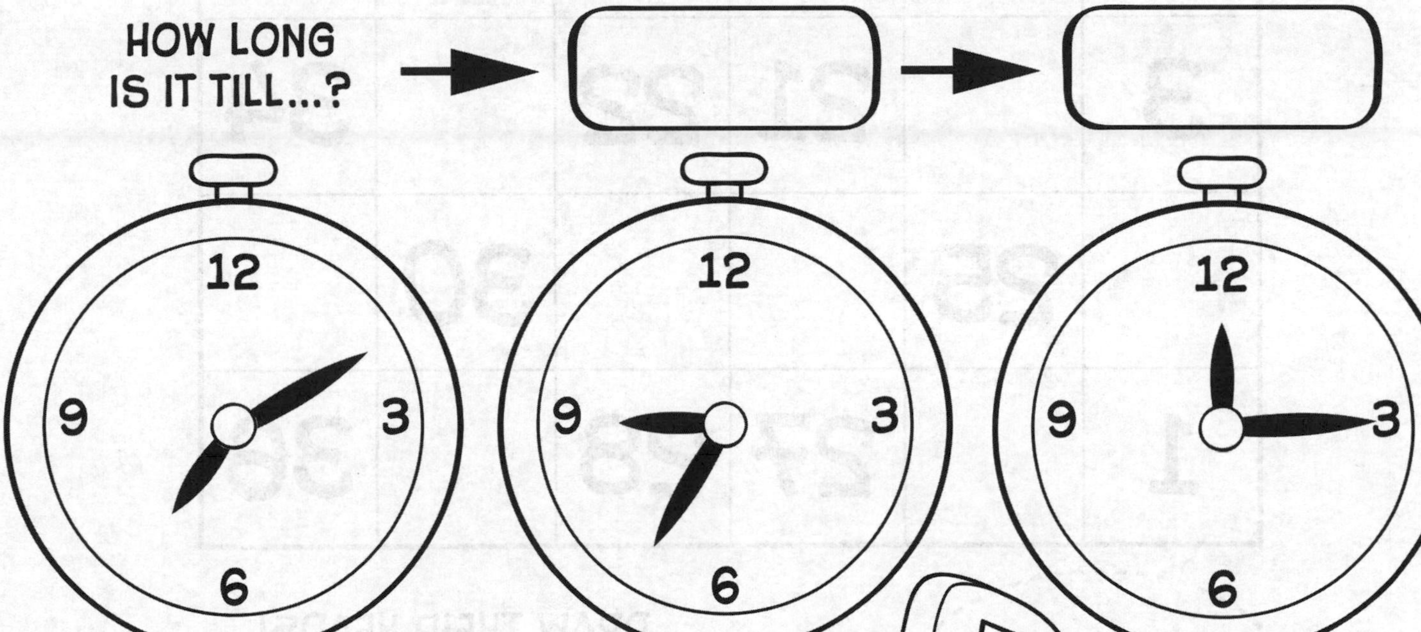

COLOR THE BEST TOOLS TO BUILD THIS BIRDHOUSE.

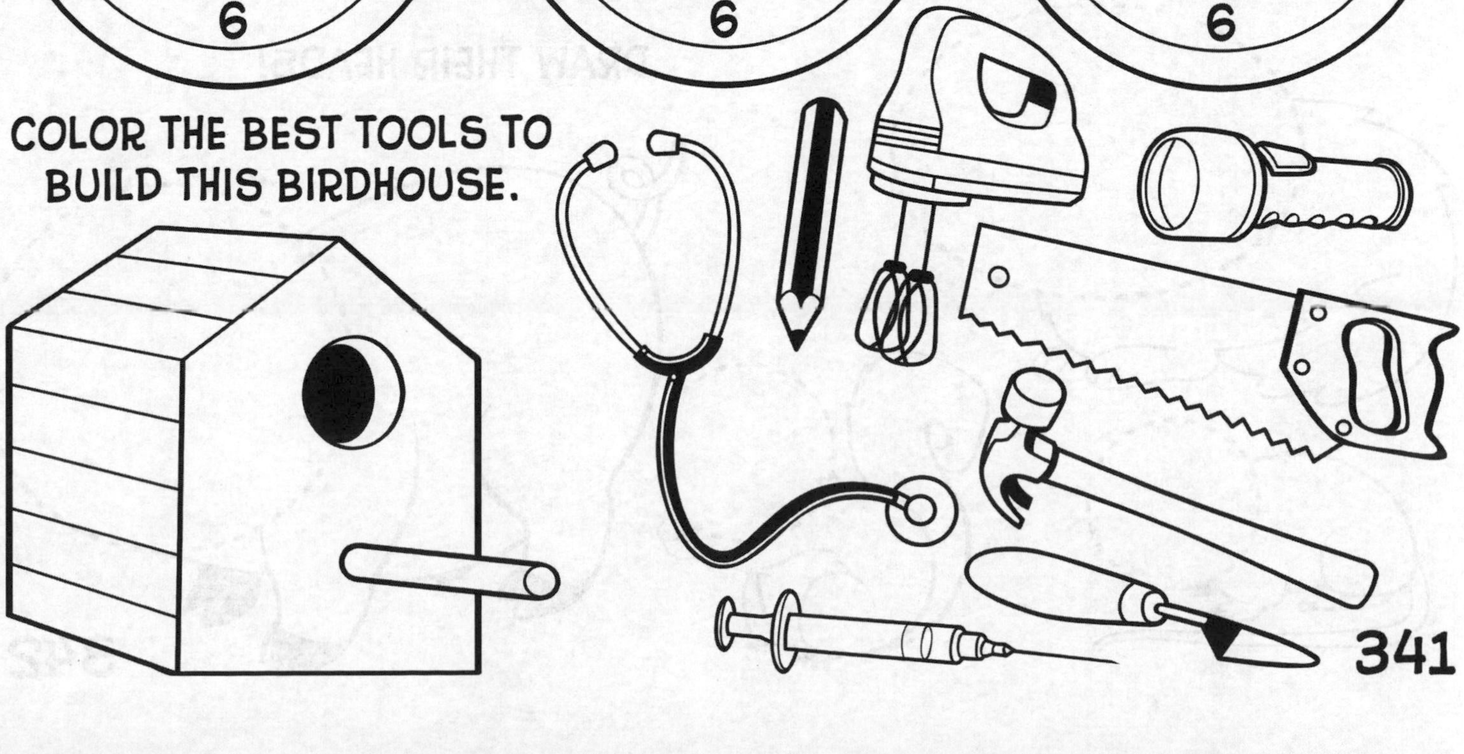

FILL THE MISSING NUMBERS FROM 1 TO 25, IN ORDER TO KEEP MOVING FROM LEFT TO RIGHT, UP OR DOWN, PANEL BY PANEL, WITHOUT REPEATING ANY NUMBERS, NOR SKIPPING ANY PANELS.

8		12	13		15
	10			17	
6		20	19		33
3		21	22		34
	25			30	
1		27	28		36

DRAW THEIR HEADS!

WHAT IS THE NAME OF THIS ANIMAL?

WHERE DOES IT LIVE?

COLOR THE BEST TOOLS TO BAKE THIS CAKE.

WHO USED TO WEAR THESE ANCIENT HELMETS?

343

WHICH ONE WEIGHS LESS?

6X10-9

25X2+2

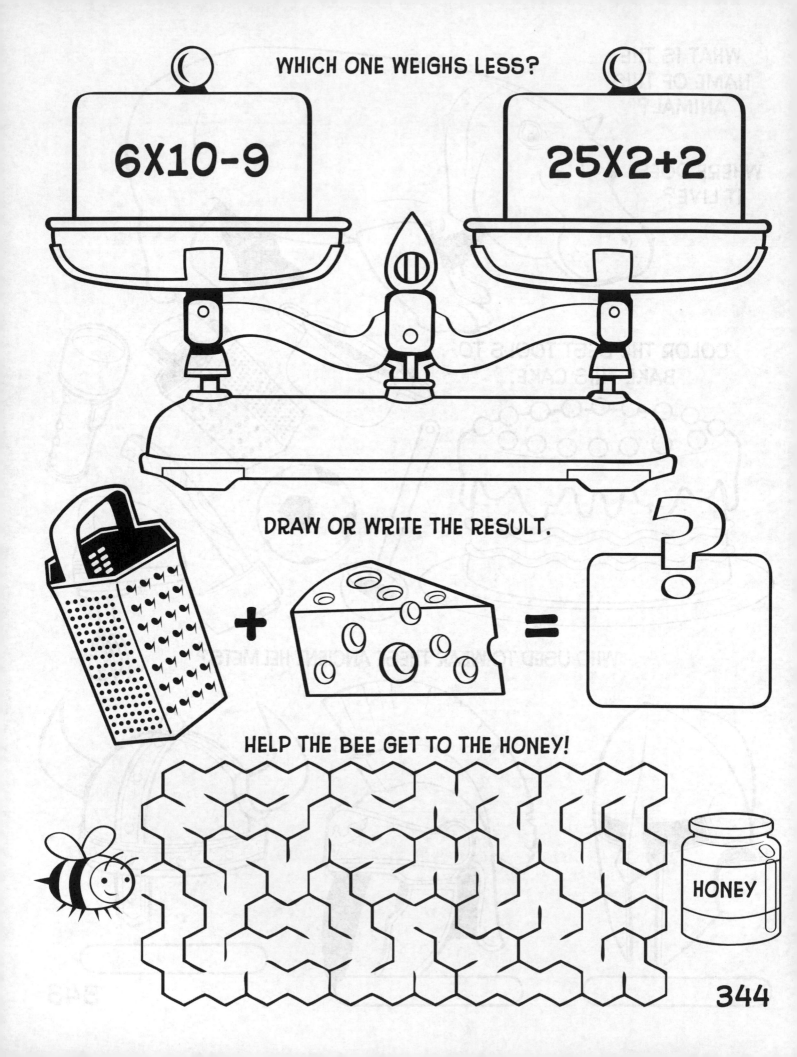

DRAW OR WRITE THE RESULT.

+ = ?

HELP THE BEE GET TO THE HONEY!

HONEY

344

HELP THE LITTLE EXPLORER ESCAPE FROM THE CAVE!

345

INSIDE EACH CIRCLE, DRAW A FRUIT MATCHING THE INITIALS BELOW.

C   B   P

WHICH WAY IS
THIS WHEEL
TURNING?

CROSSWORDS.

1.

2.

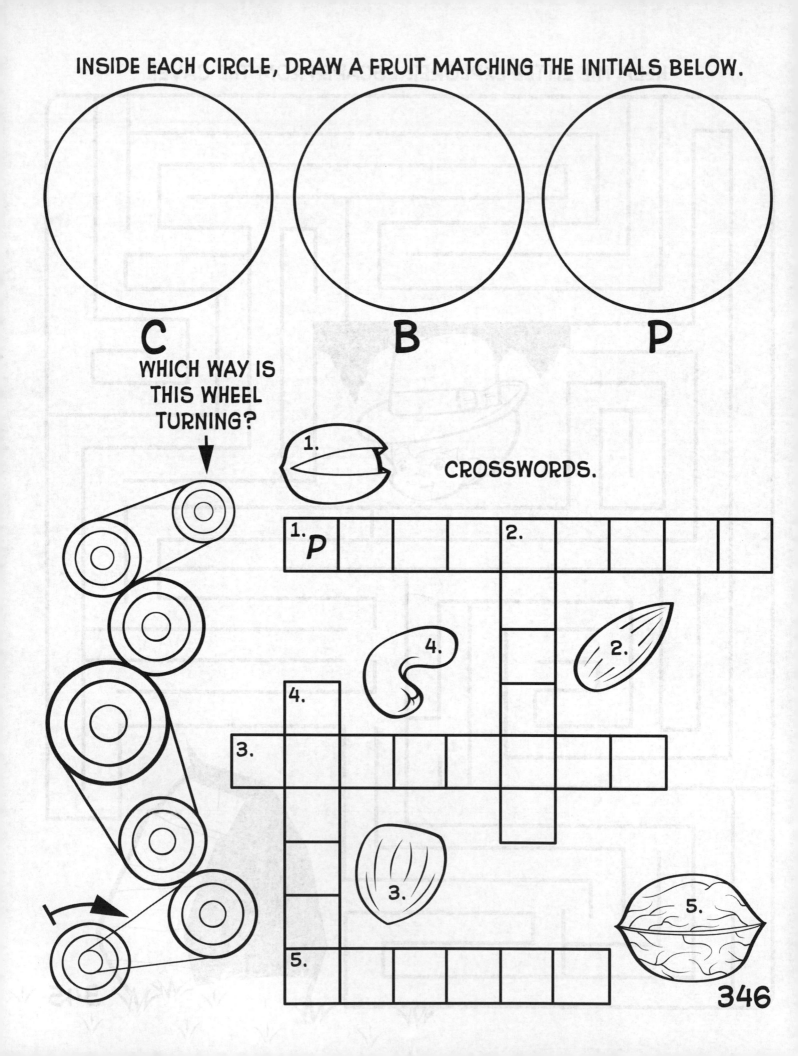

FIND THE TWO FRUIT COMBINATIONS THAT ARE ALIKE.

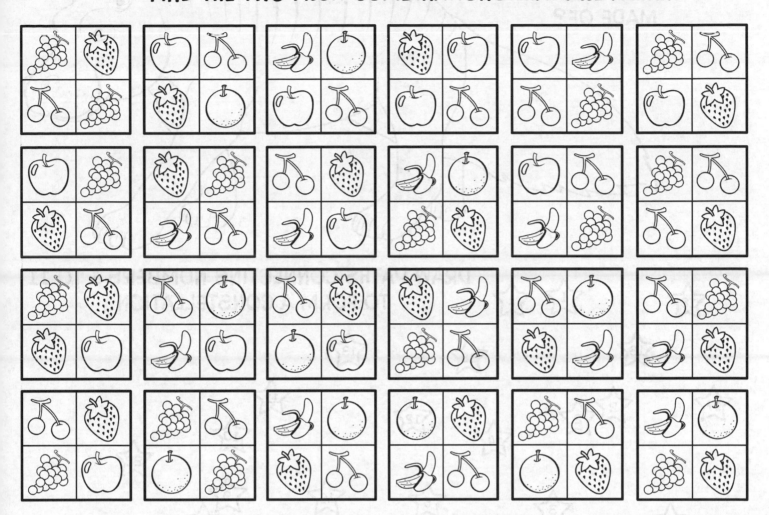

WHAT SHOULDN'T BE HERE?

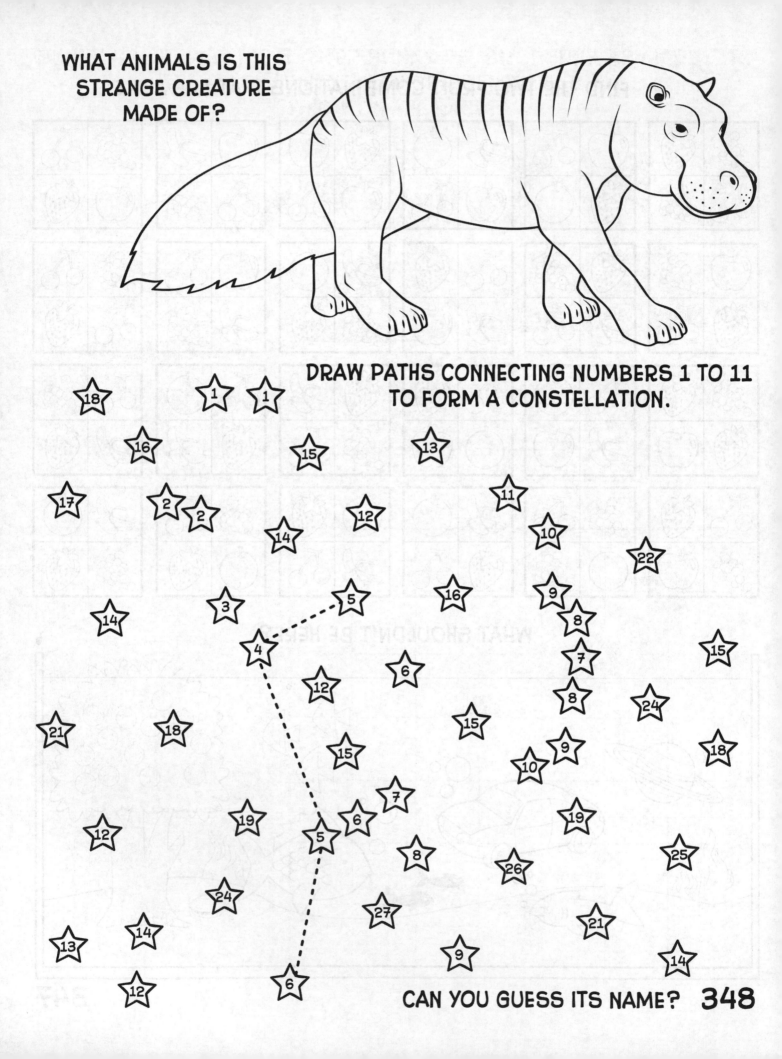

WHAT ANIMALS IS THIS STRANGE CREATURE MADE OF?

DRAW PATHS CONNECTING NUMBERS 1 TO 11 TO FORM A CONSTELLATION.

CAN YOU GUESS ITS NAME? 348

AT 20 MPH, THE BOAT HAS SAILED 1/4 OF THE DISTANCE
TO THE TINY ISLAND IN 12 MINUTES. WHAT'S THE TOTAL DISTANCE?

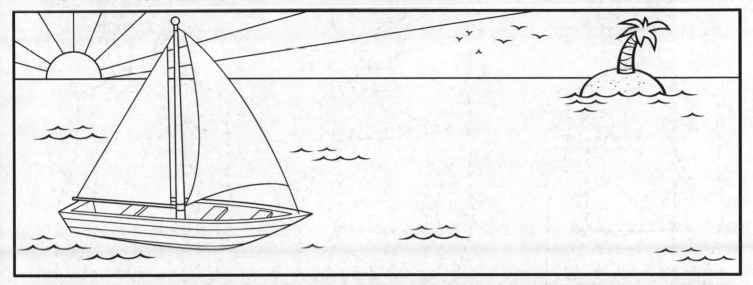

CONNECT EACH NUMBERED CIRCLE WITH ONLY VERTICAL OR HORIZONTAL,
NON OVERLAPPING LINES. THE NUMBER ON EACH CIRCLE INDICATES
THE NUMBER OF LINES EACH ONE IS ALLOWED.

② ③ ③ ①

①

② ④ ②

①

③ ④ ③

① ①

① ① ②

② ③ ② ②

349

DRAW A VIKING, A COWBOY, AND A SPARTAN WARRIOR!

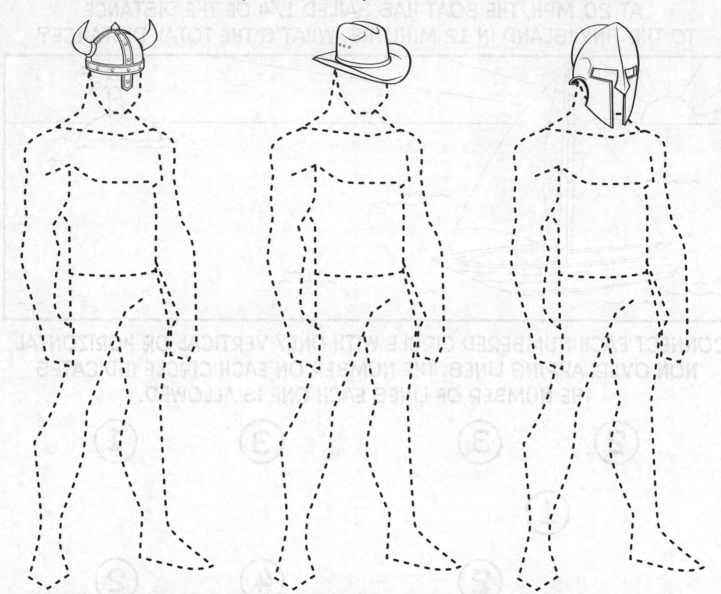

CAN YOU GUESS WHAT THE PHOTOGRAPHER TAKING A PICTURE OF?

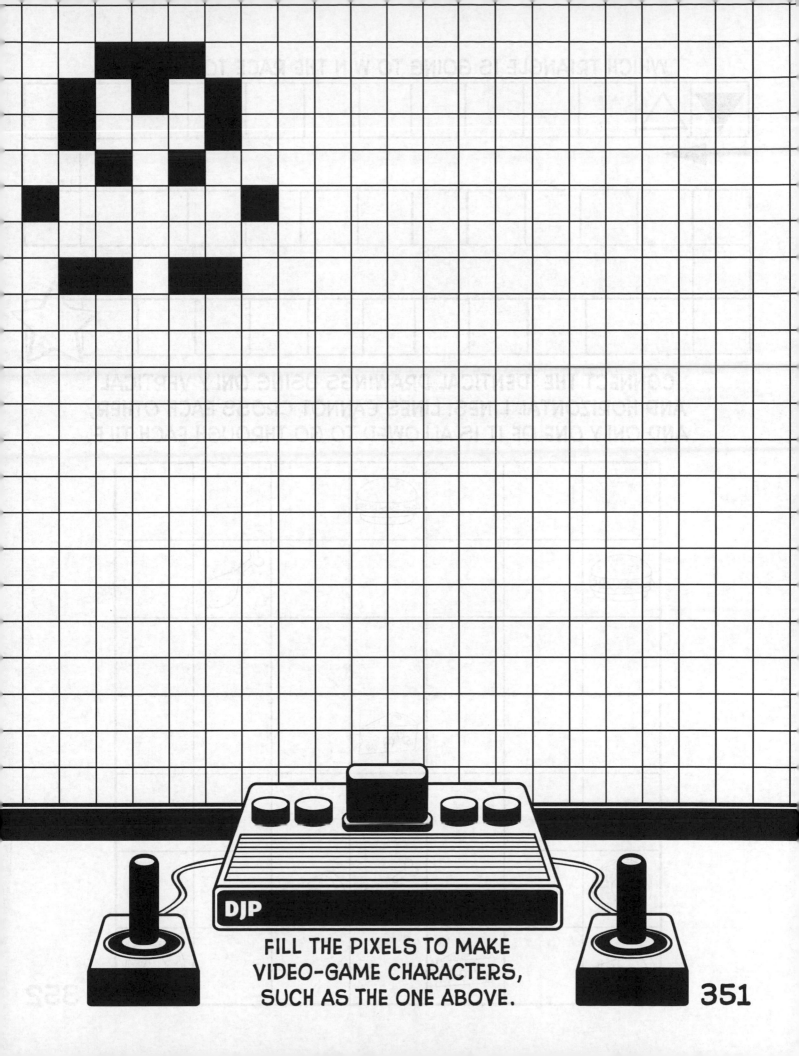

FILL THE PIXELS TO MAKE
VIDEO-GAME CHARACTERS,
SUCH AS THE ONE ABOVE.

351

WHICH TRIANGLE IS GOING TO WIN THE RACE TO THE END?

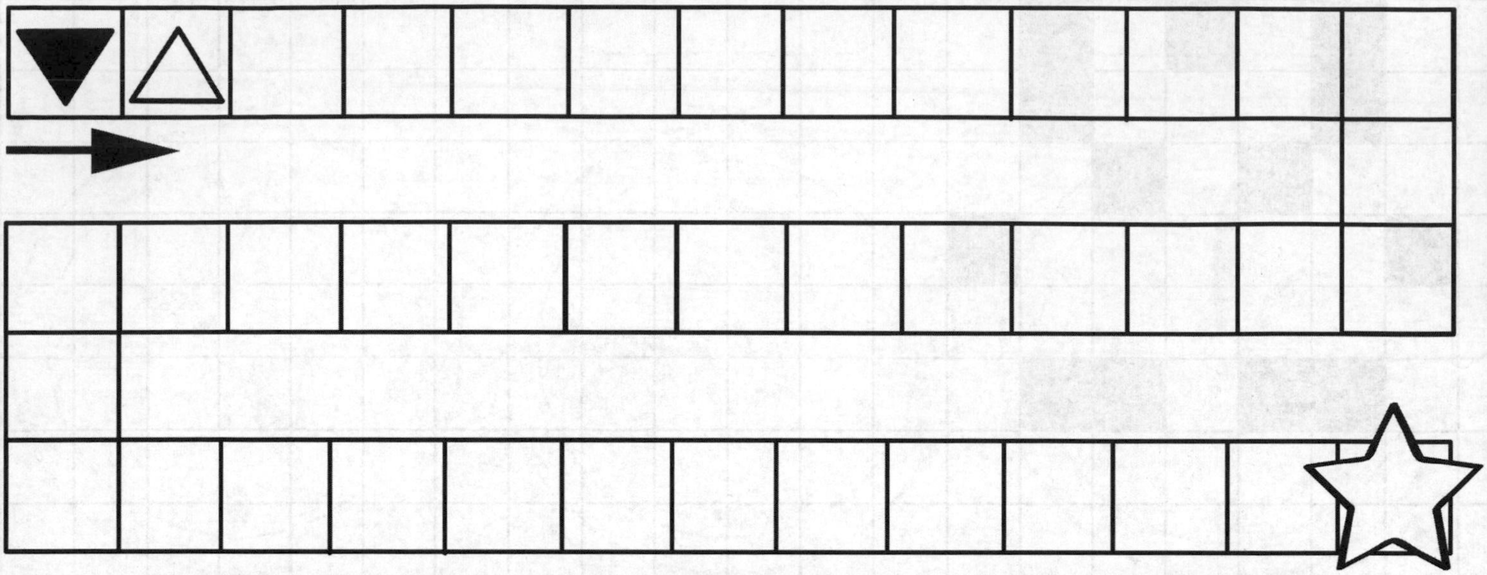

CONNECT THE IDENTICAL DRAWINGS USING ONLY VERTICAL AND HORIZONTAL LINES. LINES CANNOT CROSS EACH OTHER, AND ONLY ONE OF IT IS ALLOWED TO GO THROUGH EACH TILE.

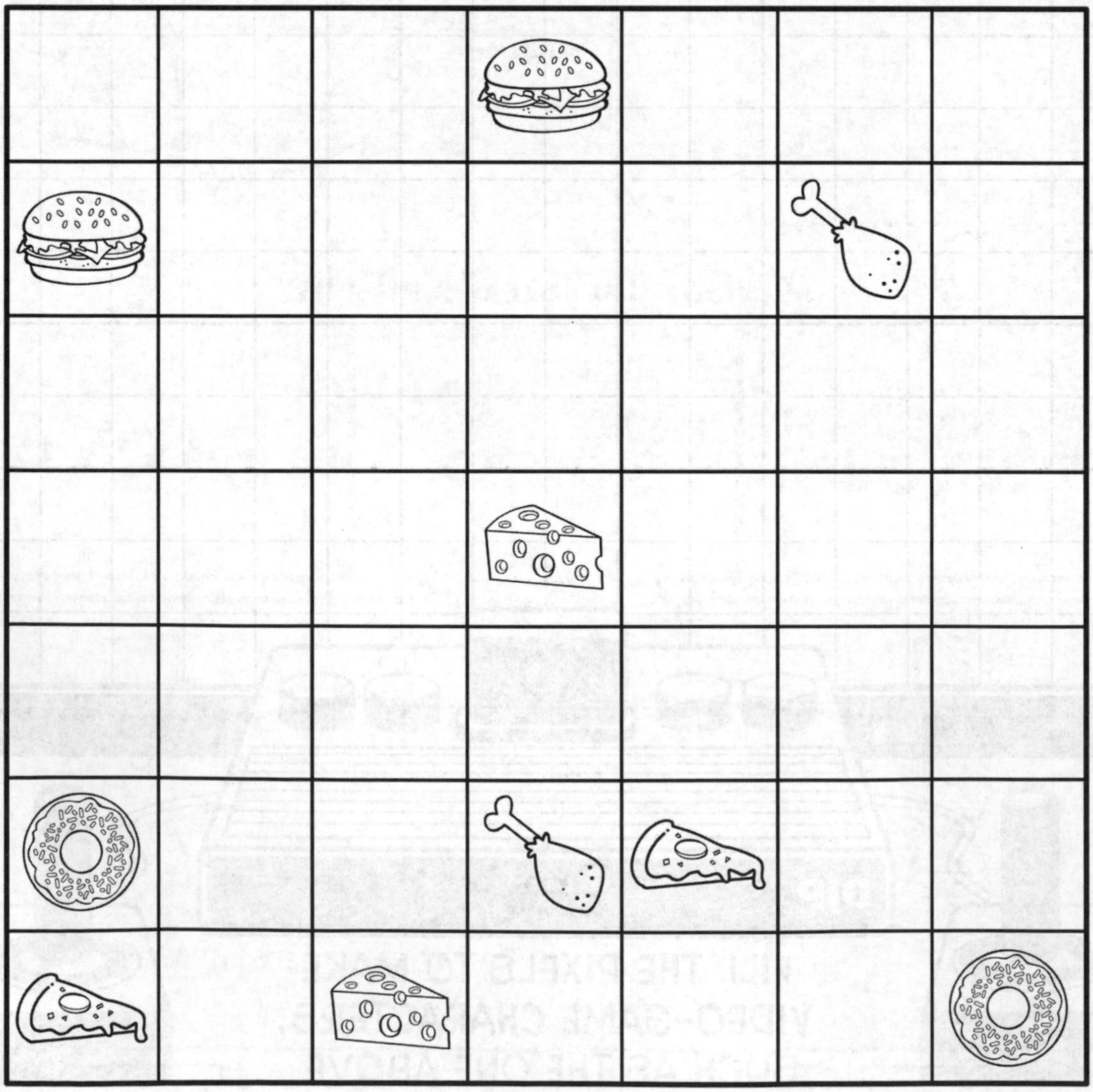

352

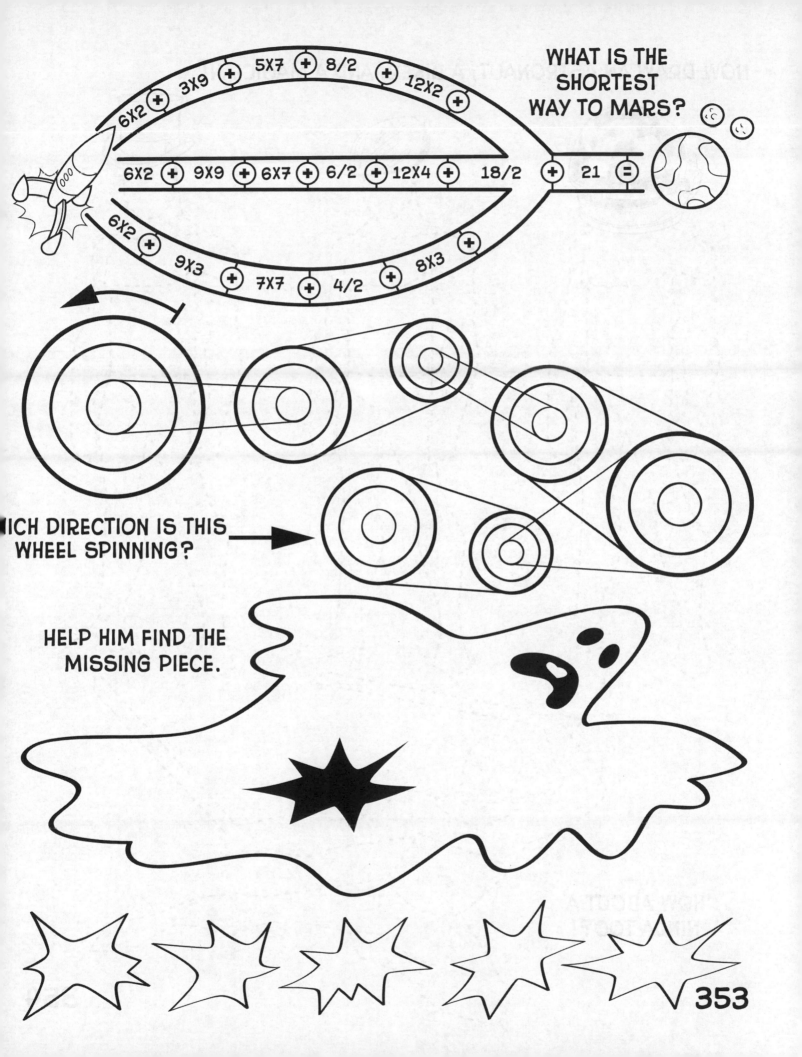

WHAT IS THE SHORTEST WAY TO MARS?

6X2 + 3X9 + 5X7 + 8/2 + 12X2

6X2 + 9X9 + 6X7 + 6/2 + 12X4 + 18/2 + 21 =

6X2 + 9X3 + 7X7 + 4/2 + 8X3

WHICH DIRECTION IS THIS WHEEL SPINNING?

HELP HIM FIND THE MISSING PIECE.

353

NOW DRAW AN ASTRONAUT, A BIKER, AND A MAGICIAN!

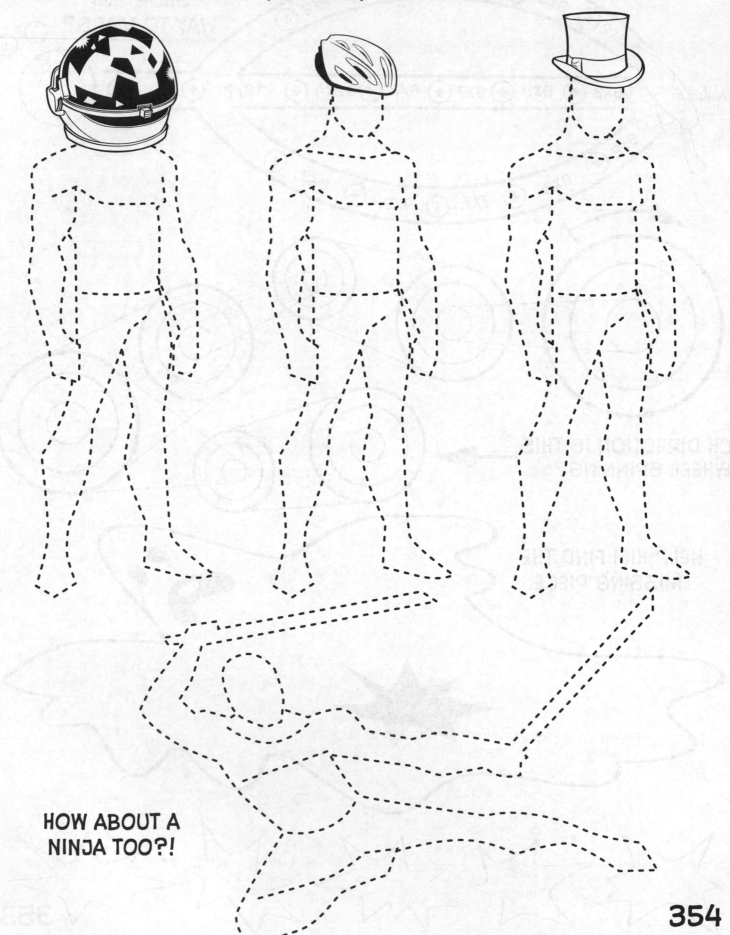

HOW ABOUT A
NINJA TOO?!

DO YOU KNOW THE COLORS
OF THE RAINBOW? COLOR IT!

SELECT AND COLOR ONLY
THE INGREDIENTS YOU NEED TO
MAKE A SALAD IN THIS BOWL.

WHO
LIVES
IN
HERE?

IN THIS NEW GAME OF TIC-TAC-TOE, THE GOAL IS
TO AVOID VERTICAL, HORIZONTAL, OR DIAGONAL
LINES OF UP TO FOUR CROSSES OR CIRCLES EACH.

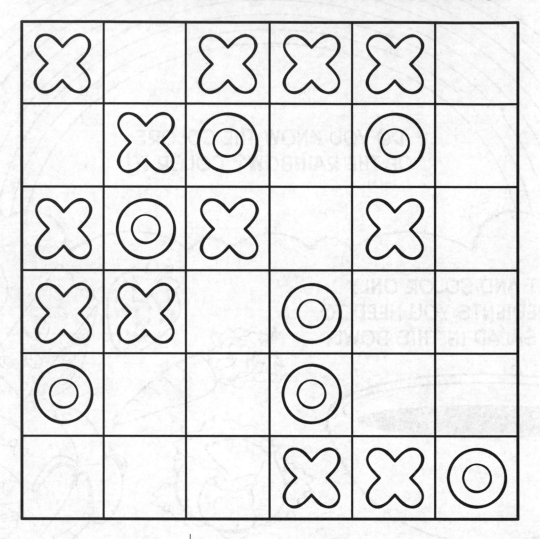

IF THIS BOAT CATCHES 2
BIG FISH EVERY HOUR, AND
10 SMALLER FISH EVERY 10
MINUTES, HOW MANY WILL
IT HAVE WHEN THE DAY IS
OVER?

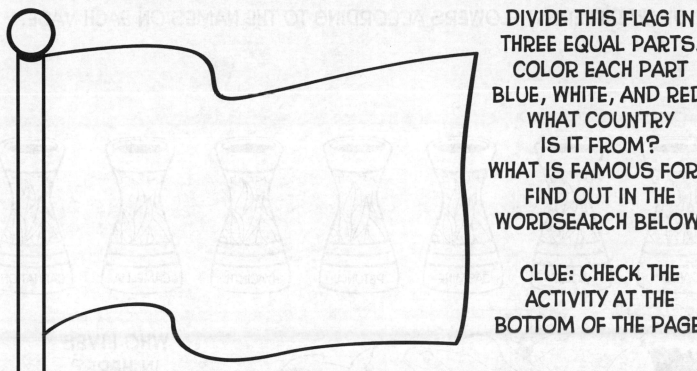

DIVIDE THIS FLAG IN
THREE EQUAL PARTS.
COLOR EACH PART
BLUE, WHITE, AND RED.
WHAT COUNTRY
IS IT FROM?
WHAT IS FAMOUS FOR?
FIND OUT IN THE
WORDSEARCH BELOW!

CLUE: CHECK THE
ACTIVITY AT THE
BOTTOM OF THE PAGE.

```
R O L A N D G A R R O S S F C R O I S S A N T B C
L O U V R E M U S E U M R F C O Q A U V I N C A H
C Y D Z P S U H D I K O O S D A U N C Z A A A G O
C H A M P A G N E Q I P E L J V P D R Y D P M U C
I S F W H S N O I D A T L B I S Q N E V S O E E O
T O K E P C I L S P R W W I N E J R T M R L M T L
R W O C A N O R M A N D Y W G Y R O E O B E B T A
O L W T R U W T C A I N G R J I E E T N S O E E T
E D Y L I S Q S C B I Y L V F G W N H T A N R D E
N E B A S H E J O H X C G O U K S P M M S U T J B
N O T R E D A M E C A T H E D R A L E A T I L J R
Z M L T E B O C Y J D N P K C Z A N Q R E O J T E
R P L N P I Q T O U R D E F R A N C E T R A O S A
F S E I F F E L T O W E R L Y R P H W R I C X F D
E R J A C Q U E S L O U I S D A V I D E X S O R V
```

DRAW OR WRITE THE RESULT.

DRAW DIFFERENT FLOWERS ACCORDING TO THE NAMES ON EACH VASE.

DAHLIA   VIOLET   JASMINE   PETUNIA   HYACINTH   CAMELLIA   CARNATION

WHO LIVES IN HERE?

IT TAKES THIS TRAIN 10 MINUTES TO COVER 200 FT.
HOW LONG WILL IT TAKE IT TO TRAVEL 160 MILES?

MIAMI OR BUST!

IF THE PLANE FLIES AT 120 KNOTS, AND THE DISTANCE TO MIAMI IS 600 MILES, HOW LONG WILL IT TAKE IT TO GET THERE?

1 KNOT = 1.15 MI/H.

HOW MANY PENCILS CAN YOU COUNT?

IF THE BOAT'S LENGTH OVERALL MEASURES TWICE ITS HEIGHT, AND IS FOUR TIMES SHORTER THAN THE ORCA'S LENGTH, THEN HOW LONG IS THE WHALE?

SOLVE.

12-3	+ 6	-		X 7	- 14	X		+ 5	/ 3	X 8	=

CONNECT EACH NUMBERED CIRCLE WITH ONLY VERTICAL OR HORIZONTAL, NON OVERLAPPING LINES. THE NUMBER ON EACH CIRCLE INDICATES THE NUMBER OF LINES EACH ONE IS ALLOWED.

(2) (2) (3) (2)

(1)

(2) (4) (3)

(1) (1) (2)

(2)

(1) (2) (2)

(3) (4) (4) (3) (3)

(2) (3) (3) (3) (2)

HOW MANY CIRCLES ARE IN THIS TABLE?
HOW MANY STARS? AND SQUARES?

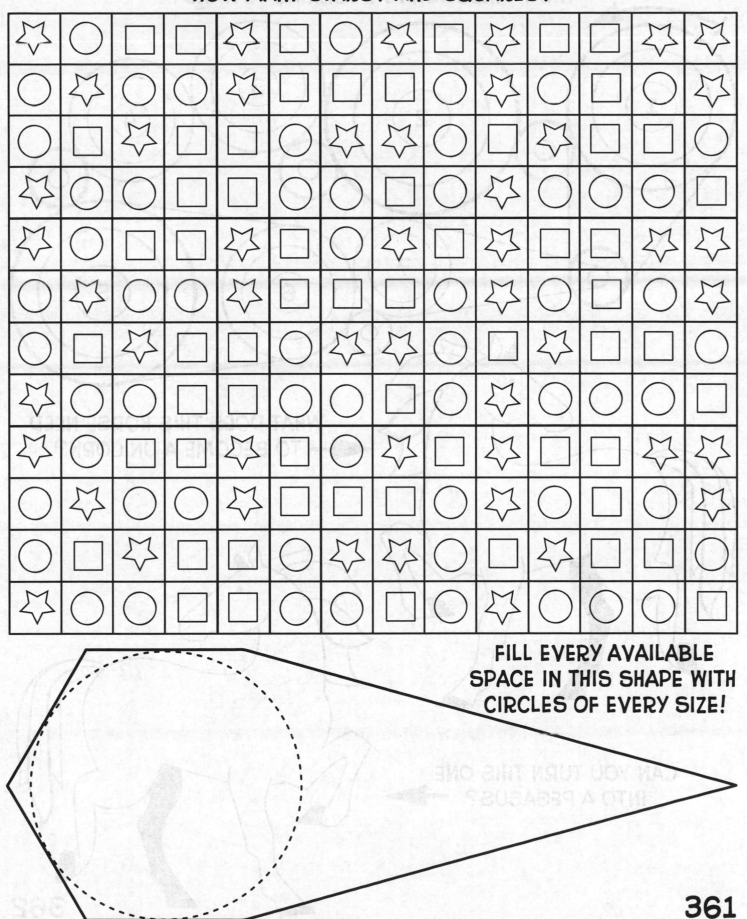

FILL EVERY AVAILABLE
SPACE IN THIS SHAPE WITH
CIRCLES OF EVERY SIZE!

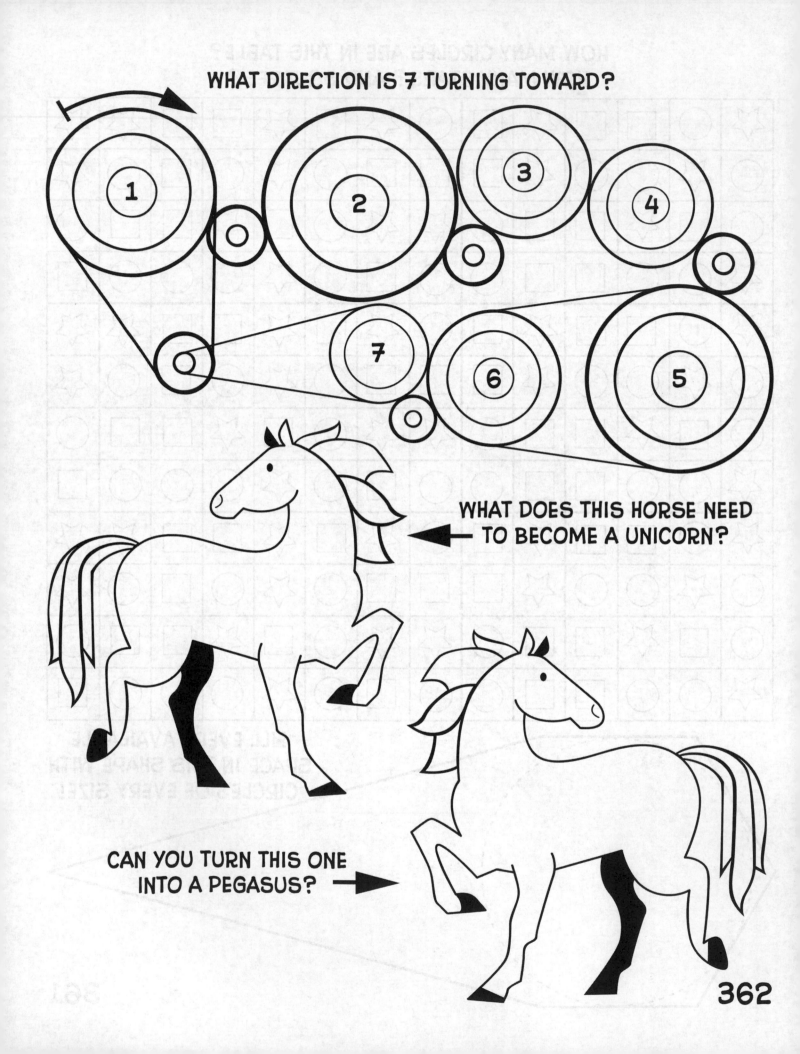

WHAT DIRECTION IS 7 TURNING TOWARD?

WHAT DOES THIS HORSE NEED TO BECOME A UNICORN?

CAN YOU TURN THIS ONE INTO A PEGASUS? →

362

NOW CREATE MORE COMPLEX
VIDEO-GAME CHARACTERS,
SUCH AS THE ONE ABOVE.

CAN YOU FIND THE MISSING
SYMBOL IN THIS ANCIENT
EGYPTIAN PYRAMID?

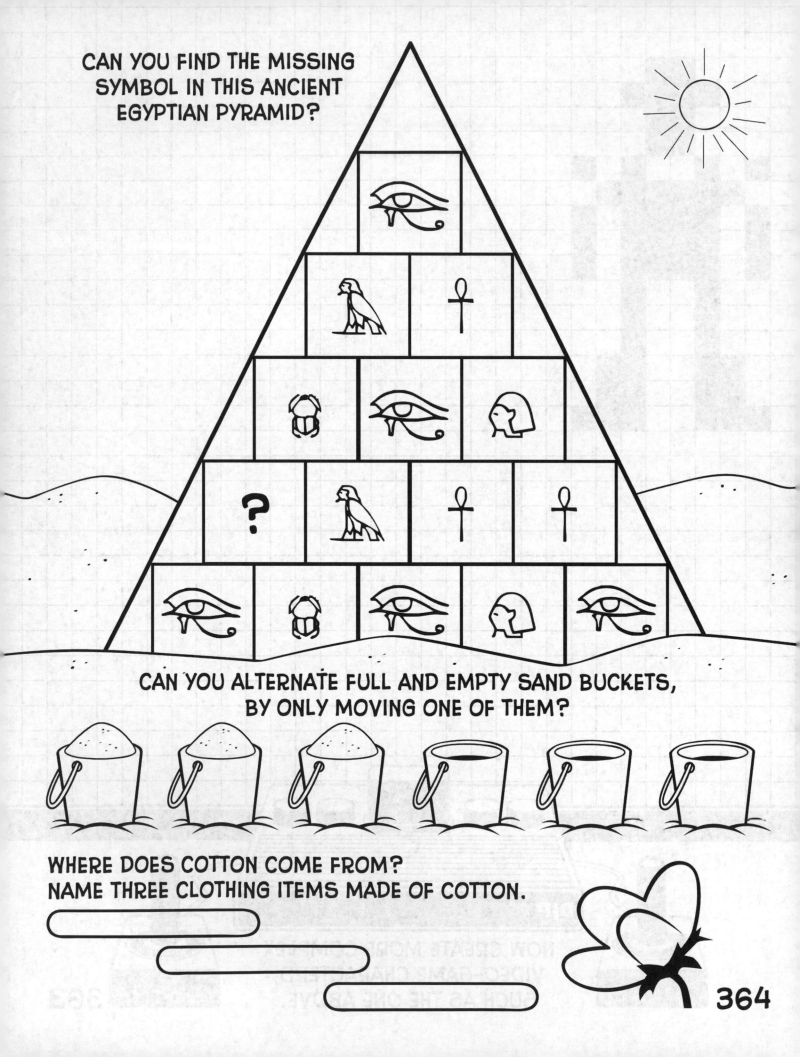

CAN YOU ALTERNATE FULL AND EMPTY SAND BUCKETS,
BY ONLY MOVING ONE OF THEM?

WHERE DOES COTTON COME FROM?
NAME THREE CLOTHING ITEMS MADE OF COTTON.

364

HOW CAN THIS SHEET BE SPLIT, SO EACH OF THE KIDS GETS A PIECE OF THE SAME SIZE AND SHAPE?

TO CRACK THIS GAME OF TIC-TAC-TOE, THE GOAL IS TO AVOID VERTICAL, HORIZONTAL, OR DIAGONAL LINES OF UP TO FOUR CROSSES OR CIRCLES.

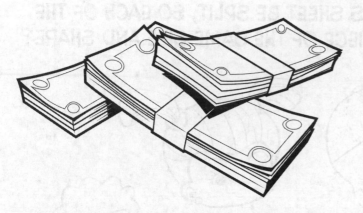

YOUR GRANDMOTHER GIVES YOU A 15 DOLLAR ALLOWANCE IN TWO BILLS.
ONE OF THE BILLS IS FIVE DOLLARS. WHAT IS THE OTHER BILL?

IN WHICH BOX DO YOU END UP IF YOU FOLLOW THE ARROWS?

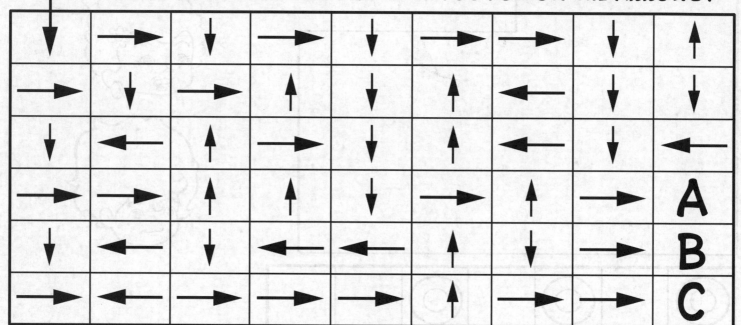

IN THIS CLASSIC GAME, CAN YOU MAKE THE "BULL" TURN ITS HEAD BY MOVING ONLY TWO MATCHES?

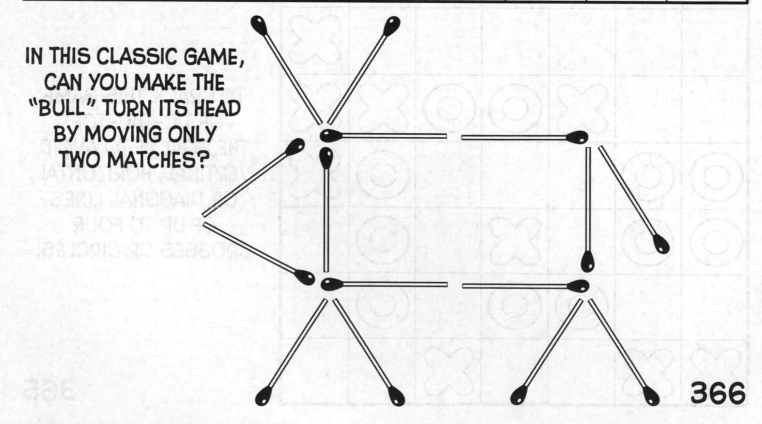

366

CONNECT THE IDENTICAL DRAWINGS USING ONLY VERTICAL AND HORIZONTAL LINES. LINES CANNOT CROSS EACH OTHER, AND ONLY ONE LINE IS ALLOWED TO GO THROUGH EACH TILE.

FIGURE OUT THE NUMERICAL VALUE OF EACH OBJECT.

CONNECT EACH FISH TO ITS CORRESPONDING HOOK!

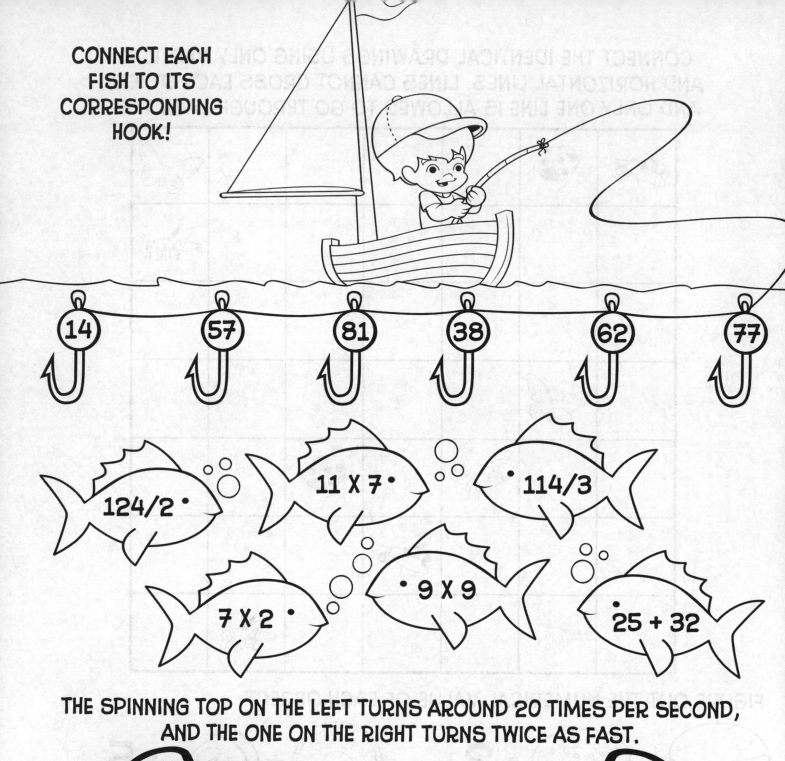

14 57 81 38 62 77

124/2

11 X 7

114/3

7 X 2

9 X 9

25 + 32

THE SPINNING TOP ON THE LEFT TURNS AROUND 20 TIMES PER SECOND, AND THE ONE ON THE RIGHT TURNS TWICE AS FAST.

HOW MANY TIMES DO THEY TURN IN ONE AND A HALF MINUTES?

CAN YOU GET RID OF
THREE MATCHES, AND
BE LEFT WITH THREE
TRIANGLES?

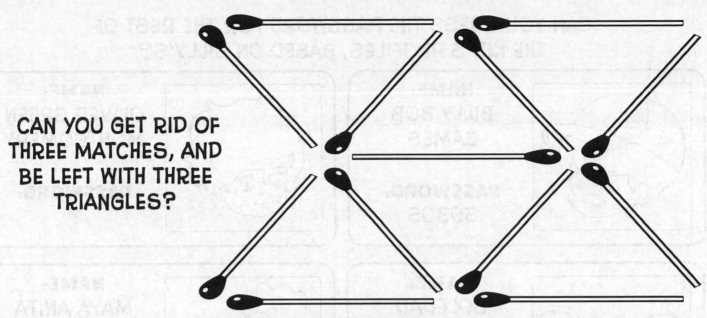

CRACK THE SUDOKU!
EACH ELEMENT CAN ONLY BE PLACED ONCE ON EACH LINE,
ONCE ON EACH ROW, AND ONCE IN EACH 3 BY 2 CELLS GRID.

369

CAN YOU GUESS THE PASSWORD FOR THE REST OF THE KID'S PROFILES, BASED ON BILLY'S?

NAME:
BILLY BOB JAMES

PASSWORD:
50305

NAME:
OLIVER GREEN MONTGOMERY

PASSWORD:
?

NAME:
SOLEDAD ROBERTSON

PASSWORD:
?

NAME:
MAYA ANITA RODRIGUEZ

PASSWORD:
?

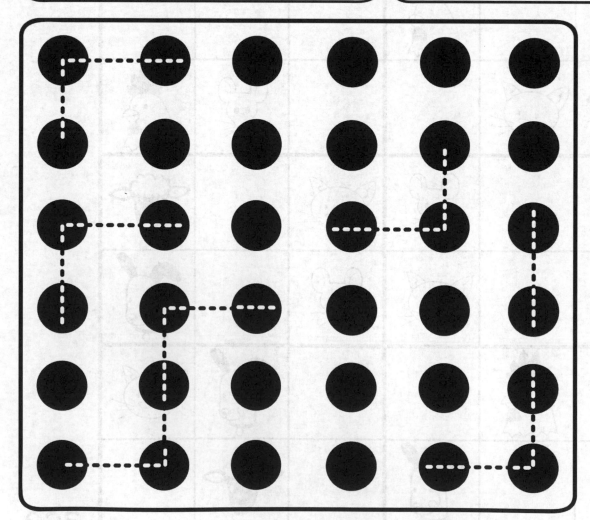

JOIN ALL DOTS USING A SINGLE LINE, WHICH GOES FROM ONE DOT TO THE NEXT, CROSSING EACH ONE ONLY ONCE!

WHERE DOES SILK COME FROM?
NAME THREE CLOTHING ITEMS
MADE OF SILK.

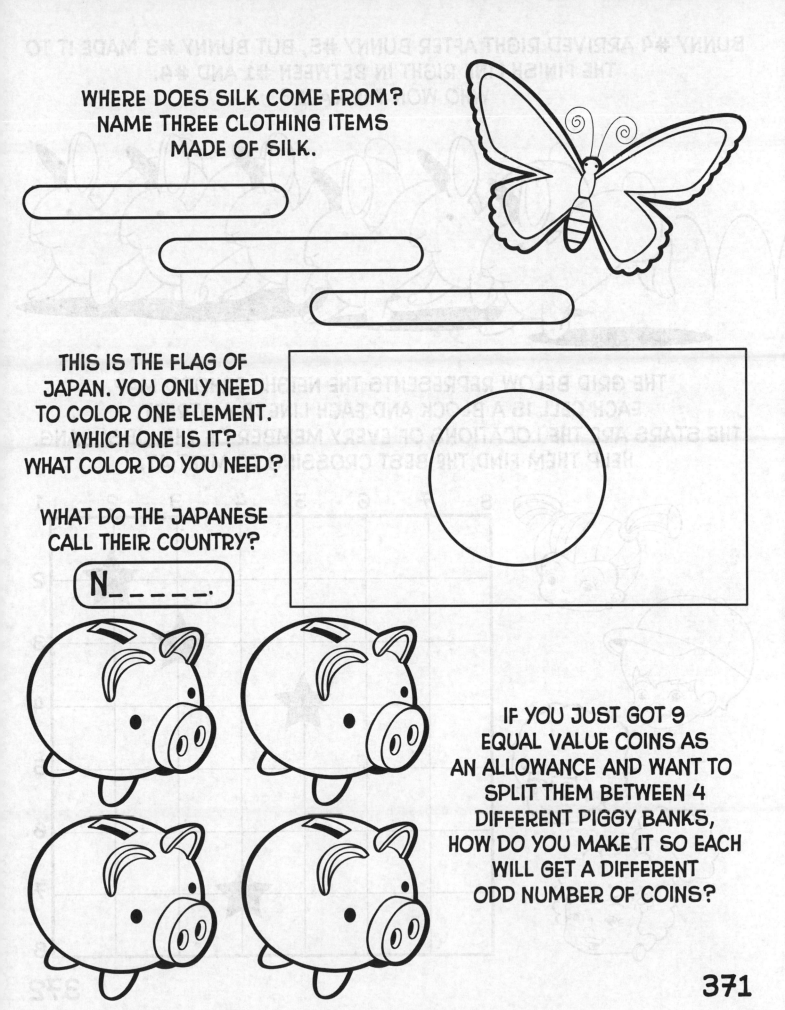

THIS IS THE FLAG OF
JAPAN. YOU ONLY NEED
TO COLOR ONE ELEMENT.
WHICH ONE IS IT?
WHAT COLOR DO YOU NEED?

WHAT DO THE JAPANESE
CALL THEIR COUNTRY?

N_ _ _ _ _ _ .

IF YOU JUST GOT 9
EQUAL VALUE COINS AS
AN ALLOWANCE AND WANT TO
SPLIT THEM BETWEEN 4
DIFFERENT PIGGY BANKS,
HOW DO YOU MAKE IT SO EACH
WILL GET A DIFFERENT
ODD NUMBER OF COINS?

371

BUNNY #4 ARRIVED RIGHT AFTER BUNNY #5, BUT BUNNY #3 MADE IT TO THE FINISH LINE RIGHT IN BETWEEN #1 AND #4. WHO WON THE RACE?

THE GRID BELOW REPRESENTS THE NEIGHBORHOOD MAP.
EACH CELL IS A BLOCK AND EACH LINE IS A STREET.
THE STARS ARE THE LOCATIONS OF EVERY MEMBER OF THE KIDS' GANG.
HELP THEM FIND THE BEST CROSSING TO MEET AT.

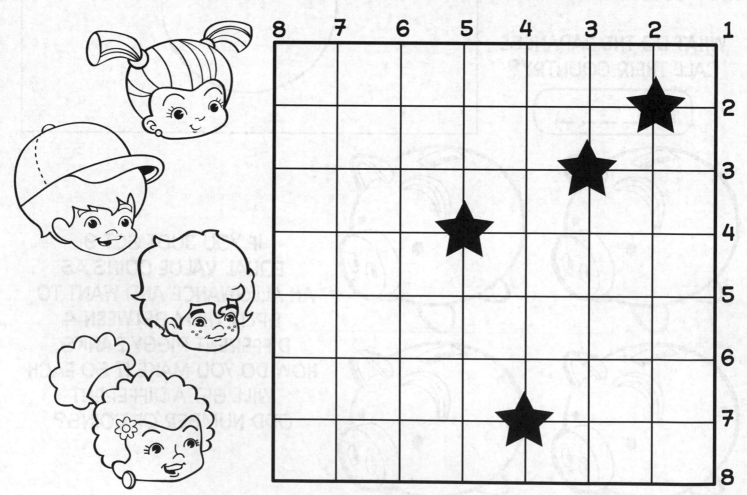

COLOR THE ONE THAT DOESN'T HIBERNATE.

ARRANGE THESE MATCHES SO ONLY TWO ARE LEFT AND NONE GOES MISSING.

THIS MOUSE HAS INVITED 8 MICE TO DINNER, BUT TO AVOID GETTING CAUGHT WITH THIS BIG WHEEL OF CHEESE, IT NEEDS TO SLICE IT IN ONLY 3 STROKES, TO TAKE ALL 8 SLICES AWAY FAST! HOW DOES IT DO IT?

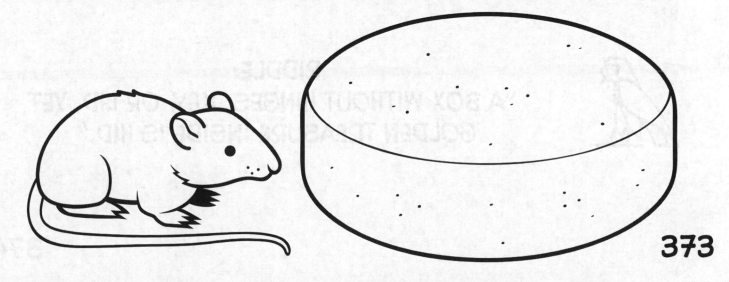

JOIN ALL DOTS USING A SINGLE LINE, WHICH GOES FROM ONE DOT TO THE NEXT, CROSSING EACH ONE ONLY ONCE!

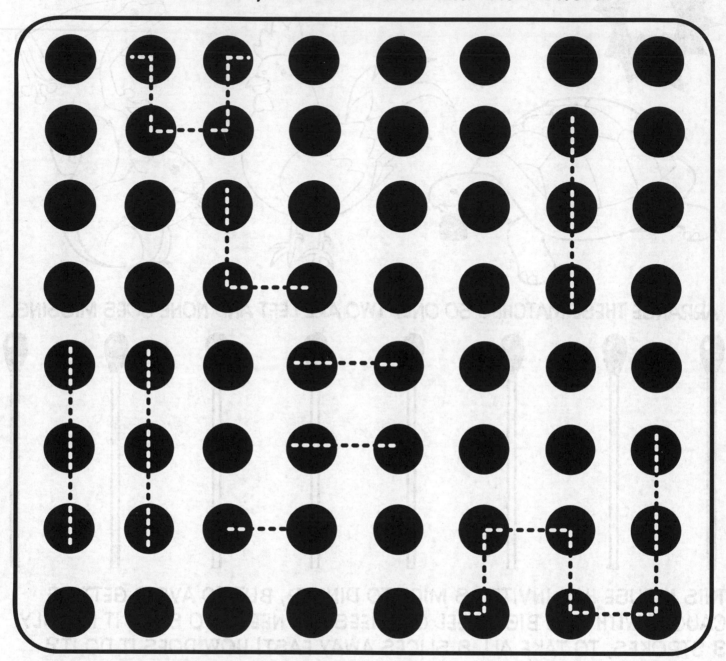

RIDDLE:
"A BOX WITHOUT HINGES, KEY, OR LID, YET GOLDEN TREASURE INSIDE IS HID."

JIMMY GETS 5 DOLLARS FROM HIS DAD EVERY WEEK, 10 FROM HIS MOM EVERY MONTH, AND 20 FROM GRANNY EVERY BIRTHDAY.

IF HE SAVES IT ALL, AND DOESN'T SPEND A PENNY, HOW MUCH MONEY WILL HE HAVE IN 10 YEARS?

CAN YOU DRAW THESE IN A DIFFERENT ORDER EACH TIME?.

IF YOU TURN THE DIALS, HOW MANY POSSIBLE COMBINATIONS WILL YOU GET?

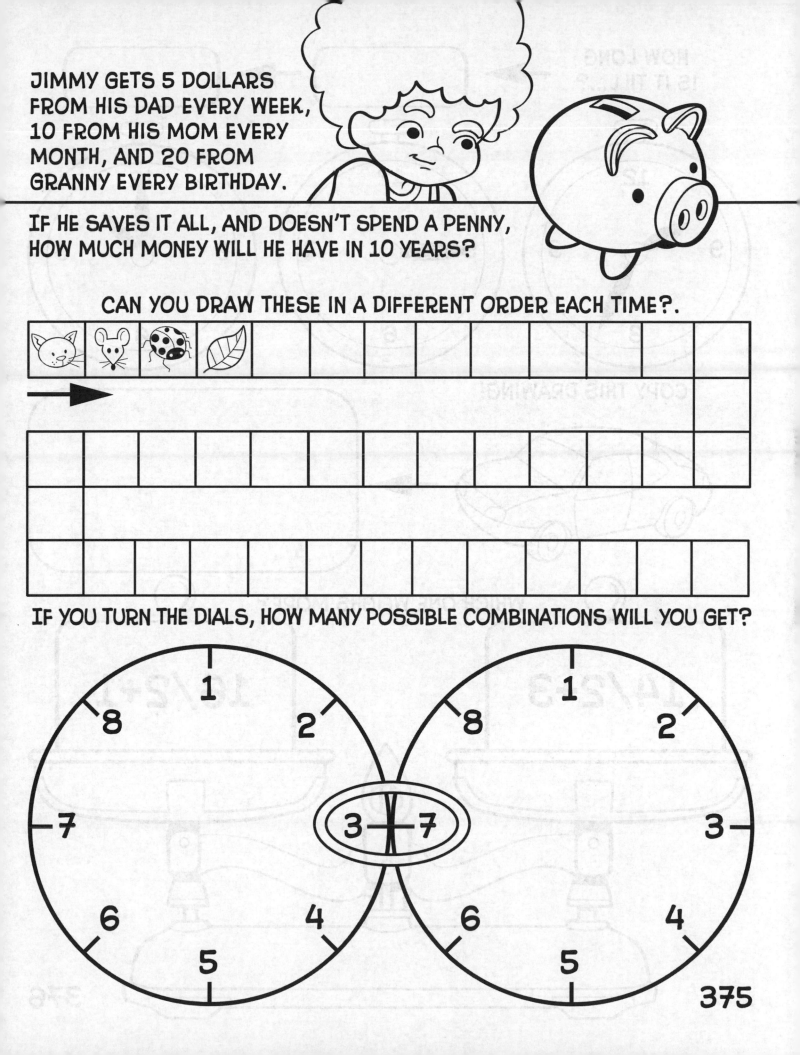

375

HOW LONG IS IT TILL...? → [ ] → [ ]

COPY THIS DRAWING!

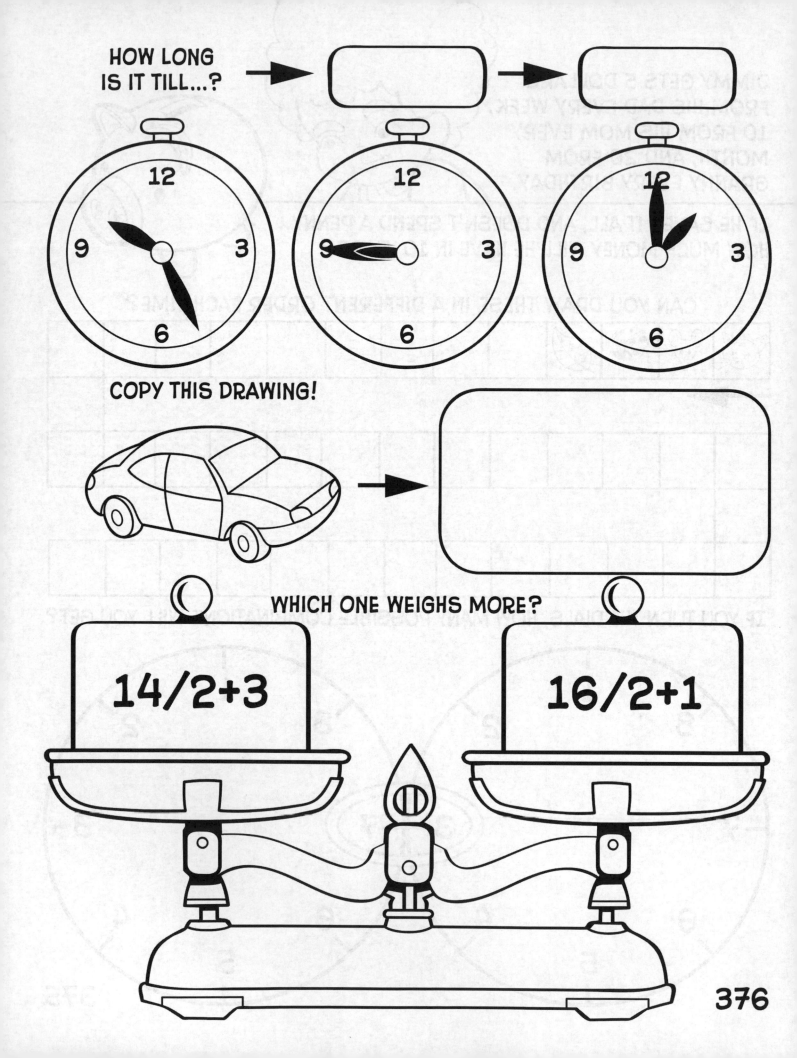

WHICH ONE WEIGHS MORE?

14/2+3

16/2+1

376

WRITE A STORY ABOUT MR. BADGER.

_____
_____
_____
_____
_____
_____
_____
_____
_____
_____
_____
_____
_____
_____
_____
_____
_____
_____
_____
_____
_____
_____
_____
_____
_____
_____
_____

THE END.

WILL THE WHEELS FALL LEFT OR RIGHT?

INSIDE THIS HEART, DRAW THE PERSON YOU LOVE THE MOST IN THE WHOLE, WIDE WORLD!

WHERE DOES WOOL COME FROM?

NAME THREE CLOTHING ITEMS MADE OF WOOL.

DECEPTIVELY SIMPLE! CAN YOU CHANGE THE "DONKEY" POSITION BY MOVING ONLY ONE MATCH?

DESIGN EVEN MORE DETAILED
VIDEO-GAME "SPRITES"
LIKE THE ONE ABOVE!

COMPLETE EACH COLUMN SO THE SUM OF THESE NUMBERS IS ALWAYS 231.

↓ 1	38	54	21	5	18	96	42	27	16	30	210
30											
120											
80											

WHAT IS THE NAME OF THIS ANIMAL?

WHAT KIND OF MAMMAL IS IT?

CAN YOU FIND 15 GREAT AMERICAN PAINTERS IN THIS WORDSEARCH?
CLUE: ONE OF THEM WAS KNOWN TO SPLATTER PAINT ON THE CANVAS!

```
F R A N C I S L U I S M O R A K J P K F J
T H E L E N F R A N K E N T H A L E R Q A
M B Z J O H N S I N G E R S A R G E N T C
T L H V E E D W A R D H O P P E R D T E K
X Z D U E Q F H T Q G R F I O B F W L Y S
R O Y L I C H T E N S T E I N X Q O J C O
E D G A R P A Y N E Y P F W X C C H C C N
P K R A C D N Y G P R U E I L S X T Y Z P
M A R K R O T H K O K X B T A O V C B Z O
G E O R G I A O K E E F E M E O O G Q G L
J I R D W I N S L O W H O M E R L M F Z L
O Z Z L C T T P H B G H D G U B M U I Y O
L A N D R E W W Y E T H M J B E D A J S C
F R E D E R I C R E M I N G T O N A X B K
```

380

IF YOU TURN THE DIALS, HOW MANY POSSIBLE COMBINATIONS WILL YOU GET?

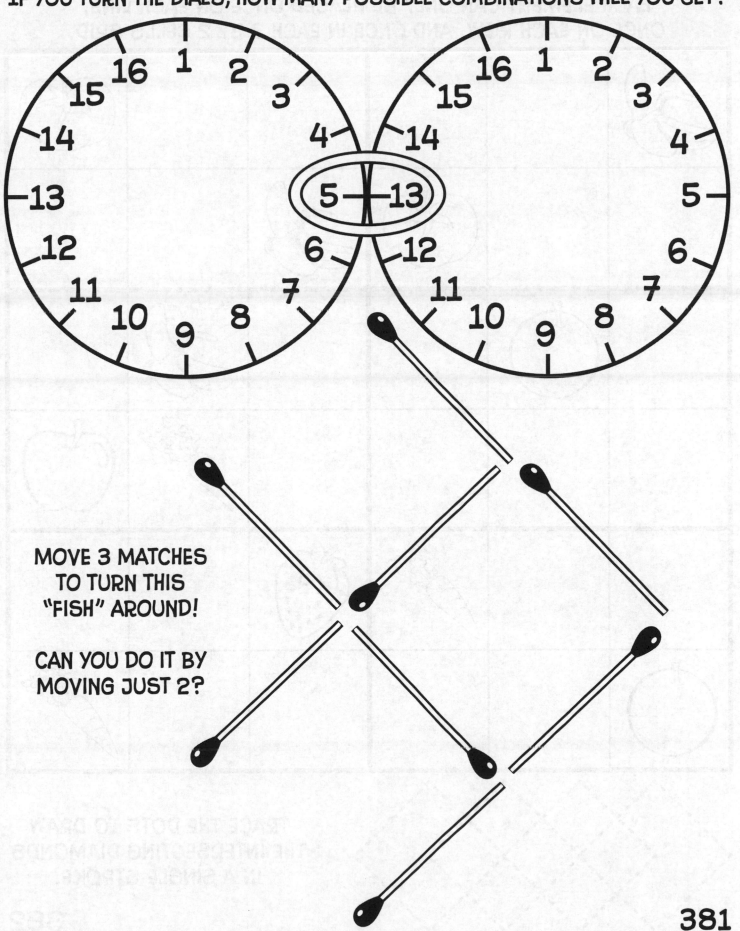

MOVE 3 MATCHES
TO TURN THIS
"FISH" AROUND!

CAN YOU DO IT BY
MOVING JUST 2?

CRACK THE SUDOKU!
EACH ELEMENT CAN ONLY BE PLACED ONCE ON EACH LINE, ONCE ON EACH ROW, AND ONCE IN EACH 3 BY 2 CELLS GRID.

TRACE THE DOTS TO DRAW
THE INTERSECTING DIAMONDS
IN A SINGLE STROKE.

FIND THE WAY OUT! WRITE A STORY ABOUT MS. TORTOISE.

THE END.

RIDDLE:
"THERE ARE TWO MONKEYS ON A TREE AND ONE JUMPS OFF. WHY DOES THE OTHER MONKEY JUMP TOO?"

LOOK FOR THE SYMBOL THAT APPEARS TWICE IN THE WHOLE GRID, AND COLOR BOTH ALIKE.

384

ONLY THREE BLACK SHAPES WILL FIT THE DIAMOND.
WHICH ONES DO NOT?

CAN YOU SET THIS TABLE RIGHT?
SEE THE RIGHT WAY TO DO IT ON THE NEXT PAGE!

SURPRISE YOUR PARENTS BY SETTING THE DINNER TABLE AT HOME!

NAME EACH NUMBERED ITEM BELOW.

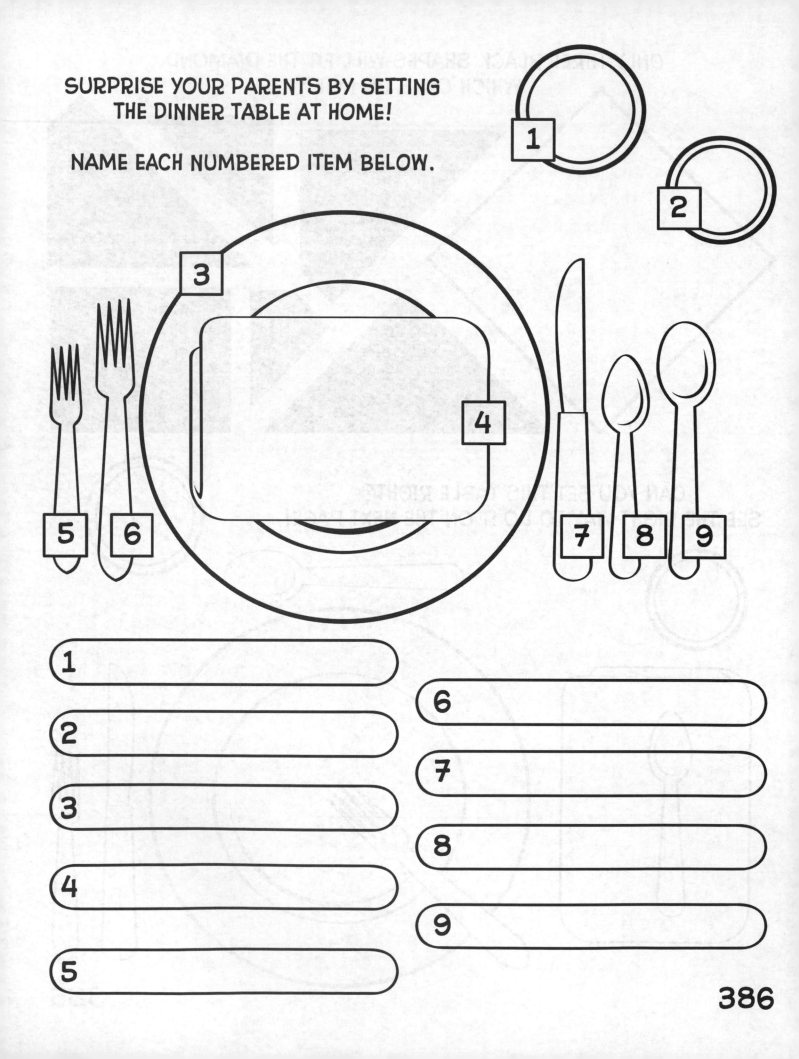

1 _____

2 _____

3 _____

4 _____

5 _____

6 _____

7 _____

8 _____

9 _____

TRACE THE DOTS TO DRAW IT ALL IN A
SINGLE STROKE, WITHOUT ONCE LIFTING
YOUR PENCIL OR PEN FROM THE PAGE!

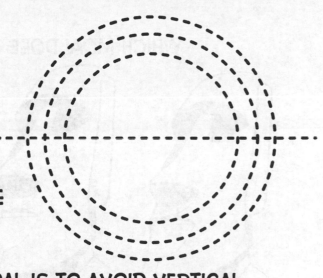

RIDDLE:
"FLAT AS A LEAF, ROUND AS A
RING; HAS TWO EYES, CAN'T SEE
A THING." WHAT IS IT?

IN THIS NEW GAME OF TIC-TAC-TOE, THE GOAL IS TO AVOID VERTICAL,
HORIZONTAL, OR DIAGONAL LINES OF UP TO FOUR CROSSES OR CIRCLES.

X			O		X	X	
		X	O	O		X	X
X				X			X
	O		O	X	X		
	O	O		O		O	
X			O		O	O	O
					O	X	O
X	X		X		X		X

387

WHICH MOAI DOES NOT LOOK LIKE THE OTHERS?

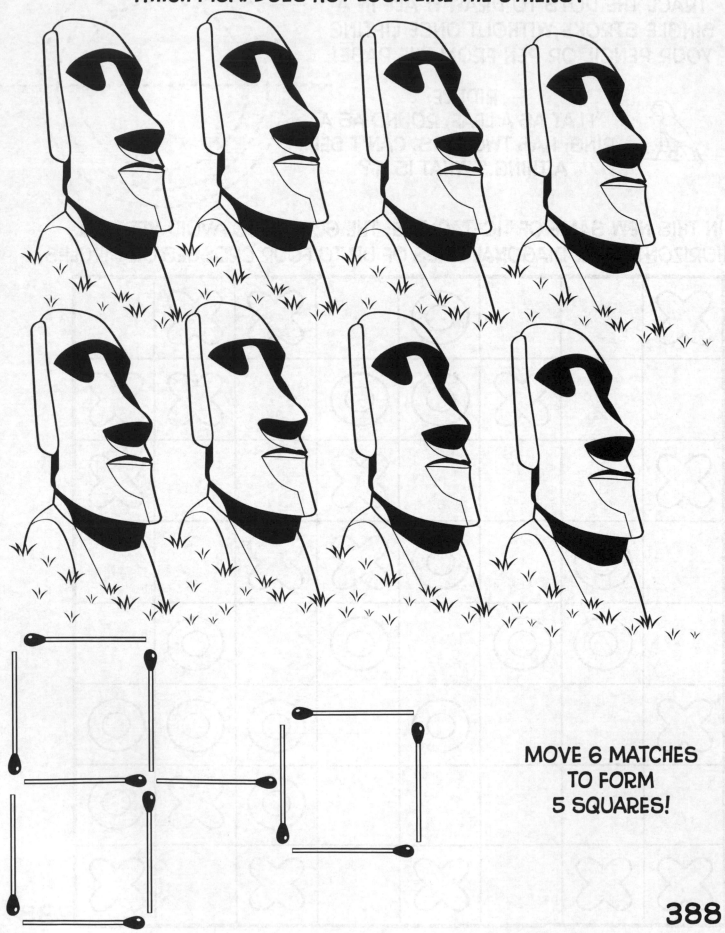

MOVE 6 MATCHES
TO FORM
5 SQUARES!

FOLLOW EACH PATH TO FIND OUT WHICH TAPES ACTUALLY BELONG TO THIS MUSIC CASSETTE!

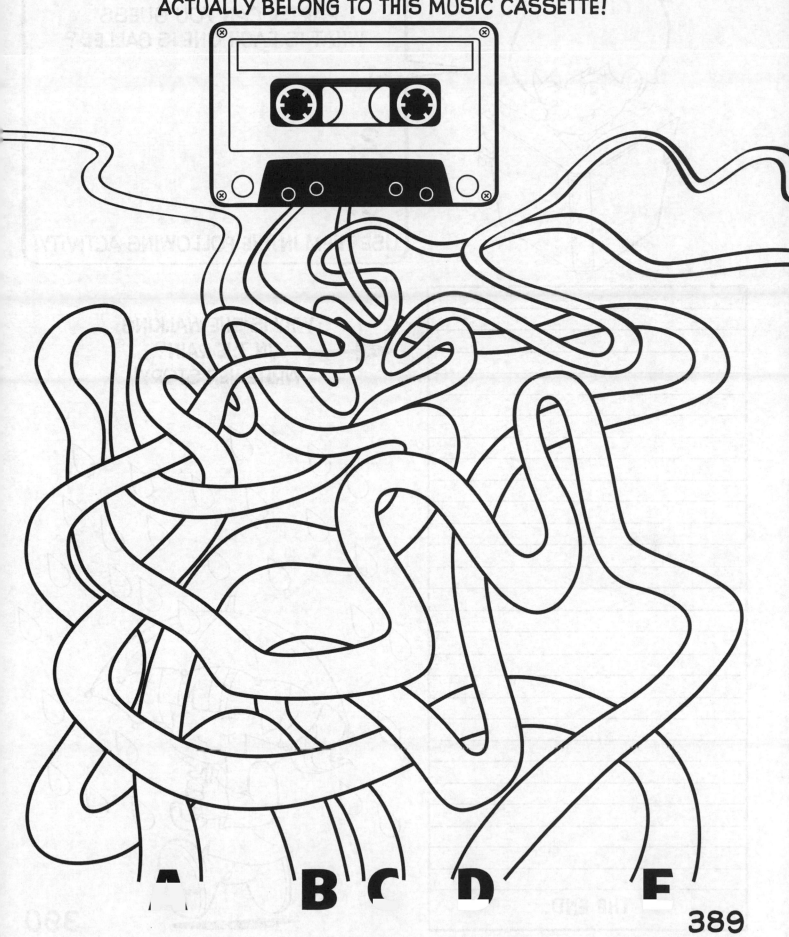

389

EVERY GOOD STORY HAS THREE PARTS. CAN YOU GUESS WHAT IS EACH ONE IS CALLED?

1.

2.

3.

USE THEM IN THE FOLLOWING ACTIVITY!

WHY IS SHE WALKING IN THE RAIN? WRITE HER STORY!

THE END.

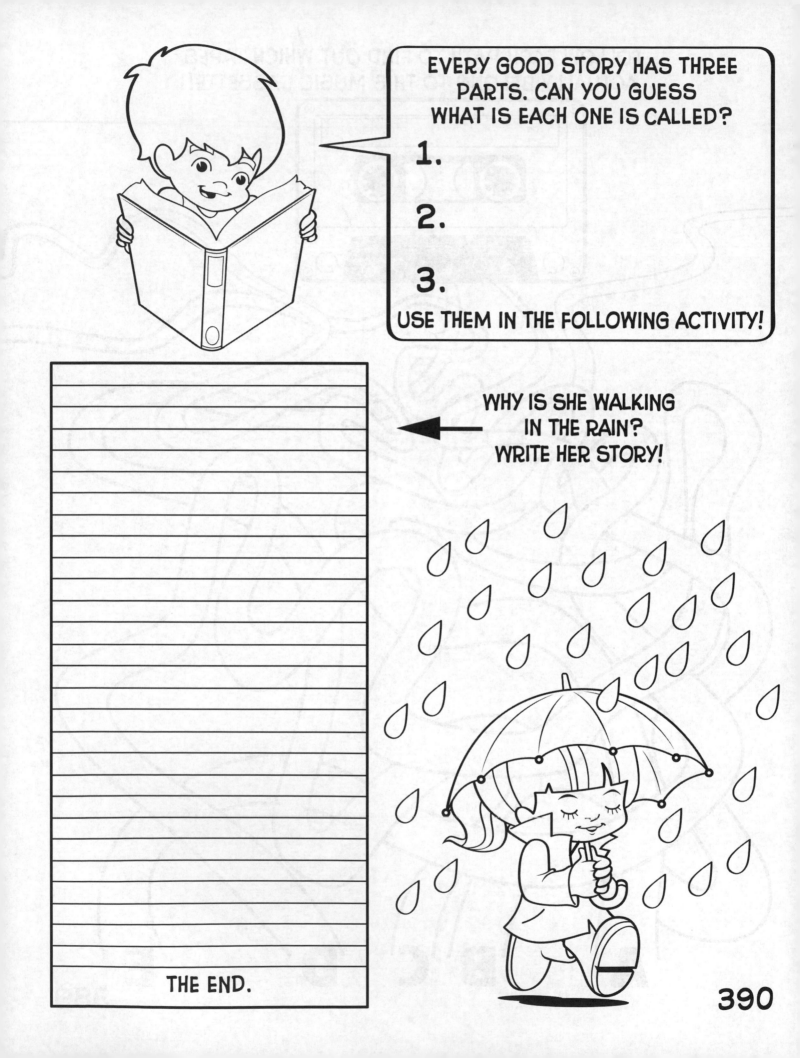

CRACK THE SUDOKU!
EACH ELEMENT CAN ONLY BE PLACED ONCE ON EACH LINE, ONCE ON EACH ROW, AND ONCE IN EACH 3 BY 2 CELLS GRID.

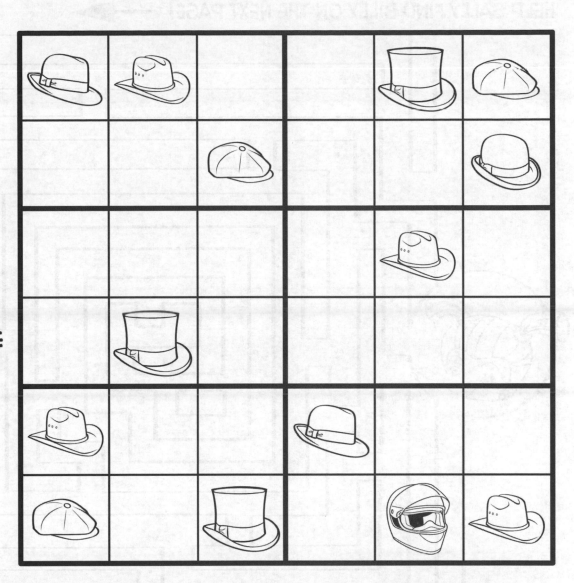

```
K H W D E N N I S T H E M E N A C E I S
A L I T T L E O R P H A N A N N I E C T
T U E C T O Q Z B K W J G Y B D A P A E
Z C M Q H K P P O P E Y E A A E F R L V
E H L M A N D R A K E L Y N R Y F I V E
N A E I S R Z T R G I C A P N X F N I C
J R D O F J A Q A A A G P C E A V C N A
A L V W D K F P B R R A L L Y C M E A N
M I O F Y D F E T O C B O F G H A V N Y
M E K Z U P L K M Y W T T T O Q R A D O
E B A N T T C X D F W R N C O P Y L H N
R R E T E I E N A J E X D H G Z W I O P
K O K E D R A J N B Y L Z Z L I O A B M
I W B F W J M R L A Z A I O E P R N B T
D N Z L F D D I M A R V I N G P T T E Q
S Z Z T X Z D D N L B O M X T Y H O S P
```

HOW MUCH DO YOU KNOW ABOUT COMICS? THIS WORDSEARCH CONTAINS THE NAMES OF 20 CLASSIC CHARACTERS FROM THE FUNNIES FOR YOU TO FIND.

CLUE:
NONE OF THEM IS A SUPERHERO!

HELP SALLY FIND BILLY ON THE NEXT PAGE! ———→

DRAW THE MISSING
ASTEROID BELT!

← OR PLAY WITH A FRIEND TO SEE WHO FINDS THE OTHER ONE FIRST!

WHERE WERE THESE TOYS
FIRST INVENTED?

393

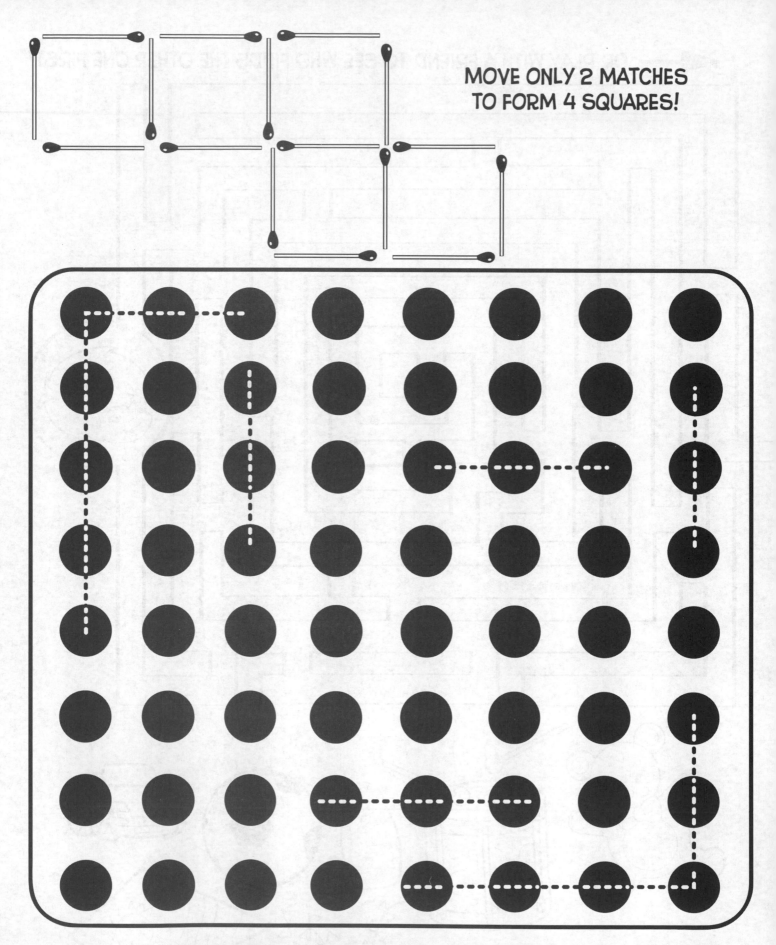

MOVE ONLY 2 MATCHES TO FORM 4 SQUARES!

JOIN ALL DOTS USING A SINGLE LINE, WHICH GOES FROM ONE DOT TO THE NEXT, CROSSING EACH ONE ONLY ONCE!

394

THESE FLAGS BELONG TO NORTH KOREA AND SOUTH KOREA.

WHAT DO YOU KNOW ABOUT THESE TWO COUNTRIES?

THEIR FLAGS ARE BOTH RED, WHITE, AND BLUE.

COLOR THEM!

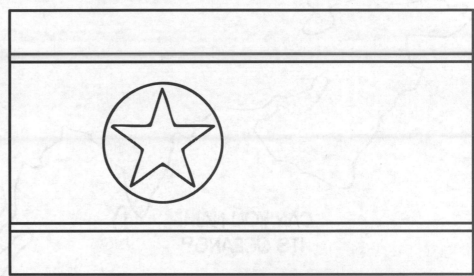

FIND THE HIPPO'S MATCHING SILHOUETTE.

395

WHAT CONTINENT IS THIS?

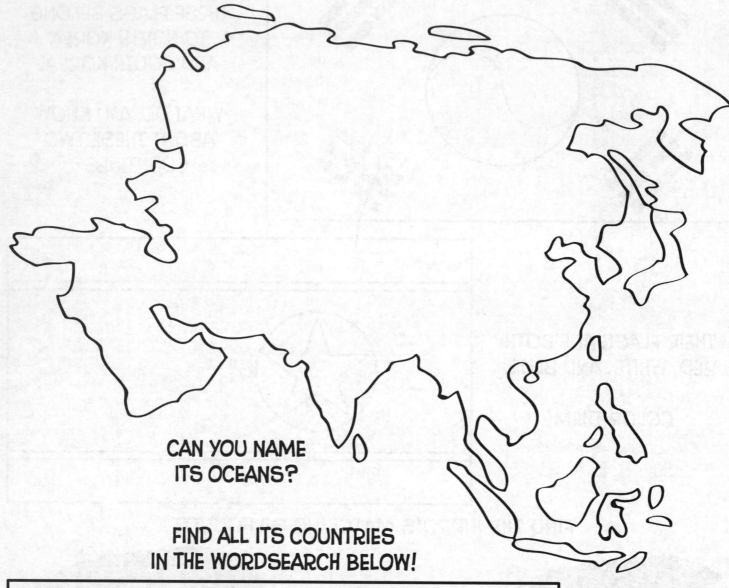

CAN YOU NAME ITS OCEANS?

FIND ALL ITS COUNTRIES IN THE WORDSEARCH BELOW!

```
X M S Q P C T U O N P H I L I P P I N E S C I S Y R I A U A
P A K I S T A N A A B A N G L A D E S H V H T H A I L A N D
P P C Q E A J R N N O A K C A F W H D I R A Q X M A C A O N
E R I P W R I F K U W A I T A O K A I N D I A D P R D L D V
G H U S B M K U N I T E D A R A B E M I R A T E S S J F T N
N B Y S Q E I C A M B O D I A T C F Z M Y A N M A R D I A E
W A L N S N S T F Y W S L A O S U V I E T N A M A I X T R H
C H I N A I T A Z E R B A I J A N R M A L D I V E S S O T Y
D R J O V A A N O R T H K O R E A Z K M I O F N P I P D E A
B A O B I I N D O N E S I A D K Y H K M A U U Q K A P K A Z
U I M S A U D I A R A B I A N W A O G O E R A E G M R I T F
J N A L A F G H A N I S T A N E H J E N B N B N Z U S E B Q
B O N Y L H U E K Y L P L X Q N J N O G I Z I B T Y N J H A
G Q R L H A Q B M J Q I S R A E L X R O U S Q S A A C A L T
Q P W D Q Y Z H K Y R G Y Z S T A N G L L P R L T D H P A A
L P Y K A Z A K H S T A N Z J E C L I I C R A U N A V A H R
Z L E B A N O N S O U T H K O R E A A A X M H C Q O N N Q F
P A L E S T I N I A N T E R R I T O R Y S B X Y E M E N Y K
```

CLUE:
SEE TWO OF THESE COUNTRIES IN THE PREVIOUS PAGE!

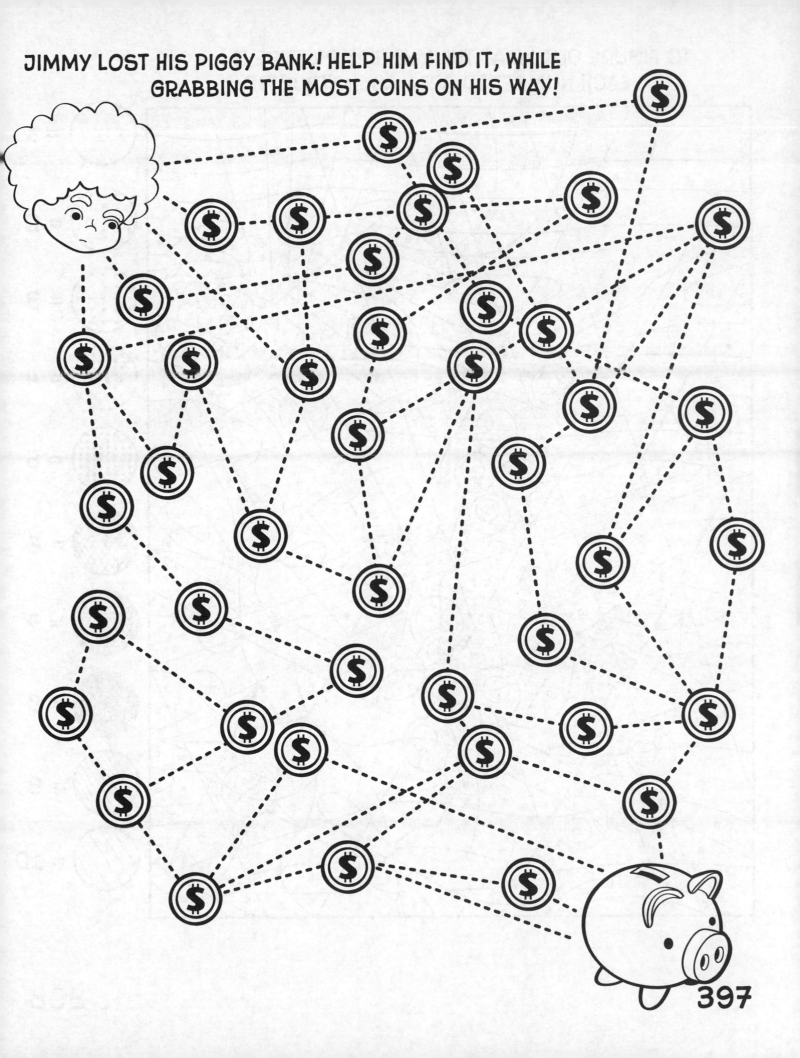

JIMMY LOST HIS PIGGY BANK! HELP HIM FIND IT, WHILE GRABBING THE MOST COINS ON HIS WAY!

397

TO FIGURE OUT WHAT THE MYSTERY PICTURE IS, FILL EACH NUMBERED AREA AS INSTRUCTED.

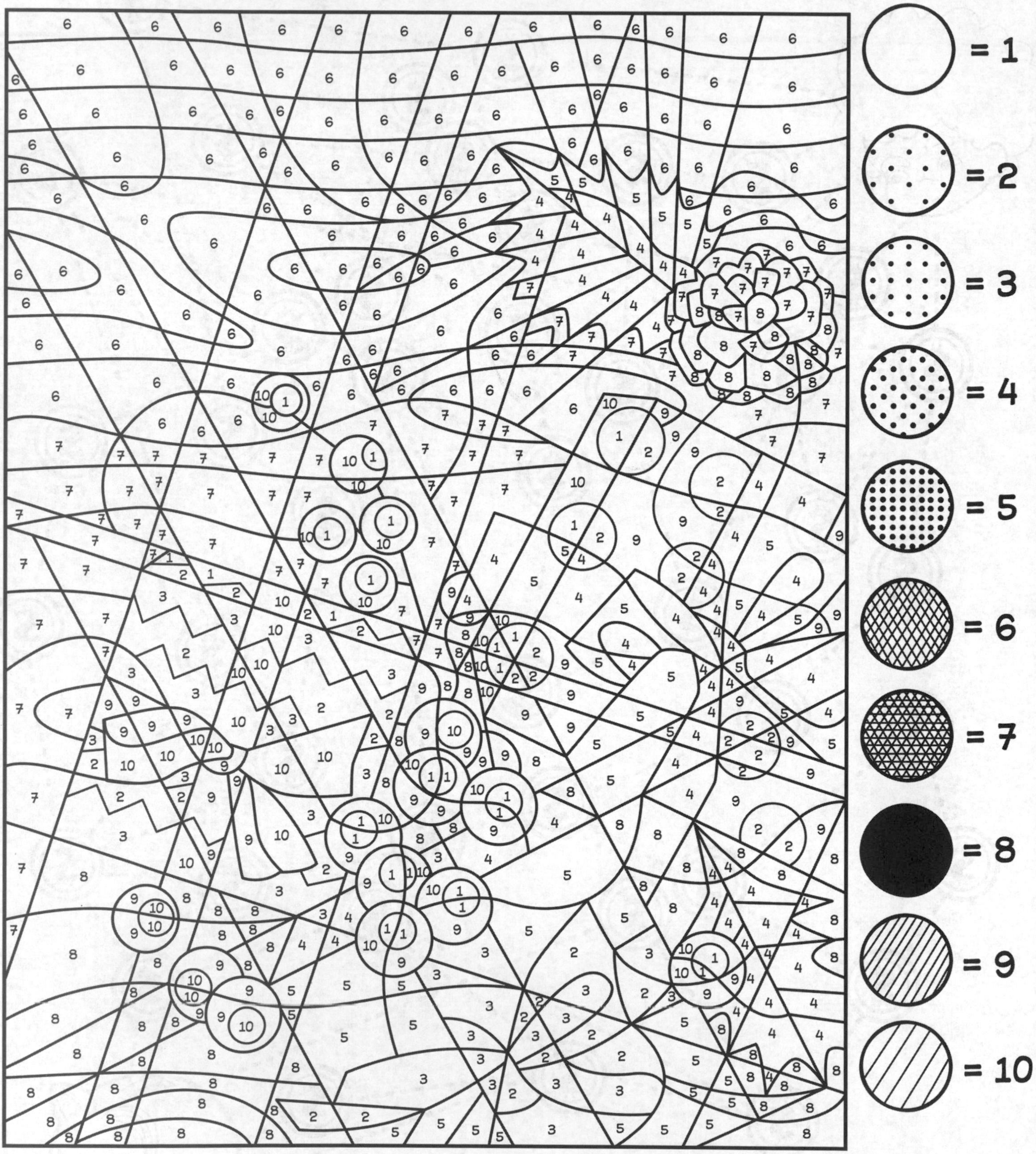

○ = 1
⦿ = 2
⦿ = 3
⦿ = 4
⦿ = 5
⦿ = 6
⦿ = 7
● = 8
⦿ = 9
⦿ = 10

HOW MANY CANDY CANES AND BAUBLES CAN YOU COUNT? COLOR THE CANES RED AND WHITE, THE BALLS BLUE, AND A VERY MERRY CHRISTMAS TO ALL OF YOU!

THIS BOOK WAS COMPLETED BY:

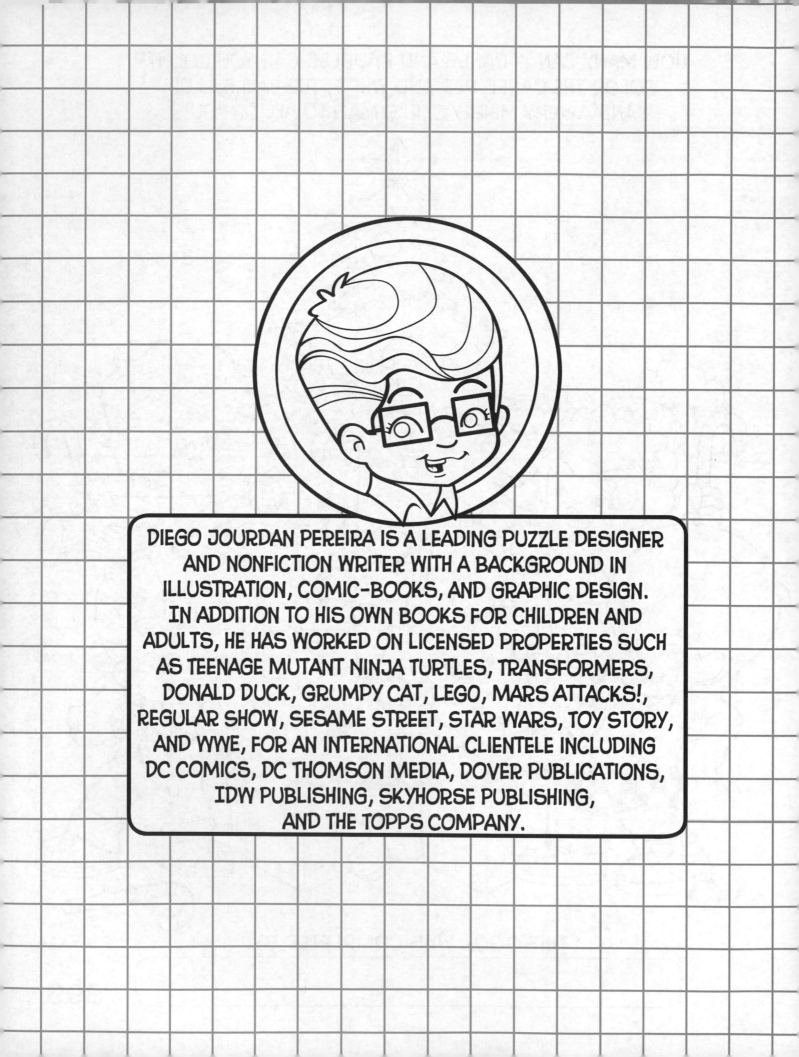

DIEGO JOURDAN PEREIRA IS A LEADING PUZZLE DESIGNER
AND NONFICTION WRITER WITH A BACKGROUND IN
ILLUSTRATION, COMIC-BOOKS, AND GRAPHIC DESIGN.
IN ADDITION TO HIS OWN BOOKS FOR CHILDREN AND
ADULTS, HE HAS WORKED ON LICENSED PROPERTIES SUCH
AS TEENAGE MUTANT NINJA TURTLES, TRANSFORMERS,
DONALD DUCK, GRUMPY CAT, LEGO, MARS ATTACKS!,
REGULAR SHOW, SESAME STREET, STAR WARS, TOY STORY,
AND WWE, FOR AN INTERNATIONAL CLIENTELE INCLUDING
DC COMICS, DC THOMSON MEDIA, DOVER PUBLICATIONS,
IDW PUBLISHING, SKYHORSE PUBLISHING,
AND THE TOPPS COMPANY.

6

THE POOR ZEBRA GOT SCARED AND LOST HER STRIPES!
CAN YOU DRAW THEM?

BE CREATIVE!

WHAT ABOUT THE TIGER'S?

COLOR THEM BOTH!
YOU CAN
DO IT!

6

7

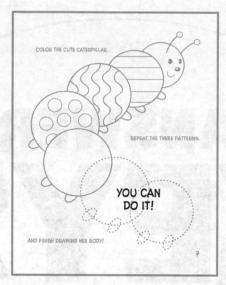

COLOR THE CUTE CATERPILLAR.

REPEAT THE THREE PATTERNS.

YOU CAN
DO IT!

AND FINISH DRAWING HER BODY!

7

8

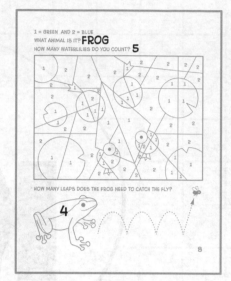

1 = GREEN AND 2 = BLUE
WHAT ANIMAL IS IT? FROG
HOW MANY WATERLILIES DO YOU COUNT? 5

HOW MANY LEAPS DOES THE FROG NEED TO CATCH THE FLY?

4

8

9

FILL EACH FISH WITH A DIFFERENT PATTERN.

HOW MANY FISH DO YOU COUNT? 4

BE CREATIVE!

DECORATE AND COLOR THE SEASHELLS TOO!

9

10

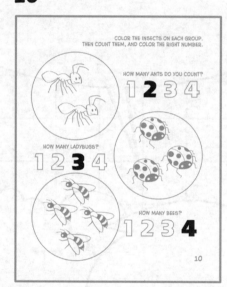

COLOR THE INSECTS ON EACH GROUP.
THEN COUNT THEM, AND COLOR THE RIGHT NUMBER.

HOW MANY ANTS DO YOU COUNT?
1 2 3 4

HOW MANY LADYBUGS?
1 2 3 4

HOW MANY BEES?
1 2 3 4

10

11

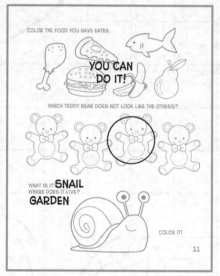

COLOR THE FOOD YOU HAVE EATEN.

YOU CAN
DO IT!

WHICH TEDDY BEAR DOES NOT LOOK LIKE THE OTHERS?

WHAT IS IT? SNAIL
WHERE DOES IT LIVE?
GARDEN

COLOR IT!

11

12

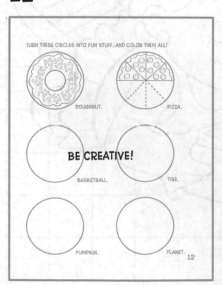

TURN THESE CIRCLES INTO FUN STUFF, AND COLOR THEM ALL!

DOUGHNUT.

PIZZA.

BE CREATIVE!

BASKETBALL.

TIRE.

PUMPKIN.

PLANET.

12

13

IF THE CABBAGE IS ALL GREEN, WHAT COLORS IS THE CARROT?

ORANGE & GREEN

DECORATE THE GHOST'S SHEET TO MAKE HIM HAPPY!

BE CREATIVE!

COUNT AND COLOR THE STARS YOU SEE. 11

13

14

TRACE THE DOTS TO DRAW THE WATER
THE ELEPHANT IS SPRAYING.

COLOR THIS
RUBBER DUCK
YELLOW!

YOU CAN
DO IT!

CONNECT EACH ANIMAL TO THE NOISE IT MAKES.

MEOW!   CHIRP!   BARK!   CLICK!

14

15

DRAW THE MYSTERIOUS TREASURE
HIDDEN UNDERGROUND.
WHAT ELSE CAN BE FOUND BELOW? DRAW IT!

ABOVE.

BE CREATIVE!

BELOW.

16

DRAW A TREAT TO FEED THE CAT.

YOU CAN DO IT!

HOW MANY APPLES
DO YOU COUNT?

COLOR THE BIG ONES
RED, THE SMALL ONES
GREEN, AND THE REST
YELLOW.

R   G   R

G   Y   G   R   Y

DRAW A HAPPY FACE, A SAD FACE, AND AN ANGRY FACE.

YOU CAN DO IT!

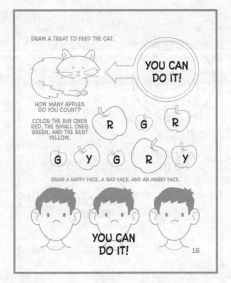

17

WHICH PUPPY DOES NOT LOOK LIKE THE OTHERS?

DECORATE THE BUTTERFLY WINGS AND COLOR THEM.

BE CREATIVE!

18

CONNECT THE DOTS TO
COMPLETE THIS
VERY TALL ANIMAL.

GIRAFFE
COLOR HER SPOTS!

YOU CAN
DO IT!

WHO CLIMBED
UP THE LADDER
TO GREET HER?   THE CAT.

WHO CLIMBED
DOWN?   THE MOUSE

UP

DOWN

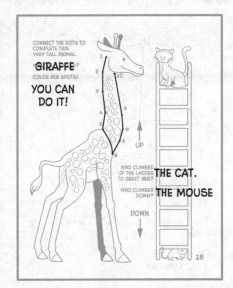

19

DRAW THE LIONS' MANE—
ONE STRAIGHT AND THE OTHER CURLY.

YOU CAN
DO IT!

DRAW TWO MORE LIONS
WITH DIFFERENT MANES.

BE CREATIVE!

20

1 = BLUE , 2 = GREEN, AND 3 = BROWN
WHAT IS IT? A TURTLE.

WHICH PATH WILL TAKE THE BUNNY TO THE EASTER EGG?

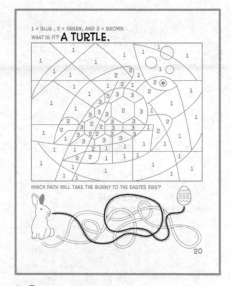

21

CONNECT THE DOTS TO DRAW THE ROCKET,
THEN DRAW THE ASTRONAUT LOOKING OUT THE WINDOW,
AND COLOR EVERYTHING!

YOU CAN
DO IT!

22

WHAT ANIMAL IS IT?

ARMADILLO

TRACE THE DOTTED LINE TO HELP THE LITTLE HUMMINGBIRD
REACH THE FLOWER.

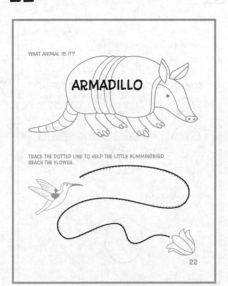

23

COLOR THE FRUITS IN EACH GROUP.
COUNT THEM AND COLOR THE RIGHT NUMBER.

HOW MANY APPLES DO YOU COUNT?

1 2 3 4
5 **6** 7 8

HOW MANY BANANAS DO YOU COUNT?

1 2 3 4
5 6 7 8

HOW MANY ORANGES DO YOU COUNT?

1 2 3 4
5 6 **7** 8

24

COLOR AND NAME
EACH FRUIT.

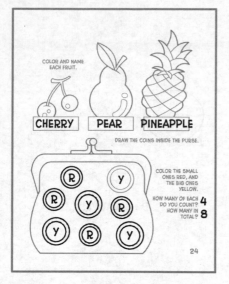

CHERRY | PEAR | PINEAPPLE

DRAW THE COINS INSIDE THE PURSE.

COLOR THE SMALL
ONES RED, AND
THE BIG ONES
YELLOW.

HOW MANY OF EACH
DO YOU COUNT? **4**
HOW MANY IN
TOTAL? **8**

24

25

COLOR THE
BIGGEST DRUM.

DRAW A LINE OVER THE DOTS.
WHAT IS IT? COLOR IT RED!

**YOU CAN
DO IT!**

DRAW YOUR FAVORITE TOY!

**YOU CAN
DO IT!**

25

26

TORTOISE

WHAT ANIMAL IS THIS?
CAN YOU COLOR IT?

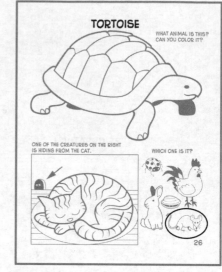

ONE OF THE CREATURES ON THE RIGHT
IS HIDING FROM THE CAT.

WHICH
ONE IS IT?

26

27

FILL THIS PAGE WITH THE DOG'S MUD PRINTS!

**YOU CAN
DO IT!**

27

28

DRAW FOUR RAISINS ON TOP OF THE ROLL, AND THEN COLOR THE CUP.

**YOU CAN
DO IT!**

FILL THE HEDGEHOG'S BACK WITH SPINES,
AND DRAW ANOTHER ONE JUST LIKE IT.

**YOU CAN
DO IT!**

WHICH PENGUIN DOES NOT LOOK LIKE THE OTHERS?

28

29

TRACE THE DOTS TO
DRAW THE SAIL AND
THE FLAG.

WHAT SHOULD BILLY
USE AS BAIT TO
CATCH FISH?

DRAW THE MISSING
FISHING LINE.

COLOR ALL SIMILAR FISH THE SAME.
HOW MANY OF EACH GROUP CAN YOU COUNT?

ONE OF THEM IS MISSING!
WHERE IS IT?

**YOU CAN
DO IT!**

DRAW THE BAIT!

2

4

7

1

WHAT KIND OF
FISH IS THIS?
STINGRAY

29

30

FIND THE MISSING PIECE.

DRAW MOMMA GOOSE AND
BABY GEESE OVER THE
DOTS, WITHOUT LIFTING
YOUR HAND.

**YOU CAN
DO IT!**

DECORATE AND COLOR
THIS SET OF NESTING DOLLS.

BE CREATIVE!

30

31

A WHOLE LOT OF HATS! CAN YOU GUESS THEIR NAMES?

COWBOY FEDORA BOWLER FLATCAP TOPHAT

DRAW THREE SCOOPS OF ICECREAM ON THE FIRST CONE,
TWO ON THE SECOND ONE, AND ONE ON THE THIRD ONE.
COLOR EACH LIKE YOUR FAVORITE FLAVORS!

WHICH ONES ARE NOT A FRUIT?

31

32

WRITE THE NUMBERS MISSING ON THE CARS.
COLOR ONE LOCOMOTIVE RED,
AND THE OTHER GREEN.

1 | 2 | 3 | 4 | 5

6 | 7 | 8 | 9 | 10

**YOU CAN
DO IT!**

DRAW THE SPOTS
MISSING FROM THIS COW!

32

33

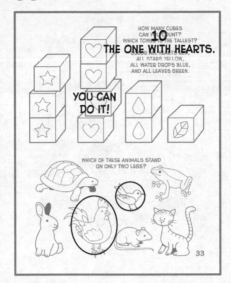

HOW MANY CUBES CAN YOU COUNT?
10
WHICH TOWER IS THE TALLEST?
THE ONE WITH HEARTS.
ALL STARS YELLOW, ALL WATER DROPS BLUE, AND ALL LEAVES GREEN.

YOU CAN DO IT!

WHICH OF THESE ANIMALS STAND ON ONLY TWO LEGS?

33

34

WHAT ANIMAL IS THIS? WHERE DOES IT LIVE?
KANGAROO. AUSTRALIA.
CAN YOU DRAW THE SPIRAL ON THE LOLLIPOP, TRACING THE DOTS FROM THE STAR AT THE CENTER ALL THE WAY OUT?

DECORATE AND COLOR THE GIFT WRAPPING!

BE CREATIVE!

34

35

WHAT DOES THE MOUSE EAT?

DRAW YOUR MOM'S PORTRAIT.   DRAW YOUR DAD'S PORTRAIT.

BE CREATIVE!

HOW MANY TIMES DID THE RABBIT LEAP TO GET THE CARROT?
6

35

36

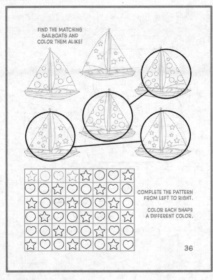

FIND THE MATCHING SAILBOATS AND COLOR THEM ALIKE!

COMPLETE THE PATTERN FROM LEFT TO RIGHT.

COLOR EACH SHAPE A DIFFERENT COLOR.

36

37

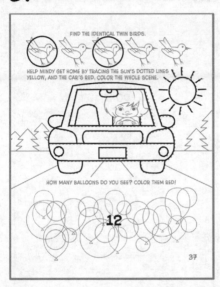

FIND THE IDENTICAL TWIN BIRDS.

HELP MINDY GET HOME BY TRACING THE SUN'S DOTTED LINES YELLOW, AND THE CAR'S RED. COLOR THE WHOLE SCENE.

HOW MANY BALLOONS DO YOU SEE? COLOR THEM RED!
12

37

38

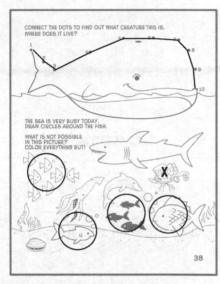

CONNECT THE DOTS TO FIND OUT WHAT CREATURE THIS IS. WHERE DOES IT LIVE?

THE SEA IS VERY BUSY TODAY. DRAW CIRCLES AROUND THE FISH.

WHAT IS NOT POSSIBLE IN THIS PICTURE? COLOR EVERYTHING BUT!

38

39

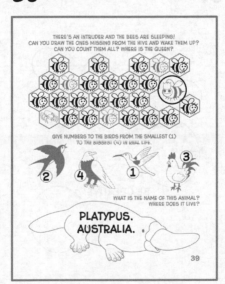

THERE'S AN INTRUDER AND THE BEES ARE SLEEPING! CAN YOU DRAW THE ONES MISSING FROM THE HIVE AND WAKE THEM UP? CAN YOU COUNT THEM ALL? WHERE IS THE QUEEN?

GIVE NUMBERS TO THE BIRDS FROM THE SMALLEST (1) TO THE BIGGEST (4) IN REAL LIFE.

2   **4**   **1**   **3**

WHAT IS THE NAME OF THIS ANIMAL? WHERE DOES IT LIVE?
PLATYPUS. AUSTRALIA.

39

40

FILL THIS PAGE WITH BLUE BUBBLES! ➡

YOU CAN DO IT!

SOAP

WHAT ARE BUBBLES MADE OF? UNSCRAMBLE THE LETTERS TO FIND OUT!

40

41

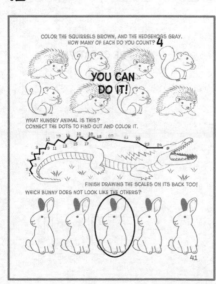

COLOR THE SQUIRRELS BROWN, AND THE HEDGEHOGS GRAY. HOW MANY OF EACH DO YOU COUNT?
4

YOU CAN DO IT!

WHAT HUNGRY ANIMAL IS THIS? CONNECT THE DOTS TO FIND OUT AND COLOR IT.

FINISH DRAWING THE SCALES ON ITS BACK TOO!
WHICH BUNNY DOES NOT LOOK LIKE THE OTHERS?

41

42

HELP JIMMY FIND HIS SNEAKERS BY COLORING THEM BLUE!

COLOR THE COWBOY BOOTS BROWN, THE HIGH HEELS RED, AND THE REST AS YOU WISH!

YOU CAN DO IT!

DRAW THE GARDEN SNAIL'S SHELL BY TRACING THE DOTTED LINE. WHAT DOES IT EAT?

42

43

GUIDE THE PLANE THROUGH THE CLOUDS SO IT LANDS SAFELY!

43

44

1 = BROWN
2 = BLUE
3 = GREEN
4 = YELLOW

FIND THE EAGLE'S SHADOW.

WHAT ANIMAL IS IT?

AN OWL.

DRAW A SLEEPY FACE, A SURPRISED FACE, AND A SERIOUS FACE.

YOU CAN DO IT!

44

45

FIND THE SEVEN DIFFERENCES.

CAN YOU DRAW A DINOSAUR IN THIS PREHISTORIC LANDSCAPE?

BE CREATIVE!

COLOR THE ONES YOU CAN OPEN.

45

46

FILL THIS PAGE WITH BLUE RAINDROPS!

YOU CAN DO IT!

COLOR ANNIE'S UMBRELLA RED, HER COAT YELLOW, AND HER BOOTS GREEN.

46

47

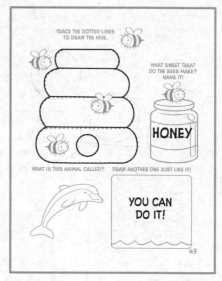

TRACE THE DOTTED LINES TO DRAW THE HIVE.

WHAT SWEET TREAT DO THE BEES MAKE? NAME IT!

HONEY

WHAT IS THIS ANIMAL CALLED? DRAW ANOTHER ONE JUST LIKE IT!

YOU CAN DO IT!

47

48

DRAW DIFFERENT HAIRCUTS FOR THE BOY!

BE CREATIVE!

DRAW THE LION'S OTHER HALF AND COLOR THE WHOLE PICTURE.

DOES THE SPIDER CATCH THE FLY?

48

49

WHAT'S MISSING FROM THIS CAMEL? CAN YOU DRAW IT?

HUMP

WHICH ONE OF THESE ANIMALS DOES NOT LAY EGGS?

49

50

COLOR THE FOOD THAT TASTES SWEET.

COLOR ONLY THE STRIPPED T-SHIRTS.

DECORATE THE ONE IN THE MIDDLE ANY WAY YOU LIKE!

BE CREATIVE!

50

51

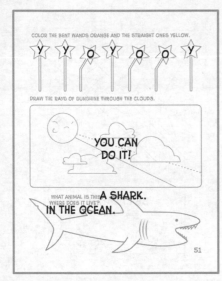

COLOR THE BENT WANDS ORANGE AND THE STRAIGHT ONES YELLOW.

Y Y Y O Y O O Y

DRAW THE RAYS OF SUNSHINE THROUGH THE CLOUDS.

YOU CAN DO IT!

WHAT ANIMAL IS THIS? **A SHARK.** WHERE DOES IT LIVE? **IN THE OCEAN.**

51

52

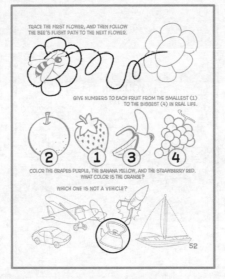

TRACE THE FIRST FLOWER, AND THEN FOLLOW THE BEE'S FLIGHT PATH TO THE NEXT FLOWER.

GIVE NUMBERS TO EACH FRUIT FROM THE SMALLEST (1) TO THE BIGGEST (4) IN REAL LIFE.

2   1   3   4

COLOR THE GRAPES PURPLE, THE BANANA YELLOW, AND THE STRAWBERRY RED. WHAT COLOR IS THE ORANGE?

WHICH ONE IS NOT A VEHICLE?

52

53

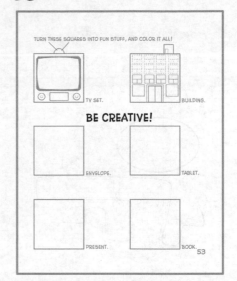

TURN THESE SQUARES INTO FUN STUFF, AND COLOR IT ALL!

TV SET.   BUILDING.

BE CREATIVE!

ENVELOPE.   TABLET.

PRESENT.   BOOK.

53

54

COLOR THE SWALLOWS BLUE AND THE BUTTERFLIES PINK!

YOU CAN DO IT!

CROW!   SQUEAK!   MOO!   CHATTER!

CONNECT EACH ANIMAL TO THE NOISE IT MAKES.

54

55

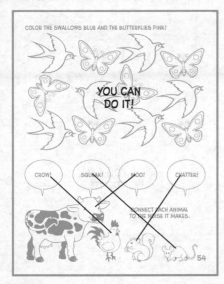

DRAW THE KITTY'S LONG TAIL, AND THEN COLOR HIM ORANGE.

DO YOU HAVE A PET? DRAW IT HERE.

YOU CAN DO IT!

YOU CAN DO IT!

FILL THE JAR WITH CANDY. COLOR HALF OF THEM RED, AND THE REST BLUE.

COUNT THEM ALL.

55

56

WHOOPS! HOW MANY DOUGHNUTS DID SALLY DROP?

WHICH ONE OF THESE DOES NOT BELONG IN THE KITCHEN?

15

56

57

DRAW THE SHEEP'S COAT OF WOOL— ONE WAVY AND THE OTHER CURLY.

YOU CAN DO IT!

DRAW TWO MORE SHEEP WITH DIFFERENT COATS.

BE CREATIVE!

57

58

WHAT IS NOT POSSIBLE IN THIS PICTURE? WHY?

DOLPHINS LIVE IN THE OCEAN. THE HALF MOON CAN'T BE SEEN NEXT TO THE SUN.

1 = GRAY
2 = PINK
3 = WHITE
4 = YELLOW
5 = ORANGE

WHAT ANIMAL IS IT? **A CAT.** DRAW A CIRCLE AROUND ITS FAVORITE FOOD BELOW.

58

59

ONE OF THESE ANIMALS CAN'T SWIM. CAN YOU GUESS WHICH ONE?

WHAT IS THIS ANIMAL CALLED?   DRAW ANOTHER ONE JUST LIKE IT!

YOU CAN DO IT!

FINISH THIS DRAWING.

59

60

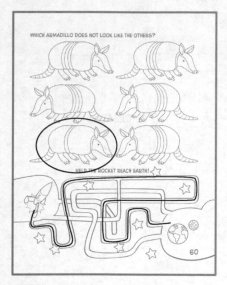

WHICH ARMADILLO DOES NOT LOOK LIKE THE OTHERS?

HELP THE ROCKET REACH EARTH!

60

61

FILL THE SKY WITH FALLING SNOWFLAKES! →

YOU CAN DO IT!

COLOR THE CARROT ORANGE AND THE PINE TREES GREEN.

COLOR THE CABIN BROWN, AND THE SNOWMAN'S BUTTONS RED.

61

62

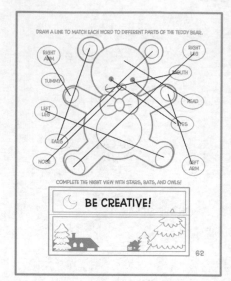

DRAW A LINE TO MATCH EACH WORD TO DIFFERENT PARTS OF THE TEDDY BEAR.

RIGHT ARM
RIGHT LEG
TUMMY
MOUTH
LEFT LEG
HEAD
EARS
EYES
NOSE
LEFT ARM

COMPLETE THE NIGHT VIEW WITH STARS, BATS, AND OWLS!

BE CREATIVE!

62

63

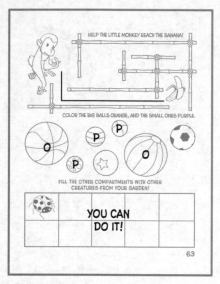

HELP THE LITTLE MONKEY REACH THE BANANA!

COLOR THE BIG BALLS ORANGE, AND THE SMALL ONES PURPLE.

P P P O O

FILL THE OTHER COMPARTMENTS WITH OTHER CREATURES FROM YOUR GARDEN!

YOU CAN DO IT!

63

64

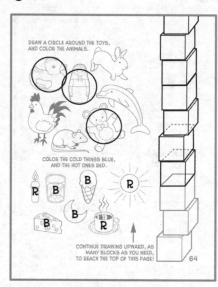

DRAW A CIRCLE AROUND THE TOYS, AND COLOR THE ANIMALS.

COLOR THE COLD THINGS BLUE, AND THE HOT ONES RED.

R B B R B B R

CONTINUE DRAWING UPWARD, AS MANY BLOCKS AS YOU NEED, TO REACH THE TOP OF THIS PAGE!

64

65

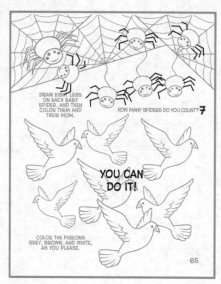

DRAW EIGHT LEGS ON EACH BABY SPIDER, AND THEN COLOR THEM AND THEIR MOM.

HOW MANY SPIDERS DO YOU COUNT? 7

YOU CAN DO IT!

COLOR THE PIGEONS GREY, BROWN, AND WHITE, AS YOU PLEASE.

65

66

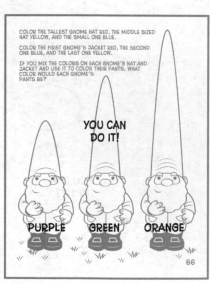

COLOR THE TALLEST GNOME HAT RED, THE MIDDLE SIZED HAT YELLOW, AND THE SMALL ONE BLUE.

COLOR THE FIRST GNOME'S JACKET RED, THE SECOND ONE BLUE, AND THE LAST ONE YELLOW.

IF YOU MIX THE COLORS ON EACH GNOME'S HAT AND JACKET AND USE IT TO COLOR THEIR PANTS, WHAT COLOR WOULD EACH GNOME'S PANTS BE?

YOU CAN DO IT!

PURPLE GREEN ORANGE

66

67

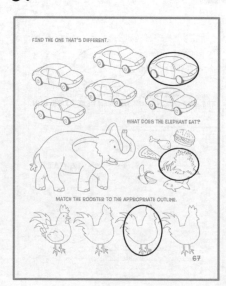

FIND THE ONE THAT'S DIFFERENT.

WHAT DOES THE ELEPHANT EAT?

MATCH THE ROOSTER TO THE APPROPRIATE OUTLINE.

67

68

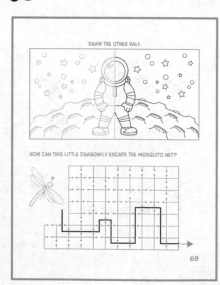

DRAW THE OTHER HALF.

HOW CAN THIS LITTLE DRAGONFLY ESCAPE THE MOSQUITO NET?

68

69

WHICH PINEAPPLE DOES NOT LOOK LIKE THE OTHERS?

WHAT PIECE DOES NOT MATCH THE DRAWING?

TRACE A LINE OVER THE DOTS, WITHOUT LIFTING YOUR HAND.

WHAT IS IT? **A BOAT.**

YOU CAN DO IT!

70

FILL THE JAR WITH LICORICE. COLOR HALF OF THEM RED, AND THE REST PURPLE.

COUNT THEM ALL.

YOU CAN DO IT!

DRAW THE NOSE WITHOUT LIFTING YOUR HAND.

YOU CAN DO IT!

WHICH ONE OF THESE ANIMALS IS NOT A MAMMAL?

71

WHAT'S MISSING FROM MR. SCARECROW'S HEAD?

WHAT DO WE CALL THE BLACK BIRD PERCHED ON HIS ARM?

CROW

BE CREATIVE!

DECORATE THE SHIRT, AND COLOR THE BIB BLUE.

CHOOSE A FACE TO DRAW ON IT'S HEAD.

WHAT ARE THESE CALLED? COLOR THEM!

PUMPKINS

YOU CAN DO IT!

72

COLOR THE CAT WITH THE LONGEST TAIL PURPLE, AND THE ONE WITH THE SHORTEST ORANGE.

1 = BLACK
2 = RED
3 = DARK GREEN
4 = LIGHT GREEN
5 = BLUE

LADYBUG
WHERE DOES IT LIVE?
GARDEN

COLOR ONLY THE ROUND THINGS.

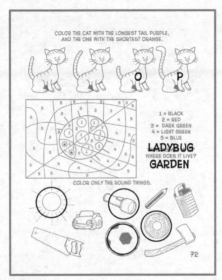

73

HOW MANY TRIANGLES DO YOU SEE? COLOR THEM YELLOW. **22**

FIND THE SIX DIFFERENCES.

COLOR THE BROKEN LOLLIPOPS GREEN, AND THE STRAIGHT ONES RED. WHICH ONE ISN'T A LOLLIPOP? WHAT IS IT? COLOR IT PINK.

R G R R G

COTTON CANDY

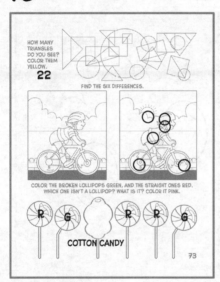

74

HELP ICHA'S KISS FIND ITS WAY TO DIEGO'S CHEEK!

FILL THESE WITH HEARTS!

YOU CAN DO IT!

75

COLOR ONLY THE THINGS PEOPLE WEAR.

COLOR THE BASKET WITH THE MOST APPLES IN IT.

COLOR THE BIG PEARS YELLOW, AND THE SMALL ONES GREEN. COLOR ALL CHERRIES RED.

R
G R
R G Y
R Y

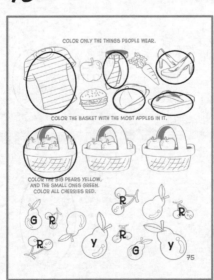

76

FIND THE ONE THAT'S DIFFERENT.

TRACE THE SWALLOW'S FLIGHT PATH TO HER LITTLE ONES.

77

WHICH ONE DOESN'T BELONG? **THE SPIDER.**
WHY? **SPIDERS ARE ARACHNIDS, NOT INSECTS.**

DRAW THE OTHER HALF, AND PAINT FRECKLES ON HIS FACE.

WHAT IS THE NAME OF THIS TOOL?

HAMMER

CARPENTRY

78

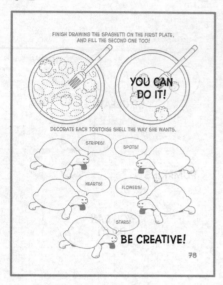

FINISH DRAWING THE SPAGHETTI ON THE FIRST PLATE, AND FILL THE SECOND ONE TOO!

YOU CAN DO IT!

DECORATE EACH TORTOISE SHELL THE WAY SHE WANTS.

STRIPES! SPOTS! HEARTS! FLOWERS! STARS!

BE CREATIVE!

78

79

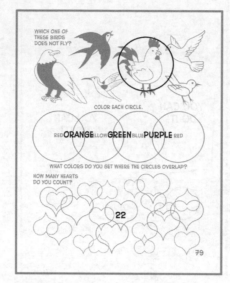

WHICH ONE OF THESE BIRDS DOES NOT FLY?

COLOR EACH CIRCLE.

RED **ORANGE** YELLOW **GREEN** BLUE **PURPLE** RED

WHAT COLORS DO YOU GET WHERE THE CIRCLES OVERLAP?

HOW MANY HEARTS DO YOU COUNT?

22

79

80

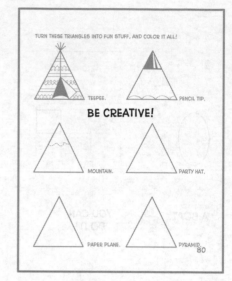

TURN THESE TRIANGLES INTO FUN STUFF, AND COLOR IT ALL!

TEEPEE. PENCIL TIP.

BE CREATIVE!

MOUNTAIN. PARTY HAT.

PAPER PLANE. PYRAMID.

80

81

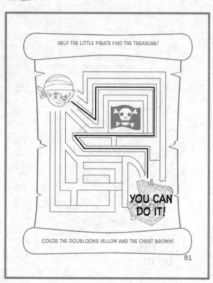

HELP THE LITTLE PIRATE FIND THE TREASURE!

YOU CAN DO IT!

COLOR THE DOUBLOONS YELLOW AND THE CHEST BROWN!

81

82

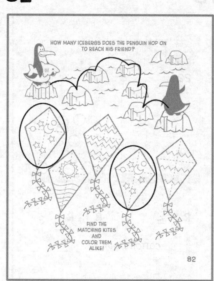

HOW MANY ICEBERGS DOES THE PENGUIN HOP ON TO REACH HIS FRIEND?

FIND THE MATCHING KITES AND COLOR THEM ALIKE!

82

83

CAN YOU COUNT THE NUMBER OF SPOTS ON THE DALMATIAN ON THE LEFT, AND MIRROR THEM ON THE SPOTLESS ONE?

42

YOU CAN DO IT!

COLOR THE TALLEST ONE PURPLE, AND THE SMALLEST YELLOW.

P

Y

83

84

DO YOU LIKE THIS PUPPY? DRAW ANOTHER ONE JUST LIKE IT, AND COLOR THE FRISBEE RED!

YOU CAN DO IT!

FOLLOW EACH THREAD TO FIND OUT WHICH BALLOON IS SHE HOLDING, AND COLOR IT BLUE!

84

85

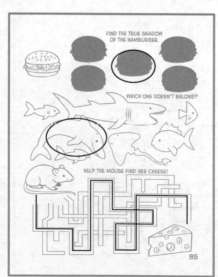

FIND THE TRUE SHADOW OF THE HAMBURGER.

WHICH ONE DOESN'T BELONG?

HELP THE MOUSE FIND HER CHEESE!

85

86

CAN YOU COUNT ALL THE BUBBLES IN THIS GLASS OF WATER?

YOU CAN DO IT!

COLOR THE RABBIT THAT MADE IT HIGHER UPSTAIRS!

COLOR THE VASE WITH THE MOST FLOWERS.

HOW MANY FLOWERS DO ALL VASES HAVE IN TOTAL?

12

86

87

COLOR ONLY THE THINGS THAT FLY.

THE BIRTHDAY CAKE ON THE RIGHT NEEDS FOUR CANDLES LIKE THIS ONE. CAN YOU DRAW THEM?

YOU CAN DO IT!

COLOR THE PRESENT THAT IS NOT LIKE THE OTHERS.

87

88

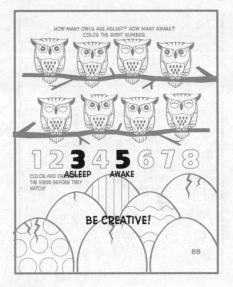

HOW MANY OWLS ARE ASLEEP? HOW MANY AWAKE? COLOR THE RIGHT NUMBER.

1 2 **3** 4 **5** 6 7 8
ASLEEP AWAKE

COLOR AND DECORATE THE EGGS BEFORE THEY HATCH!

BE CREATIVE!

88

89

CAN YOU DRAW WHAT'S ON AMY'S MIND?

BE CREATIVE!

WHICH TOOL DO PAINTERS NOT USE?

CONNECT THE DOTS TO SEE WHAT SHE'S PAINTING!

89

90

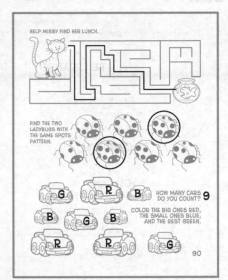

HELP MISSY FIND HER LUNCH.

FIND THE TWO LADYBUGS WITH THE SAME SPOTS PATTERN.

G R B
B G B
R R G

HOW MANY CARS DO YOU COUNT? **9**

COLOR THE BIG ONES RED, THE SMALL ONES BLUE, AND THE REST GREEN.

90

91

COLOR THE BUTTERFLY ON THE LEFT, AND DRAW ANOTHER JUST LIKE IT.

YOU CAN DO IT!

CAN YOU DRAW THE LOVE LETTER ENVELOPE WITHOUT LIFTING YOUR HAND?

YOU CAN DO IT!

THIS GLASS IS FILLED WITH ORANGE SODA.

YOU CAN DO IT!

AND THIS ONE WITH

COLOR THEM!

91

92

FIND THE DIFFERENCES BETWEEN THESE TWO SCENES...

YOU CAN DO IT!

... AND COLOR THEM ACCORDINGLY!

DO YOU KNOW THIS ANIMAL? **PANDA**
WHERE DOES IT LIVE? **CHINA**
WHAT DOES IT EAT? **BAMBOO**

92

93

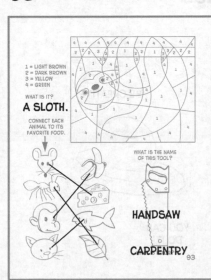

1 = LIGHT BROWN
2 = DARK BROWN
3 = YELLOW
4 = GREEN

WHAT IS IT?

A SLOTH.

CONNECT EACH ANIMAL TO ITS FAVORITE FOOD.

WHAT IS THE NAME OF THIS TOOL?

HANDSAW

CARPENTRY

93

94

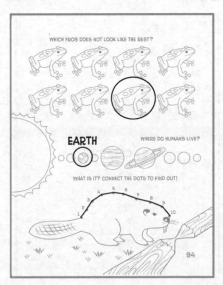

WHICH FROG DOES NOT LOOK LIKE THE REST?

EARTH

WHERE DO HUMANS LIVE?

WHAT IS IT? CONNECT THE DOTS TO FIND OUT!

94

95

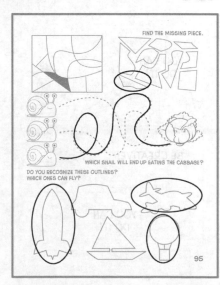

FIND THE MISSING PIECE.

WHICH SNAIL WILL END UP EATING THE CABBAGE?

DO YOU RECOGNIZE THESE OUTLINES? WHICH ONES CAN FLY?

95

96

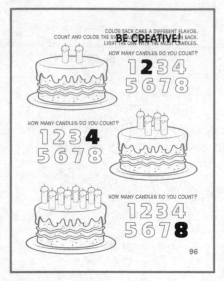

COLOR EACH CAKE A DIFFERENT FLAVOR.
COUNT AND COLOR THE RIGHT NUMBER OF CANDLES IN EACH.
LIGHT THE ONE WITH THE MOST CANDLES.

BE CREATIVE!

HOW MANY CANDLES DO YOU COUNT?
1 2 3 4 5 6 7 8

HOW MANY CANDLES DO YOU COUNT?
1 2 3 **4** 5 6 7 8

HOW MANY CANDLES DO YOU COUNT?
1 2 3 4 5 6 7 **8**

97

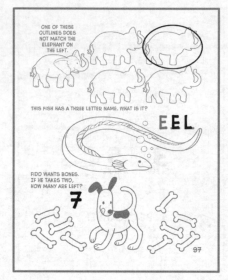

ONE OF THESE OUTLINES DOES NOT MATCH THE ELEPHANT ON THE LEFT.

THIS FISH HAS A THREE LETTER NAME. WHAT IS IT?
E E L

FIDO WANTS BONES. IF HE TAKES TWO, HOW MANY ARE LEFT?
7

98

COLOR THE TWO IDENTICAL MICE.

COUNT THE NUMBER OF STARS AND STRIPES, AND THEN COLOR THE FLAG.
YOU CAN DO IT!

BILLY'S KITE GOT TANGLED WITH OTHERS. HELP HIM FIND IT!

99

WHAT IS SALLY KNITTING?
FOLLOW THE WOOL THREAD TO THE RIGHT PIECE OF CLOTHING, AND COLOR EACH ACCORDING TO THE LIST BELOW.
YOU CAN DO IT!

1 = RED
2 = ORANGE
3 = YELLOW
4 = GREEN
5 = BLUE
6 = PURPLE

100

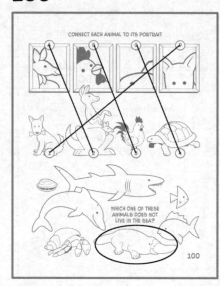

CONNECT EACH ANIMAL TO ITS PORTRAIT

WHICH ONE OF THESE ANIMALS DOES NOT LIVE IN THE SEA?

102

WRITE THE FIRST LETTER OF YOUR NAME, AND TURN IT INTO A BIRD!
D → **BE CREATIVE!**

IT'S COLD AND THESE HANDS NEED GLOVES. CAN YOU DESIGN THEM?
BE CREATIVE!
LEFT   RIGHT

YOU CAN DO IT!

GIVE HER DIFFERENT HAIRCUTS.

103

DRAW FEATHERS FOR EACH ONE! →
YOU CAN DO IT!

WHAT SONG IS IT SINGING? WRITE IT DOWN.
BE CREATIVE!

YOU CAN DO IT!

DRAW AND COLOR YOUR OWN SUNSET.

104

DRAW AND COLOR YOUR OWN SNOWMAN ARMY!

BE CREATIVE!

105

DRAW THE HEADS AND FACES OF THE PEOPLE WEARING THESE HATS.
BE CREATIVE!

CONNECT THE DOTS!

WHAT DOES THIS ANIMAL EAT? DRAW IT!

YOU CAN DO IT!

106

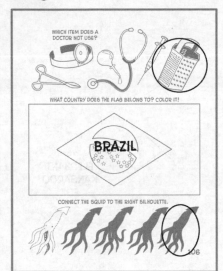

WHICH ITEM DOES A DOCTOR NOT USE?

WHAT COUNTRY DOES THE FLAG BELONG TO? COLOR IT!

BRAZIL

CONNECT THE SQUID TO THE RIGHT SILHOUETTE.

106

107

FILL THIS PAGE WITH MUSIC NOTES!

YOU CAN DO IT!

WHAT IS THE NAME OF THIS MUSICAL INSTRUMENT?

SAXOPHONE

107

108

TRACE THE DOTS TO DRAW THE FISH IN A SINGLE STROKE.

YOU CAN DO IT!

FIND THE SIX DIFFERENCES.

WHAT ANIMALS IS THIS CREATURE MADE OF?

RHINOCEROS
TIGER
RACOON

108

109

DRAW THE OTHER HALF AND COLOR IT!

ONE OF THESE DOESN'T BELONG IN THE GROUP. WHY?

HERMIT CRAB DOESN'T HAVE A SHELL OF ITS OWN

109

110

COLOR AND DECORATE THE ELEPHANTS ANYWAY YOU LIKE!
HOW MANY ARE MARCHING EAST?
HOW MANY ARE MARCHING WEST?

BE CREATIVE!
9 MARCH EAST.
6 MARCH WEST.

110

111

THE LITTLE MONKEY LOVES BANANAS. WHAT OTHER FRUITS DOES HE LIKE TO EAT?

YOU CAN DO IT!

DRAW THEM HERE!

PETER, THE GNOME, IS PLAYING THE DRUM.

WHAT OTHER INSTRUMENTS ARE THE REST OF HIS BAND MEMBERS PLAYING? DRAW THEM!

YOU CAN DO IT!

111

112

COLOR THE FIRST MASK BROWN, AND THEN CREATE YOUR OWN MONSTERS FOR HALLOWEEN!

WEREWOLF   VAMPIRE

BE CREATIVE!

ZOMBIE   MUTANT

ALIEN   DEVIL   112

113

COUNT THE NUMBER OF ORANGES. WHICH TREE HAS MORE OF THEM?

13   12

COLOR THE ONES THAT CAN'T FLY.

113

114

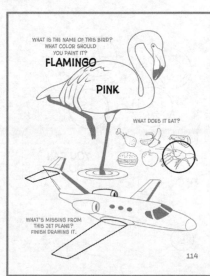

WHAT IS THE NAME OF THIS BIRD? WHAT COLOR SHOULD YOU PAINT IT?

FLAMINGO

PINK

WHAT DOES IT EAT?

WHAT'S MISSING FROM THIS JET PLANE? FINISH DRAWING IT.

114

115

HELP THE ANT FIND ITS LEAF.

COLOR THE TWO IDENTICAL CATS.

DECORATE YOUR DAD'S TIE ANYWAY YOU LIKE!

BE CREATIVE!

116

BREAKFAST IS THE MOST IMPORTANT MEAL OF THE DAY.

TRACE THE DOTTED LINES TO DRAW THE FRIED EGGS.

WHICH ONE IS THE YOLK? WHAT COLOR IS IT? YELLOW

WHAT DO WE CALL THE AREA AROUND IT? EGG WHITE

YOU CAN DO IT!

CAN YOU DRAW SAUSAGES AND BACON IN THIS EMPTY FRYING PAN?

COLOR BOTH PANS BLUE.

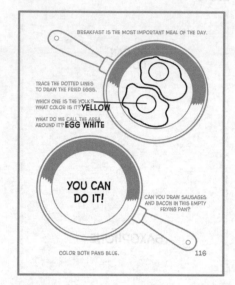

117

CONNECT EACH PERSON TO THE RIGHT TOOL.

WHAT ANIMALS IS THIS STRANGE CREATURE MADE OF?

WHAT DOES THE SHARK EAT?

ELEPHANT KANGAROO FOX

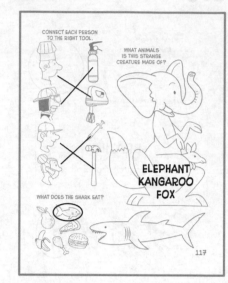

118

COUNT THE CHICKENS AND COLOR THE RIGHT NUMBER.

HOW MANY ROOSTERS DO YOU COUNT?

1 2 3 4
5 **6** 7 8

HOW MANY HENS DO YOU COUNT?

9 **10** 11 12
13 14 15 16

HOW MANY CHICKS DO YOU COUNT?

17 18 19 20
21 22 23 24

119

TRACE THE DOTTED LINES TO FINISH DRAWING THE TRAIN.

FIND THE PIECE OF THE DRAWING ON THE RIGHT THAT DOESN'T BELONG TO THE ONE ON THE LEFT.

WHICH COW DOES NOT LOOK LIKE THE OTHERS?

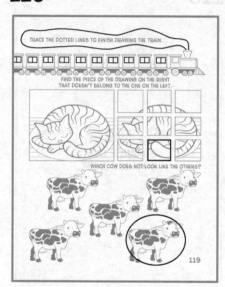

120

CONNECT EACH ANIMAL TO THE GRID IT BELONGS TO, BUT BEWARE, ONLY ONE ANIMAL GOES IN EACH GRID!

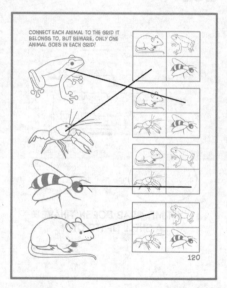

121

COLOR ONLY THE RED FOODS.

DO YOU LIKE THIS TORTOISE? DRAW ANOTHER ONE JUST LIKE HER!

YOU CAN DO IT!

WHAT DOES THE PLATYPUS EAT?

122

DRAW THE SECOND CHERRY, AND THE STRAWBERRY.

YOU CAN DO IT!

CAN YOU DRAW A RASPBERRY INSIDE THIS CIRCLE?

CRACK THE SUDOKU! EACH FRUIT CAN ONLY BE PLACED ONCE ON EACH LINE, ONCE ON EACH ROW, AND ONCE IN EACH FOUR CELL GRID.

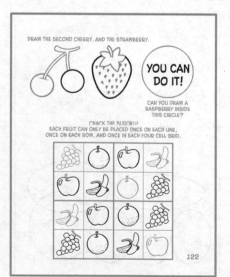

123

WHICH RABBIT WILL GET THE CARROT? FOLLOW THE DOTTED LINES TO FIND OUT.

FIND THE SIX DIFFERENCES.

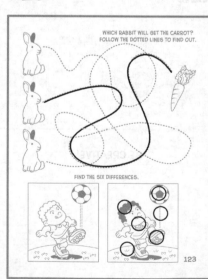

124

CAN YOU BEAT DAPHNE AT DOMINOES? COMPLETE THE SERIES BY DRAWING THE RIGHT ANIMAL ON EACH END.

124

125

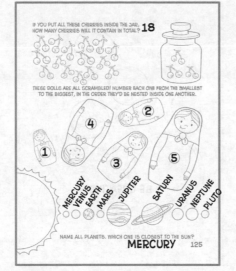

IF YOU PUT ALL THESE CHERRIES INSIDE THE JAR, HOW MANY CHERRIES WILL IT CONTAIN IN TOTAL? **18**

THESE DOLLS ARE ALL SCRAMBLED! NUMBER EACH ONE FROM THE SMALLEST TO THE BIGGEST, IN THE ORDER THEY'D BE NESTED INSIDE ONE ANOTHER.

MERCURY VENUS EARTH MARS JUPITER SATURN URANUS NEPTUNE PLUTO

NAME ALL PLANETS. WHICH ONE IS CLOSEST TO THE SUN? **MERCURY** 125

126

IF THE DOG CHASES THE CAT, THE CAT CHASES THE MOUSE, AND THE MOUSE EATS THE CHEESE, WHICH ONE IS NOT BEING CHASED?

HELP THE DOLPHIN FIND THE TUNA! 126

127

CAN YOU FIND THE SMALLER COMBINATIONS IN THE BIG GRID BELOW? COLOR THEM WHEN YOU DO!

127

128

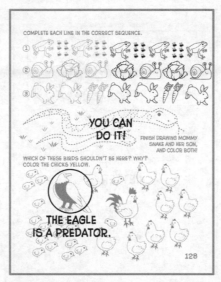

COMPLETE EACH LINE IN THE CORRECT SEQUENCE.

YOU CAN DO IT!

FINISH DRAWING MOMMY SNAKE AND HER SON, AND COLOR BOTH!

WHICH OF THESE BIRDS SHOULDN'T BE HERE? WHY? COLOR THE CHICKS YELLOW.

THE EAGLE IS A PREDATOR.

128

129

FILL THIS TREE WITH APPLES AND LEAVES! HOW MANY DID YOU DRAW?

YOU CAN DO IT!

WHAT'S HIDING BEHIND THE TRUNK? **A CAT.**

YOU CAN DO IT!

CARVE YOUR INITIALS INSIDE THE HEART.

129

130

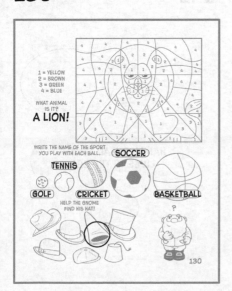

1 = YELLOW
2 = BROWN
3 = GREEN
4 = BLUE

WHAT ANIMAL IS IT? **A LION!**

WRITE THE NAME OF THE SPORT YOU PLAY WITH EACH BALL.

SOCCER
TENNIS
GOLF
CRICKET
BASKETBALL

HELP THE GNOME FIND HIS HAT!

130

131

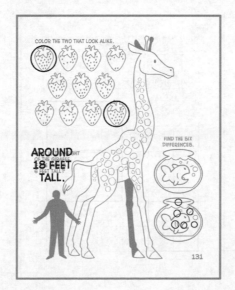

COLOR THE TWO THAT LOOK ALIKE.

AROUND **18 FEET** TALL.

FIND THE SIX DIFFERENCES.

131

132

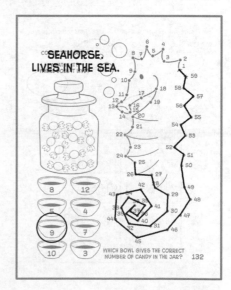

SEAHORSE, LIVES IN THE SEA.

WHICH BOWL GIVES THE CORRECT NUMBER OF CANDY IN THE JAR? 132

133

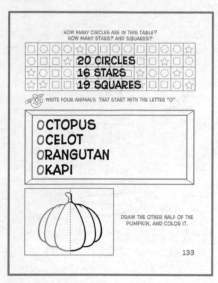

HOW MANY CIRCLES ARE IN THIS TABLE?
HOW MANY STARS? AND SQUARES?

20 CIRCLES
16 STARS
19 SQUARES

WRITE FOUR ANIMALS THAT START WITH THE LETTER "O".

OCTOPUS
OCELOT
ORANGUTAN
OKAPI

DRAW THE OTHER HALF OF THE
PUMPKIN, AND COLOR IT.

133

134

DRAW A CIRCLE AROUND THE FOODS THAT AREN'T GOOD FOR YOU,
AND COLOR THE HEALTHY ONES.

DRAW YOURSELF A HEALTHY MEAL!

FILL THE PLATE ON THE LEFT WITH
THE MAIN COURSE.

BE CREATIVE!

AND THE ONE AT YOUR RIGHT
WITH A HEALTHY DESSERT.

134

135

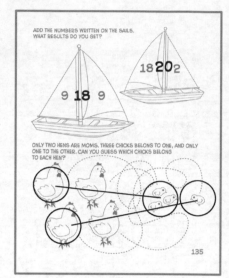

ADD THE NUMBERS WRITTEN ON THE SAILS.
WHAT RESULTS DO YOU GET?

18 20 2

9 18 9

ONLY TWO HENS ARE MOMS. THREE CHICKS BELONS TO ONE, AND ONLY
ONE TO THE OTHER. CAN YOU GUESS WHICH CHICKS BELONG
TO EACH HEN?

135

136

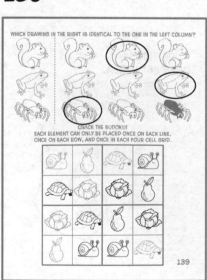

THIS PIG LOVES PLAYING IN THE MUD, SO GRAB A BROWN CRAYON, FILL
THIS PAGE WITH MUD SPLATTERS OF EVERY SHAPE AND SIZE,
AND THEN COLOR THE PIG PINK!

**YOU CAN
DO IT!**

136

137

FIND THE 10 DIFFERENCES.

WHAT IS INSIDE THIS BOTTLE?

LETTER

IN WHAT BOX WILL CAR #1 AND CAR #2 MEET,
KNOWING THAT #2 GOES TWO TIMES FASTER
THAN #1? COLOR #1 BLUE, AND #2 RED.

137

138

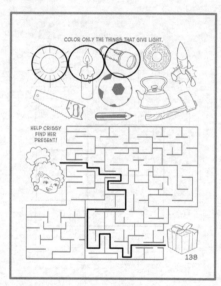

COLOR ONLY THE THINGS THAT GIVE LIGHT.

HELP CRISSY
FIND HER
PRESENT!

138

139

WHICH DRAWING IN THE RIGHT IS IDENTICAL TO THE ONE IN THE LEFT COLUMN?

CRACK THE SUDOKU!
EACH ELEMENT CAN ONLY BE PLACED ONCE ON EACH LINE,
ONCE ON EACH ROW, AND ONCE IN EACH FOUR CELL GRID.

139

140

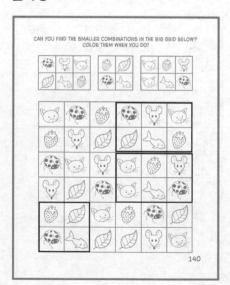

CAN YOU FIND THE SMALLER COMBINATIONS IN THE BIG GRID BELOW?
COLOR THEM WHEN YOU DO!

140

141

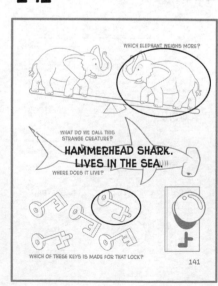

WHICH ELEPHANT WEIGHS MORE?

WHAT DO WE CALL THIS
STRANGE CREATURE?

**HAMMERHEAD SHARK.
LIVES IN THE SEA.**

WHERE DOES IT LIVE?

WHICH OF THESE KEYS IS MADE FOR THAT LOCK?

141

142

IF THE GORILLA EATS TWO BANANAS PER DAY, HOW MANY DAYS WILL IT TAKE HIM TO EAT THEM ALL? **5**

HOW MANY WATERLILIES DOES THE FROG JUMP ON IF IT GOES AROUND THE POND THREE TIMES? **21**

WHICH ONE IS NOT A TOY?

143

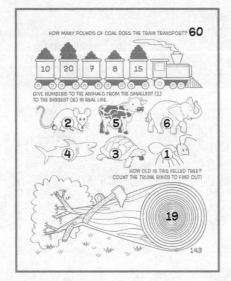

HOW MANY POUNDS OF COAL DOES THE TRAIN TRANSPORT? **60**

10 20 7 8 15

GIVE NUMBERS TO THE ANIMALS FROM THE SMALLEST (1) TO THE BIGGEST (6) IN REAL LIFE.

2 5 6
4 3 1

HOW OLD IS THIS FELLED TREE? COUNT THE TRUNK RINGS TO FIND OUT! **19**

144

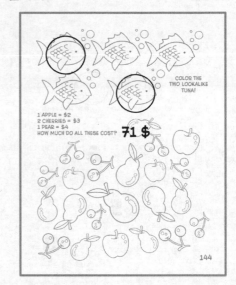

COLOR THE TWO LOOKALIKE TUNA!

1 APPLE = $2
2 CHERRIES = $3
1 PEAR = $4
HOW MUCH DO ALL THESE COST? **71 $**

145

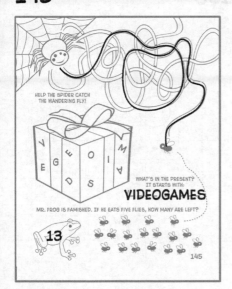

HELP THE SPIDER CATCH THE WANDERING FLY!

WHAT'S IN THE PRESENT? IT STARTS WITH: **VIDEOGAMES**

MR. FROG IS FAMISHED. IF HE EATS FIVE FLIES, HOW MANY ARE LEFT? **13**

146

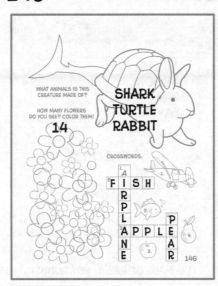

WHAT ANIMALS IS THIS CREATURE MADE OF?
SHARK
TURTLE
RABBIT

HOW MANY FLOWERS DO YOU SEE? COLOR THEM! **14**

CROSSWORDS.

F I S H
A
I R
P
L A P P L E
A
N P E A R
E

147

CREATE YOUR OWN FLAG!

BE CREATIVE!

MATCH THESE ANIMALS TO THEIR PROPER FEET!

148

ONE OF THEM HAS NO LUNGS... WHICH ONE?

IF YOU ADD ALL THE NUMBERS IN THE SQUARES, AND SUBTRACT ALL THE NUMBERS IN THE CIRCLES, WHAT WILL THE RESULT BE? **46**

5 4 21 3 16 14
12 10 8 0
3 7 9 24
6 1 2 18

DO YOU KNOW THIS INSECT? **BEETLE**
WHERE HAVE YOU SEEN IT? **THE GARDEN**
CAN IT FLY? **SOME CAN.** COLOR IT BRIGHTLY!

YOU CAN DO IT!

149

THE KIDS HAVE GONE OUTSIDE TO PLAY!

TRACE THE DOTTED LINE TO FINISH THE SWINGS.

FOLLOW THE THREAD TO FIND OUT WHICH TOP IS SALLY REALLY THROWING FOR A SPIN.

BE CREATIVE! CREATE AN ORIGINAL DESIGN TO DECORATE BILLY'S CAP.

COLOR THE BIG MARBLES GREEN, AND THE SMALL ONES BLUE.

YOU CAN DO IT!

150

CROSSWORDS.

C A T
L A D Y B U G
I
B I R D
D R A G O N F L Y

WHICH BOWL GIVES THE CORRECT NUMBER, FOR THE NUMBER OF CHERRIES IN THE JAR?

4 14 6
16 7 12

WHICH ANIMALS HERE EAT THE NECTAR FROM FLOWERS?

151

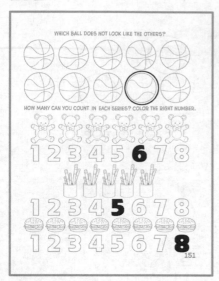

WHICH BALL DOES NOT LOOK LIKE THE OTHERS?

HOW MANY CAN YOU COUNT IN EACH SERIES? COLOR THE RIGHT NUMBER.

1 2 3 4 5 **6** 7 8

1 2 3 4 **5** 6 7 8

1 2 3 4 5 6 7 **8**

151

152

FIND THE STALLION'S CORRESPONDING SHADOW.

WHICH RABBIT GOT THE MOST CARROTS? COLOR HIS STASH!

152

153

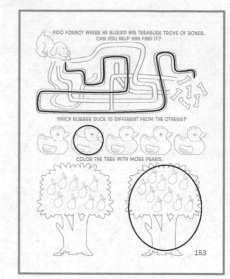

FIDO FORGOT WHERE HE BURIED HIS TREASURE TROVE OF BONES. CAN YOU HELP HIM FIND IT?

WHICH RUBBER DUCK IS DIFFERENT FROM THE OTHERS?

COLOR THE TREE WITH MORE PEARS.

153

154

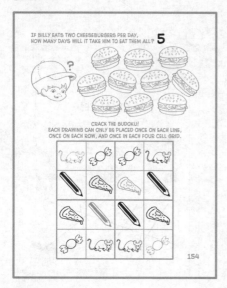

IF BILLY EATS TWO CHEESEBURGERS PER DAY, HOW MANY DAYS WILL IT TAKE HIM TO EAT THEM ALL? **5**

CRACK THE SUDOKU!
EACH DRAWING CAN ONLY BE PLACED ONCE ON EACH LINE, ONCE ON EACH ROW, AND ONCE IN EACH FOUR CELL GRID.

154

155

WRITE FOUR ANIMALS THAT START WITH THE LETTER "B".

BADGER
BABOON
BEAR
BEAVER

WHAT COLOR IS THE LIGHT?

YELLOW

WHICH ONE DOES NOT BELONG? WHY?

IT'S MADE OF RESIN, NOT RUBBER.

155

156

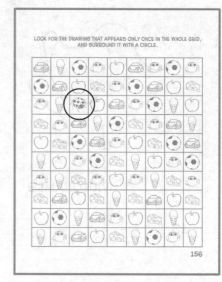

LOOK FOR THE DRAWING THAT APPEARS ONLY ONCE IN THE WHOLE GRID, AND SURROUND IT WITH A CIRCLE.

156

157

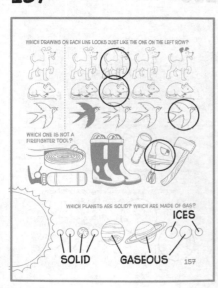

WHICH DRAWING ON EACH LINE LOOKS JUST LIKE THE ONE ON THE LEFT ROW?

WHICH ONE IS NOT A FIREFIGHTER TOOL?

WHICH PLANETS ARE SOLID? WHICH ARE MADE OF GAS?

ICES

SOLID   GASEOUS

157

158

DAPHNE WANTS A DOMINOES REMATCH! TO WIN, DRAW THE CORRESPONDING FRUIT ON EACH END.

158

159

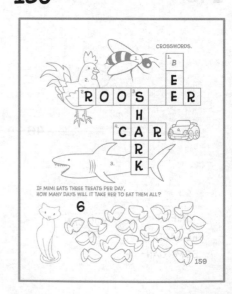

CROSSWORDS.

B
E
ROOSER ER
H
CAR
K

IF MIMI EATS THREE TREATS PER DAY, HOW MANY DAYS WILL IT TAKE HER TO EAT THEM ALL?

6

159

160

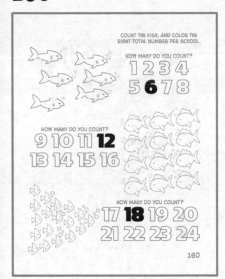

COUNT THE FISH, AND COLOR THE RIGHT TOTAL NUMBER PER SCHOOL.

HOW MANY DO YOU COUNT?
1 2 3 4
5 **6** 7 8

HOW MANY DO YOU COUNT?
9 10 11 **12**
13 14 15 16

HOW MANY DO YOU COUNT?
17 **18** 19 20
21 22 23 24

160

161

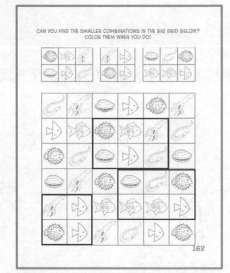

CROSS-OUT THE PIG THAT APPEARS IN THE IMAGE ONLY ONCE.

X

EVERY ANIMAL HAS A SHADOW. WHICH ONE HAS NONE?

161

162

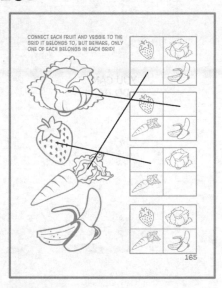

CAN YOU FIND THE SMALLER COMBINATIONS IN THE BIG GRID BELOW? COLOR THEM WHEN YOU DO!

162

163

COMPLETE THE UNDERWATER VIEW WITH FISH, AND OTHER MARINE LIFE!

BE CREATIVE!

WHICH OUTLINE DOES NOT MATCH THE FROG'S DRAWING?

DRAW DIFFERENT FLOWER BOUQUETS ACCORDING TO THE FLOWERS NAMED ON EACH VASE.

YOU CAN DO IT!

ROSES   DAISIES   BEGONIAS   MARIGOLDS   163

164

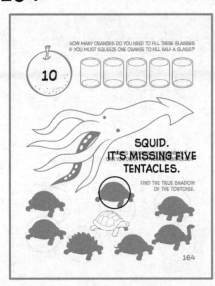

HOW MANY ORANGES DO YOU NEED TO FILL THESE GLASSES IF YOU MUST SQUEEZE ONE ORANGE TO FILL HALF A GLASS?

10

SQUID. IT'S MISSING FIVE TENTACLES.

FIND THE TRUE SHADOW OF THE TORTOISE.

164

165

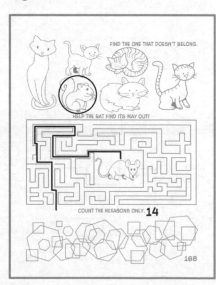

CONNECT EACH FRUIT AND VEGGIE TO THE GRID IT BELONGS TO, BUT BEWARE, ONLY ONE OF EACH BELONGS IN EACH GRID!

165

166

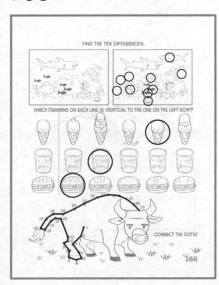

FIND THE TEN DIFFERENCES.

WHICH DRAWING ON EACH LINE IS IDENTICAL TO THE ONE ON THE LEFT ROW?

CONNECT THE DOTS!

166

167

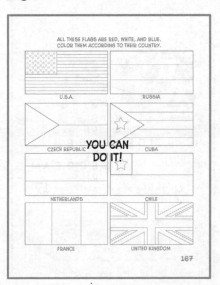

ALL THESE FLAGS ARE RED, WHITE, AND BLUE. COLOR THEM ACCORDING TO THEIR COUNTRY.

U.S.A.   RUSSIA

YOU CAN DO IT!

CZECH REPUBLIC   CUBA

NETHERLANDS   CHILE

FRANCE   UNITED KINGDOM

167

168

FIND THE ONE THAT DOESN'T BELONG.

HELP THE RAT FIND ITS WAY OUT!

COUNT THE HEXAGONS ONLY. **14**

168

419

169

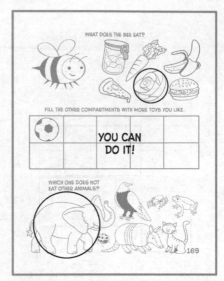

WHAT DOES THE BEE EAT?

FILL THE OTHER COMPARTMENTS WITH MORE TOYS YOU LIKE.

YOU CAN
DO IT!

WHICH ONE DOES NOT
EAT OTHER ANIMALS?

169

170

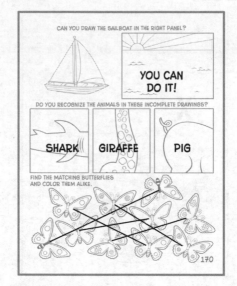

CAN YOU DRAW THE SAILBOAT IN THE RIGHT PANEL?

YOU CAN
DO IT!

DO YOU RECOGNIZE THE ANIMALS IN THESE INCOMPLETE DRAWINGS?

SHARK GIRAFFE PIG

FIND THE MATCHING BUTTERFLIES
AND COLOR THEM ALIKE.

170

171

DO YOU RECOGNIZE THESE SILHOUETTES? WHICH ONE DOES NOT BELONGS?

YOU CAN
DO IT!

WHAT'S MISSING FROM
THIS PICTURE?
DRAW IT BY TRACING
THE DOTTED LINE.

HOW MANY APPLES
DO YOU NEED TO FILL
THESE GLASSES IF
YOU MUST SQUEEZE
TWO APPLES TO FILL
A GLASS?

20

171

172

FILL THIS PAGE WITH FALLING LEAVES
FOR SALLY TO RAKE!

YOU CAN
DO IT!

172

173

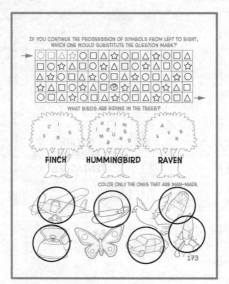

IF YOU CONTINUE THE PROGRESSION OF SYMBOLS FROM LEFT TO RIGHT,
WHICH ONE WOULD SUBSTITUTE THE QUESTION MARK?

WHAT BIRDS ARE HIDING IN THE TREES?

FINCH HUMMINGBIRD RAVEN

COLOR ONLY THE ONES THAT ARE MAN-MADE.

173

174

EACH RABBIT CAN ONLY TAKE ONE CARROT.
HOW MANY WILL THEY LEAVE BEHIND?

10

CAMEL
CAPYBARA
CARDINAL
CAT

WRITE FOUR ANIMALS THAT START WITH THE LETTER "C".

174

175

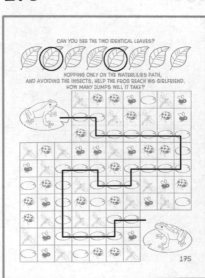

CAN YOU SEE THE TWO IDENTICAL LEAVES?

HOPPING ONLY ON THE WATERLILIES PATH,
AND AVOIDING THE INSECTS, HELP THE FROG REACH HIS GIRLFRIEND.
HOW MANY JUMPS WILL IT TAKE?

175

176

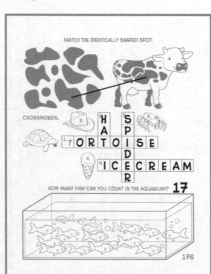

MATCH THE IDENTICALLY SHAPED SPOT.

CROSSWORDS.

HAT
SPIDER
TORTOISE
ICECREAM

HOW MANY FISH CAN YOU COUNT IN THE AQUARIUM? 17

176

177

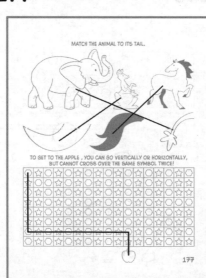

MATCH THE ANIMAL TO ITS TAIL.

TO GET TO THE APPLE, YOU CAN GO VERTICALLY OR HORIZONTALLY,
BUT CANNOT CROSS OVER THE SAME SYMBOL TWICE!

177

178

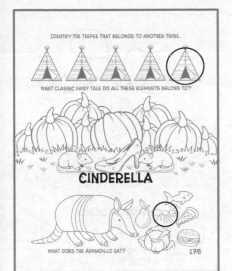

IDENTIFY THE TEEPEE THAT BELONGS TO ANOTHER TRIBE.

WHAT CLASSIC FAIRY TALE DO ALL THESE ELEMENTS BELONG TO?

CINDERELLA

WHAT DOES THE ARMADILLO EAT?

178

179

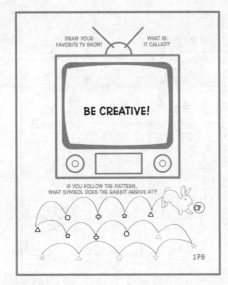

DRAW YOUR FAVORITE TV SHOW! WHAT IS IT CALLED?

BE CREATIVE!

IF YOU FOLLOW THE PATTERN, WHAT SYMBOL DOES THE RABBIT ARRIVE AT?

179

180

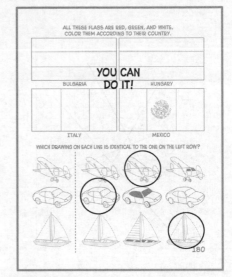

ALL THESE FLAGS ARE RED, GREEN, AND WHITE. COLOR THEM ACCORDING TO THEIR COUNTRY.

YOU CAN DO IT!

BULGARIA — HUNGARY

ITALY — MEXICO

WHICH DRAWING ON EACH LINE IS IDENTICAL TO THE ONE ON THE LEFT ROW?

180

181

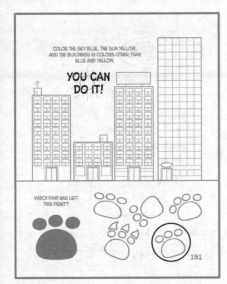

COLOR THE SKY BLUE, THE SUN YELLOW, AND THE BUILDINGS IN COLORS OTHER THAN BLUE AND YELLOW.

YOU CAN DO IT!

WHICH PAW HAS LEFT THIS PRINT?

181

182

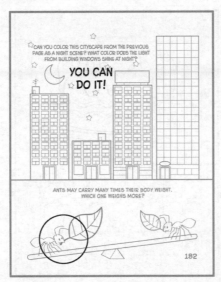

CAN YOU COLOR THIS CITYSCAPE FROM THE PREVIOUS PAGE AS A NIGHT SCENE? WHAT COLOR DOES THE LIGHT FROM BUILDING WINDOWS SHINE AT NIGHT?

YOU CAN DO IT!

ANTS MAY CARRY MANY TIMES THEIR BODY WEIGHT. WHICH ONE WEIGHS MORE?

182

183

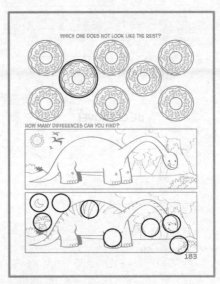

WHICH ONE DOES NOT LOOK LIKE THE REST?

HOW MANY DIFFERENCES CAN YOU FIND?

183

184

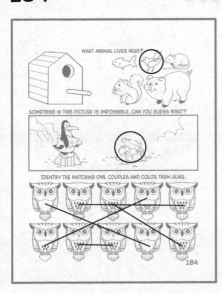

WHAT ANIMAL LIVES HERE?

SOMETHING IN THIS PICTURE IS IMPOSSIBLE. CAN YOU GUESS WHAT?

IDENTIFY THE MATCHING OWL COUPLES AND COLOR THEM ALIKE.

184

185

THESE TWO ARE RELATED. CAN YOU GUESS THE NAME OF THEIR FAMILY?

CRUSTACEAN

WRITE FOUR ANIMALS THAT START WITH THE LETTER "S".

SCORPION
SALAMANDER
SEAHORSE
SERVAL

DECORATE AND COLOR THIS CAKE TO MATCH YOUR FAVORITE FLAVORS.

BE CREATIVE!

185

186

EACH APE CAN ONLY TAKE TWO BANANAS. HOW MANY WILL THEY LEAVE BEHIND? **12**

COMPLETE THIS BY CREATING YOUR OWN SYMBOLS MOVING FORWARD.

BE CREATIVE!

HELP THE SWALLOWS MEET!

186

187

CONNECT EACH ANIMAL TO THE GRID IT BELONGS TO, BUT BEWARE, ONLY ONE ANIMAL BELONGS IN EACH GRID!

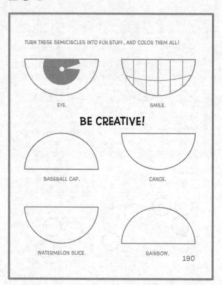

188

HOW MANY PLANES DO YOU COUNT? **13**

COLOR THE BIG ONES RED, THE SMALL ONES YELLOW, AND THE REST GREEN.

IF THE BOWLING BALL KNOCKS SEVEN PINS, HOW MANY ARE LEFT STANDING? **3**

WHAT ANIMALS IS THIS WEIRD CREATURE MADE OF?

SPIDER CHICKEN CAT

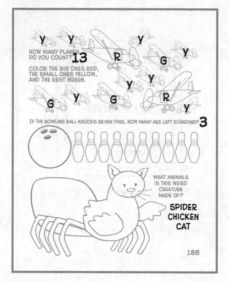

189

WHICH ONE WILL GET TO THE LETTUCE?

COPY IT! →

YOU CAN DO IT!

WHAT DO THESE HAVE IN COMMON?

THEY ARE ALL ORANGE.

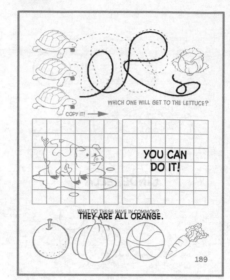

190

TURN THESE SEMICIRCLES INTO FUN STUFF, AND COLOR THEM ALL!

EYE.

SMILE.

BE CREATIVE!

BASEBALL CAP.

CANOE.

WATERMELON SLICE.

RAINBOW.

191

DRAW THE OTHER HALF.

HOW MANY CARROTS DO YOU NEED TO FILL THESE GLASSES IF YOU MUST GRIND THREE TO FILL A GLASS? **63**

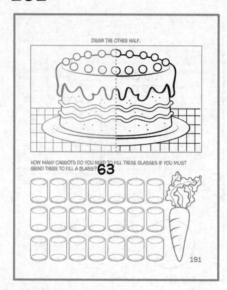

192

MATCH THE MOUSE TO THE APPROPRIATE SHADOW.

TAKING THE TUNNELS AND AVOIDING DELAYS, DRIVE THE CAR SAFELY TO MAKE IT HOME ON TIME.

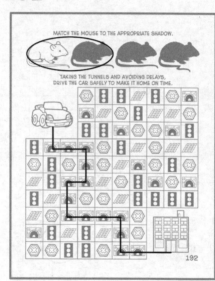

193

THEY CAN ONLY WEAR FOUR HORSESHOES EACH. HOW MANY WILL THEY LEAVE BEHIND?

28

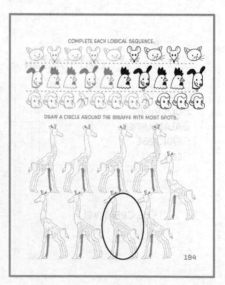

194

COMPLETE EACH LOGICAL SEQUENCE.

DRAW A CIRCLE AROUND THE GIRAFFE WITH MOST SPOTS.

195

FILL THE WATER WITH FRIENDLY FISH, AND COLOR IT ALL! →

YOU CAN DO IT!

196

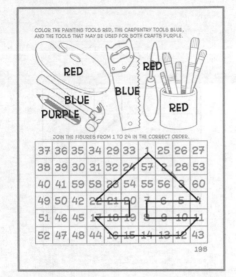

WHERE DO YOU FIND THESE PIECES IN THE DRAWING?

WHO LIVES IN HERE?

196

197

HOW DOES THE FLY GET TO THE ICECREAM?

1 = GREEN
2 = PURPLE
3 = BLUE
4 = GRAY
5 = YELLOW

WHAT IS IT?

GODZILLA!

197

198

COLOR THE PAINTING TOOLS RED, THE CARPENTRY TOOLS BLUE, AND THE TOOLS THAT MAY BE USED FOR BOTH CRAFTS PURPLE.

RED
RED
BLUE
BLUE
PURPLE
RED

JOIN THE FIGURES FROM 1 TO 24 IN THE CORRECT ORDER.

37	36	35	34	29	33	1	25	26	27
38	39	30	31	32	24	57	2	28	53
40	41	59	58	23	54	55	56	3	60
49	50	42	22	21	20	7	6	5	4
51	46	45	17	18	19	8	9	10	11
52	47	48	44	16	15	14	13	12	43

198

199

IF EACH HAMBURGER COSTS TWO DOLLARS, HOW MUCH DO THEY ALL COST?

30 DOLLARS

WHAT CHANGED IN THE SECOND AND THIRD IMAGES, COMPARED TO THE FIRST?

THE DISTANCE FROM EARTH AS THE ROCKET APPROACHES MARS.

WHAT COUNTRY IS IT?
DO YOU REMEMBER THE COLORS OF ITS FLAG?
COLOR THE MAP THE SAME WAY.

RUSSIA

199

200

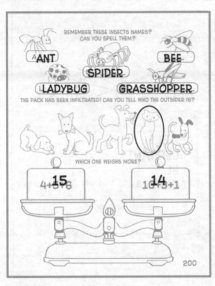

REMEMBER THESE INSECTS NAMES? CAN YOU SPELL THEM?

ANT
BEE
SPIDER
LADYBUG
GRASSHOPPER

THE PACK HAS BEEN INFILTRATED! CAN YOU TELL WHO THE OUTSIDER IS?

WHICH ONE WEIGHS MORE?

15
4+5+6

14
10+3+1

200

202

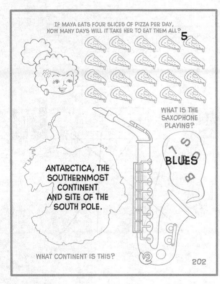

IF MAYA EATS FOUR SLICES OF PIZZA PER DAY, HOW MANY DAYS WILL IT TAKE HER TO EAT THEM ALL? 5

WHAT IS THE SAXOPHONE PLAYING?

BLUES

ANTARCTICA, THE SOUTHERNMOST CONTINENT AND SITE OF THE SOUTH POLE.

WHAT CONTINENT IS THIS?

202

203

WHAT IS THE AVERAGE NUMBER OF APPLES IN THESE BASKETS? 3.6

WHICH DRAWING IN THE RIGHT IS IDENTICAL TO THE ONE IN THE LEFT COLUMN?

TO CATCH THE MOUSE, THE CAT NEEDS TO GO THROUGH THE ODD NUMBERS.

203

204

DRAW A CIRCLE AROUND THE ITEMS YOU PUT ON YOUR FEET. COLOR THE ONES THAT COVER YOUR HEAD.

IT'S A COW.

CAN YOU SPELL THE NAME OF THIS ANIMAL? C _ _
WHAT DOES IT EAT? G _ _ _ _
WHERE DOES IT LIVE? F _ _ _

IT EATS GRASS AND LIVES IN A FARM.

COMPLETE EACH LINE IN THE CORRECT SEQUENCE.

204

205

WHICH ONE OF THESE ANIMALS IS BEST CAPABLE OF WITHSTANDING FREEZING TEMPERATURES?

HOW MANY SWALLOWS ARE FLYING EAST? COLOR THEM BLUE.
HOW MANY FLY WEST? COLOR THEM PURPLE.

**9 FLY EAST,
8 FLY WEST.**

205

206

CAN YOU FIND THE SMALLER COMBINATIONS IN THE BIG GRID BELOW?
COLOR THEM WHEN YOU DO!

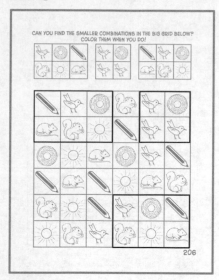

207

IF YOU CONTINUE THE PROGRESSION OF SYMBOLS FROM LEFT TO RIGHT,
WHICH ONE WOULD SUBSTITUTE THE QUESTION MARK?

COLOR PLANE #1 RED, PLANE
#2 BLUE, AND #3 YELLOW.
THEN TRACE EACH PLANE'S
AEROBATIC FLIGHT PATH
USING THEIR COLORS.

IN WHAT ORDER SHOULD THESE
PLANES TAKE FLIGHT IN ORDER TO
AVOID CRASHING EACH OTHER?

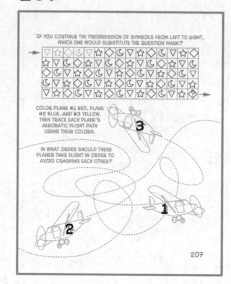

208

JUMPING ONLY FROM ONE WEBBING TO THE OTHER, WHILE
AVOIDING THE DANGERS, HELP THE SPIDER REACH HER MEAL.

CAN YOU SEE THE TWO IDENTICAL DRAGONFLIES?

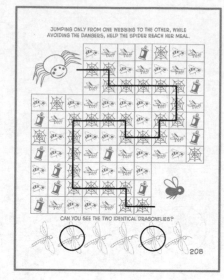

209

IT'S GETTING LATE, AND THE KIDS NEED TO BE
BACK HOME BEFORE THE SUN SETS.
TRACE THE DOTTED PATHS TO FIND OUT WHERE
EACH ONE LIVES.

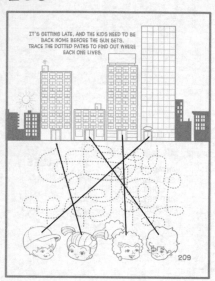

210

CONNECT EACH ONE OF THESE TO ITS APPROPRIATE FOOTPRINT.

WRITE FOUR ANIMALS THAT START WITH THE LETTER "E".

EAGLE
ELEPHANT
EEL
ECHIDNA

DRAW THE HANDS OF THE CLOCKS.

12:00   12:15   12:30

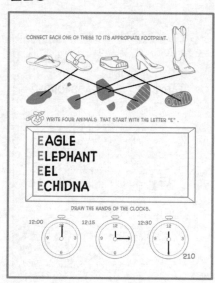

211

THE MORE LEAVES A CATERPILLAR EATS, THE MORE IT GROWS.
COUNT THE LEAVES ON EACH PLANT AND DRAW AN EQUAL NUMBER
OF CIRCLES FOR EACH CATERPILLAR.

WHAT DO CATERPILLARS TURN INTO, AND WHAT IS THE
TRANSFORMATION PROCESS CALLED?

METAMORPHOSIS

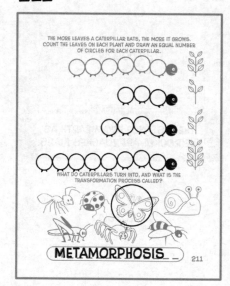

212

WHICH ONE WEIGHS MORE?

8 20 4   15 21 2

BE CREATIVE!

DECORATE AND COLOR THE THREE TEEPEES.
DRAW THE PEOPLE THAT LIVE INSIDE.

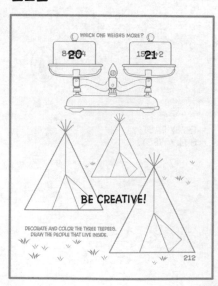

213

SOLVE THE ADDITIONS, AND WRITE YOUR RESULTS BELOW.

= 4

= 8

= 6

= 7

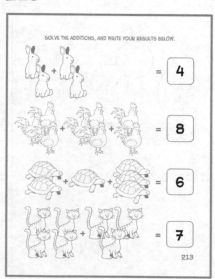

214

ALL THESE FLAGS ARE BLUE AND WHITE.
COLOR THEM ACCORDING TO THEIR COUNTRY.

ARGENTINA   ISRAEL

HONDURAS   YOU CAN   GREECE
            DO IT!

FINLAND   URUGUAY

SAN MARINO   SOMALIA

215

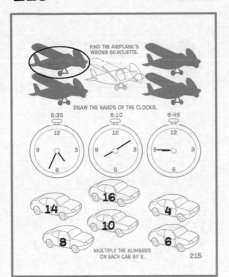

FIND THE AIRPLANE'S WRONG SILHOUETTE.

DRAW THE HANDS OF THE CLOCKS.

5:35   8:10   9:45

MULTIPLY THE NUMBERS ON EACH CAR BY 2.

14   16   4
10   8   6

215

216

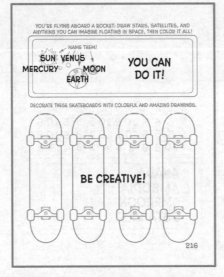

YOU'RE FLYING ABOARD A ROCKET: DRAW STARS, SATELLITES, AND ANYTHING YOU CAN IMAGINE FLOATING IN SPACE, THEN COLOR IT ALL!

NAME THEM!
SUN VENUS
MERCURY   MOON
EARTH

YOU CAN DO IT!

DECORATE THESE SKATEBOARDS WITH COLORFUL AND AMAZING DRAWINGS.

BE CREATIVE!

216

217

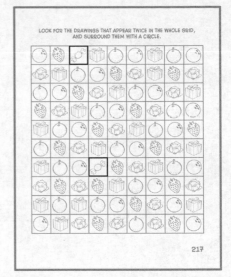

LOOK FOR THE DRAWINGS THAT APPEAR TWICE IN THE WHOLE GRID, AND SURROUND THEM WITH A CIRCLE.

217

218

CRACK THE SUDOKU!
REMEMBER EACH SYMBOL CAN ONLY BE PLACED ONCE ON EACH LINE, ONCE ON EACH ROW, AND ONCE IN EACH FOUR CELL GRID.

TO BEAT DAPHNE AT DOMINOES YOU NEED TO DRAW THE RIGHT AMOUNT OF MISSING DOTS ON EACH HEAD, OR WRITE THE TOTAL NUMBER ABOVE EACH TILE.

8   9   11   8

218

219

DRAW YOUR OWN COMIC-BOOK COVER.

DESIGN THE COVER TITLE.

BE CREATIVE!

DRAW THE CITY THEY PROTECT IN THE BACKGROUND.

GIVE THESE HEROES CAPES, MASKS, AND OTHER GEAR!

AND COLOR IT ALL!   219

220

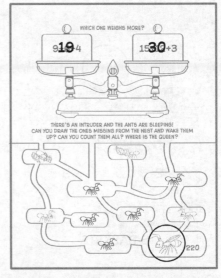

WHICH ONE WEIGHS MORE?

19 9+4   30 15+3

THERE'S AN INTRUDER AND THE ANTS ARE SLEEPING! CAN YOU DRAW THE ONES MISSING FROM THE NEST AND WAKE THEM UP? CAN YOU COUNT THEM ALL? WHERE IS THE QUEEN?

220

221

THERE ARE TEN MAMMALS TO BE FOUND IN THIS WORDSEARCH.

CLUE: ONE OF THEM IS PICTURED BELOW!

WHAT'S ITS NAME? WHERE DOES IT LIVE? WHAT DOES IT EAT?

ANTEATER
SOUTH AMERICA
ANTS

221

222

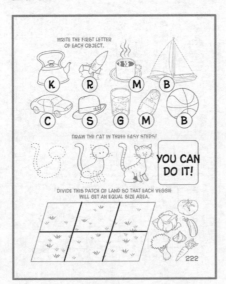

WRITE THE FIRST LETTER OF EACH OBJECT.

K   R   M   B
C   S   G   M   B

DRAW THE CAT IN THREE EASY STEPS!

YOU CAN DO IT!

DIVIDE THIS PATCH OF LAND SO THAT EACH VEGGIE WILL GET AN EQUAL SIZE AREA.

222

223

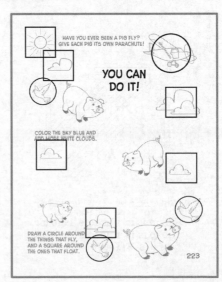

HAVE YOU EVER SEEN A PIG FLY? GIVE EACH PIG ITS OWN PARACHUTE!

YOU CAN DO IT!

COLOR THE SKY BLUE AND ADD MORE WHITE CLOUDS.

DRAW A CIRCLE AROUND THE THINGS THAT FLY, AND A SQUARE AROUND THE ONES THAT FLOAT.

223

224

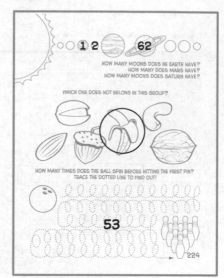

1 2 62

HOW MANY MOONS DOES HE EARTH HAVE?
HOW MANY DOES MARS HAVE?
HOW MANY MOONS DOES SATURN HAVE?

WHICH ONE DOES NOT BELONGS IN THIS GROUP?

HOW MANY TIMES DOES THE BALL SPIN BEFORE HITTING THE FIRST PIN?
TRACE THE DOTTED LINE TO FIND OUT!

53

225

EACH CAR CONSUMES 1 GALLON PER BOX. CAR #1 HAS 12 GALLONS IN ITS
TANK. CAR #2 HAS 38 GALLONS, AND #3 HAS 28 GALLONS.
WHICH ONE GETS STOPPED BY TRAFFIC LIGHTS? #1

WHICH ONE STOPS AT THE "X" SIGN? #3

WHICH ONE MAKES IT HOME? #2

COMPLETE EACH ROW SO THE SUM OF THESE NUMBERS IS ALWAYS 27.

→	9	7	14	11	5	18	3	20	18	13	4	15
9	5	5	5	10	2	10	3	3	5	10	6	
5	5	5	5	10	2	10	2	3	5	10	3	
4	10	3	6	2	5	4	2	3	4	3	3	

C ANADA
C AMBODIA
C AMEROON
C OSTA RICA

WRITE FOUR COUNTRIES THAT START WITH THE LETTER "C".

226

ADD THE MISSING NUMBER TO LEVEL THE WEIGHT.

80

35
+
45

COLOR THE
STRONGMAN'S
LEOTARD!

COMPLETE AND COLOR THE
FELINES TO TURN ONE INTO
A TIGER, AND THE OTHER
A PANTHER.

YOU CAN
DO IT!

COLOR THE BALL, ALTERNATING
RED, WHITE, AND BLUE.

227

DRAW A CIRCLE AROUND THE FOOD THAT DOESN'T BELONG.

IF FOUR APPLES FROM THE TREE ON THE LEFT WILL FILL A BASKET,
HOW MANY BASKETS WILL YOU NEED?
KEEP IN MIND THE APPLES ON THE SECOND TREE
ARE TWICE AS BIG.

2   3

5 BASKETS

228

YOU CAN
DO IT!

FILL THE CIRCLES TO MAKE LETTERS, SUCH AS THE "A" ABOVE.
CAN YOU WRITE YOUR NAME VERTICALLY OR HORIZONTALLY?

229

SALLY HAS SENT BILLY A CODED MESSAGE.
CAN YOU DECIPHER IT?

A B C D E F G H I J K L M
N O P Q R S T U V W X Y Z

I   LOVE   YOU

HOW MANY MOVES DOES THE HORSE NEED TO CHECK THE KING? 5

230

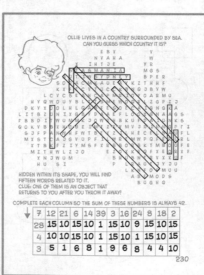

OLLIE LIVES IN A COUNTRY SURROUNDED BY SEA.
CAN YOU GUESS WHICH COUNTRY IT IS?

HIDDEN WITHIN ITS SHAPE, YOU WILL FIND
FIFTEEN WORDS RELATED TO IT.
CLUE: ONE OF THEM IS AN OBJECT THAT
RETURNS TO YOU AFTER YOU THROW IT AWAY!

COMPLETE EACH COLUMN SO THE SUM OF THESE NUMBERS IS ALWAYS 42.

→	7	12	21	6	14	39	3	16	24	8	18	2
28	15	10	15	10	1	15	10	9	15	10	15	
4	10	15	6	10	15	1	15	10	1	15	10	15
3	5	16	8	1	9	6	8	4	4	1	10	

231

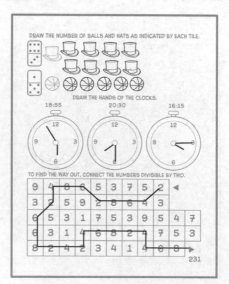

DRAW THE NUMBER OF BALLS AND HATS AS INDICATED BY EACH TILE.

DRAW THE HANDS OF THE CLOCKS.

18:55   20:30   16:15

TO FIND THE WAY OUT, CONNECT THE NUMBERS DIVISIBLE BY TWO.

9	4	8	6	5	3	7	5	2	◄
2	5	9	2	8	6	4	3	9	
6	5	3	1	7	5	3	9	4	7
6	3	1	4	6	8	2	7	5	3
8	2	4	2	3	4	1	6	8	→

232

CONNECT EACH DOS TO ITS
CORRESPONDING SHADOW.

DRAW WHAT'S MISSING FROM EACH TRAIN.
THE TRAIN GOING LEFT HAS BLUE WHEELS,
AND THE TRAIN GOING RIGHT RED WHEELS.

YOU CAN
DO IT!

233

CRACK THE SUDOKU!
EACH DRAWING CAN ONLY BE PLACED ONCE ON EACH LINE,
ONCE ON EACH ROW, AND ONCE IN EACH FOUR CELL GRID.

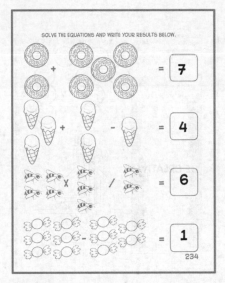

THE ROOSTER AND THE HEN HAD MANY CHICKS.
FIGURE OUT HOW MANY BY COUNTING ALL THE
BROKEN EGG SHELLS.
DRAW THE MISSING CHICKS.
12

233

234

SOLVE THE EQUATIONS AND WRITE YOUR RESULTS BELOW.

○ + ○ = **7**

🍦 + 🍦 - 🍦 = **4**

🐝 x 🐝 / 🐝 = **6**

🍬 - 🍬 = **1**

234

235

WHAT DO YOU GET WHEN YOU BLOW THROUGH THIS RING?
BUBBLES

WRITE FOUR COUNTRIES THAT START WITH
THE LETTER "A".

ANGOLA
AUSTRALIA
ARMENIA
ARGENTINA

WHICH ONE WEIGHS MORE?

20 **21**

235

236

SOMETHING'S WRONG OR AMISS WITH THESE FLAGS.
CAN YOU FIX AND COLOR THEM ACCORDINGLY?
IT'S OK TO GO BACK TO PREVIOUS PAGES TO CHECK THEM OUT.

U.S.A   ISRAEL

HONDURAS   CUBA

YOU CAN
DO IT!

FINLAND   URUGUAY

ITALY   MEXICO

236

237

TRACE THE DOTTED
LINES TO COMPLETE
THE OWLS.
HOW MANY ARE IN
THE TREE?
14

WHICH OWL IS
DIFFERENT FROM THE
OTHERS? COLOR IT
A LIGHTER SHADE OF
BROWN THAN THE
REST OF THEM.

237

238

COMPLETE EACH COLUMN SO THE SUM OF THESE NUMBERS WILL ALWAYS BE 36.

18	4	10	1	32	6	3	8	27	13	4	12
9	15	10	15	1	10	15	10	5	10	10	10
5	15	10	15	1	5	15	10	3	10	2	10
4	2	6	5	1	15	3	8	1	3	20	4

HELP ICHA MAKE THREE NECKLACES
BY DRAWING THE MISSING BEADS
IN THE RIGHT SEQUENCE.

YOU CAN
DO IT!

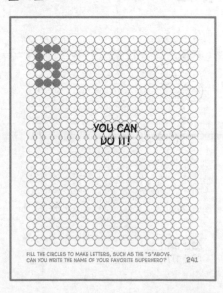

195

MULTIPLY THE NUMBER OF SPOTS ON EACH LADYBUG BY 5.
IF YOU ADD THE RESULTS, WHAT WILL THE TOTAL RESULT BE?

238

239

SURROUND THE DUCKIES WITH A LINE IN GROUPS OF THREE,
BUT BE CAREFUL NOT TO INCLUDE THE FROGS IN ANY OF THE GROUPS!

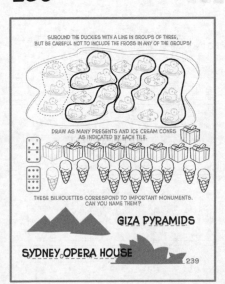

DRAW AS MANY PRESENTS AND ICE CREAM CONES
AS INDICATED BY EACH TILE.

THESE SILHOUETTES CORRESPOND TO IMPORTANT MONUMENTS.
CAN YOU NAME THEM?

GIZA PYRAMIDS

SYDNEY OPERA HOUSE

239

240

SPELL THE NAME OF EACH ANIMAL ALOUD, AND WRITE IT DOWN.

CAT   MOUSE   DOG   BIRD

FIND THE NAMES OF TEN DIFFERENT COLORS,
AND FILL THE CIRCLES WITH EACH ONE AS YOU DO.

L	A	P	E	J	B	E	N	Y	V	K
D	Y	U	K	Q	H	B	Z	D	T	E
X	L	R	S	X	Q	Y	K	W	G	F
B	L	P	O	L	Z	Q	K	N	S	A
C	S	L	D	B	Y	A	A	U	V	E
B	H	E	C	R	W	R	R	H	E	R
G	R	F	Z	O	O	D	O	R	O	V
D	L	O	L	I	V	E	P	P	E	P
Z	C	W	E	G	M	L	Y	W	D	R
D	E	T	N	N	P	I	N	K	B	S
V	G	R	A	Y	G	R	E	E	N	L

240

241

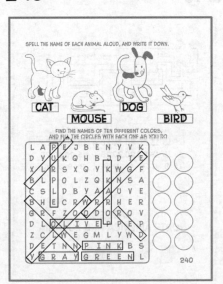

YOU CAN
DO IT!

FILL THE CIRCLES TO MAKE LETTERS, SUCH AS THE "S" ABOVE.
CAN YOU WRITE THE NAME OF YOUR FAVORITE SUPERHERO?

241

242

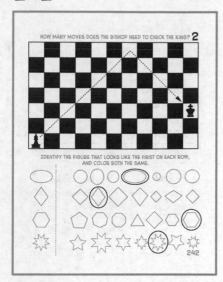

HOW MANY MOVES DOES THE BISHOP NEED TO CHECK THE KING? **2**

IDENTIFY THE FIGURE THAT LOOKS LIKE THE FIRST ON EACH ROW, AND COLOR BOTH THE SAME.

243

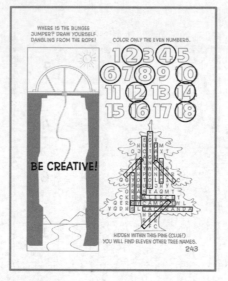

WHERE IS THE BUNGEE JUMPER? DRAW YOURSELF DANGLING FROM THE ROPE!

COLOR ONLY THE EVEN NUMBERS.

1 2 3 4 5
6 7 8 9 10
11 12 13 14
15 16 17 18

BE CREATIVE!

HIDDEN WITHIN THIS PINE (CLUE!) YOU WILL FIND ELEVEN OTHER TREE NAMES.

244

WRITE ANYTHING YOU LIKE ON THE BANNER.

BE CREATIVE!

WHICH ONE REQUIRES BATTERIES?

WHICH ONE IS NOT MAN-MADE?

COLOR THE MUSHROOMS RED, BUT LEAVE AS MANY WHITE SPOTS AS THE NUMBER ON EACH ONE INDICATES.

YOU CAN DO IT!

245

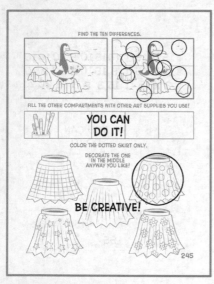

FIND THE TEN DIFFERENCES.

FILL THE OTHER COMPARTMENTS WITH OTHER ART SUPPLIES YOU USE!

YOU CAN DO IT!

COLOR THE DOTTED SKIRT ONLY.

DECORATE THE ONE IN THE MIDDLE ANYWAY YOU LIKE!

BE CREATIVE!

246

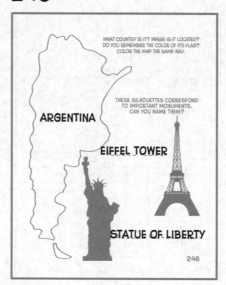

WHAT COUNTRY IS IT? WHERE IS IT LOCATED? DO YOU REMEMBER THE COLOR OF ITS FLAG? COLOR THE MAP THE SAME WAY.

ARGENTINA

THESE SILHOUETTES CORRESPOND TO IMPORTANT MONUMENTS. CAN YOU NAME THEM?

EIFFEL TOWER

STATUE OF LIBERTY

247

WRITE FOUR COUNTRIES THAT START WITH THE LETTER "U".

URUGUAY
UGANDA
UKRAINE
UNITED KINGDOM

IF EACH ICE CREAM COSTS FOUR DOLLARS, **64 DOLLARS**

HOW MUCH DO THESE COST ALL TOGETHER?

DRAW AS MANY FRUITS ON EACH TREE AS INDICATED BY THE RESPECTIVE TILE.

248

HOW MANY CUPCAKES CAN YOU COUNT? COLOR THE RIGHT NUMBER.

HOW MANY HAVE SPRINKLED HEARTS? COLOR THE RIGHT NUMBER. **3**

1 2 3
4 5 6
7 8 9
10 11
12 13
14 15
16 17
18 19
20

HOW MANY HAVE A CHERRY ON TOP? COLOR THE RIGHT NUMBER. **4**

HOW MANY HAVE SPRINKLES? COLOR THE NUMBER. **ALSO 4**

YOU CAN DO IT!

249

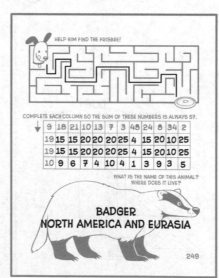

HELP HIM FIND THE FRISBEE!

COMPLETE EACH COLUMN SO THE SUM OF THESE NUMBERS IS ALWAYS 57.

9	18	21	10	13	7	3	48	24	8	34	2
19	15	15	20	20	25	4	21	5	20	10	25
19	15	15	20	20	20	25	4	15	20	10	25
10	9	6	7	4	10	4	1	3	9	3	5

WHAT IS THE NAME OF THIS ANIMAL? WHERE DOES IT LIVE?

BADGER
NORTH AMERICA AND EURASIA

250

BE CREATIVE!

FILL THE EMPTY JARS WITH ALL THE ICKY, YUCKY, GOOEY, AND HALLOWEENY STUFF YOU CAN IMAGINE! THEN WRITE THEIR NAMES ON EACH LABEL, AND COLOR IT ALL.

251

CROSSWORDS.

POPLAR
OAK
MAPLE
ELM

DRAW THE WATER AND THE GOLDFISH IN THE BOWL, THEN COLOR IT ALL!

BE CREATIVE!

WHAT ELSE CAN YOU DRAW TO MAKE IT NICER FOR THE FISH TO LIVE IN THERE?

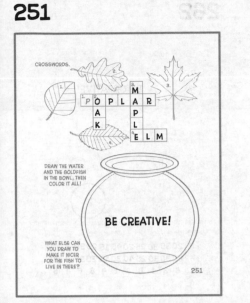

251

252

JIMMY DREW HOPSCOTCH BOARDS FOR ALL HIS FRIENDS, BUT SOME NUMBERS ARE MISSING. CAN YOU HELP HIM FILL THE EMPTY BOXES?

COUNT ONLY THE APPLES.

15

FIND ALL THE DIFFERENCES BETWEEN THESE TWO.

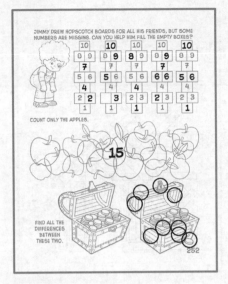

252

253

DESIGN YOUR OWN KITE, ANYWAY YOU LIKE.

BE CREATIVE!

COMPLETE THIS BY CREATING YOUR OWN SYMBOLS MOVING FORWARD.

BE CREATIVE!

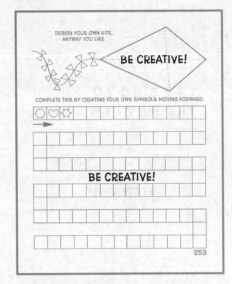

253

254

WRITE THE NAME OF EACH, AND DRAW A LINE TO CONNECT THE ONES THAT RHYME.

BEE — KEY
NOSE — FROG
CAKE — ROSE
LOG — RAKE

FIND THE MISSING PIECE.

254

255

COLOR THE FIRST MASK, AND THEN CREATE YOUR OWN CHARACTERS FOR HALLOWEEN!

PRINCESS   FAIRY

BE CREATIVE!

MERMAID   SORCERESS

SUPERHEROINE   PIRATE

255

256

FIND THE HAMMERHEAD SHARK'S NON-CORRESPONDING SHADOW.

WHAT COUNTRY IS IT? WHERE IS IT LOCATED? DO YOU REMEMBER THE SYMBOL ON ITS FLAG?

CHILE, SOUTHAMERICA, A STAR.

WHICH ONE WEIGHS MORE?

40   45

256

257

CAN YOU HELP THE SQUIRREL FIND HER TREE?

WHICH ONE DOESN'T BELONG? WHY?

SQUARE SHAPED

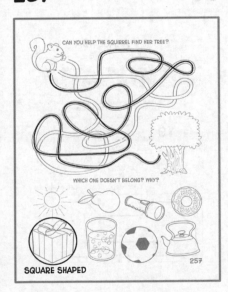

257

258

DRAW THE DOVE IN THREE EASY STEPS!

YOU CAN DO IT!

COLOR THE GEOMETRICAL SHAPE EACH OBJECT IS MOSTLY BASED ON.

TURN EACH PIECE OF SCRAP METAL INTO THREE COOL ROBOTS!

BE CREATIVE!

258

259

HELP OLLIE FIND THE TREASURE CHESTS HIDDEN ON THE ISLAND!

YOU CAN DO IT!

COLOR THE ISLAND'S MAP TO MAKE IT LOOK REAL, AND GIVE NAMES TO ALL THE PLACES IN IT!

259

260

SALLY HAS SENT BILLY ANOTHER SECRET MESSAGE. CAN YOU BREAK THE CODE?

LET'S GO TO THE MOVIES.

DRAW YOURSELF AND YOUR BEST FRIEND AS THE MEANEST COWBOY OR COWGIRL OF THE OLD WEST!

WANTED   WANTED

BE CREATIVE!

WRITE BOTH YOUR NAMES BELOW THE PICTURES.

261

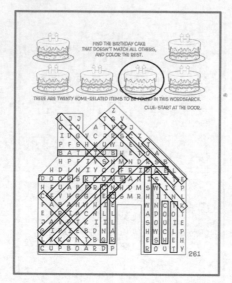

FIND THE BIRTHDAY CAKE THAT DOESN'T MATCH ALL OTHERS, AND COLOR THE REST.

THERE ARE TWENTY HOME-RELATED ITEMS TO BE FOUND IN THIS WORDSEARCH.
CLUE: START AT THE DOOR.

262

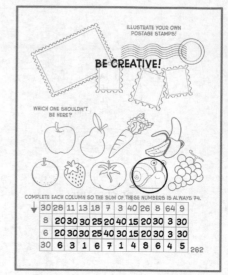

ILLUSTRATE YOUR OWN POSTAGE STAMPS!

BE CREATIVE!

WHICH ONE SHOULDN'T BE HERE?

COMPLETE EACH COLUMN SO THE SUM OF THESE NUMBERS IS ALWAYS 74.

263

YOU CAN DO IT!

FILL THE CIRCLES TO MAKE LETTERS, SUCH AS THE "U" ABOVE.
CAN YOU WRITE THE NAME OF YOUR TOWN AND COUNTRY?

264

DRAW MORE CUPCAKES, OR CROSS THEM OUT UNTIL THERE'S 15 ON EACH TRAY.

CAN YOU ALSO HELP HER FINISH BAKING HER COOKIES?

DRAW THE MISSING GINGERBREAD MEN IN EACH ROW.

265

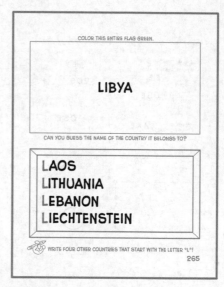

COLOR THIS ENTIRE FLAG GREEN.

LIBYA

CAN YOU GUESS THE NAME OF THE COUNTRY IT BELONGS TO?

LAOS
LITHUANIA
LEBANON
LIECHTENSTEIN

WRITE FOUR OTHER COUNTRIES THAT START WITH THE LETTER "L"!

266

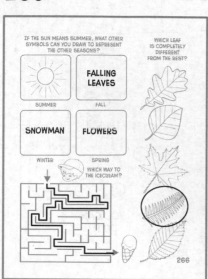

IF THE SUN MEANS SUMMER, WHAT OTHER SYMBOLS CAN YOU DRAW TO REPRESENT THE OTHER SEASONS?

WHICH LEAF IS COMPLETELY DIFFERENT FROM THE REST?

FALLING LEAVES

SUMMER   FALL

SNOWMAN   FLOWERS

WINTER   SPRING

WHICH WAY TO THE ICECREAM?

267

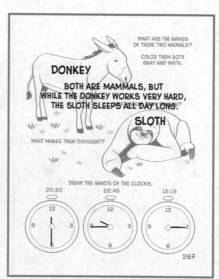

WHAT ARE THE NAMES OF THESE TWO ANIMALS?

COLOR THEM BOTH GRAY AND WHITE.

DONKEY

BOTH ARE MAMMALS, BUT WHILE THE DONKEY WORKS VERY HARD, THE SLOTH SLEEPS ALL DAY LONG.

SLOTH

WHAT MAKES THEM DIFFERENT?

DRAW THE HANDS OF THE CLOCKS.

00:30   22:45   15:15

268

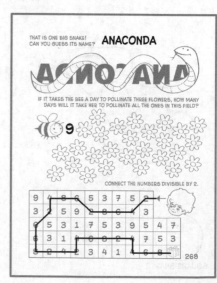

THAT IS ONE BIG SNAKE! CAN YOU GUESS ITS NAME?   ANACONDA

IF IT TAKES THE BEE A DAY TO POLLINATE THREE FLOWERS, HOW MANY DAYS WILL IT TAKE HER TO POLLINATE ALL THE ONES IN THIS FIELD?

9

CONNECT THE NUMBERS DIVISIBLE BY 2.

269

FIND THE SIX DIFFERENCES.

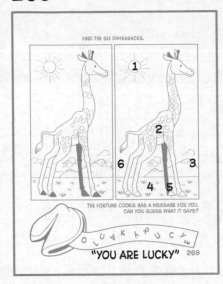

THE FORTUNE COOKIE HAS A MESSAGE FOR YOU. CAN YOU GUESS WHAT IT SAYS?

"YOU ARE LUCKY" 269

270

COMPLETE THE SERIES.

$5 = \bigcirc + \star$
$\frac{5}{3} = \square + \square$
$4 = \square + \star$

FIND THE ONE SHADOW THAT DOESN'T MATCH THE SQUIRREL.

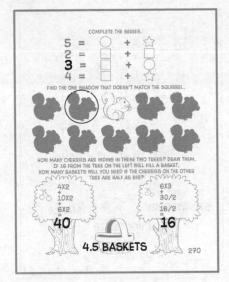

HOW MANY CHERRIES ARE HIDING IN THESE TWO TREES? DRAW THEM. IF 16 FROM THE TREE ON THE LEFT WILL FILL A BASKET, HOW MANY BASKETS WILL YOU NEED IF THE CHERRIES ON THE OTHER TREE ARE HALF AS BIG?

4X2 + 10X2 + 6X2 = **40**

6X3 + 30/2 + 16/2 = **16**

4.5 BASKETS 270

271

DROMEDARY   BACTRIAN

EACH ONE OF THESE TWO CAMELS IS CALLED BY A DIFFERENT NAME. DO YOU KNOW THEM?

TO PAINT A DOOR YOU NEED A WHOLE CAN OF PAINT.

TO PAINT A WINDOW FRAME YOU NEED TWO.

TO PAINT THE WALL ON EACH FLOOR THREE.

HOW MANY CANS WILL YOU NEED TO PAINT ALL THESE BUILDINGS?

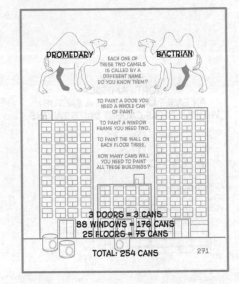

3 DOORS = 3 CANS
88 WINDOWS = 176 CANS
25 FLOORS = 75 CANS

TOTAL: 254 CANS 271

272

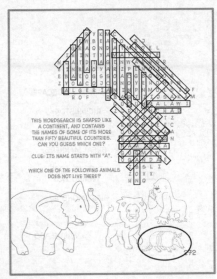

THIS WORDSEARCH IS SHAPED LIKE A CONTINENT, AND CONTAINS THE NAMES OF SOME OF ITS MORE THAN FIFTY BEAUTIFUL COUNTRIES. CAN YOU GUESS WHICH ONE?

CLUE: ITS NAME STARTS WITH "A".

WHICH ONE OF THE FOLLOWING ANIMALS DOES NOT LIVE THERE?

272

273

DRAW AND COLOR YOUR FAVORITE FLAGS FROM SOME OF THE COUNTRIES ON THE PREVIOUS PAGE'S WORDSEARCH.

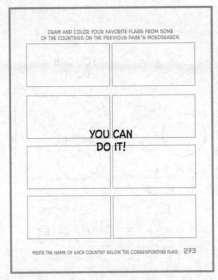

YOU CAN DO IT!

WRITE THE NAME OF EACH COUNTRY BELOW THE CORRESPONDING FLAG. 273

274

COMPLETE THE PATTERN AS BEST YOU CAN.

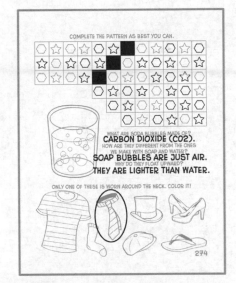

WHAT ARE SODA BUBBLES MADE OF? **CARBON DIOXIDE (CO2).** HOW ARE THEY DIFFERENT FROM THE ONES WE MAKE WITH SOAP AND WATER? **SOAP BUBBLES ARE JUST AIR.** WHY DO THEY FLOAT UPWARD? **THEY ARE LIGHTER THAN WATER.**

ONLY ONE OF THESE IS WORN AROUND THE NECK. COLOR IT!

274

275

TURN EACH PIECE OF SCRAP METAL INTO THREE COOL ROBOTS!

BE CREATIVE!

COMPLETE THE SERIES.

$\frac{3}{5} = \star + \bigcirc$
$\frac{4}{4} = \star + \bigcirc$

COPY HER! →

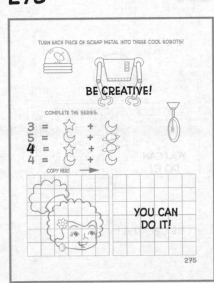

YOU CAN DO IT!

275

276

FILL IN THE BLANK SPACES TO GET THE GIVEN RESULTS.

10	+	75	-	**1**	+	18	-	**2**	=	100
88	-	81	+	24	-	6	+	**53**	=	78
6	+	42	-	**48**	+	48	-	**8**	=	56
35	-	18	+	**3**	-	6	+	**7**	=	21

DRAW AND COLOR YOUR OWN COMIC-STRIP!

YOU CAN DO IT!

276

277

HELP THE DONKEY FIND ITS LUNCH!

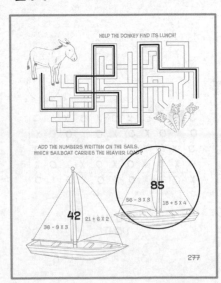

ADD THE NUMBERS WRITTEN ON THE SAILS. WHICH SAILBOAT CARRIES THE HEAVIER LOAD?

42 21 + 6 X 2 36 - 9 X 3

85 56 - 3 X 3 18 + 5 X 4

277

278

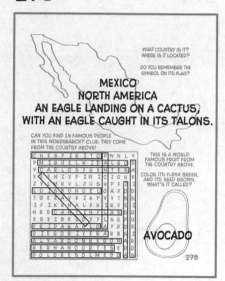

WHAT COUNTRY IS IT?
WHERE IS IT LOCATED?

DO YOU REMEMBER THE
SYMBOL ON ITS FLAG?

MEXICO
NORTH AMERICA
AN EAGLE LANDING ON A CACTUS,
WITH AN EAGLE CAUGHT IN ITS TALONS.

CAN YOU FIND 14 FAMOUS PEOPLE
IN THIS WORDSEARCH? CLUE: THEY COME
FROM THE COUNTRY ABOVE!

THIS IS A WORLD
FAMOUS FRUIT FROM
THE COUNTRY ABOVE.

COLOR ITS FLESH GREEN,
AND ITS SEED BROWN.
WHAT'S IT CALLED?

AVOCADO

278

279

CRACK THE SUDOKU!
EACH DRAWING CAN ONLY BE PLACED ONCE ON EACH LINE,
ONCE ON EACH ROW, AND ONCE IN EACH FOUR CELL GRID.

CAN YOU GUESS EACH
DOUGHNUT'S FLAVOR?
COLOR THEM ACCORDINGLY!

STRAWBERRY
CHOCOLATE
MAPLE

279

280

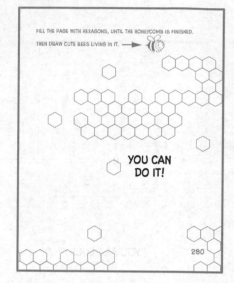

FILL THE PAGE WITH HEXAGONS, UNTIL THE HONEYCOMB IS FINISHED.

THEN DRAW CUTE BEES LIVING IN IT. →

YOU CAN
DO IT!

280

281

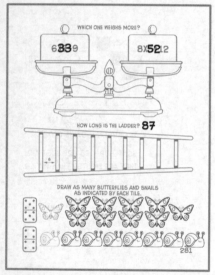

WHICH ONE WEIGHS MORE?

6 33 9   8X 52 12

HOW LONG IS THE LADDER? 87

DRAW AS MANY BUTTERFLIES AND SNAILS
AS INDICATED BY EACH TILE.

281

282

WHAT IS THE NAME OF THIS BIRD?
WHAT DOES IT EAT?

DRAW ANOTHER ONE JUST LIKE IT.

YOU CAN
DO IT!

FIND THE TWO IDENTICAL MUSHROOMS.

5	2	3	3	6	3	5	27
4	1	1	2	1	8	9	26
9	3	4	5	7	11	14	53

FILL THE BLANKS SO THE RESULTS OF ADDING THE NUMBERS
MATCH BOTH VERTICALLY AND HORIZONTALLY.

282

283

HOW MANY OF EACH TYPE OF
ICECREAM CAN YOU COUNT?
WRITE THE CORRECT NUMBER.

7

11

18

CAN YOU GUESS THE NAME
OF THIS COUNTRY?
WHAT IS IT FAMOUS FOR?

JAPAN

BEAUTIFUL LANDSCAPE

RICH HISTORY

INSPIRING ART

GREAT MANNERS

CUTTING EDGE
TECHNOLOGY

GIANT MONSTERS
IT IS MADE OF
MANY ISLANDS.
WHAT DO WE CALL A
GROUP OF ISLANDS?

A RCHIPELAGO

283

284

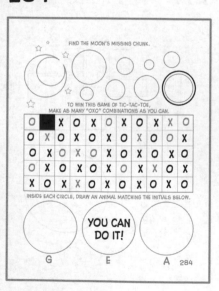

FIND THE MOON'S MISSING CHUNK.

TO WIN THIS GAME OF TIC-TAC-TOE,
MAKE AS MANY "OXO" COMBINATIONS AS YOU CAN.

O		X	O	X	O	X	O	X	X	O
O	X	O	X	O	X	O	X	O	O	X
O	X	O	X	O	X	O	X	O	X	O
O	X	O	X	O	X	O	X	X	O	X
X	O	X	X	O	X	O	X	O	X	O

INSIDE EACH CIRCLE, DRAW AN ANIMAL MATCHING THE INITIALS BELOW.

YOU CAN
DO IT!

G   E   A   284

285

THIS BEACH LOOKS EMPTY!
CAN YOU FILL IT WITH CHILDREN HAVING FUN?
SOME MAY BE SWIMMING.
SOME MAY BE PLAYING IN THE SAND.

CAN YOU DRAW MORE
BRIGHTLY COLORED
UMBRELLAS?

BE CREATIVE!

YOU CAN
DO IT!

USING THESE ELEMENTS,
DRAW YOUR OWN SAND CASTLE.

285

286

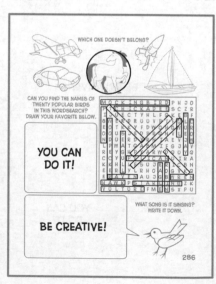

WHICH ONE DOESN'T BELONG?

CAN YOU FIND THE NAMES OF
TWENTY POPULAR BIRDS
IN THIS WORDSEARCH?
DRAW YOUR FAVORITE BELOW.

YOU CAN
DO IT!

BE CREATIVE!

WHAT SONG IS IT SINGING?
WRITE IT DOWN.

286

287

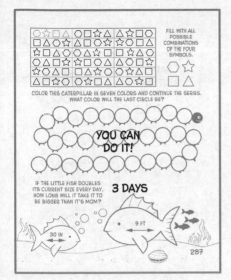

FILL WITH ALL POSSIBLE COMBINATIONS OF THE FOUR SYMBOLS.

COLOR THIS CATERPILLAR IN SEVEN COLORS AND CONTINUE THE SERIES. WHAT COLOR WILL THE LAST CIRCLE BE?

YOU CAN DO IT!

IF THE LITTLE FISH DOUBLES ITS CURRENT SIZE EVERY DAY, HOW LONG WILL IT TAKE IT TO BE BIGGER THAN IT'S MOM?

3 DAYS

30 IN   9 FT

288

FILL THE SHELVES WITH AS MANY BOOKS AS YOU CAN.

YOU CAN DO IT!

BE CREATIVE!

CAN YOU ILLUSTRATE THE COVER OF HIS BOOK?

WHAT IS IT ABOUT?

289

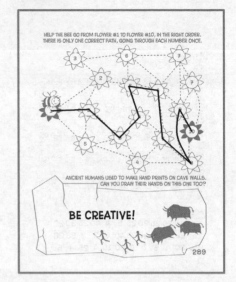

HELP THE BEE GO FROM FLOWER #1 TO FLOWER #10, IN THE RIGHT ORDER. THERE IS ONLY ONE CORRECT PATH, GOING THROUGH EACH NUMBER ONCE.

ANCIENT HUMANS USED TO MAKE HAND PRINTS ON CAVE WALLS. CAN YOU DRAW THEIR HANDS ON THIS ONE TOO?

BE CREATIVE!

290

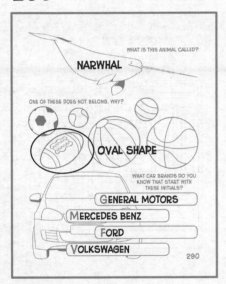

WHAT IS THIS ANIMAL CALLED?

NARWHAL

ONE OF THESE DOES NOT BELONG. WHY?

OVAL SHAPE

WHAT CAR BRANDS DO YOU KNOW THAT START WITH THESE INITIALS?

GENERAL **M**OTORS
MERCEDES **B**ENZ
FORD
VOLKSWAGEN

291

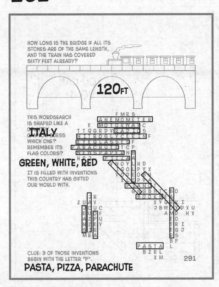

HOW LONG IS THE BRIDGE IF ALL ITS STONES ARE OF THE SAME LENGTH, AND THE TRAIN HAS COVERED SIXTY FEET ALREADY?

120FT

THIS WORDSEARCH IS SHAPED LIKE A COUNTRY, GUESS WHICH ONE? REMEMBER ITS FLAG COLORS?

ITALY

GREEN, WHITE, RED

IT IS FILLED WITH INVENTIONS THIS COUNTRY HAS GIFTED OUR WORLD WITH.

CLUE: 3 OF THOSE INVENTIONS BEGIN WITH THE LETTER "P".

PASTA, PIZZA, PARACHUTE

292

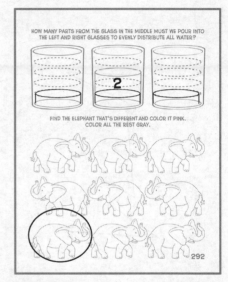

HOW MANY PARTS FROM THE GLASS IN THE MIDDLE MUST WE POUR INTO THE LEFT AND RIGHT GLASSES TO EVENLY DISTRIBUTE ALL WATER?

2

FIND THE ELEPHANT THAT'S DIFFERENT AND COLOR IT PINK. COLOR ALL THE REST GRAY.

293

WHAT TIME IS IT?

THIS STRANGE CREATURE IS MADE OF 3 ANIMALS. CAN YOU WRITE THEIR NAMES?

PIG
SQUIRREL
HEDGEHOG

294

CONNECT THESE ANIMALS TO THEIR FAVORITE FOOD!

WHICH ONE DOES NOT BELONG IN THIS SET OF TOOLS?

CAN YOU NAME ALL THE PLANETS? WHICH ONE IS CLOSEST, AND WHICH ONE IS FARTHEST FROM THE SUN?

MERCURY (CLOSEST), VENUS, EARTH, MARS, JUPITER, SATURN, URANUS, NEPTUNE, AND DWARF PLANET PLUTO (FARTHEST)!

295

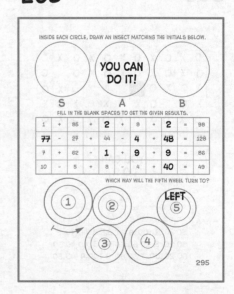

INSIDE EACH CIRCLE, DRAW AN INSECT MATCHING THE INITIALS BELOW.

YOU CAN DO IT!

S   A   B

FILL IN THE BLANK SPACES TO GET THE GIVEN RESULTS.

1	+	85	+	**2**	+	8	+	**2**	= 98
77	-	27	+	44	-	4	+	**48**	= 128
7	+	62	-	**1**	+	9	+	**9**	= 86
10	-	5	+	8	-	4	+	**40**	= 49

WHICH WAY WILL THE FIFTH WHEEL TURN TO?

LEFT

296

HOW WILL SHE FEEL WHEN SHE MAKES IT TO THE QUESTION MARK?

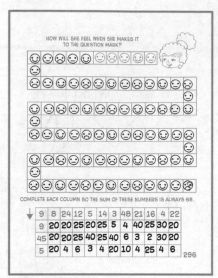

COMPLETE EACH COLUMN SO THE SUM OF THESE NUMBERS IS ALWAYS 68.

↓	9	8	24	12	5	14	3	48	21	16	4	22
9	20	20	25	20	25	5	4	40	25	30	20
45	20	20	25	40	20	40	6	3	2	30	20
5	20	4	6	3	4	20	10	4	25	4	6

296

297

SUBTRACT THE NUMBER OF BEES FROM THE TOTAL OF BUTTERFLIES YOU COUNT.

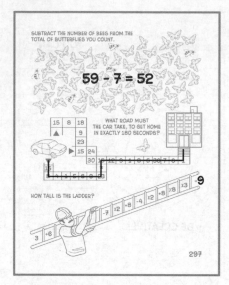

59 - 7 = 52

WHAT ROAD MUST THE CAR TAKE, TO GET HOME IN EXACTLY 180 SECONDS?

HOW TALL IS THE LADDER?

297

298

CIRCLE EVERY OTHER LETTER TO DECODE THE SECRET MESSAGE THAT CAME WITH THIS PRESENT.

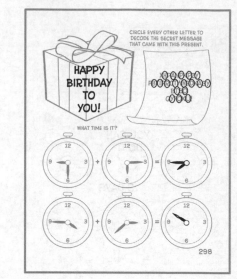

HAPPY BIRTHDAY TO YOU!

WHAT TIME IS IT?

298

299

HELP THE ALIEN FIND THE SHORTEST WAY BACK TO ITS HOME PLANET, PASSING THROUGH ONLY TEN STARS.

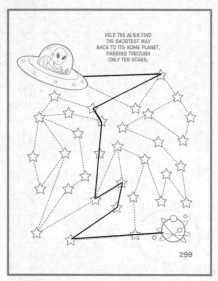

299

300

YOU CAN DO IT!

AMY IS ABOUT TO MAKE HER STAGE DEBUT. CAN YOU DRAW HER REFLECTION IN THE MIRROR?

FIND 15 TERMS RELATED TO THEATER (CLUE!) IN THIS WORDSEARCH!

300

302

HOW IS THE GANG GOING TO MAKE IT OUT OF THE MAZE?

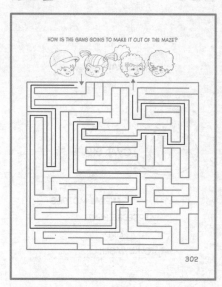

302

303

TO WIN THIS GAME OF TIC-TAC-TOE, MAKE AS MANY "OXO" COMBINATIONS AS YOU CAN.

O	X	O	X	O	X	O	X	O	O
O	X	O	X	O	X	O	X	O	X
X	O	X	O	■	X	O	X	O	X
O	X	O	X	O	X	O	X	O	X
O	X	O	X	O	X	O	X	O	O

INSIDE EACH CIRCLE, DRAW A VEGGIE MATCHING THE INITIALS BELOW.

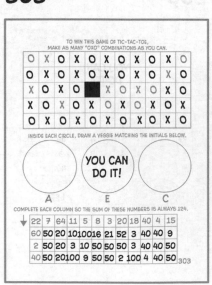

A   YOU CAN DO IT!   C
           E

COMPLETE EACH COLUMN SO THE SUM OF THESE NUMBERS IS ALWAYS 124.

↓	22	7	64	11	5	8	3	20	18	40	4	15
60	50	20	10	10	10	16	21	52	3	40	40	9
2	50	20	3	10	50	50	3	40	40	50
40	50	20	100	9	50	50	2	100	4	40	50

303

304

SPELL THESE BIRTHDAY WORDS THE RIGHT WAY!

KEAC   CAKE
FTIG   GIFT
PYPAH   HAPPY
LDSCANE CANDLES
USTSEG GUESTS

FIND THE DONKEY'S CORRESPONDING SILHOUETTE.

304

305

COMPLETE.

3 - 2 -1 + 5 + 4 -1 + 6 -1 + 2 = 15

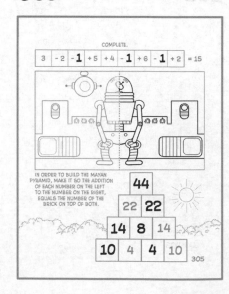

IN ORDER TO BUILD THE MAYAN PYRAMID, MAKE IT SO THE ADDITION OF EACH NUMBER ON THE LEFT TO THE NUMBER ON THE RIGHT, EQUALS THE NUMBER OF THE BRICK ON TOP OF BOTH.

	44	
22		22
14	8	14
10	4	4	10

305

306

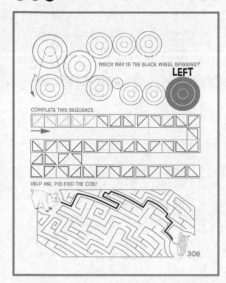

WHICH WAY IS THE BLACK WHEEL SPINNING?

LEFT

COMPLETE THIS SEQUENCE.

HELP MR. PIG FIND THE COB!

307

CAN YOU FIND THE FRUIT COMBINATIONS ON THE RIGHT WITHIN THE MAIN GRID?

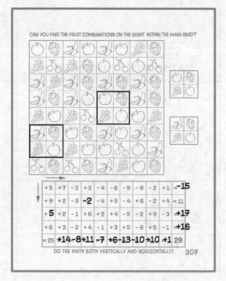

+5	+7	-2	+3	-4	-6	-9	-8	-2	+1	=-15
+9	+2	+1	-2	-4	+5	-4	+6	-2	+4	=11
+5	+2	-1	+6	+2	+4	-5	-2	+9	-3	=17
+6	+3	-2	+4	-1	+3	+5	-6	+5	-1	=16
=25	+14	-8	+11	-7	+6	-13	-10	+10	+1	29

DO THE MATH BOTH VERTICALLY AND HORIZONTALLY!

308

HOW MUCH DO YOU KNOW ABOUT OUR PLANET? TEST YOUR KNOWLEDGE BY CRACKING THIS WORDSEARCH!

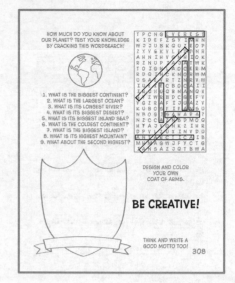

1. WHAT IS THE BIGGEST CONTINENT?
2. WHAT IS THE LARGEST OCEAN?
3. WHAT IS ITS LONGEST RIVER?
4. WHAT IS ITS BIGGEST DESERT?
5. WHAT IS ITS BIGGEST INLAND SEA?
6. WHAT IS THE COLDEST CONTINENT?
7. WHAT IS THE BIGGEST ISLAND?
8. WHAT IS ITS HIGHEST MOUNTAIN?
9. WHAT ABOUT THE SECOND HIGHEST?

DESIGN AND COLOR YOUR OWN COAT OF ARMS.

BE CREATIVE!

THINK AND WRITE A GOOD MOTTO TOO!

309

DRAW PATHS CONNECTING NUMBERS 1 TO 9 TO FORM A CONSTELLATION.

URSA MAJOR

CAN YOU GUESS ITS NAME?

CONNECT ALL THE TOTALS THAT EQUAL 9!

310

DRAW MAYA'S PET. IT CAN BE ANY ANIMAL YOU CHOOSE! COLOR THE WHOLE PICTURE.

BE CREATIVE!

FILL THE MISSING NUMBERS FROM 1 TO 16, IN ORDER TO KEEP MOVING FROM LEFT TO RIGHT, UP OR DOWN, PANEL BY PANEL, WITHOUT REPEATING ANY NUMBERS, NOR SKIPPING ANY PANELS.

10	11	16	15
9	12	13	14
8	1	2	3
7	6	5	4

IF THE FIRST WHEEL OF CHEESE WEIGHS 12 POUNDS, WHAT IS THE SECOND WHEEL'S WEIGHT?

10 LB

311

FILL EACH "TETRIS" BLOCK WITH A DIFFERENT COLOR. THEN FIGURE OUT HOW TO PROPERLY STACK ALL OF THEM INSIDE GRIDS "A" AND "B".

THERE'S ONLY TWO POSSIBLE WAYS TO DO SO!

YOU CAN DO IT!

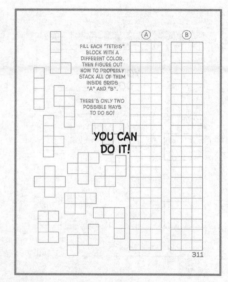

312

HOW MANY THREADS WILL THE SPIDER NEED TO REPAIR HER WEB?

BETWEEN 10 AND 12

WHAT ANIMAL IS THIS? **WALRUS** WHERE DOES IT LIVE? **THE ARCTIC**

CONNECT THE DOTS TO FIND OUT!

IMAGINE YOU'RE AN ANCIENT HUMAN, AND DRAW YOUR OWN CAVE WALL PAINTINGS.

BE CREATIVE!

313

COMPLETE THE SEQUENCES.

21	15	9	5	3	5	9	15	21
16	10	8	4	2	4	8	10	16
8	6	4	2	0	2	6	8	8

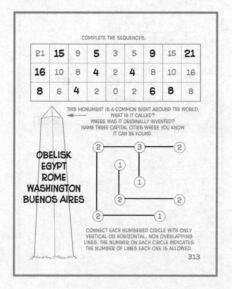

THIS MONUMENT IS A COMMON SIGHT AROUND THE WORLD. WHAT IS IT CALLED? WHERE WAS IT ORIGINALLY INVENTED? NAME THREE CAPITAL CITIES WHERE YOU KNOW IT CAN BE FOUND.

OBELISK
EGYPT
ROME
WASHINGTON
BUENOS AIRES

CONNECT EACH NUMBERED CIRCLE WITH ONLY VERTICAL OR HORIZONTAL, NON OVERLAPPING LINES. THE NUMBER ON EACH CIRCLE INDICATES THE NUMBER OF LINES EACH ONE IS ALLOWED.

314

HOW MANY PENCILS WOULD THE OCTOPUS NEED TO FINISH WRITING THE LETTER SOONER?

7

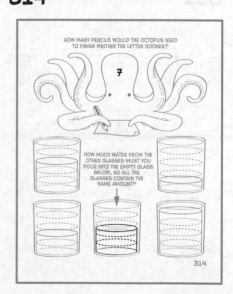

HOW MUCH WATER FROM THE OTHER GLASSES MUST YOU POUR INTO THE EMPTY GLASS BELOW, SO ALL THE GLASSES CONTAIN THE SAME AMOUNT?

315

COMPLETE THIS SEQUENCE
TO FIND OUT WHICH INSECTS
WILL REPLACE THE QUESTION MARKS.

316

WHAT STRANGE ANIMAL IS THIS?
WHERE DOES IT LIVE?
WHAT DOES IT EAT?

SEA ELEPHANTS, OR ELEPHANT SEALS,
LIVE IN BOTH THE NORTHERN AND
SOUTHERN HEMISPHERES, AND EAT
MAINLY FISH AND SQUIDS.

DRAW A CIRCLE AROUND THE
ANIMAL WE COMPARE IT TO.

COLOR BOTH THE SAME!

IN ORDER TO BUILD THE MAYAN
PYRAMID, MAKE IT SO THE ADDITION
OF EACH NUMBER ON THE LEFT
TO THE NUMBER ON THE RIGHT,
EQUALS THE NUMBER OF THE
BRICK ON TOP OF BOTH.

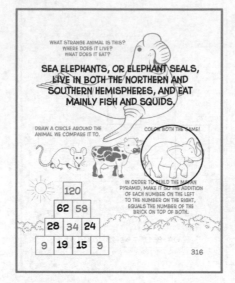

317

HELP AMY COLOR THIS
PICTURE IN THE STYLE
OF DUTCH PAINTER, PIET
MONDRIAN! TO DO SO,
FILL EACH PANEL USING
ONLY PRIMARY COLORS,
BUT NEVER PAINT JOINT
PANELS USING THE SAME
COLOR (YOU MAY CHEAT
BY NOT COLORING A FEW).

YOU CAN
DO IT!

BE CREATIVE!

NOW DRAW AND PAINT
YOUR OWN "MONDRIAN",
USING ONLY STRAIGHT
LINES, AND THREE
COLORS!

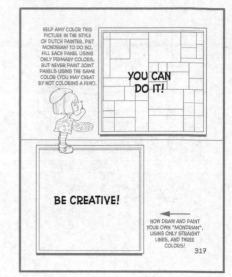

318

DID YOU KNOW YOU CAN FILL ANY SHAPE WITH AN INFINITE NUMBER OF
CIRCLES? WHAT'S THE BIGGEST CIRCLE YOU CAN DRAW IN THIS RECTANGLE?
GO AHEAD AN FILL EVERY AVAILABLE SPACE WITH SMALLER ONES!

YOU CAN
DO IT!

CAN YOU FIND THE NEW FOUR FRUIT COMBINATIONS AT THE RIGHT?

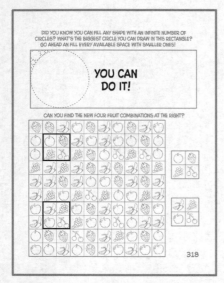

319

WHAT TIME IS IT?

SOLVE.

6+4 + 3 -4 + 5 -2+8 X 2 - 6 X 2 + 5 = 9

CAN YOU FIND ALL 14 FELINE SPECIES
IN THIS WORDSEARCH?

CLUE:
"FELINE" MEANS CAT!

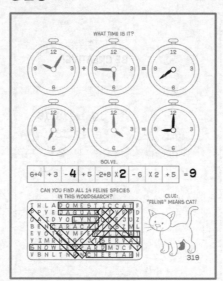

320

THESE ANIMALS ARE RACING TO THE CITY
OF MELBOURNE, IN AUSTRALIA.
IF THE KANGAROO'S LEAPS ARE 10 FEET LONG,
THE DOG'S 4 FEET LONG, THE RABBIT'S 6 FEET LONG,
THE FROG'S 5 FEET, AND THE GRASSHOPPER'S 2,
HOW MANY WILL IT TAKE EACH ONE TO ARRIVE?

17,952 FT

MELBOURNE
34 MILES

44,880 FT

29,920 FT

35,904 FT

89,760 FT

ONLY ONE OF THEM
IS CRISS CROSS FROM
THE KANGAROO

COUNT THE SNOWFLAKES! 285

IF SNOWMAN IS 5 FEET TALL, AND IT SNOWS 7 INCHES PER HOUR,
HOW LONG WILL IT TAKE FOR THE SNOW TO FULLY COVER HIM UP? 9 HOURS

321

RIDING A BIKE DOESN'T POLLUTE!
DRAW MORE BIKES AND THEIR RIDERS ON EVERY ROUTE, AND COLOR
ALL WHICH ONES GO RIGHT, AND WHICH GO LEFT?

YOU CAN
DO IT!

322

CAN YOU DO THE MATH?

-2	+5	3
+3	-1	+3
-4	+5	-2
+1	X2	22

LEFT
B

RIGHT
C

WHICH WAY DO WHEELS
"B" AND "C" TURN TO?

A

COMPLETE THE SERIES!

52 60 68 76 84 92 100 108

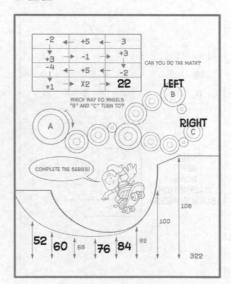

323

CONNECT EACH NUMBERED CIRCLE WITH ONLY VERTICAL OR HORIZONTAL,
NON OVERLAPPING LINES. THE NUMBER ON EACH CIRCLE INDICATES
THE NUMBER OF LINES EACH ONE IS ALLOWED.

WHAT EUROPEAN
COUNTRY IS THIS?

ESTONIA

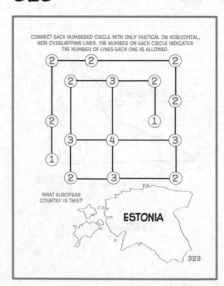

324

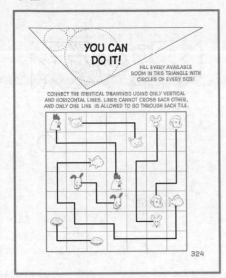

YOU CAN DO IT!

FILL EVERY AVAILABLE ROOM IN THIS TRIANGLE WITH CIRCLES OF EVERY SIZE!

CONNECT THE IDENTICAL DRAWINGS USING ONLY VERTICAL AND HORIZONTAL LINES. LINES CANNOT CROSS EACH OTHER, AND ONLY ONE LINE IS ALLOWED TO GO THROUGH EACH TILE.

324

325

COMPLETE THIS TABLE WITH + AND − SIGNS.

3	+	5	+	2	+	5	+	6	+	9	= 30
8	+	3	−	6	−	5	+	2	+	1	= 3
4	+	5	+	9	+	6	+	8	−	7	= 25
6	+	3	−	5	+	9	−	8	+	2	= 7

FILL EACH EMPTY CIRCLE SO THE SUM OF EACH LINE IS ALWAYS 10.

7   3   3
4   3   3
5   2   1
    2

THESE ARE CALLED "MOAI". THEY COME FROM EASTER ISLAND OR "RAPA NUI".

WHERE ARE THESE ANCIENT STATUES FROM? WHAT ARE THEY CALLED?

325

326

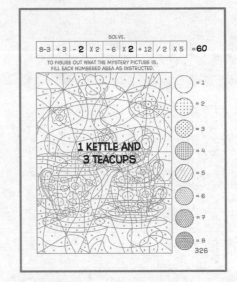

SOLVE.

$8-3 + 3 - 2 \times 2 - 6 \times 2 + 12 / 2 \times 5 = 60$

TO FIGURE OUT WHAT THE MYSTERY PICTURE IS, FILL EACH NUMBERED AREA AS INSTRUCTED.

1 KETTLE AND 3 TEACUPS

= 1
= 2
= 3
= 4
= 5
= 6
= 7
= 8

326

327

OLLIE IS A VEGETARIAN: DRAW A CIRCLE AROUND THE FOOD HE CAN EAT, AND COLOR IT.

WHAT IS THE NAME OF THIS ANIMAL? IS IT A FISH? WHERE DOES IT LIVE? WHAT DOES IT EAT?

AN ORCA. MAMMAL. LIVES IN THE SEA. EATS MEAT.

YOU CAN DO IT!

DRAW ANOTHER TYPE OF WHALE YOU LIKE!

327

328

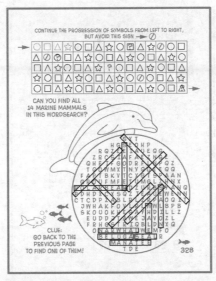

CONTINUE THE PROGRESSION OF SYMBOLS FROM LEFT TO RIGHT, BUT AVOID THIS SIGN ⊘

CAN YOU FIND ALL 14 MARINE MAMMALS IN THIS WORDSEARCH?

CLUE: GO BACK TO THE PREVIOUS PAGE TO FIND ONE OF THEM!

328

329

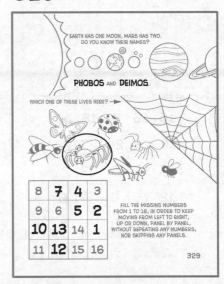

EARTH HAS ONE MOON, MARS HAS TWO. DO YOU KNOW THEIR NAMES?

PHOBOS AND DEIMOS.

WHICH ONE OF THESE LIVES HERE?

8	7	4	3
9	6	5	2
10	13	14	1
11	12	15	16

FILL THE MISSING NUMBERS FROM 1 TO 16, IN ORDER TO KEEP MOVING FROM LEFT TO RIGHT, UP OR DOWN, PANEL BY PANEL, WITHOUT REPEATING ANY NUMBERS, NOR SKIPPING ANY PANELS.

329

330

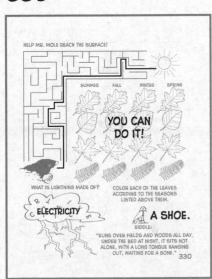

HELP MR. MOLE REACH THE SURFACE!

SUMMER   FALL   WINTER   SPRING

YOU CAN DO IT!

WHAT IS LIGHTNING MADE OF?

ELECTRICITY

COLOR EACH OF THE LEAVES ACCORDING TO THE SEASONS LISTED ABOVE THEM.

A SHOE.

RIDDLE:
"RUNS OVER FIELDS AND WOODS ALL DAY, UNDER THE BED AT NIGHT, IT SITS NOT ALONE, WITH A LONG TONGUE HANGING OUT, WAITING FOR A BONE."

330

331

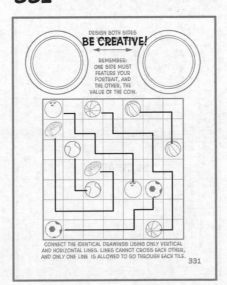

DESIGN BOTH SIDES
BE CREATIVE!

REMEMBER: ONE SIDE MUST FEATURE YOUR PORTRAIT, AND THE OTHER, THE VALUE OF THE COIN.

CONNECT THE IDENTICAL DRAWINGS USING ONLY VERTICAL AND HORIZONTAL LINES. LINES CANNOT CROSS EACH OTHER, AND ONLY ONE LINE IS ALLOWED TO GO THROUGH EACH TILE.

331

332

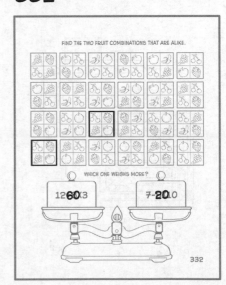

FIND THE TWO FRUIT COMBINATIONS THAT ARE ALIKE.

WHICH ONE WEIGHS MORE?

12 60 X 3   7 - 20 0

332

333

WOULD YOU HELP SALLY DESIGN HER BLANKET? BY DIVIDING A SQUARE DIAGONALLY, AND FILLING ONE HALF BLACK, YOU MAKE A TRIANGLE. IF YOU DO THAT TO OTHER SQUARES YOU CAN CREATE ANY PATTERN YOU CAN IMAGINE!

BE CREATIVE!

334

ONE OF THESE DOES NOT BELONG IN THIS GROUP.

YOU CAN DO IT!

CAN YOU THINK OF ANOTHER ANIMAL THAT'S BLACK AND WHITE? DRAW IT HERE!

WHICH WAY DOES HE NEED TO FOLLOW IN ORDER TO PICK ALL THE EGGS?

335

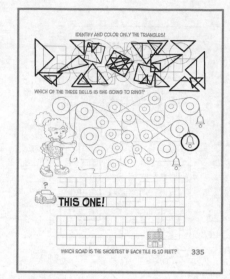

IDENTIFY AND COLOR ONLY THE TRIANGLES!

WHICH OF THE THREE BELLS IS SHE GOING TO RING?

THIS ONE!

WHICH ROAD IS THE SHORTEST IF EACH TILE IS 10 FEET?

336

WHO WEARS THESE MODERN HELMETS?

BIKER   ASTRONAUT   CYCLIST

15	16	17	18	19
14	25	24	23	20
13	10	9	22	21
12	11	8	7	6
1	2	3	4	5

FILL THE MISSING NUMBERS FROM 1 TO 25, IN ORDER TO KEEP MOVING FROM LEFT TO RIGHT, UP OR DOWN, PANEL BY PANEL, WITHOUT REPEATING ANY NUMBERS, NOR SKIPPING ANY PANELS.

337

WHICH ONE OF THESE FOOTPRINTS BELONGS TO THE BOOT ON THE LEFT?

HOW TALL IS THIS BRIDGE, IF ITS LENGTH IS 4 TIMES ITS HEIGHT?

3 ft.

4FT

IN ORDER TO BUILD THE MAYAN PYRAMID, MAKE IT SO THE ADDITION OF EACH NUMBER ON THE LEFT TO THE NUMBER ON THE RIGHT, EQUALS THE NUMBER OF THE BRICK ON TOP OF BOTH.

426

202 224

93 109 115

42 51 58 57

19 23 28 30 27

338

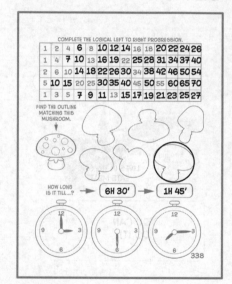

COMPLETE THE LOGICAL LEFT TO RIGHT PROGRESSION.

1		4	6		8	10	12	14		16		18	20	22	24	26
1		4	7	10		13	16	19		22		25	28	31	34	37	40
2		6	10		14	18	22	26	30		34	38	42	46	50	54
3		5	7	9	11	13	15	17	19	21	23	25	27

FIND THE OUTLINE MATCHING THIS MUSHROOM.

HOW LONG IS IT TILL...? → 6H 30' → 1H 45'

339

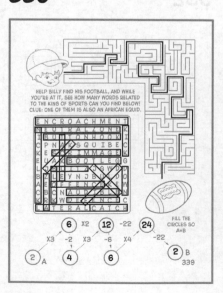

HELP BILLY FIND HIS FOOTBALL, AND WHILE YOU'RE AT IT, SEE HOW MANY WORDS RELATED TO THE KING OF SPORTS CAN YOU FIND BELOW! CLUE: ONE OF THEM IS ALSO AN AFRICAN EQUID.

ENCROACHMENT
NEUTRALZONE
BUTTONHOOK
CPN SQUIBEC
KE IMMAGE
BOOTLEG G
BLEYNJBD W
FENEN
NAUB N
WDENC

LATERALCATCH

FILL THE CIRCLES SO A=B

6 →x2→ 12 →-22→ 24

x3 -2   x3   -6   x4   -22

2 → 4 → 6 → 2
A   B

340

WOULD YOU LIKE TO DESIGN AN EVEN MORE COMPLEX BLANKET PATTERN FOR SALLY?

BE CREATIVE!

341

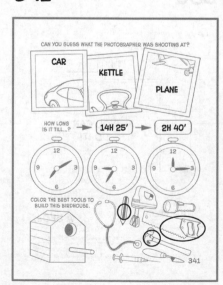

CAN YOU GUESS WHAT THE PHOTOGRAPHER WAS SHOOTING AT?

CAR   KETTLE   PLANE

HOW LONG IS IT TILL...? → 14H 25' → 2H 40'

COLOR THE BEST TOOLS TO BUILD THIS BIRDHOUSE.

342

FILL THE MISSING NUMBERS FROM 1 TO 25, IN ORDER TO KEEP MOVING FROM LEFT TO RIGHT, UP OR DOWN, PANEL BY PANEL, WITHOUT REPEATING ANY NUMBERS, NOR SKIPPING ANY PANELS.

8	9	12	13	14	15
7	10	11	18	17	16
6	5	20	19	32	33
3	4	21	22	31	34
2	25	24	23	30	35
1	26	27	28	29	36

DRAW THEIR HEADS!

YOU CAN DO THIS!

342

343

WHAT IS THE NAME OF THIS ANIMAL? **HIPPOPOTAMUS**

WHERE DOES IT LIVE? **AFRICA**

COLOR THE BEST TOOLS TO BAKE THIS CAKE.

WHO USED TO WEAR THESE ANCIENT HELMETS?

SPARTAN   **ROMAN**   **VIKING**   343

344

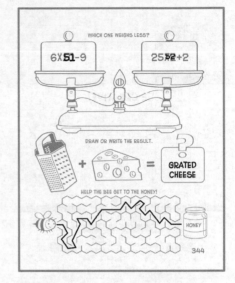

WHICH ONE WEIGHS LESS?

6X51-9   25×52+2

DRAW OR WRITE THE RESULT.

+ = GRATED CHEESE

HELP THE BEE GET TO THE HONEY!

HONEY   344

345

HELP THE LITTLE EXPLORER ESCAPE FROM THE CAVE!

345

346

INSIDE EACH CIRCLE, DRAW A FRUIT MATCHING THE INITIALS BELOW.

YOU CAN DO THIS!

C   B   P

WHICH WAY IS THIS WHEEL TURNING?

LEFT

CROSSWORDS.

P I S T A C H I O
C A S H E W
H A Z E L N U T
W A L N U T

346

347

FIND THE TWO FRUIT COMBINATIONS THAT ARE ALIKE.

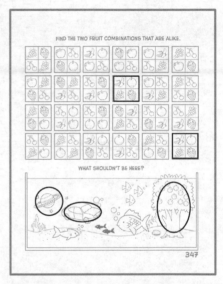

WHAT SHOULDN'T BE HERE?

347

348

WHAT ANIMALS IS THIS STRANGE CREATURE MADE OF?

TIGER
ANTEATER
HIPPOPOTAMUS

DRAW PATHS CONNECTING NUMBERS 1 TO 11 TO FORM A CONSTELLATION.

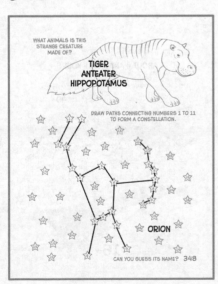

ORION

CAN YOU GUESS ITS NAME? 348

349

AT 20 MPH, THE BOAT HAS SAILED 1/4 OF THE DISTANCE TO THE TINY ISLAND IN 12 MINUTES. WHAT'S THE TOTAL DISTANCE?

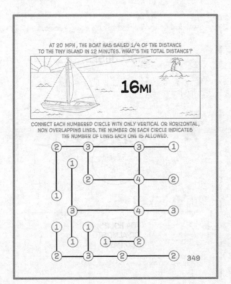

16MI

CONNECT EACH NUMBERED CIRCLE WITH ONLY VERTICAL OR HORIZONTAL, NON OVERLAPPING LINES. THE NUMBER ON EACH CIRCLE INDICATES THE NUMBER OF LINES EACH ONE IS ALLOWED.

349

350

DRAW A VIKING, A COWBOY, AND A SPARTAN WARRIOR!

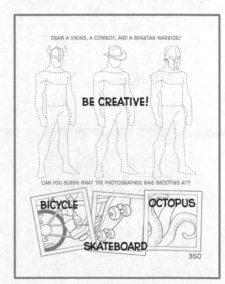

BE CREATIVE!

CAN YOU GUESS WHAT THE PHOTOGRAPHER WAS SHOOTING AT?

BICYCLE   **OCTOPUS**
SKATEBOARD   350

351

BE CREATIVE!

FILL THE PIXELS TO MAKE
VIDEO-GAME CHARACTERS,
SUCH AS THE ONE ABOVE.

351

352

WHICH TRIANGLE IS GOING TO WIN THE RACE TO THE END?

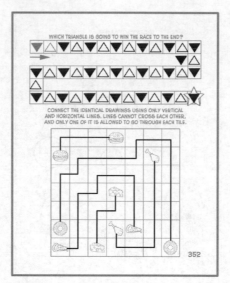

CONNECT THE IDENTICAL DRAWINGS USING ONLY VERTICAL
AND HORIZONTAL LINES. LINES CANNOT CROSS EACH OTHER,
AND ONLY ONE OF IT IS ALLOWED TO GO THROUGH EACH TILE.

352

353

WHAT IS THE
SHORTEST
WAY TO MARS?

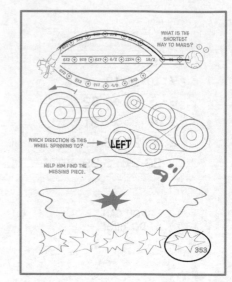

WHICH DIRECTION IS THIS
WHEEL SPINNING TO? → **LEFT**

HELP HIM FIND THE
MISSING PIECE.

353

354

NOW DRAW AN ASTRONAUT, A BIKER, AND A MAGICIAN!

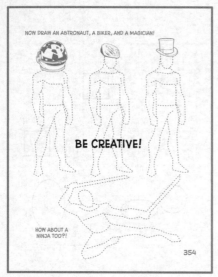

BE CREATIVE!

HOW ABOUT A
NINJA TOO?!

354

355

**YOU CAN
DO THIS!**

DO YOU KNOW THE COLORS
OF THE RAINBOW? COLOR IT!

SELECT AND COLOR ONLY
THE INGREDIENTS YOU NEED TO
MAKE A SALAD IN THIS BOWL.

WHO
LIVES
IN
HERE?

355

356

IN THIS NEW GAME OF TIC-TAC-TOE, THE GOAL IS
TO AVOID VERTICAL, HORIZONTAL OR DIAGONAL
LINES OF UP TO FOUR CROSSES OR CIRCLES EACH.

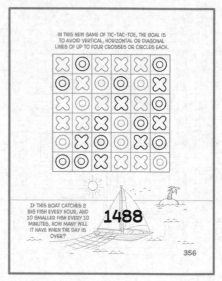

IF THIS BOAT CATCHES 2
BIG FISH EVERY HOUR, AND
10 SMALLER FISH EVERY 10
MINUTES, HOW MANY WILL
IT HAVE WHEN THE DAY IS
OVER? **1488**

356

357

DIVIDE THIS FLAG IN
THREE EQUAL PARTS.
COLOR EACH PART
BLUE, WHITE, AND RED.
WHAT COUNTRY
IS IT FROM?
WHAT IS FAMOUS FOR?
FIND OUT IN THE
WORDSEARCH BELOW!

FRANCE

CLUE: CHECK THE
ACTIVITY AT THE
BOTTOM OF THE PAGE.

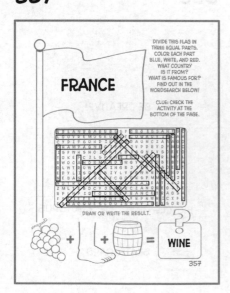

DRAW OR WRITE THE RESULT.

+ + = **WINE**

357

358

DRAW DIFFERENT FLOWERS ACCORDING TO THE NAMES ON EACH VASE.

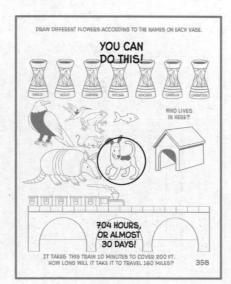

**YOU CAN
DO THIS!**

WHO LIVES
IN HERE?

**704 HOURS,
OR ALMOST
30 DAYS!**

IT TAKES THIS TRAIN 10 MINUTES TO COVER 200 FT.
HOW LONG WILL IT TAKE IT TO TRAVEL 160 MILES?

358

359

MIAMI OR BUST!

ABOUT 4 AND A HALF HOURS.

IF THE PLANE FLIES AT 120 KNOTS, AND THE
DISTANCE TO MIAMI IS 600 MILES,
HOW LONG WILL IT TAKE IT TO GET THERE?

1 KNOT = 1.15 MI/H.

HOW MANY PENCILS CAN YOU COUNT? **49**

IF THE BOAT'S LENGTH OVERALL
MEASURES TWICE ITS HEIGHT,
AND IS FOUR TIMES SHORTER
THAN THE ORCA'S LENGTH,
THEN HOW LONG IS THE WHALE? **16** FT

359

360

SOLVE.

$12-3 + 6 - \mathbf{5} \times 7 - 14 \times \mathbf{5} + 5 / 3 \times 8 = \cancel{760}$

CONNECT EACH NUMBERED CIRCLE WITH ONLY VERTICAL OR HORIZONTAL, NON OVERLAPPING LINES. THE NUMBER ON EACH CIRCLE INDICATES THE NUMBER OF LINES EACH ONE IS ALLOWED.

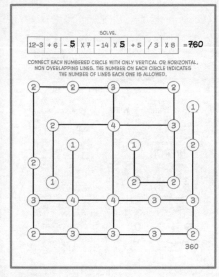

360

361

HOW MANY CIRCLES ARE IN THIS TABLE? HOW MANY STARS? AND SQUARES?

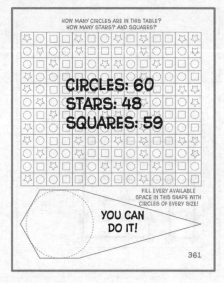

CIRCLES: 60
STARS: 48
SQUARES: 59

FILL EVERY AVAILABLE SPACE IN THIS SHAPE WITH CIRCLES OF EVERY SIZE!

YOU CAN DO IT!

361

362

WHAT DIRECTION IS 7 TURNING TOWARD?

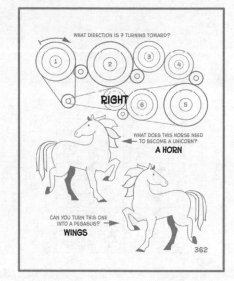

RIGHT

WHAT DOES THIS HORSE NEED TO BECOME A UNICORN?

A HORN

CAN YOU TURN THIS ONE INTO A PEGASUS?

WINGS

362

363

BE CREATIVE!

NOW CREATE MORE COMPLEX VIDEO-GAME CHARACTERS, SUCH AS THE ONE ABOVE.

363

364

CAN YOU FIND THE MISSING SYMBOL IN THIS ANCIENT EGYPTIAN PYRAMID?

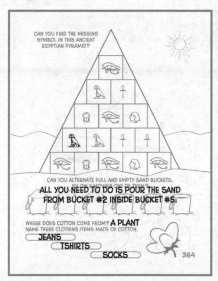

CAN YOU ALTERNATE FULL AND EMPTY SAND BUCKETS,

ALL YOU NEED TO DO IS POUR THE SAND FROM BUCKET #2 INSIDE BUCKET #5.

WHERE DOES COTTON COME FROM? A PLANT
NAME THREE CLOTHING ITEMS MADE OF COTTON.

JEANS
TSHIRTS
SOCKS

364

365

HOW CAN THIS SHEET BE SPLIT, SO EACH OF THE KIDS GETS A PIECE OF THE SAME SIZE AND SHAPE?

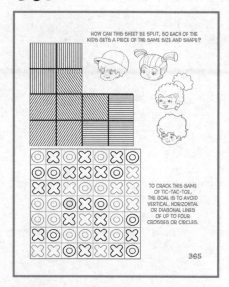

TO CRACK THIS GAME OF TIC-TAC-TOE, THE GOAL IS TO AVOID VERTICAL, HORIZONTAL OR DIAGONAL LINES OF UP TO FOUR CROSSES OR CIRCLES.

365

366

YOUR GRANDMOTHER GIVES YOU
THE OTHER BILL IS A
10 DOLLAR BILL.
ONE OF THE BILLS IS FIVE DOLLARS.

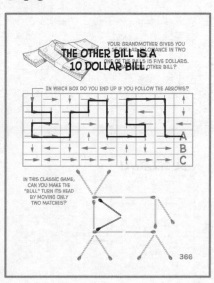

IN WHICH BOX DO YOU END UP IF YOU FOLLOW THE ARROWS?

A
B
C

IN THIS CLASSIC GAME, CAN YOU MAKE THE "BULL" TURN ITS HEAD BY MOVING ONLY TWO MATCHES?

366

367

CONNECT THE IDENTICAL DRAWINGS USING ONLY VERTICAL AND HORIZONTAL LINES. LINES CANNOT CROSS EACH OTHER, AND ONLY ONE LINE IS ALLOWED TO GO THROUGH EACH TILE.

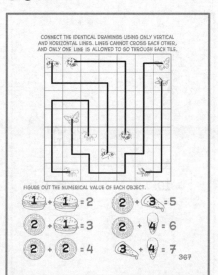

FIGURE OUT THE NUMERICAL VALUE OF EACH OBJECT.

1 + 🍔 = 2   2 + 🍕 = 5

2 + 1 = 3   2 + 4 = 6

2 + 2 = 4   3 + 4 = 7

367

368

CONNECT EACH FISH TO ITS CORRESPONDING HOOK!

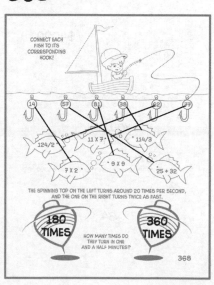

14   57   81   38   62   27

124/2   11 X 7   114/3

7 X 2   9 X 9   25 + 32

THE SPINNING TOP ON THE LEFT TURNS AROUND 20 TIMES PER SECOND, AND THE ONE ON THE RIGHT TURNS TWICE AS FAST.

180 TIMES   360 TIMES

HOW MANY TIMES DO THEY TURN IN ONE AND A HALF MINUTES?

368

369

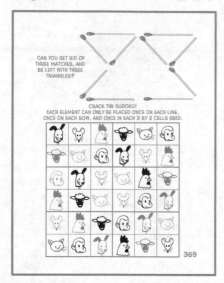

CAN YOU GET RID OF THREE MATCHES, AND BE LEFT WITH THREE TRIANGLES?

CRACK THE SUDOKU!
EACH ELEMENT CAN ONLY BE PLACED ONCE ON EACH LINE, ONCE ON EACH ROW, AND ONCE IN EACH 3 BY 2 CELLS GRID.

370

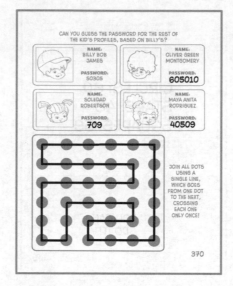

CAN YOU GUESS THE PASSWORD FOR THE REST OF THE KID'S PROFILES, BASED ON BILLY'S?

NAME: BILLY BOB JAMES
PASSWORD: 50305

NAME: OLIVER GREEN MONTGOMERY
PASSWORD: 605010

NAME: SOLEDAD ROBERTSON
PASSWORD: 709

NAME: MAYA ANITA RODRIGUEZ
PASSWORD: 40509

JOIN ALL DOTS USING A SINGLE LINE, WHICH GOES FROM ONE DOT TO THE NEXT, CROSSING EACH ONE ONLY ONCE!

371

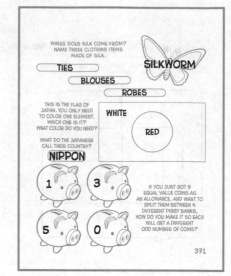

WHERE DOES SILK COME FROM? NAME THREE CLOTHING ITEMS MADE OF SILK.

SILKWORM

TIES
BLOUSES
ROBES

THIS IS THE FLAG OF JAPAN. YOU ONLY NEED TO COLOR ONE ELEMENT. WHICH ONE IS IT? WHAT COLOR DO YOU NEED?

WHITE
RED

WHAT DO THE JAPANESE CALL THEIR COUNTRY?

NIPPON

1   3
5   0

IF YOU JUST GOT 9 EQUAL VALUE COINS AS AN ALLOWANCE, AND WANT TO SPLIT THEM BETWEEN 4 DIFFERENT PIGGY BANKS, HOW DO YOU MAKE IT SO EACH WILL GET A DIFFERENT ODD NUMBER OF COINS?

372

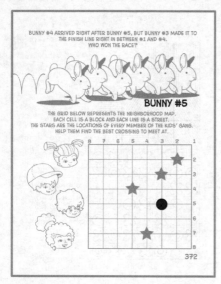

BUNNY #4 ARRIVED RIGHT AFTER BUNNY #5, BUT BUNNY #3 MADE IT TO THE FINISH LINE RIGHT IN BETWEEN #1 AND #4. WHO WON THE RACE?

BUNNY #5

THE GRID BELOW REPRESENTS THE NEIGHBORHOOD MAP. EACH CELL IS A BLOCK AND EACH LINE IS A STREET. THE STARS ARE THE LOCATIONS OF EVERY MEMBER OF THE KIDS' GANG. HELP THEM FIND THE BEST CROSSING TO MEET AT.

373

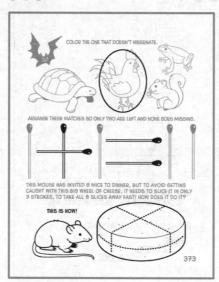

COLOR THE ONE THAT DOESN'T HIBERNATE.

ARRANGE THESE MATCHES SO ONLY TWO ARE LEFT AND NONE GOES MISSING.

THIS MOUSE HAS INVITED 8 MICE TO DINNER, BUT TO AVOID GETTING CAUGHT WITH THIS BIG WHEEL OF CHEESE, IT NEEDS TO SLICE IT IN ONLY 3 STROKES, TO TAKE ALL 8 SLICES AWAY FAST! HOW DOES IT DO IT?

THIS IS HOW!

374

JOIN ALL DOTS USING A SINGLE LINE, WHICH GOES FROM ONE DOT TO THE NEXT, CROSSING EACH ONE ONLY ONCE!

RIDDLE:
"A BOX WITHOUT HINGES, KEY, OR LID, YET GOLDEN TREASURE INSIDE IS HID."

AN EGG.

375

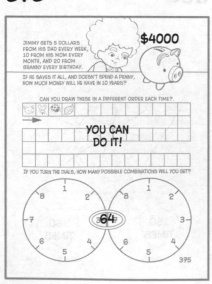

JIMMY GETS 5 DOLLARS FROM HIS DAD EVERY WEEK, 10 FROM HIS MOM EVERY MONTH, AND 20 FROM GRANNY EVERY BIRTHDAY.

$4000

IF HE SAVES IT ALL, AND DOESN'T SPEND A PENNY, HOW MUCH MONEY WILL HE HAVE IN 10 YEARS?

CAN YOU DRAW THESE IN A DIFFERENT ORDER EACH TIME?

YOU CAN DO IT!

IF YOU TURN THE DIALS, HOW MANY POSSIBLE COMBINATIONS WILL YOU GET?

64

376

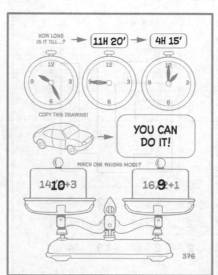

HOW LONG IS IT TILL...?

11H 20'   →   4H 15'

COPY THIS DRAWING!

YOU CAN DO IT!

WHICH ONE WEIGHS MORE?

$14 \times 10 + 3$ $16.9 \times 2 + 1$

377

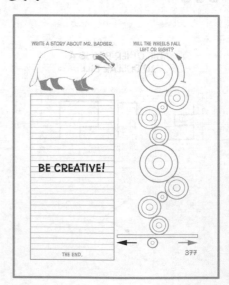

WRITE A STORY ABOUT MR. BADGER.

WILL THE WHEELS FALL LEFT OR RIGHT?

BE CREATIVE!

THE END.

378

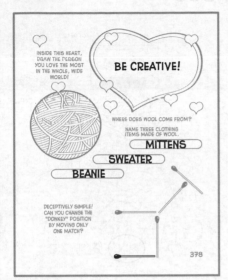

INSIDE THIS HEART, DRAW THE PERSON YOU LOVE THE MOST IN THE WHOLE, WIDE WORLD!

BE CREATIVE!

WHERE DOES WOOL COME FROM?

NAME THREE CLOTHING ITEMS MADE OF WOOL.

MITTENS

SWEATER

BEANIE

DECEPTIVELY SIMPLE! CAN YOU CHANGE THE "DONKEY" POSITION BY MOVING ONLY ONE MATCH?

379

BE CREATIVE!

DESIGN EVEN MORE DETAILED VIDEO-GAME "SPRITES" LIKE THE ONE ABOVE!

380

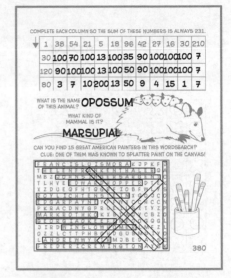

COMPLETE EACH COLUMN SO THE SUM OF THESE NUMBERS IS ALWAYS 231.

WHAT IS THE NAME OF THIS ANIMAL? OPOSSUM

WHAT KIND OF MAMMAL IS IT? MARSUPIAL

CAN YOU FIND 15 GREAT AMERICAN PAINTERS IN THIS WORDSEARCH? CLUE: ONE OF THEM WAS KNOWN TO SPLATTER PAINT ON THE CANVAS!

381

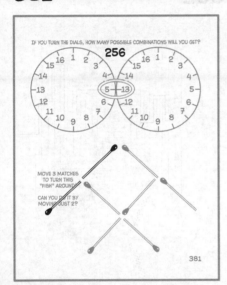

IF YOU TURN THE DIALS, HOW MANY POSSIBLE COMBINATIONS WILL YOU GET?

256

MOVE 3 MATCHES TO TURN THIS "FISH" AROUND!

CAN YOU DO IT BY MOVING JUST 2?

382

CRACK THE SUDOKU! EACH ELEMENT CAN ONLY BE PLACED ONCE ON EACH LINE, ONCE ON EACH ROW, AND ONCE IN EACH 3 BY 2 CELLS GRID.

YOU CAN DO IT!

TRACE THE DOTS TO DRAW INTERSECTING DIAMONDS IN A SINGLE STROKE.

383

FIND THE WAY OUT!

WRITE A STORY ABOUT MS. TORTOISE.

BE CREATIVE!

THE END.

384

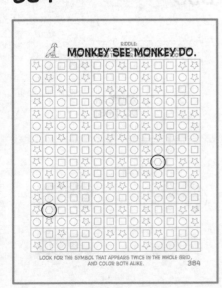

RIDDLE: MONKEY SEE MONKEY DO.

LOOK FOR THE SYMBOL THAT APPEARS TWICE IN THE WHOLE GRID, AND COLOR BOTH ALIKE.

385

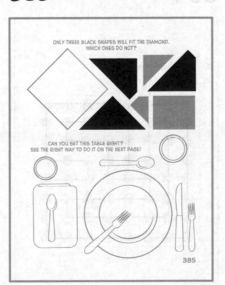

ONLY THREE BLACK SHAPES WILL FIT THE DIAMOND. WHICH ONES DO NOT?

CAN YOU SET THIS TABLE RIGHT? SEE THE RIGHT WAY TO DO IT ON THE NEXT PAGE!

386

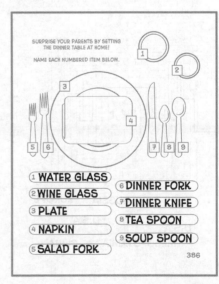

SURPRISE YOUR PARENTS BY SETTING THE DINNER TABLE AT HOME!

NAME EACH NUMBERED ITEM BELOW.

1 WATER GLASS
2 WINE GLASS
3 PLATE
4 NAPKIN
5 SALAD FORK
6 DINNER FORK
7 DINNER KNIFE
8 TEA SPOON
9 SOUP SPOON

387

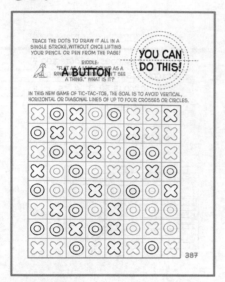

TRACE THE DOTS TO DRAW IT ALL IN A SINGLE STROKE, WITHOUT ONCE LIFTING YOUR PENCIL OR PEN FROM THE PAGE!

RIDDLE: "FLAT AS A RING, ROUND AS A THING, YOU CAN'T SEE A THING." WHAT IS IT?

A BUTTON

YOU CAN DO THIS!

IN THIS NEW GAME OF TIC-TAC-TOE, THE GOAL IS TO AVOID VERTICAL, HORIZONTAL OR DIAGONAL LINES OF UP TO FOUR CROSSES OR CIRCLES.

388

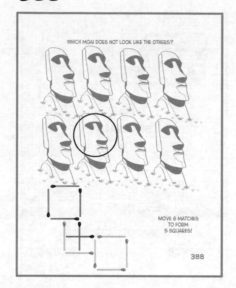

WHICH MOAI DOES NOT LOOK LIKE THE OTHERS?

MOVE 6 MATCHES TO FORM 5 SQUARES!

389

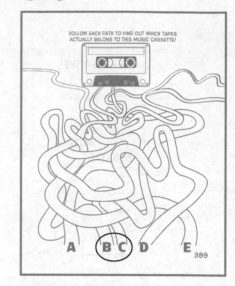

FOLLOW EACH PATH TO FIND OUT WHICH TAPES ACTUALLY BELONG TO THIS MUSIC CASSETTE!

A B C D E

390

EVERY GOOD STORY HAS THREE PARTS, CAN YOU GUESS WHAT IS EACH ONE CALLED?

1. BEGINNING
2. MIDDLE
3. END

USE THEM IN THE FOLLOWING ACTIVITY!

WHY IS SHE WALKING UNDER THE RAIN? WRITE HER STORY!

YOU CAN DO THIS!

THE END.

391

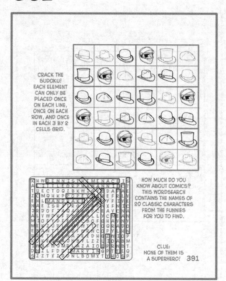

CRACK THE SUDOKU! EACH ELEMENT CAN ONLY BE PLACED ONCE ON EACH LINE, ONCE ON EACH ROW, AND ONCE IN EACH 3 BY 2 CELLS GRID.

HOW MUCH DO YOU KNOW ABOUT COMICS? THIS WORDSEARCH CONTAINS THE NAMES OF 20 CLASSIC CHARACTERS FROM THE FUNNIES FOR YOU TO FIND.

CLUE: NONE OF THEM IS A SUPERHERO!

392

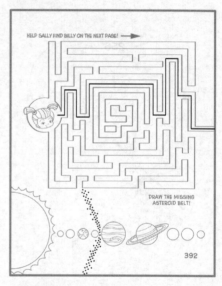

HELP SALLY FIND BILLY ON THE NEXT PAGE! →

DRAW THE MISSING ASTEROID BELT!

393

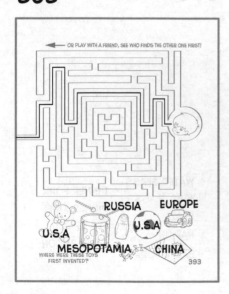

← OR PLAY WITH A FRIEND, SEE WHO FINDS THE OTHER ONE FIRST!

RUSSIA EUROPE

U.S.A U.S.A

MESOPOTAMIA CHINA

WHERE WERE THESE TOYS FIRST INVENTED?

394

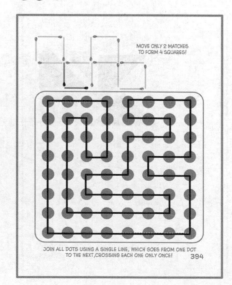

MOVE ONLY 2 MATCHES TO FORM 4 SQUARES!

JOIN ALL DOTS USING A SINGLE LINE, WHICH GOES FROM ONE DOT TO THE NEXT, CROSSING EACH ONE ONLY ONCE!

395

THESE FLAGS BELONG TO NORTH KOREA AND SOUTH KOREA.

WHAT DO YOU KNOW ABOUT THESE TWO COUNTRIES?

YOU CAN DO THIS!

THEIR FLAGS ARE BOTH RED, WHITE, AND BLUE.

COLOR THEM!

FIND THE HIPPO'S MATCHING SILHOUETTE.

396

WHAT CONTINENT IS THIS? **ASIA**

CAN YOU NAME ITS OCEANS?

ARCTIC
PACIFIC
INDIAN

FIND ALL ITS COUNTRIES IN THE WORDSEARCH BELOW!

CLUE: SEE TWO OF THESE COUNTRIES IN THE PREVIOUS PAGE!

396

397

JIMMY LOST HIS PIGGY BANK! HELP HIM FIND IT, GRABBING THE MOST COINS ON HIS WAY!

397

398

TO FIGURE OUT WHAT THE MYSTERY PICTURE IS, FILL EACH NUMBERED AREA AS INSTRUCTED.

CHRISTMAS PRESENTS

= 1
= 2
= 3
= 4
= 5
= 6
= 7
= 8
= 9
= 10

398

399

HOW MANY CANDY CANES AND BAUBLES CAN YOU COUNT? COLOR THE CANES RED AND WHITE, THE BALLS BLUE, AND A VERY MERRY CHRISTMAS TO ALL OF YOU!

11 CANES
35 BAUBLES

THIS BOOK WAS COMPLETED BY:
YOUR NAME

399

445